THE MEDIEVAL CLOISTER IN ENGLAND AND WALES

JOURNAL OF THE BRITISH ARCHAEOLOGICAL ASSOCIATION

Edited by

Martin Henig and John McNeill

VOLUME 159 *for* 2006

D1157853

THE BRITISH ARCHAEOLOGICAL ASSOCIATION

President

NICOLA COLDSTREAM, M.A., Ph.D., F.S.A.

The British Archaeological Association was founded in 1843 to promote the study of archaeology, art and architecture and the preservation of our national antiquities. It encourages original research and publishes new work on art and antiquities of Roman to post-medieval date.

The Association embraces a wide spectrum of antiquarian and art historical interests (with architectural history strongly represented) and its capacity to engage in debate across these disciplines is a major strength. Regular lectures held in London provide one channel of communication; others include an annual conference held over several days (whose proceedings are published for the benefit of members at large) and an annual journal.

LECTURE SERIES

The lectures take place on the first Wednesday of each month from October to May. Meetings are normally held in the rooms of the Society of Antiquaries of London, Burlington House, Piccadilly, London W1J 0BE, UK. Members may introduce guests. Non-members not being so introduced are welcome to attend occasional individual lectures, but are asked to introduce themselves to the Director or one or other of the officers on arrival.

ANNUAL CONFERENCES

The Association holds an annual conference at a centre of established importance in the medieval period, usually in the British Isles and occasionally in mainland Europe, collating the results of recent research on major cathedrals, minsters and abbeys, and including visits to places of relevant interest.

PUBLICATIONS

The *Journal of the British Archaeological Association* contains original papers within the Association's areas of interest; it is published annually and is free to members. Articles for consideration should be submitted to the Honorary Editor, who will supply notes for contributors on request.

The Association also publishes the proceedings of its conferences in the *Transactions* series. These consist of papers delivered and others specially commissioned with the aim of producing monographs of permanent value.

MEMBERSHIP

Membership of the Association is open to anyone interested in art, architecture and archaeology. Applications for membership are welcome and should be sent to the Hon. Membership Secretary with a cheque for the current year's subscription (John Jenkins, Esq., 75 Budmouth Avenue, Weymouth, Dorset DT3 6QJ, UK).

Rates:
Ordinary Member	£33.00
Student	£15.00
Retired Member	£22.00

The BAA is a Registered Charity (no. 1014821) and a company limited by guarantee and registered in England (no. 2747476).

Contents

Forensic Archaeology: advances in theory and practice, edited by JOHN HUNTER *and* MARGARET COX; *The Past from Above, edited by* CHARLOTTE TRÜMPLER; *Roman Mosaics of Britain. Volume II. South-West Britain, by* STEPHEN R. COSH *and* DAVID S. NEAL; *Imago Dei. Sculpted Images of the Crucifix in the Art of Early Modern Malta, by* SANDRO DE BONO; *Observation and Image-Making in Gothic Art, by* JEAN A. GIVENS; *A History of Ely Cathedral, edited by* PETER MEADOWS *and* NIGEL RAMSAY; *Gold and Gilt, Pots and Pins. Possessions and People in Medieval Britain, by* DAVID A. HINTON; *Decorated Medieval Floor Tiles of Somerset, by* BARBARA J. LOWE; *Greater Medieval Houses of England and Wales. Vol III, Southern England, by* ANTHONY EMERY, *Acton Court: The evolution of an early Tudor courtier's house, by* KIRSTY RODWELL *and* ROBERT BELL; *The Idea of the Castle in Medieval England and Wales, by* ABIGAIL WHEATLEY; *Stonehenge, by*

JULIAN RICHARDS; *Birdoswald Roman Fort*, *by* TONY WILMOTT; *Goodrich Castle*, *by* JEREMY ASHBEE; *Lindisfarne Priory*, *by* JOANNA STORY; *Belsay Hall*, *Castle and Gardens*, *by* ROGER WHITE; *Apsley House: The Wellington Collection*, *by* JULIUS BRYANT; *Old Sarum*, *by* JOHN MCNEILL; *Kenilworth Castle*, *by* RICHARD K. MORRIS; *Caerwent Roman Town*, *by* RICHARD J. BREWER; *Chepstow Castle*, *by* RICK TURNER; *Blaenavon Ironworks and World Heritage Landscape*, *by* PETER WAKELIN; *The Victoria History of the Counties of England. A History of the County of Chester Vol. V Part 1, The City of Chester: General History and Topography; Vol. V Part 2, The City of Chester: Culture, Buildings, Institutions*, *edited by* C. P. LEWIS *and* A. T. THACKER; *Medieval Trim, History and Archaeology*, *by* RICHARD POTTERTON; *New Winchelsea Sussex. A Medieval Port Town*, *by* DAVID *and* BARBARA MARTIN; *Archaeological fantasies. How pseudoarchaeology misrepresents the past and misleads the public*, *edited by* GARRETT G. FAGAN; *The Beautiful Burial in Roman Egypt. Art, Identity, and Funerary Religion*, *by* CHRISTINA RIGGS; *Celtic Gods. Comets in Irish Mythology*, *by* PATRICK MCCAFFERTY *and* MIKE BAILLIE; *The Sutton Hoo Sceptre and the Roots of Celtic Kingship Theory*, *by* MICHAEL J. ENRIGHT; *Early Anglo-Saxon buckets. A Corpus of Copper Alloy- and Iron-bound, Stave-built vessels*, *by* JEAN M. COOK; *Anglo-Saxons. Studies presented to Cyril Roy Hart*, *edited by* SIMON KEYNES *and* ALFRED P. SMYTH; *Sandlands. The Suffolk Coast and Heaths*, *by* TOM WILLIAMSON; *Hedgerow History: Ecology, History & Landscape Character*, *by* GERRY BARNES *and* TOM WILLIAMSON; *'Outrageous Waves'. Global Warming and Coastal Change in Britain through Two Thousand Years*, BASIL CRACKNELL; *Royston Grange. 6000 Years of Peakland Landscape*, *by* RICHARD HODGES; *The Malvern Hills. An Ancient Landscape*, *by* MARK BOWDEN et al.; *Barentin's Manor. Excavations of the moated manor at Harding's Field, Chalgrove, Oxfordshire 1976–9*, *by* PHILIP PAGE, KATE ATHERTON *and* ALAN HARDY; *The Catesby Family and their Brasses at Ashby St Ledgers, Northamptonshire*, *edited by* JEROME BERTRAM; *A History of the Stained Glass of St George's Chapel, Windsor Castle*, *edited by* SARAH BROWN; *The Choir-Stalls at Amiens Cathedral*, *by* CHARLES TRACY *and* HUGH HARRISON; *A History of English Glassmaking AD 43–1800*, *by* HUGH WILLMOTT

PRESIDENTS

1843 The Lord Albert Denison Conynham
1850 James Heywood, Esq.
1851 Sir Oswald Mosley, Bart.
1852 His Grace the Duke of Newcastle
1853 Ralph Bernal, Esq.
1855 The Earl of Perth and Melfont
1857 The Earl of Albemarle
1858 The Marquis of Ailesbury
1859 The Earl of Carnarvon
1860 Beriah Botfield, Esq.
1861 Sir H. Stafford Northcote, Bart., C.B.
1862 John Lee, Esq.
1863 R. Monkton Milnes, Esq.
1864 George Tomline, Esq.
1865 The Duke of Cleveland, K.G.
1866 The Rt Hon. the Lord Boston
1867 Sir Charles H. Rouse Boughton, Bart.
1868 The Earl Bathurst
1869 The Lord Lytton
1870 ChandosWren Hoskyns, Esq.
1871 Sir William Coles Medlycott, Bart.
1872 The Earl of Dartmouth
1873 The Duke of Norfolk, E.M.
1874 The Most Noble the Marquis of
       Hertford
1875 Kirkman D. Hudson, Esq.
1876 The Most Noble the Marquis of
       Hertford
       The Earl of Mount Edgcumbe
1877 Sir Watkin Williams Wynn, Bart.
1878 The Earl of Hardwicke
1879 The Lord Waveney
1880 The Rt Hon. the Earl Nelson
1881 The Very Revd Lord Alwyne Compton
1882 His Grace the Duke of Somerset, K.G.
1883 The Rt Hon. the Earl of Granville, K.G.
1884 The Rt Revd the Lord Bishop of St
       David's

1885 The Duke of Norfolk, K.G., E.M.
1886 The Rt Revd the Lord Bishop of
       Durham
1887 Sir J. Allanson Picton
1888 The Most Hon. the Marquess of Bute,
       K.T.
1889 The Rt Hon. the Earl of Winchilsea and
       Nottingham
1891 The Most Hon. the Marquess of Ripon,
       K.G.
1894 The Rt Hon. the Earl of Northbrook,
       G.C.S.I.
1895 His Grace the Duke of Sutherland, K.G.
1896 Col. Sir Walter Wilkin
1897 The Rt Hon. the Lord Mostyn
1898 The Rt Revd the Lord Bishop of
       Peterborough
1899 The Most Hon. the Marquess of Granby
1901 Thomas Hodgkin, Esq.
1902 Lt-Col. Clifford Probyn
1903 R. E. Leader, Esq.
1905 M. J. Sutton, Esq.
1906 Charles E. Keyser, Esq.
1930 Francis Weston, Esq.
1938 A. H. Thompson, Esq.
1944 Miss Rose Graham
1951 Lawrence Tanner, Esq.
1957 John F. Nichols, Esq.
1960 [Lord] Eric G. M. Fletcher
1963 [Sir] David M. Wilson
1968 T. S. R. Boase, Esq.
1971 Professor D. E. Strong
1974 Cecil Farthing, Esq.
1977 Professor Peter Lasko
1980 Professor Peter Kidson
1983 Dr Richard D. H. Gem
1989 Laurence Keen, Esq.
2004 Dr Nicola Coldstream

BRITISH ARCHAEOLOGICAL ASSOCIATION
CONGRESSES AND CONFERENCES

1844	Canterbury	1893	Winchester	1950	Sherborne
1845	Winchester	1894	Manchester	1951	Matlock
1846	Gloucester	1985	Stoke-on-Trent	1952	Brighton
1847	Warwick	1896	London	1953	King's Lynn
1848	Worcester	1897	Conway	1954	Malvern
1849	Chester	1898	Peterborough	1955	Bury St Edmunds
1850	Manchester and Lancaster	1899	Buxton	1956	Harrogate
		1900	Leicester	1957	Leamington Spa
1851	Derby	1901	Newcastle	1958	Lincoln
1852	Newark	1902	Westminster	1959	Salisbury
1853	Rochester	1903	Sheffeld	1960	Hereford
1854	Chepstow	1904	Bath	1961	Exeter
1855	Isle of Wight	1905	Reading	1962	Bath
1856	Bridgwater & Bath	1906	Nottingham	1963	Peterborough
1857	Norwich	1907	Weymouth	1964	Hull
1858	Salisbury	1908	Carlisle	1975	Worcester
1859	Newbury	1910	Warwick	1976	Ely
1860	Shrewsbury	1911	London	1977	Durham
1861	Exeter	1912	Gloucester	1978	Wells and Glastonbury
1862	Leicester	1913	Cambridge	1979	Canterbury
1863	Leeds	1914	Canterbury	1980	Winchester
1864	Ipswich	1915	Isle of Wight	1981	Gloucester and Tewkesbury
1865	Durham	1916	Southampton		
1866	Hastings	1917	Brighton	1982	Lincoln
1867	Ludlow	1918	London	1983	Hull & Beverley
1868	Cirencester	1919	Colchester	1984	London
1869	St Albans	1920	Shrewsbury	1985	Exeter
1870	Hereford	1921	Lincoln	1986	Edinburgh and St Andrews
1871	Weymouth	1922	Bath		
1872	Wolverhampton	1923	York	1987	Lichfield
1873	Sheffield	1924	Hastings	1988	York
1874	Bristol	1925	Norwich	1989	Rouen
1875	Evesham	1926	Chester	1990	Hereford
1876	Bodmin & Penzance	1927	Exeter	1991	Salisbury
1877	Llangollen	1928	Ipswich	1992	Chester
1878	Wisbech	1929	Newport	1993	Utrecht
1879	Yarmouth & Norwich	1930	Great Malvern	1994	Bury St Edmunds
1880	Devizes	1931	Peterborough	1995	Southwell and Nottinghamshire
1881	Great Malvern	1932	Weymouth		
1882	Plymouth	1933	Nottingham	1996	Bristol
1883	Dover	1934	Sheringham	1997	Glasgow
1884	Tenby	1935	East Kent	1998	Windsor
1885	Brighton	1936	Hereford	1999	St Albans
1886	Darlington & Bishop Auckland	1937	Colchester	2000	Angers
		1938	Banbury	2001	Carlisle
1887	Liverpool	1939	Shrewsbury	2002	Rochester
1888	Glasgow	1940	Kingston upon Thames	2003	Mainz
1889	Lincoln	1947	Northampton	2004	Cardiff
1890	Oxford	1948	Gloucester	2005	King's Lynn
1891	York	1949	Chester	2006	Prague
1892	Cardiff				

Preface

This volume of the Journal which, apart from the Reviews section, is dedicated to the medieval cloister in England and Wales, has its origins in a conference held at Rewley House, Oxford, on 2–4 April 2004. At that time it seemed that a considerable amount of research had been devoted to specific cloisters, though few attempts had been made to discuss cloisters in general, excepting the New York cloisters conference of 1973 and at a conference held in Tübingen in 1999 — both of which were concerned with cloisters across Europe. The New York conference resulted in the publication of a special volume of *Gesta* (vol. XII, 1973), and the transactions of the Tübingen conference were published under the editorship of Peter Klein as *Der mittelalterliche Kreuzgang* in 2004. Finding a publisher for the transactions of a specialised conference is not easy, however, and the decision of the Council of the British Archaeological Association to make available to its members and to the wider world most of the papers delivered at the Oxford conference in a special thematic issue of the journal is a cause for some celebration. Of the ten papers delivered at the conference, seven are published here and, after it was agreed that the 2006 Journal would be a cloisters volume, three more papers were submitted: by Jenny Alexander on the cloister at Lincoln Cathedral, by Jackie Hall on Cistercian east ranges, and by Stuart Harrison on Augustinian and Benedictine cloisters.

In the course of editing this issue of the journal the editors have incurred many debts, and would particularly like to thank Ron Baxter, Eric Fernie and John Goodall for illuminating the Rewley House cloister conference with papers that are not — and were never intended to be — published here, Eileen Rubery for producing such helpful notes, and Linda Fisher for her enormously efficient and good-natured sub-editorial work. Our greatest debt is owed to John Osborn. Without outside help the Association can only afford to produce journals above a certain length by dipping into its own reserves, and it was John's agreement to underwrite any cost overrun that made this volume viable. Indeed, without it a BAA cloisters volume on this scale would have been quite impossible. The Association extends its heartfelt thanks.

Martin Henig
John McNeill

The Continental Context

JOHN McNEILL

There are an uncountably large number of medieval cloisters in various states of preservation surviving in mainland western Europe. In order to make sense of this material, and tease it into acting as a continental context for claustral design in England and Wales, the following paper concentrates on four aspects of the Latin medieval cloister: its origins, uses, architecture and imagery. None of these exist in watertight compartments, and they will flow into and out of each other, but one — the origins of the medieval cloister — is fundamental and might be cauterised and treated separately, if only briefly. The rest of the paper concentrates on the cloister between the 11th and 13th centuries. There is little in it that has not already been published, but it was felt it would be useful to bring some of this material together in English. The paper was originally written to be read aloud, hence its rather colloquial presentation, and the detail which should have turned it into an article is in the endnotes.

ORIGINS

THE earliest standing cloisters to survive in continental Europe are fragmentary and date from the first half of the 11th century.[1] The Simeonstift at Trier was begun *c.* 1036 and utilises piers in the lower walks and columns with crutch-capitals in the upper arcades (Fig. 1). The heavily restored north walk of St-Guilhem-le-Désert is datable to shortly after 1025.[2] The north walk at St-Philibert, Tournus was built during the abbacy of Ardain some time between 1028 and 1056 (Fig. 2).[3] And elements of the lower sections of the south and east cloister walks of Sant Pere de Rodes are still discernible — difficult to pin down exactly but probably to be dated to the 1020s or 1030s.[4] To these we might add the heavily restored rubble arches attached to the lower church of Saint-Martin-du-Canigou, and a certain amount of standing evidence for early-11th-century east ranges, of which much the most revealing is the chapter-house entrance at Charlieu, which can be associated with work done while Odilo was abbot of Cluny, that is before 1049 (Fig. 3).[5] Jotsuald's *Vita Odilonis* also tells us that Odilo constructed a cloister in stone at Cluny,

admirably decorated with marble columns from the furthest parts of that province, transported by the headlong currents of the Daurade and Rhone. In which he was wont to glory and to remark in jest that he had found it in wood and left it in marble, in imitation of Caesar Augustus, of whom chroniclers say he found Rome made of brick and left it in marble.[6]

In other words, Odilo replaced a wooden cloister at Cluny with one whose arcades were supported on marble columns. There is also a strong likelihood that the columns of this cloister were grouped in pairs, as in the chapter-house entrance at Charlieu, and, indeed, in most 12th-century cloisters. As thing stand, Charlieu, along with the

JBAA, vol. 159 (2006), 1–47
© British Archaeological Association 2006
DOI: 10.1179/174767006X147433

FIG. 1.   Simeonstift, Trier: north walk *John McNeill*

FIG. 2.   Saint-Philibert, Tournus: north walk to west *John McNeill*

FIG. 3.   Saint-Fortunat, Charlieu: chapter-house entrance *John McNeill*

Simeonstift at Trier, Sant Pere de Rodes and St-Benigne at Dijon, are the earliest east cloister ranges to survive in western Europe.[7] But the underlying principles of the medieval cloister go back much further, and were certainly well understood by the late Carolingian period, as is demonstrated by the famous St-Gall plan (Fig. 4).[8]

This is drawn on five sheets of parchment, and is impressively large (1.12 m × 0.77 m — about the size of a small dining table for four people). The preamble states:

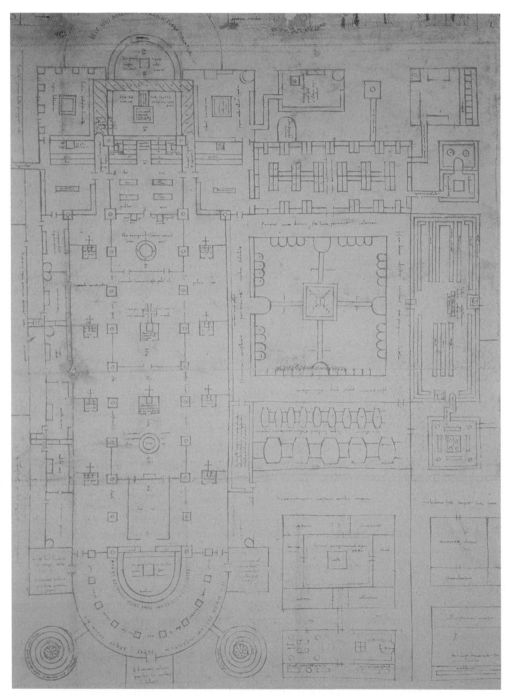

FIG. 4.   St-Gall plan. detail showing monastic church and cloister
MS Cod. Sang. 1092, Stiftsbibliothek, St-Gall

'I have sent you, Gozbert, dearest son, this modest example of the disposition of a monastery, that you may dwell upon it in spirit.' Gozbert was the abbot of St-Gall from 816 to 837, and there is evidence that the plan was drawn up at Reichenau (most tituli are in the hand of a Reichenau scribe) under the direction of Haito, sometime abbot of Reichenau and bishop of Basle, who retired from the abbacy at Reichenau in 823 and died in 836.

As it is drawn out, the St-Gall plan is of little use to a builder. The indications of wall thicknesses are too inconsistent and one is usually left to guess at relative floor levels. But it has been carefully thought out. The tituli indicate that the east, south and west cloister ranges are two-storey. The east range has a warming room below, connected via a passage to the monks' laundry and bath house, with a dormitory above, also connected via a passage to a privy (or reredorter). The south range consists of a ground-storey refectory, with the monks' vestiary above, while the west range has a ground-storey cellar and first-storey larder. Two entrances from the claustral precinct to the church are shown. One at the north-east angle of the cloister, and another, by implication a night-stair (since it is the dormitory that is shown on the plan, even though the titulus tells us this was at first-storey level), bringing the monks from the dormitory into the south transept. Between the cellar and the church, there is a parlour, where the monks could meet with members of their family, and wash the feet of visitors. And at the centre of the garth there is the famous juniper tree that so puzzled Walter Horn and Ernest Born, with four branch-like symbols extending to the corners of a square by the word *SAVINA*.[9] There is one other telling detail discernible in the St-Gall plan. In drawing out the north cloister arcade, the scribe switched to full vertical projection, making it clear that the cloister arcades were to stand on a plinth or stylobate.

Most of the features one associates with later medieval monastic cloisters are therefore present at St-Gall — two of which are absolutely fundamental, and distinguish monastic cloisters from other types of arcaded courtyard. The cloister is organised so as to create a series of circulatory passages connecting a variety of communal buildings — in other words it is positioned at the centre of monastic life — and the walks are separated from the garth by a stylobate. Both these features distance the monastic cloister from the atrium — as is exemplified by the late-11th-century atrium at Salerno, surrounded on three sides by public streets and designed to facilitate easy concourse (Fig. 5).[10] And both these features become pretty much standard. Monastic orders with fewer demands on communal buildings, such as the Carthusians, do move the great cloister away from the church, it is true, though the monks still eat and sleep in cells arranged around a cloister walk.[11] Equally, other sorts of cloister, such as infirmary cloisters, may be purposefully removed from the principal monastic precinct. But when it comes to single cloister foundations it is only really the cloisters attached to non-residentiary collegiate churches, basically cathedrals, and, rather oddly, what are called the 'cloisters' attached to educational institutions created by William of Wykeham and Henry Chichele, that are removed from the main centres of life, and even this floating off of the cloister is rejected by the big educational colleges of late-15th- and early-16th-century Oxford (Fig. 6).[12]

The sylobate is, I think, universal, and has a function — or at least this is true of the period before the development of traceried cloisters brought new ways of stressing the distinctness of walk and garth, and indeed new reading habits.[13] It is used as a bench by monks when reading, or, in the earlier Middle Ages, by monks engaged in teaching the *pueri* or *juvenes* who had been offered as oblates. In monastic customaries it is usually referred to as *cancellus* or *cancelli*, the bench or balustrade, as in Ulrich of

4

Zell's late-11th-century description of how each of the pueri had his own *truncus* (plank or small seat), which was positioned along the inner wall of the cloister, while their monastic guardians sat opposite them, *in cancellis*, on the balustrades and between the columns.[14] Stylobates are nearly always constructed at a convenient height for sitting, and one has become so inured to seeing cloister walks constructed in this way that when a stylobate is omitted by an overenthusiastic 19th-century restorer with a few bits of medieval cloister to piece back together, as happened at the Savignac nunnery of L'Abbaye-Blanche near Mortain, the results can be quite shocking (Fig. 7).[15]

The one element missing from the St-Gall plan is a chapter-house — a titulus indicating that meetings of the monks were to take place in the north walk of the cloister.[16] The earliest evidence we have for a room specifically set aside for chapter meetings comes from the History of the Abbots of Fontenelle and concerns the cloister created by Abbot Ansegis at what is now known as the abbey of St-Wandrille some time between 822 and 833. This is a difficult text, interpreted by Wolfgang Braunfels as meaning the chapter-house was constructed at ground-storey level beneath the dormitory and formed part of the east range.[17]

Besides all this he [Ansegis] also ordered another building to be put up on the north side of St Peter's by the apse, which it is proper to call the assembly or court-house — Bouleterion in Greek — because the brethren are wont to gather there to take counsel over anything whatsoever. There is also a daily reading from a pulpit there, and deliberation over what the authority of the Rule advises should be done. Ansegis also ordained that a memorial should be put up there to his name, so that when God set an end to his life on this earth, he might be laid to rest there by his fellows.

It is equally possible that this room could have been a freestanding structure east of the cloister east range, or that it was entered from the church, but, whatever view one takes of its position, it is certainly what is understood as a chapter-house in the later Middle Ages, even unto the association, at the very period when the chapter-house as a distinct building first emerges, of a chapter-house with burial and remembrance.[18]

So, the underlying principles of the medieval cloister were clearly understood by the second quarter of the 9th century, but what were the imperatives driving its development? There is much about the organisation of buildings on the St-Gall plan, and at Fontenelle that suggests they were not the result of a continuing organic architectural development, but that they have been thought out from first principles — that they are the result of clear-headed functional planning. It is this that distinguishes them from the sort of arrangement seen on the Hariulf manuscript at St-Riquier. But there must have been an architectural point of departure — a suggestion — a sort of pre-history of the medieval monastic cloister, bound up in the experiments of the late 8th century, or even earlier. These have been much discussed, and their origins have been sought in Roman courtyard houses, peristyle gardens, atria, eastern monasticism and the Late Antique *villa rustica*, the last being much favoured as the seed from which the medieval monastic cloister grew. Particularly since Frederick Behn excavated the Altenmünster at Lorsch in the 1920s, and interpreted his findings as meaning that between 765 and 774 Abbot Gundeland had converted a Frankish *villa rustica* to monastic use, adding a church on the south side.[19] But as the sort of structures that lie somewhere between the Altenmünster and the St-Gall plan are an involved subject, and the site at Lorsch is under complete review, it would be better leave it here, though I would add that looked at formally and non-archaeologically the courtyard house and related peristyle garden do seem to have more in common with the monastic cloister than the generally open yards of the *villa rustica*.[20]

5

Fig. 5.   Salerno Cathedral: atrium to east
John McNeill

Fig. 6.   New College, Oxford: detail of David Loggan view of 1675. The cloister is in the foreground, to the west of the college chapel, with the fellows quadrangle to its right

Fig. 7.   L'Abbaye-Blanche: reconstructed cloister walk against south wall of nave
John McNeill

Fig. 8.   San Benedetto, Conversano: south
walk from garth
John McNeill

Fig. 9   San Benedetto, Bríndisi: north walk
from garth
John McNeill

PLANNING AND DEVELOPMENT

THE great age of cloister building is the great age of monastic building, and the overwhelming majority of European cloisters were at least first established between *c*. 1000 and *c*. 1250. The problem with assessing this period in England and Wales is that only rarely does anything other than the backs of cloister walks survive *in situ*.[21] Many splendid fragments remain, and much can be done to reconstruct the design of individual 12th-century cloister walks, but it is not until one arrives at the traceried cloister walks of the mid-13th century and later that substantially complete walks survive.[22]

By contrast, in Europe surviving cloisters come thick and fast from the last quarter of the 11th century onwards — San Benedetto, Conversano, begun 1085, San Benedetto, Bríndisi, begun 1090, Nieul-sur-l'Autize probably in building during the 1090s, Moissac, completed 1100 — though looking at Europe as a whole does mask significant regional and chronological variations (Figs 8 and 9).[23] Most are situated in the angle between nave and transept or, in the absence of a transept, liturgically west of the apse; at Nieul-sur-l'Autize the cloister sits in the angle between nave and transept, at Bríndisi and Conversano, neither of which have transepts, the cloister adjoins the long wall of the church to the west of the apse. However, as in England, there are exceptions where the east cloister range projects east of the presbytery, as at St-Trophime at Arles, Sta Sofia at Benevento, and San Pere de Rodes, all of which are the result of the peculiarities of their site. At Arles, the archbishop's palace and courtyard already occupied the angle between the nave and transepts,[24] at Benevento the church is centrally-planned with a public square to the west,[25] and at Rodes, which is a particularly demanding site, the underlying bedrock rises steeply to the south-west of the nave.[26] One might make similar points about Old Sarum or Rochester cathedrals as regards topography or the disposition of pre-existing buildings, and there is no reason to suppose that any of the above cloisters belong to a functionally related group.[27] They are simply cloisters displaced for site-specific reasons.

Most continental cloisters also consist of four walks arranged around a garth, though, again, there are exceptions. At the Augustinian priory of Serrabone, in the

FIG. 10.   Serrabone: cloister walk to west
John McNeill

FIG. 11.   Santa Maria di Cerrate: church and
'loggia' from south-west
John McNeill

Pyrenees, for instance, there is a single walk which acts as a processional route connecting the dormitory and refectory, which were to the west, with the south transept, and seems to have some of the characteristics of a cloister walk, in that it housed a book press, arranged its arcades on a stylobate, and, in overlooking a steep ravine, looked onto a garden of sorts (Fig. 10).[28] At Santa Maria di Cerrate, just outside Lecce (Apulia), there is an enormous loggia aligned along the north side of the church, both of which date from the very end of the 12th century and which I suspect was conceived in the spirit of a cloister walk (Fig. 11). There is a laver adjacent to the walk, admittedly 17th century but likely to have replaced an earlier well-head on the same site, and just north of this are an olive press and cellar, refectory and western guest range, though the site of the late-12th-century dormitory is unknown. The whole thing is remarkably like a late Roman villa, specialising in the production of olive oil and organised to support a small Benedictine community.[29]

Many cloisters were also rebuilt in the later Middle Ages, though, as in England and Wales, it is exceptional to find an existing monastic site completely replanned and rebuilt after the late 12th century, as had generally been the case after the Norman Conquest. Indeed, patterns of planning and rebuilding are broadly comparable between England and continental Europe, and there are plenty of examples of the wholesale reconstruction of sites, and institutions, in the late 11th and 12th centuries. This happened at St-Georges de Boscherville, where the late-11th-century Augustinian church and conventual precincts were swept away after 1114 and the site replanned for a Benedictine community.[30] And Toulouse, where although the early-12th-century reconstruction of recently Cluniac Notre-Dame-de-la-Daurade retained its 5th-century axial rotunda, the late-11th- and early-12th-century rebuildings of the cathedral and St-Sernin involved the complete replanning of their respective sites and the construction of vast new conventual precincts and cloisters.[31] This sort of total precinct planning applied to existing sites — as distinct from completely new foundations — becomes rare after the middle of the 12th century, almost certainly because there is far less need after the middle of the 12th century to replace small buildings with large buildings. The main exceptions to this are cathedrals, particularly Spanish cathedrals,[32] and a handful of rather grand, Augustinian and Benedictine houses, most of them in northern France — as at St-Jean-des-Vignes, Soissons — where all elements of the earlier Romanesque abbey were obliterated in the course of a wholesale 13th-century rebuilding, or St-Nicaise at Reims, which was completely rebuilt between 1229 and 1311.[33]

Otherwise, once the cloister had been established, or perhaps it would be better to say once the conventual precincts had been laid out, if they are rebuilt they are usually rebuilt piecemeal — each project (such as new chapter-house, new refectory) being regarded as a relatively discrete programme, as St-Benigne, Dijon, where after 1272 a new dormitory was built above the existing early-11th-century chapter-house and dormitory undercroft, or Charroux where the reverse process applied, and a 13th-century chapter-house was constructed beneath a dormitory retained from the late-11th-century precinct, which in turn had followed a major revamp of the second quarter of the 12th century, from which one rather splendid, unpublished capital survives— (Figs 12 and 13).[34] But, as in England, the most common form of remodelling is the replacement of wooden-roofed Romanesque cloister walks by late medieval vaulted and traceried walks, as obviously eventually happened to the east walk at Charroux and is evident at St-Aubin at Angers (Fig. 14), or Cadouin (Fig. 15), where an elaborate historiated pendant vault was created in the last decade of the 15th century, or San Isidoro at León (Fig. 16), where, within the largely 12th-century claustral square, Juan Badajoz added a magnificent set of vaulted cloister walks in the second quarter of the 16th century which, as is not uncommon in 15th- and 16th-century Spain, dispensed with tracery in favour of an open stylobate.[35]

FIG. 12.   St-Sauveur, Charroux: east cloister range
John McNeill

FIG. 13.   St-Sauveur, Charroux: double capital
John McNeill

FIG. 14.   St-Aubin, Angers: elevation of the outer face of the chapter-house façade
Service Archéologique Maine-et-Loire

FIG. 15.   Abbaye de Cadouin: east walk to
south
John McNeill

FIG. 16.   San Isidoro, León: north cloister
walk to west
John McNeill

GARTHS, WALKS, AND LIFE IN THE CLOISTER

THE garth is the area about which least is known and, although archaeologists have recently begun to wake up to the importance of the unbuilt spaces within monasteries, the garth remains little understood. As already mentioned, the St-Gall plane features a juniper tree at its centre, which Paul Meyvaert has argued may have been the medieval monastic equivalent of the unknown biblical hyssop of Psalm 50 — *asperges me hysoppo et mondabor* — and to have provided branches for asperging altars on major feast days.[36] The 11th-century *Horologium Stellare Monasticum* also speaks of juniper in the cloister.[37] But the planting which is most commonly encountered in accounts of monastic cloisters — at least prior to the widespread adoption of formal parterres in the 17th century — is grass, and grass kept short as lawn. 'The green lawn of the cloister refreshes the eyes of beholders and brings to their minds the delightfulness of Paradise', as Hugh of Fouilloy put it.[38] At Rochester, the late-14th-century account rolls record regular payments for mowing the grass in the cloister.[39]

Most garths also have evidence of a cloister laver, generally opposite the refectory, and a few covered lavers have even survived — most famously the heavily restored examples at two Catalan Cistercian monasteries, Poblet and Santes Creus, along with San Zeno, Verona, Valmagne, Maulbronn and the like (Fig. 17).[40] But there is also sometimes evidence of additional basins or wells in cloisters, and the documentary evidence suggests we should expect to find many more.[41] The 11th-century Cluniac customaries of Bernard of Cluny and Ulrich of Zell point to a lot of washing going on in the cloister.[42] The monks washed their hands and faces at set times in the main monastic laver, being careful when drying their hands not to use the towels set aside by the kitchen brethren for drying their pots and pans.[43] However, when using soap to lather their faces the monks were to use basins specially set up for the purpose. During Holy Week groups of laymen were brought into the cloister to have their feet washed by the whole community.[44] The monks' garments also had to be periodically washed — and Bernard speaks of a large washboard being set up in the cloister garth, hollowed at the centre and divided into sections so that 'shirts could be washed here and undergarments there'.[45] Large portions of the cloister would then be strung with lines on which to dry the clothes, though usage seems to have had regard to appropriate appearance and the walk by the chapter-house was exempt from clothes lines.[46] Footwear was also washed, and we are told that the slippers of the children were not to be hung on lines to dry like those of the monks, but were to be laid out to dry in the garth.[47] When the clothes had dried they were taken down, folded and placed on benches in the walks. The shaving of tonsures also took place in the cloister, and Bernard describes the occasion in considerable detail. The monks were seated or lined up in two rows, one against the wall, the other group wielding razors or holding basins. When the seated group has been tonsured the two groups swap around. The chanting of Psalms accompanies the shaving. The *cameraius*, who had charge of the razors, was even exempt from the prohibition on noisy activities in the cloister during periods of silence, and was allowed to sharpen his knives in the cloister in the days leading up to a regular shave, provided 'he kept a little apart from the brethren who were reading'.[48] Certain other tasks could also be performed in the cloister walks (Fig. 18). The Eynsham customary talks of bookbinding and the preparation of parchment being permissible in the cloister, though, as is usual in these sorts of accounts, cautions that this should be done quietly, during periods when talking was allowed, and not on Sundays or feast days.[49]

FIG. 17.   Poblet: lavabo
John McNeill

FIG. 18.   Santes Creus: north cloister walk
to east. Monks would have used the
masonry bench backing on to the nave for
the *mandatum*, collation, and shaving. It is
more likely the low bench beneath the
tracery was used for reading
John McNeill

The rhythms of daily life could transform, or indeed place particular pressures, on individual walks. In Cistercian houses, the ritual public reading before compline known as *collatio* took place in the cloister walk adjacent to the church.[50] It also seems likely that in Cluniac and independent Benedictine houses the walk adjacent to the church was singled out for the formal period set aside for reading — *lectio*.[51] The chapter meeting, processions to and from the refectory, the church, into and out of the dormitory, would all animate particular walks at certain times of the day (and night). The period set aside for talking — *locutio* — was the period at which the greatest variety of activities took place in the cloister — the time when there would be the greatest movement and all walks would be in use, though one should not equate *locutio* with open-ended conversation. The Benedictine Rule suggests it is a time when practical matters could be settled, and expressly states the cellarer should be present at *locutio* so he might provide the monks with what they needed. Moreover, there were periods, such as Lent, when there was no talking in the cloister, and considerably more time was allocated to reading.[52]

Customs obviously varied between different groups of monasteries, and the extent to which all monastic cloisters were regarded by their monks as the busy and beating heart of the monastery it is difficult to say, as it is difficult to gauge the traffic between cloister walk and garth. The provision of openings in the stylobate, other than the refectory-laver link, is surprisingly varied, and as far as I have been able to observe it does not follow a particular pattern in houses of particular orders. The who and when (or indeed, how) of movement from walk to garth is not something that can be pieced together from monastic customaries.[53] But what can be gleaned from the customaries is that monks spent a lot of time in the cloister — most of it in silence, though depending on the monastic order, and the liturgical season (or whether a fellow monk had recently died, as silence was observed in the cloister between the death and burial of a member of the monastic community), periods of talking were allowed. It is reasonable to suppose that most of this time was spent in the walks, or on the stylobate. Much of it was certainly spent reading, or in prayer, and it is clear that by the end of the 11th century, if not earlier, the cloister had become the place for reading *par excellence*. Portable book chests, or, increasingly from the early 12th century, book cupboards were provided in the cloister. And surviving Lenten lists do offer an occasional glimpse of what monks were reading, which can be surprisingly varied.[54]

ARTICULATION

HOWEVER, to return to the main plot, and in the absence of any substantially original medieval garths, the character of a cloister is largely the result of its arcades, which in turn are determined by how the walks are covered. If the walks are vaulted, relatively thick walls are necessary, and the columns might be arranged in small groups so as to allow substantial piers to support relieving arches, as happened in the late 11th century at Brindisi, and is frequent in 12th-century Provence (Figs 9 and 19).[55] Alternatively, the columns might be arranged in deeply-spaced pairs to support a consistently thick wall, as occurs in 12th-century Catalonia,[56] or a designer might even use compound piers, as at the cathedral of Le Puy. If a timber roof was used, the arches could be supported on a continuous line of columns. The most common form this took was to arrange the columns in pairs, as at Silos (Fig. 20), but occasionally a single line of columns might be used — as in the largely reconstructed south and west cloister walks at St-Michel de Cuxa, initially built under Abbot Gregory (1137–46), or the cathedral of Roda de Isábena.[57] A distinctive variant, apparently initiated at Moissac, was to alternate single and double columns.[58] This remained relatively unusual, and enjoyed its greatest popularity in south-western France and the Pyrenees, turning up at La Daurade and the cathedral in Toulouse, St-Pons-de-Thomières, St-Lizier, and San Juan de la Peña.[59] However, what can now appear as outliers are interesting, in that this alternating rhythm is used in what is arguably the earliest Dominican precinct to survive in Europe, the cloister added to the north of Santa Sabina in Rome, around the time Pope Honorius III made over the church to the Dominican Order in 1219 (Fig. 21).[60] It also turns up in a sumptuous variant in the cloister of Notre-Dame-en-Vaux at Châlons-sur-Marne, and may well have been a feature of early gothic cloisters in northern France (Fig. 22).[61]

Notre-Dame-en-Vaux also introduces one of the great themes of the late-12th- and early-13th-century cloister — what one might describe as claustral microarchitecture. For this is the period which witnesses the most elaborate experiments with claustral columns and arches. There are column figures in various guises and a quite astonishing variety of supports at Châlons-sur-Marne, with eight-column clusters articulating the angles, and sumptuously carved and faceted columns orchestrated in sophisticated rhythmic changes beneath the arcades. Nor were cloister arcades incorporating column figures peculiar to early Gothic France.[62] There are several sites in northern and central Italy from which claustral column figures have survived, as with those now in the Museo Nazionale in Ravenna, which probably came originally from the cloister of San Vitale (Fig. 23).[63] Continuing the microarchitectural theme, one finds cosmati inlay at San Paolo fuori le mura, Rome around 1200 (and indeed further south),[64] syncopated arcading at Mont-St-Michel,[65] richly polished stones and faceted supports in Provence,[66] exquisitely carved columns in Anjou (Figs 24 and 25),[67] intersecting arches at San Pedro, and a sort of arcuated handwriting or Kufic verse at San Juan de Duero, both of them in Soria (Fig. 26).[68] This is also, of course, the period which sees the invention of the glazed and traceried cloister, certainly known by the second quarter of the 13th century, and which, like its plate-traceried forebears of the very beginning of the 13th century, was widely adopted in Cistercian monasteries, as at Heiligenkreuz by c. 1230, or the north walk at Noirlac of perhaps the 1240s (Fig. 27).[69]

HISTORIATED CLOISTERS

THE date when historiated capitals were first used in a cloister is unknown, and the only evidence of their use prior to Moissac is a tantalising refererence in the Chronicle of St-Florent, which tells us that some time before his death in 1022 abbot Roger of Blois had built a cloister decorated with sculptures which were painted and enriched with verse inscriptions, and that under abbot Frederick (1022–55), these sculptures so enraged a monk of Marmoutier that he attacked them with a hammer, destroying the heads of many figures.[70] So it seems there were partisans of image-free cloisters long before Bernard of Clairvaux. The other text which is usually pressed into service when discussing the origins of the historiated cloister is the mention of sumptuous sculpture — *claustrum quidam, quamquam sumptuosis expensis, mira arte sculptoria decoravit* — in the cloister at St-Bertin c. 1080–85, but this does not specifically mention figure sculpture.[71] All surviving cloister sculpture pre-Moissac, or at least all sculpture that has been recognised as having originated in a cloister that pre-dates 1100, is non-narrative — either foliate or geometric, as at Tournus, or animate, as at Brindisi.[72] The cloister at Moissac itself was built some forty or so years after the abbey of

FIG. 19.   Abbaye de Sénanque: east
cloister walk from garth
John McNeill

FIG. 20.   Santo Domingo de Silos: east cloister
walk to south
John McNeill

FIG. 21 (*above left*).   Santa Sabina, Rome: north
cloister walk to east
John McNeill

FIG. 22 (*above right*).   Notre-Dame-en-Vaux,
Châlons-sur-Marne: five-column section of cloister
arcade
John McNeill

FIG. 23 (*left*).   Museo Nazionale, Ravenna: figure of
Saint John from former cloister of San Vitale
John McNeill

FIG. 24.   St-Nicolas, Angers: displaced
column probably originally from cloister or
chapter-house entry
John McNeill

FIG. 25.   St-Nicolas, Angers: displaced
column probably originally from cloister or
chapter-house entry
John McNeill

FIG. 26.   San Juan de Duero: cloister arcade
John McNeill

FIG. 27.   Noirlac: north cloister walk to west
John McNeill

Moissac was affiliated to Cluny, the work being undertaken while Ansquitil was abbot and being complete in the year 1100 (Fig. 28).[73] Circumstantial evidence suggests it was started in 1096. Despite the insertion of a new roof and new arches under Abbot Bertrand de Montaigut (1260–95), the capitals are likely to be in their original positions — as stylistically they fall into groups that coincide with specific walks. And despite a herculean scholarly effort to discern a unifying programme, no convincing explanation has so far been advanced to demonstrate why any sequence of more than three capitals are arranged as they are.[74]

Notwithstanding this, it is very Cluniac — Durandus, the first Cluniac abbot of Moissac, is positioned opposite the chapter-house entrance. The martyrdoms of Saints Peter and Paul are depicted together on a capital next to the paired images of the two titular saints of Cluny. Those saints who were particularly venerated at Cluny, and were accorded octaves and special offices — such as John the Baptist, Benedict, Martin and Lawrence — are all there. So is the Exaltation of the Cross, a capital to be seen in the context of the feast of the Inventio Sanctae Crucis, celebrated with great solemnity at Cluny on 14 September from the time of Odilo.[75] When the Moissac cloister was first planned a number of associates of the Bernard Gelduin workshop from Toulouse were employed — perhaps regarded as specialist relief sculptors — to carve the angle figures. Gelduin workshop sculptors are also responsible for producing what are probably three trial pieces, one of them in marble, which were subsequently pressed into service.[76] But in the event something happened, and the Toulouse sculptors left. Perhaps it was decided it was too expensive to employ marble for the capitals and abaci, perhaps the trial narrative capitals were not good enough, or the Toulouse sculptors were called to another job — or died? But for whatever reason, a group of sculptors whose background probably lies around Albi were brought in, and produced

FIG. 29.   Moissac: Saint Martin divides
his cloak
John McNeill

the overwhelming majority of capitals at Moissac.[77] They developed a very distinctive narrative method, simplifying the shape of the capital so as to enhance the legibility of the scenes, and experimenting with what Meyer Schapiro usefully characterised as closed and open fields. Closed field is the dominant compositional mode at Moissac, where each face of the capital carries a single image or episode from a story. See, for example, the Saint Martin capital, or the capital depicting the Four Evangelists (Fig. 29). As most of the capitals are carved on all four faces, if you wish to read them quickly you have to be a monastic acrobat, and swing around the column and over the stylobate, strongly suggesting that each capital — or rather the two faces of the capital visible at any one time — were to be considered slowly, and that the continuation of related scenes onto the side facing the garth was a matter of compositional convenience. As Leah Rutchick has pointed out, there is more to this method than simple convenience, however. A sequential arrangement of scenes across four faces of a capital encourages anticipation — and as a monk becomes familiar with the cloister memory cuts in, and what cannot be seen might inform what can.[78] Indeed, Schapiro's south gallery master actively exploited this, experimenting with open field capitals, in which a single scene might be expanded to run across two, or even three faces of the capital. Moissac is also a literate cloister, or rather it veers between the literate and the semi-literate, between the magnificent epigraphy of the alphabet abacus and pier reliefs, and what Schapiro memorably described as the vagrant and decomposed inscriptions of the east walk.[79] It is also important to point out that not all the Moissac cloister capitals are historiated, and there are a considerable number of foliate and animate capitals relatively freely distributed across the various walks.[80]

The sculptors responsible for Moissac went on to carve the first series of capitals from the cloister of Notre-Dame-de-la-Daurade in Toulouse — see, for example, their new version of the exhaltation of the cross (Figs 30 and 31) — utilising both compositional modes and contributing a couple of extraordinary abaci, described by Alexandre du Mège in the first catalogue of the Musée des Augustins as the *toilette du prince* and *tableaux de la vie domestique* (Figs 32 and 33).[81] The faces of the *tableaux de la vie domestique* (M.111) are variously concerned with reading and writing or perhaps spelling and rhyming games, wrestlers, musicians, tumblers, and boys playing board games — and it is tempting to speculate these compositions may have acted as commentaries on the images on the capital below. As it happens this abacus is now displayed above the Incredulity of Thomas and Transfiguration of Christ — and the

FIG. 30. Moissac: Exaltation of the Cross
John McNeill

FIG. 31. Musée des Augustins,
Toulouse: Exaltation of the
Cross from La Daurade
(M.119)
John McNeill

FIG. 32. Musée des Augustins, Toulouse:
tableaux de la vie domestique (M.111)
John McNeill

FIG. 33. Musée des Augustins, Toulouse:
tableaux de la vie domestique (M.111)
John McNeill

lively struggle of the figures with their books, in contrast to the rather solemn figure sitting on his own to the left, brings to mind Ulrich of Zell's evocation of the *pueri* and *iuvenes* learning to read, seated on their *trunci*, and the renunciation of wordly games necessary to effect the transfiguration of oblates into monks. Alternatively, the abacus may have been intended to set up a starker set of contrasts between the cloister and a world of secular pleasure, though it should be noted that the joining of particular capitals with particular abaci affer they entired the Musée des Augustins is entirely arbitrary.[82] However it was that such abaci were intended to be read, the arrangement of figures on abaci is exceptional, and something which seems to belong to this early, and experimental, phase of historiated cloister design.

From this point on, the development of historiated cloisters seems to have swift. Indeed, the decision to create a historiated cloister at La Daurade ushered in a period of competitive cloister building in Toulouse which witnessed rapid changes in narrative methods — as can be seen in the capitals carved by the group of sculptors who eventually completed the cloister of La Daurade — the so-called Second Daurade Workshop.[83] One might compare the very much more dramatic figure groupings of their version of the Arrest of Christ with the earlier depiction of the scene — and point to the evidence for the expressive use of the shape of the capital, as in the Four Rivers of Paradise (Figs 34–36).[84] At the cathedral there is an enhanced sense of narrative continuity. See, for example, the magnificent capital devoted to the Adoration of the Magi (Fig. 37), or the Legend of Mary of Egypt,[85] though it should also be said that not all Toulouse cloisters went historiated. Not a single narrative capital survives from the cloister of St-Sernin.[86] And even in a predominantly historiated cloister such as La Daurade, non-narrative forms were employed of such exquisite finish that one wonders whether the monks were intended to reflect upon virtuosity itself (Fig. 38).[87]

It is also ultimately Moissac which inspired the adoption of historiated cloisters by a number of the chapters of Augustinian canons to whom the running of many southern French and northern Spanish cathedrals had been entrusted since the second half of the 11th century — as at Jaca, where the magnificent capital of David and the Musicians of *c.* 1110–20 was originally carved for the chapter-house portal,[88] or Pamplona, where a group of three historiated and six foliate double capitals of *c.* 1140 survive from the cathedral cloister.[89] Of the three historiated capitals, two are devoted to the Passion of Christ and one to an account of Job's miseries — the scenes being wrapped around the face of the capital as a frieze.

Subsequently, in the second half of the 12th century, there do seem to have been attempts to produce sequential arrangements of narrative capitals, as Pamela Patton has recently demonstrated for San Juan de la Peña, where all surviving capitals either depict scenes from Genesis or the Life of Christ, and were originally arranged in scriptural order.[90] Or, most remarkably, Santa María la Mayor at Tudela, where, running clockwise between the north-west pier and a point in the south cloister arcade, over thirty episodes between the Nativity of Christ and the Conversion of Paul are organised according to a fairly straightforward temporal sequence.[91] But most 12th-century cloisters historiated cloisters follow Moissac's lead and organise the sculpture as a diversified set of subjects and themes, some capitals or reliefs grouped in discrete areas, others arranged in isolation. The late-12th-century cloister at Sant Cugat del Vallès is an excellent example.[92]

Notre-Dame-en-Vaux at Châlons-sur-Marne was probably like this. The cloister here was demolished in 1759, but most of the debris was then used in the construction of a number of houses for the canons on the same site. The odd capital and column-figure dribbled out onto the international art market in the 19th century, but most of what survives was brought to light between 1963 and 1976, when the then decrepit 18th-century buildings were demolished and the site was systematically excavated. The spoil amounts to around two-thirds of the bases, columns and capitals of a cloister Léon Pressouyre has dated to between 1170 and 1180.[93]

There are a fair number of foliage capitals and grotesques, as at Moissac, but the narrative material broadly falls into five categories.[94] Old Testament figures — all of them carved as column figures, some of which have a typological significance, such as Moses, Abraham sacrificing Isaac, and the Widow of Sarepta. Simeon and John the Baptist probably belong with this group (Fig. 39). Some figures of Apostles, Old Testament Kings and Prophets, most of them badly damaged. Scenes from the Life of Christ — all of which are carved on capitals — as in the magnificent Wedding at Cana

FIG. 34.   Musée des Augustins, Toulouse:
Arrest of Christ by La Daurade First
Workshop (M.114)

John McNeill

FIG. 35.   Musée des Augustins, Toulouse:
Arrest of Christ by La Daurade Second
Workshop (M.131)

John McNeill

FIG. 36.   Musée des Augustins, Toulouse:
Four Rivers of Paradise capital. (M.157)

John McNeill

FIG. 37.   Musée des Augustins, Toulouse:
face of Adoration of the Magi capital from
Saint-Étienne, Toulouse

John McNeill

FIG. 38.   Musée des Augustins, Toulouse:
Unlocalised capital probably from the cloister
at La Daurade (M174)

John McNeill

capital, where the entire capital was given over to a single subject (Fig. 41). Other capitals treat each face separately, such as that which juxtaposes the Presentation in the Temple, Flight into Egypt, Baptism and Raising of Lazarus. A small eschatological group, namely two capitals showing the Weighing of Souls and the Damned, to which the Wise and Foolish Virgins might be related (and the surviving Foolish Virgins appear on both a capital and as a column figure). And selective scenes from the lives of saints, of which far and away the most interesting is an image of the fasting St Nicholas turning away from his mother's breast as an infant (Fig. 40). Some of this narrative could certainly have been organised into coherent mini-programmes. But for other subjects, such as the fasting St Nicholas, this is unlikely, and it makes more sense to see this as an image which functioned as an example of abstinence in its own right, and may have taken on a particular value during Lent.[95] The capital showing Christ washing the feet of the Apostles — again a single subject capital — may also have had a self-contained liturgical and stational purpose, though the direct evidence for this is unfortunately post-medieval, and the information that the ceremony of the washing of feet on Maundy Thursday — *mandatum* — took place beneath this capital comes from a letter of 1754.[96]

More obviously self-sufficient or integrated programmes tend to be reserved for chapter-house entrances, though some of the more important 12th-century examples are fragmentary and their reconstruction and interpretation is disputed. Toulouse, as it happens, is again a good example of this. One question here is how to interpret the figures of twelve apostles said to have been recovered from the cloister of the cathedral of Saint-Etienne.[97] Eight of these are carved as pairs and arranged to take an enormous capital block square with the wall, and four are carved singly and designed to be bedded at 45 degrees to the wall plane (Fig. 42). When Alexandre du Mège installed these in the Musée de Toulouse in the 1830s he reconstructed them as a portal which he claimed originally marked the chapter-house entrance. But du Mège is a notoriously unreliable commentator, describing seeing the figures acting as a chapter-house portal in an article he published in 1835, and flatly contradicting his earlier claim of 1823 that he saw the four single apostles standing in the corners of the chapter-house.[98] In fact, du Mège probably first saw the figures only after they were removed from Saint-Etienne. The chapter-house certainly no longer existed by April, 1812, the year in which he claimed to have seen them, and may have been demolished the previous year.[99]

Scepticism of the du Mège reconstruction reached a crescendo in 1968 when Linda Seidl published a celebrated article entitled 'a romantic forgery', and some eight years later the museum authorities quietly dismantled the arrangement of the figures as a portal.[100] Seidl went on to suggest the figures originally embellished the chapter-house interior, with the four paired apostles supporting the transverse arches of a barrel vault, and the single figures at the four corners, in part prefiguring the sort of design with which the interior of the Camera Santa at Oviedo was embellished later in the 12th century. But Seidl's reconstruction has not enjoyed universal support, at 1.15 m the figures really are too small for the sort of supporting role envisaged, and the Saint-Etienne apostles remain unanchored.[101] Notwithstanding this, a position around the chapter-house entrance remains entirely plausible, though one which may have involved the two lateral openings as well as the chapter-house itself.

When it comes to the collection of reliefs and column figures associated with the chapter-house at La Daurade, there is no dispute they were originally from the chapter-house entrance. There is a description of 1760 which mentions a figured

FIG. 39. Notre-Dame-en-Vaux, Châlons-sur-Marne: Simeon holding the Christ-Child
John McNeill

FIG. 40. Notre-Dame-en-Vaux, Châlons-sur-Marne: Saint Nicholas refuses his mother's breast
John McNeill

FIG. 41. Notre-Dame-en-Vaux, Châlons-sur-Marne: detail of Wedding at Cana capital
John McNeill

chapter-house portal and a plan made by François Franque in 1764, prior to the proposed 18th-century reconstruction of the monastic church.[102] The disputes here are over whether all the figures from the chapter-house entry have survived, what is the identity of two crowned column figures, and how they all originally fitted together. There are three prophets set within niches, a possible pairing of Solomon and Sheba, a majestic figure of David usually seen as a pair with an equally majestic, if horribly repainted, Virgin and Child, and seven column figures, two of whom are crowned of which the one with both arms intact holds an ampulla. Serafín Moralejo argued the crowned figure holding an ampulla was one of three Magi, and suggested the chapter-house portal juxtaposed a monumental narrative grouping of the Adoration of the Magi diagonally slanted across its southern jambs with prophets to the north. Solomon and Sheba faced outwards between the portal and the lateral openings, while the reliefs of David and the Virgin and Child faced each other beneath the inner order of the portal and across the chapter-house entry (Fig. 43).[103] Horste opted for a lighter

FIG. 42.   Musée des Augustins, Toulouse:
Apostles Paul and Peter from cathedral of
Saint-Étienne, Toulouse

John McNeill

and more open design, which accords better with the Franque plan and limits the losses to no more than two figures (Fig. 44). She dismissed the idea of a narrative Adoration, and interpreted the king holding the ampulla as an Old Testament figure.[104] Horste dated the sculpture early, to *c.* 1165–75. Moralejo opted for a date after *c.* 1180. Importance attaches to the dating because the formal and expressive qualities of the Daurade chapter-house figures relate them to the early Gothic portals of northern France — particularly the *Portail Royal* at Chartres Cathedral — and relations between the sculpture of north and south in the second half of the 12th century excite scholarly passions.[105] The points on which both agree are that David and the Virgin and Child originally faced each other across the chapter-house entry (Figs 45 and 46), and Solomon and Sheba looked out into the cloister walk. The reason for pressing La Daurade in this way is that the themes it brought to bear on a chapter-house entrance — Christ as the fulfilment of Old Testament prophecy, David, the Virgin and Child — are powerful themes. Along with the Incarnation, they are the themes most commonly encountered on chapter-house façades. And yet their deployment at the Daurade never seems to have solidified into a model, and there is no evidence with chapter-house façades that iconographic programmes were ever explored in broadly consistent formats, as happens with church portal sculpture.[106]

This is particularly evident in the last 12th-century chapter-house programme it seems appropriate to point up — that of Saint-Aubin at Angers — where David is

FIG. 43.   Reconstruction of chapter-house façade at La Daurade, Toulouse
Serafín Moralejo (Annuario de estudios medievales, 1983)

FIG. 44.   Reconstruction of chapter-house façade at La Daurade, Toulouse
Kathryn Horste and William Broom

also paired with the Virgin and Child, though the relationship between the two is handled in a looser and more typically western French manner than was likely to have been the case at La Daurade. Indeed, David is not here depicted as the author of the Psalms, the Virgin and Child are not beneath a canopy, and the two are separated by

25

FIG. 45.   Musée des Augustins, Toulouse:
King David from chapter-house façade at La
Daurade

John McNeill

FIG. 46.   Musée des Augustins, Toulouse:
Virgin and Child from chapter-house façade
at La Daurade

John McNeill

a considerable distance. But the reason for bringing it into the discussion is that it is an early instance of what may have been intended as a programme to be applied to a chapter-house entrance, and the relative positioning of the Virgin and Child on the chapter-house façade suggests the image had a specific role to play. The archaeological and iconographical arguments here are not easily summarised, but it is likely the east cloister walk at St-Aubin was built between *c.* 1128 and *c.* 1135.[107] As one moves south from the chapter-house entrance one sees, or rather would have seen, in the tympana contained within three consecutive arches, a single image of the Virgin and Child (the painting of the Magi and Massacre of the Innocents was added around 1160–70 in a way which radically modified the role originally played by the Virgin and Child), a damaged image of a man escaping from a dragon, and three scenes from the life of David — namely David squaring up to Goliath, killing him, and presenting his head to Saul (Figs 47–49).[108] Mary is the pivot of all this, and her importance is underscored by the choice of a double-mandorla which, as was pointed out long ago, is a means of emphasising the role of the Virgin as Queen of Heaven and extending to

FIG. 47.   St-Aubin, Angers: tympanum and arch of bays 7–8 of chapter-house façade
John McNeill

FIG. 48.   St-Aubin, Angers: tympanum and arch of bays 9–10 of chapter-house façade
John McNeill

FIG. 49.   St-Aubin, Angers: detail of tympanum of bays 11–12 of chapter-house façade
John McNeill

her the symbolic trappings of divinity.[109] And she undoubtedly is a Queen, wearing a prominent jewelled crown which is both an affirmation of her temporal royalty, inherited through the line of David, and an affirmation of her role in heaven. In the words of Peter the Venerable she is *imperatrix coelorum, dominatrix angelorum* — empress of heaven, lord of the angels.[110]

Moreover, there is a strong sense that the conflicts depicted in the next arch to the south are intended to qualify the image of the Virgin, and lend her an intercessionary role. It does not help that this is now incomplete — but in essence there is a battle being waged around the arch, and a man fleeing from a dragon in the tympanum. There is nothing of which I am aware which parallels the tympanum composition, and I would be inclined to read it straightforwardly. A soldier within the arc of a battle takes flight from a dragon and runs towards the Virgin in the neighbouring arch. The whole may also be modulated by an image of temptation below — the only capital in the south arcades which might have a role in the iconography of the south arches proper, and an image which seems to derive from the belfry at Cunault, where it is juxtaposed with the Annunciation; temptation and sin — or redemption via the Incarnation.[111] This strongly suggests that the monks of Saint-Aubin also turned to the Virgin for aid in the face of temptation, and for intercession on their behalf with Christ. And the positioning of images indicating a path away from sin and towards the Virgin at the threshold of the chapter-house seems entirely appropriate in this context.[112] In other words, the role played by the Virgin at Saint-Aubin is fundamentally that of mediatrix.[113]

Finally, David in the southernmost opening also refers to the Virgin — to leap over the spiritual battle of the middle arch, as well as to partake of it. But it is probable he equally has a far more specific and commemorative role to play within the monastery of Saint-Aubin. It is likely he was intended to allude to the exploits of Count Geoffrey Grisgonelle, the man who first ceded the community the right to freely elect their own abbot in 966. As far as I am aware it was Victor Godard-Faultrier who first noticed the parallel between the representation of David and Goliath and a story of a single combat which supposedly took place Grisegonelle and a Danish giant known as Haustuin, which supposedly took place during the siege of Paris in 978.[114] Whether this combat ever took place need not concern us. What is important is that it had evolved into an epic by the 12th century, and is recounted in all four versions of the deeds of the counts of Anjou, where Haustuin is invariably described as *alter Goliath* and Grisegonelle as *alter David*.[115]

The themes which extend across the chapter-house entrance and south arcades at Saint-Aubin are interwoven. They are partly commemorative — David as Grisegonelle as guarantor of both monastic independence and protection — and partly intercessionary. They offer mediation and hope to an ancient community.

Saint-Aubin is unusual and relatively early in doing this. It is also intensely self-conscious, which exactly befits its status as the pre-eminent comitally supported abbey in an expansionary county. But figurative sculpture is not the only way a cloister might be imbued with local meaning. Text is another vehicle, particularly in Italy and Provence. The cloister of the Augustinian canons attached to the cathedral at Vaison, for example, is overlooked by an inscription which gives thanks for the passing away of the Mistral, and goes on to indulge in some edifying numerology.[116]

I exhort you brothers to profit from the departure of Aquilon and faithfully guard the rule of the cloister so that the threefold will embrace the fourfold in such a manner that the living stones will be inspired two times six. Peace on this house.

The convention has been to see the threefold as the theological virtues embracing the fourfold (cloister) to the benefit of the twelve canons (two times six).[117] Italian cloisters can be prolix with inscriptions, which are often concerned to say something about the history of the community. At Sant' Orso, Aosta, a capital show Saint Ours presenting the first Augustinian prior, Arnolfo, to St Augustine, and underlines this on the neighbouring capital with an image of Aribertus, bishop of Aosta, making a blessing alongside an inscription which translates as 'In the year of Our Lord 1133, the regular life was introduced to this cloister'.[118] And in the cloister at Sta Sofia at Benevento, a capital celebrates the contribution of John IV, abbot between 1142 and 1177, to the rebuilding of the cloister (Fig. 50).[119]

Little in the way of text, or figurative imagery, survives from English 11th- or 12th-century cloisters. There is some in the east range of Rochester Cathedral priory, a group of capitals from Norwich Cathedral priory, a laver embellished with figurative reliefs at Wenlock priory, a capital which may have come from the 12th-century cloister at Westminster Abbey, and, of course, the portals that originally gave onto the north cloister walk at Ely Cathedral, but when it comes to cloister arcades none of the imagery that survives has an obvious textual or theological base. I do hasten to add that the absence of evidence is not evidence of absence. Far too much has disappeared for one to be able to generalise here — and in continental Europe it should be emphasised that the majority of cloister arcades are neither inscription-rich, nor historiated. Most partake of the imagery of the garden, that is they are foliate — even the one capital so far discovered from the cloister arcades at Saint-Aubin, Angers is foliate — or they confront the monks with images of grotesques and monsters. There is a growing tendency to see these monsters and hybrids as part of a wider medieval

FIG. 50.   Santa Sofia, Benevento: capital in east
walk with inscription praising Abbot John IV
John McNeill

interest in the world of deformed or unlike, unseen things, a world often encountered
on corbel tables and socles — around the edges of churches, or in the margins and
beneath the text of manuscript folios.[120] These are then interpreted as an invitation to
the monk to reflect on his terrors and temptations.[121] The monstrous apes and hybrids
and centaurs functioned as conventional depictions of corporeal deformity which
manifest in physical form the spiritual deformities, inner desires and phantasms that
disturbed the collective imagination of the monastic community. Thomas Dale has
recently published a very learned, impeccably referenced article on this, anchoring his
enquiry in St-Michel de Cuxa.[122] And he is absolutely right that sometimes monks
externalise these conflicts in a way we might think of as paradoxical, by bringing
them into the cloister, where they might be tamed through familiarity and ultimately
transcended. The actual hybrids themselves can often be precisely identified and associated with particular vices, degeneracies, or temptations, though they tend to take on
slightly different forms in different areas, as sculptural workshops develop favoured
compositions. The workshop responsible for most of the cloister capitals at St-Michel
de Cuxa, for instance, went on to Serrabone, and established a repertoire which
echoed down the next half century in the eastern Pyrenees;[123] winged creatures guard-
ing their mouths was one favourite, found at Saint-Michel de Cuxa, Serrabone,
Elne, Ripoll, St-Martin-du-Canigou, and other sites (Figs 51–53). But notwithstanding
regional preferences for particular sorts of grotesque, which probably, in fact, begin as
workshop preferences, monsters and hybrids are found throughout European cloisters
(Fig. 54).

   The development of traceried cloisters obviously changed this. Imagery of whatever
type moved, and the importance of the capital was lessened. It did not disappear
completely, and there are some notable 14th-century examples of capitals being used
to underline particular points. At Santes Creus, where the English master mason,
Reynard Foynoll, began building the west cloister walk around 1331, the south-west
angle capital depicts the Creation and Fall, organising the scenes to run from right to
left and so bring one round into the west walk, the *conversi* walk, and face to face

FIG. 51.   Elne Cathedral: capital from south
cloister walk
John McNeill

FIG. 52.   Santa Maria, Ripoll: capital from
north cloister walk
John McNeill

FIG. 53.   Serrabone: capital from cloister
walk
John McNeill

FIG. 54.   Abbaye de Maillezais: 12th-century
capital from cloister depicting 12 basilisks
John McNeill

with the greatest concentration of hybrids and grotesques in the cloister.[124] But, by and
large, in the later Middle Ages the importance of the cloister capital as a bearer
of meaning was diluted as the potential of glass, vaults and rear walls came to be
recognised.[125] Rear walls in particular became very important, as at Elne where the

Fig. 55. Elne Cathedral: Deposition plaque from inner south walk of cloister

John McNeill

cloister was repaired and vaulted around 1340, and relief panels of the Passion and Resurrection, running from the Raising of Lazarus at the north-east angle to Pentecost by the entrance into the church (Fig. 55).[126] This is a late medieval story, however, and the inclination of this paper has been to concentrate on the cloister between its origins and the 13th century. But there is much about the cloister we see only vaguely, and I would like to conclude with one of the most remarkable phenomena of all, and one which seems without parallel in England — tall cloister walks.

Tall in this instance means anything over 25 feet — or, say, 8 metres. The vast majority of cloister walks are between 12 and 20 feet (roughly 4 to 6 metres). Above 6 metres would be lofty in England — Westminster rather than Gloucester.[127] But there are a considerable number of very tall cloister walks in Spain, most, though not all, attached to cathedrals — and it can be argued they look back towards one of two, unusual, exemplars — Pamplona and Lérida. Neither cloister is closely dated or well understood, and of the two Lérida is perhaps the more revealing (Figs 56 and 57).[128] The new cathedral at Lérida was begun in 1203 to the east of the site of the former mosque, which, in turn, seems to have been modified so as to act as the cathedral after 1149.[129] Towards the end of the 13th century an arcaded courtyard was attached to this, combining some of the characteristics of an atrium with some of the characteristics of a cloister.[130] It is situated to the west of the cathedral and has a public entrance giving onto the west walk. But it was also used by the chapter, with a canonry off one walk and records of chapter meetings being held in another. In 1746 the cathedral was abandoned, and two years later the first proposals to adapt the cloister and church to military use were circulated. Shortly afterwards the traceried openings of the cloister walks were blocked up, intermediate floors were inserted and the whole was converted into a barracks, a situation which endured until 1925, when the first tentative attempts were made to remove 18th-century partitioning. The military finally left the site in 1948.[131] Much of the tracery was subsequently replaced, in many cases speculatively and on the basis of no more than few fragments.

To a medievalist the cloister is inherently problematic, but the vaults and inner walls are fine, and the height and shape of the cloister are original. It desperately needs a major archaeological survey, but despite the much that is uncertain, Lérida

FIG. 56.   Pamplona Cathedral: west cloister
walk to north
John McNeill

FIG. 57.   Lérida Cathedral: north cloister
walk to west
John McNeill

does seem important in stimulating the fashion for tall cloisters in Spain. This may seem a strange way to end, with something that has no relevance to the medieval cloister in England and Wales. But that, in a sense, is the point. Cloisters are both the most international and the most local of spaces. For most orders and for most of the time they balance the needs of a regular community — needs that were fairly consistent throughout Latin Europe — with the resources and preferences of their immediate region. The rest of this volume bears on how such a balance was struck in medieval England and Wales.

ACKNOWLEDGEMENTS

Many people have tried to help me understand medieval cloisters over the years, and what familiarity I have would never have got beyond the basics without them. For their generous conversation and the insights they have shared with me I am indebted to François Comte, Anna Eavis, Eric Fernie, the late Larry Hoey, Linda Monckton, John Montague, Eric Palazzo, Daniel Prigent, David Stocker, Neil Stratford and Tim Tatton-Brown. For kindnesses with regard to this paper, I should particularly like to thank Tara O'Connor, Carolyn Heighway, Christine Reynold, Warwick Rodwell and Jennifer Thorp. I am also enormously grateful to the authorities at the Musée des Augustins in Toulouse for allowing me to bring a tripod into the former refectory in the summer of 2000, and photograph Romanesque stonework at will.

NOTES

1. The literature on the origins and early development of monastic cloisters is extensive, but among the more wide-ranging studies, see W. Braunfels, *Monasteries of Western Europe: The Architecture of the Orders* (London 1972), particularly 9–66; W. Horn, 'On the Origins of the Medieval Cloister', *Gesta*, XII (1973), 13–52; R. Legler, *Kreuzgänge: Orte der Meditation* (Cologne 1995); B. Brenk, 'Zum Problem der Vierflügelanlage (claustrum) in frühchristlichen und frühmittelalterlichen Klöstern', in *Studien zum St. Galler Klosterplan II*, ed. P. Ochsenbein and K. Schmuki (St Gall 2002), 185–215; and three articles in the volume of transactions of the 1999 Tübingen symposium on the medieval cloister, published as *Der Mittelalterliche Kreuzgang*, ed. P. Klein (Regensburg 2004), namely W. Jacobsen, 'Die Anfänge des abendländischen Kreuzgangs', 37–56, J.-P. Caillet, 'Atrium, péristyle et cloître: des réalités si diverses?', 57–65, and R. Legler, 'Der abendländischen Kreuzgang — Erfindung oder Tradition?', 66–79.

2. On the chronology of the 11th-century work at St-Guilhem, see M Durliat, 'La Catalogne et le premier art roman', *Bull. mon.*, CXLVII (1989), 220–21. Éliane Vergnolle prefers a date in the third quarter of the 11th century. E. Vergnolle, *L'Art Romane en France* (Paris 1994), 259.

3. J. Henriet, 'Saint-Philibert de Tournus. Les campagnes de construction du XIe siècle', in *Saint-Philibert de Tournus. Histoire, Archéologie, Art*, ed. J. Thirion (Tournus 1995), 177–201, and B. St-John Vitus, 'Les bâtiments claustraux de Saint-Philibert au moyen-age', ibid., 231–48. It was in this surviving north cloister walk that 18th-century local historians maintain that Abbot Ardain was buried in 1056.

4. M. Mataro i Pladelesala and E. Riu-Barrera, 'Sant Pere de Rodes: Un monestir comtal a la perifèria de l'extingit Imperi carolingi', in *Catalunya a l'època carolíngia*, exhibition catalogue (Barcelona 1999), 236–42 (précis in English 536–39). There has been no good study of the conventual buildings at Rodes, whose status has been radically altered by the restoration work of the last fifteen years, and whose fragile earlier archaeology was anyway extensively altered in the 12th century. The early work in the east range, and elements of the lower storey of the cloister are broadly contemporary with the monastic church, which seems likely to have been built in two phases. The most plausible short account of this church is given by Marcel Durliat in 'La Catalogne et le premier art roman', 214–18, who argued that the apse and outer shell of the church were complete by 1022, with the nave arcade and vaults likely to date to the 1030s. The extreme irregularity of the plan of the cloister and east range suggests that they were begun after the monastic church had been laid out.

5. See N. Stratford, 'Les bâtiments de l'abbaye de Cluny à l'époque médiévale. Etat des questions', *Bull. Mon.*, CL (1992), 383–411, and H. Stein-Kecks, '"Claustrum" and "Capitulum": Some remarks on the Façade and Interior of the Chapter House', in *Der Mittelalterliche Kreuzgang*, ed. P. Klein (Regensburg 2004), 157–60. The design of the Charlieu chapter-house is clearly related to that originally attached to Cluny II and described by John of Farfa in the *Consuetudines Farvenses*. This tells us that the Cluny chapter-house was 45 feet long and 34 feet wide, had four windows to the east and three on the north, and was open to the west through twelve *balcones* with pairs of columns between each *balcone*. The most recent edition renders this last as 'Contra occidentem duodecim balcones et per unumquemque afixe in eis duo columnae'. See P. Dinter ed., 'Liber tramitis aevi Odilonis abbatis', in *Corpus consuetudinum monasticarum*, X (Siegburg 1980), 204. Cluny and Charlieu were not the first chapter-houses to use a perforated western wall. Clemens Kosch has convincingly identified a section of late-10th-century arcading at San Pantaleon, Cologne as belonging to a chapter-house front. See C. Kosch, 'Zur Spätromanischen Schatzkammer (dem sog. Kapitelsaal) von St. Pantaleon. Ein vorläufige Bestandsaufnahme', *Colonia Romanica*, VI (1991), 34–63. However, the adoption of this design at Cluny was clearly important in endorsing an approach to chapter-house design which gave it something of the quality of the cloister arcade itself, and so encouraged a broader aesthetic of openness and architectural permeability — characteristics which were to predominate in later-11th- and 12th-century cloister design. It has been suggested that this type of chapter-house façade was developed so as to enable novices, and other members of the community who were not formally admitted to chapter, to hear what was being said during the early parts of the chapter meeting, and perhaps also hear the homilies on the Gospel delivered on Sundays and feast days. However, Heidrun Stein-Kecks has recently pointed to inconsistencies in this explanation — not least the statement in the Cluniac customary composed by Ulrich of Zell for William, abbot of Hirsau, that nobody was allowed in the east walk while the monks were at chapter except the camerarius, whose role would then be to flush out any infractories from the parlour — and takes a more functional view, arguing that the design was first developed so as to increase light levels within the chapter-house itself. See H. Stein-Kecks, '"Claustrum" and "Capitulum"', 162–64. Subsequently, the design was found to have a number of advantages — one of the more unexpected of which is alluded to in the customary of Bernard of Cluny, that torn garments could be left on the sills of the openings into the chapter-house, which the camerarius would collect, have repaired, and then return. The provision of adequate daylight at Cluny was potentially problematic, as the chapter-house of Odilo's time formed part of the eastern range,

and although its north wall was detached from the church, and was pierced by three windows, this was sufficiently close to the monastic church to have been permanently in deep shadow. The east wall was only partly available for fenestration, as its northern section gave access to the oratory of St Mary. The effect this has can be seen at Charlieu, where the chapel of St Mary still survives in an analogous position to that of Cluny. Given that the four windows mentioned in the *consuetudines farvenses* were squeezed into no more than two-thirds of the east wall, and that the chapter-house was 34 feet east-west, the twelve openings plus portal of the west wall would have made an enormous difference to the internal light levels. But, even if this tipped the balance in favour of an open design, there is no evidence that any buildings in the south or west ranges at Cluny were similarly treated, and it is hard to avoid the conclusion that the distinction accorded the chapter-house was also designed to highlight its status. The potential for display inherent in an open design must have been recognised at the outset.

6. Quoted in Braunfels, *Monasteries*, 240.

7. The most extensive east range to survive is that at St-Bénigne, which, according to the eponymous monastic chronicle, was built under Abbot Halinard (1031–52). The greater part of the chapter-house and dormitory undercroft survive, though the first-storey dormitory was replaced after 1272. The chapter-house is now difficult to recognise, given its partitioning into display areas for the archaeological museum, but was originally a groin-vaulted four-pillar room — impressively large at 13 metres square, with a western portal flanked by pairs of subdivided openings (four in total). As at Cluny and Charlieu the chapter-house was attached to a chapel, though here dedicated to St Benedict. C. Sapin ed., *Les prémices de l'art roman en Bourgogne* (Auxerre 1999), 70–72.

8. See, in particular, W. Horn and E. Born, *The Plan of Saint Gall. A Study of the Architecture and Economy of, and Life in, a Paradigmatic Carolingian Monastery*, 3 vols (Berkeley 1979). Some of Horn and Born's assumptions have been challenged, notably by E. Fernie, 'The proportions of the St Gall plan', *Art Bulletin*, 60 (1978), 583–89, who demonstrated that the plan was not strictly modular; L. Nees, 'The Plan of St Gall and the Theory of a Programme of Carolingian Art', *Gesta*, 25 (1986), 1–8, who showed it was not a paradigm; and W. Jacobsen, *Der Klosterplan von von St. Gallen und die Karonligische Architektur: Entwicklung und Wandel von Form und Bedeutung im Fränksichen Kirchenbau zwischen 751 und 840* (Berlin 1992), who proved that the plan was not copied from a lost exemplar, but is an original drawing.

9. Savina is the common name for *juniperus sabina* — a low spreading evergreen shrub of Mediterranean origin introduced to France and Germany in the Late Antique period. See Horn and Born, *Plan of St Gall*, I, 246–48. See also P. Meyvaert, 'Monastic Gardens', in *Medieval Gardens*, ed. E. MacDougall (Dumbarton Oaks 1986), 52.

10. On matters of dating and affiliation, see L. Speciale, 'Alfano I, Montecassino e Salerno', *Arte Medievale*, vol. 2, no. 2 (1988), 267–71. For a superb portfolio of drawings and antiquarian views of the atrium, see the interim report entitled *Restauri in Corso 1999: Cattedrale di Salerno* (Salerno 1999) issued by the Soprintendenza per i Beni Ambientali Arcitettonici, Artistici e Storici di Salerno e Avellino.

11. Relations between the monastic church and what are usually known as the 'small' and 'great' cloisters are very varied, as a glance at the plans in the chapter Wolfgang Braunfels devoted to the Carthusians will show. See Braunfels, *Monasteries*, 111–24. The part-coenobitic-part-eremitic nature of the Carthusian Order imposed very particular demands on the layout of monastic buildings, and the tendency to house individual monks in two-storeyed cells arranged in terraces around the 'great' cloister made them hugely space-consuming. By the later Middle Ages, the more successful houses, that is those with more than the anticipated complement of twelve monks, either built immense 'great' cloisters, as at Pavia, or created a second 'great' cloister (making three cloisters in all), as at the chartreuse du Val de Bénédiction at Villeneuve-lès-Avignon, where Cardinal Pierre de Montirac added the St John cloister by 1372, within a decade of the death of the founder, his uncle, Pope Innocent VI. Monastic orders with similar cellular living arrangements for individual monks, such as the Hieronymites, also employed small liturgical cloisters attached to the monastic church, and separate 'great' cloisters, as, for example, at the late-15th-century monastery of El Parral, just outside Segovia. The adoption of cloisters by the mendicant orders involved a comparable change of function, and their disposition is very different from the patterns observable in Benedictine communities, often being arranged on an enormous scale, and in sequences of up to three cloisters. See, for example, Santa Chiara at Naples, or Dominican Santo Tomás at Ávila. In part, at least, this proliferation of cloisters is a response to increasing pressure on the part of influential urban families for burial within the friaries. Sadly, no general survey of mendicant conventual architecture has ever been attempted, but for a review of at least some of the problems, and a consideration of how mendicant cloisters were used, see the essays in *Lo spazio dell'umiltà: Atti del convegno di studi sull'edilizia dell'ordine dei minori* (Fara Sabina 1982).

12. The extent to which cloisters were created to serve collegiate communities before the early 12th century remains controversial, and although there is some possible evidence for the existence of cloisters attached to cathedrals in France prior to the late 10th century, these do seem isolated. The evidence for a

cloister attached to Chrodegang's Metz Cathedral is ambiguous. See C. Heitz, 'Metz et son groupe épiscopal à l'époque pré-carolingienne et carolingienne', in *Eglises de Metz dans le haut moyen âge*, ed. C. Heitz and F. Heber-Suffrin (Metz 1982), 12, who comes out in favour; and Y. Esquieu, 'La place du cloître dans l'organisation du quartier cathédral', in *Der Mittelalterliche Kreuzgang*, ed. P. Klein (Regensburg 2004), 81, who remains sceptical. The 1985 excavations on the site of the earlier medieval cathedral at Autun did reveal an area to the south of the cathedral with what appear to have been cloister walks to the south and west, which was rebuilt *c.* 1000 according to an original plan of the mid-9th-century. See C. Sapin, 'Le problème du cloître à galeries dans l'architecture canoniale', in J.-C. Picard ed., *Les chanoines dans la ville: Recherches sur la topographie des quartiers canoniaux* (Paris 1994), 33–39. Thereafter, the adoption of cloisters at French cathedrals does not really gather pace until the second half of the 12th century, though there is documentary evidence for the construction of a cloister at Nevers Cathedral during the second quarter of the 11th century, and a cloister was planned at Toulouse Cathedral *c.* 1100. See C. Sapin ed., *Les prémices de l'art roman*, 51, and Q. Cazes, 'Le cloître disparu de la cathédrale Saint-Étienne de Toulouse', in *Der Mittelalterliche Kreuzgang*, ed. P. Klein (Regensburg 2004), 269–84. The origins of collegiate cloisters in England are discussed elsewhere in this volume by John Montague, though the earliest example for which there is archaeological evidence, Old Sarum, shows no evidence of having been associated with any communal buildings. This subsequently seems to set the pattern for English secular cathedral cloisters, for although individual walks are often arranged so as to give on to chapels, chapter-houses, even libraries, their communities neither eat nor sleep around the cloister. Unlike Augustinian houses, therefore, whose canons are ordinarily residentiary, English secular cathedral cloisters do not usually back on to ranges. There is a strong sense here that the cloister, which arose to serve a communal life (and certainly came to symbolise it), could be appropriated to the regular clergy quite simply because by the 12th century the construct had become as redolent of the concept of a Rule as it was of community, even if in the particular circumstances of Old Sarum a cloister may have been intended to remind the canons of their communal roots. Subsequently, as vicars choral were incorporated into colleges, accommodation and communal rooms for the college of vicars choral might also be arranged around a cloister, as famously survives at Hereford, though such cloisters are invariably detached from the cathedral church. For extended discussions of the types of precincts created for vicars choral, see the collection of articles in R. Hall and D. Stocker ed., *Vicars Choral at English Cathedrals* (Oxford 2005), particularly R. Shoesmith, '"A Brave and Ancient Privileg'd Place", The Hereford Vicars Choral College', 44–60, and D. Stocker, 'The Development of the College of Vicars Choral at Lincoln Monster', 76–97, who cogently argues that the north, west and south ranges of the vicars college at Lincoln were fronted by walks, and that the 'design clearly aims to imitate a monastic arrangement, with a prominent "cloister" walk set in front of the residential buildings'. The English collegiate cloisters it is most difficult to explain are those created for William of Wykeham towards the end of the 14th century — namely Winchester College and New College, Oxford — along with Archbishop Henry Chichele's related foundation of All Souls College, Oxford. All three were built with cloisters that were separate from the residential quadrangles. The New College statutes explicitly state that the cloister was used for processions — *ac circa claustrum Collegii processiones fiant solennes secundum usum et consuetudinem Ecclesiae Cathedralis Sarum, salvis distinctionibus et ordinationibus inferius annotatis* ['and that solemn processions made be around the cloister of the College, according to the usage and tradition of the Cathedral Church at Sarum, with the exception of those particular usages which we shall outline below'. The text is an extract from chapter 42, kindly provided, along with its translation, by Jennifer Thorp, archivist of New College, who tells me that the reference to processions appears in all copies of the Statutes apart from NCA 3584. I am much indebted to her for this information]. After William of Wykeham obtained a papal bull in 1389, enabling the college to celebrate mass in the chapel on Sundays, erect its own bell-tower and bury its own dead, the cloister could be used for burials. It was undoubtedly this association with burials that led to the construction of a freestanding chantry chapel (Fromond's chantry) within the garth at Winchester College. The dual importance of Wykeham's cloisters as cemeteries and processional spaces is perhaps most closely paralleled by the cathedral cloisters of south-western France and northern Spain, which functioned in exactly this way. The best documented is that of Toulouse Cathedral, whose liturgical uses are described in a Processional of *c.* 1200 and whose 16th-century obituary records the deaths of nearly 900 canons between the 11th and 16th centuries. Of the 450 whose place of burial is indicated, 363 are buried in the cloister. See Q. Cazes, 'Le cloître disparu', 282. The difference, of course, is that Toulouse, and the Spanish cloisters, also gave access to a chapter-house. All Souls College of 1437–43 followed New College in divorcing its cloister from the fellows' quadrangle, but thereafter the designers of Oxford colleges merged the fellows quadrangle and cloister, as at Magdalen College after 1474, and as was the intention at what is now the Tom Quad at Christchurch College.

13. As Richard Plant once memorably observed of abaci, stylobates are a shockingly understudied subject. In architectural terms they act as a type of podium, a base on which the elevation of the cloister walk sits. Spatially, they emphasise the distinction between the walks and the garth. In conjunction with the arcades they create a permeable boundary which tends, through the openings in the stylobate, to mark out commonly used routes, as well acting as a processional marker. Functionally, the stylobate provides seating. The

13th-century Eynsham customary even describes how monks should be seated, with their legs placed decently one next to the other, not widely splayed nor crossed, and they should not crowd together, maintaining an interval of a seat, or a column, between themselves and their immediate neighbour. See A. Gransden ed., *Corpus Consuetudinum Monasticarum*, II (1963), 45. In wooden-roofed cloisters, where the arcades are supported on relatively slender and generously spaced columns, the stylobate is usually the principal permanent bench. Where stylobates incorporate piers, and the intermediate paired columns are set high, as in many Romanesque vaulted cloisters, a low stone bench might be set against the inner face of the stylobate — as survives at St-Trophime at Arles, Montmajour, or Hauterive — a more durable realisation in stone of what must often have been provided in the form of wooden benches. This is the solution that tends to be favoured in traceried cloisters — as at, say, Santes Creus, and is usual for monastic cloisters in England, as at Westminster, Norwich, Lacock and so on. Low benches are even integrated into the design of the traceried walks at Winchester and New Colleges, artfully arranged as recessed stone ledges so that as one sits the light enters the walk over one's shoulder, suggesting these also may have been used for reading — or even enjoyed a recreational function. Conversely, there are many examples of Benedictine traceried cloisters without stone benches — such as Gloucester — where one suspects wooden seating was employed, notwithstanding the provision of carrels in the south walk.

14. P. Meyvaert, 'The Medieval Monastic Claustrum', *Gesta*, XII (1973), 54. On the dating and Cluniac context of Ulrich of Zell's customary, see S. Boynton, 'The Customaries of Bernard and Ulrich as Liturgical Sources', in *From Dead of Night to End of Day: The Medieval Customs of Cluny*, ed. S. Boynton and I. Cochelin (Turnhout 2005), 109–30.

15. L'Abbaye-Blanche was founded at the beginning of the 12th century by Vitalis of Savigny, who installed his sister, Adeline, as first abbess. The fragments of stonework reconstructed as a north cloister walk mostly date from between *c.* 1180 and *c.* 1205. Cloisters whose arcades were designed to be open to the garth, without either a stylobate or tracery, start to appear in the 16th century, and become common in the 17th century, particularly as attached to the new urban houses of orders that became popular during the Counter Reformation, such as the Celestines, Theatines, and Discalced Carmelites. Many Italian cities, particularly in the south and centre, still retain several examples. Such cloisters on conversion, as at Santa Croce in Lecce, can effectively function as city squares. In France, many of the conventual precincts rebuilt during the Maurist reform, were also equipped with similar cloisters.

16. This always remained an option, and must have persisted for a considerable time in certain foundations, particularly cathedrals. In late medieval Catalonia and northern Spain, provisions were even made for summer chapter meetings to be held in the cloister walks, despite the existence of dedicated chapter-houses. Indeed in 1406, the cathedral chapter at Lérida asked for stone benches to be provided in the south walk for their summer meetings — and similar arrangements are recorded for León and Salamanca. See E. Santamaría, 'Cathedral Cloisters in the Kingdoms of León and Galicia', in *Der Mittelalterliche Kreuzgang*, ed. P. Klein (Regensburg 2004), 94.

17. Braunfels, *Monasteries*, 28–29. The translation which follows is also that given by Braunfels, on 236.

18. The commemoration of the dead in chapter-houses seems to have taken a variety of forms in the course of the Middle Ages. At 11th-century Cluny, names of the dead were read from the necrology during the chapter meeting, after which the monks retired to the adjacent chapel of Saint Mary where they sang five psalms in honour of those dead mentioned at chapter. See H. Stein-Kecks, 'Claustrum and Capitulum', 166–67. The custom of burial in chapter-houses, excepting the extraordinary reference in the History of the Abbots of Fontenelle, does not become widespread before the late 11th century, the burial of Desiderius in 1087 in the apse of the new chapter-house he had ordered to be built at Monte Cassino being the most celebrated example. See N. Stratford, 'Notes on the Norman Chapterhouse at Worcester', in *Medieval Art and Architecture at Worcester Cathedral*, ed. G. Popper, *BAA Trans.*, I (Leeds 1978), 67 n.29 for this and other late-11th-century examples. By the middle of the 12th century, the burial of former abbots was also becoming established in Cistercian chapter-houses. Indeed, it has been argued that the design of the chapter-house constructed for Aelred at Rievaulx in the 1150s was in part inspired by Roman *coemeteria subteglata* with a view to the reburial there of his predecessor, Abbot William. See P. Fergusson and S. Harrison, *Rievaulx Abbey: Community, Architecture, Memory* (New Haven 1999), 98–99. A similarly spectacular merging of the chapter-house and the mausoleum occurs in northern and central Spain, where many cathedral chapter-houses were either designed to act as episcopal mausolea, or were transformed into burial chapels at the expense of moving chapter meetings elsewhere. The best documented example of this last is the chapel established by Archbishop Juan Arias in the chapter-house of the cathedral of Santiago de Compostela in 1250, which came to act as a burial chapel for many of Arias' successors, chapter meetings being moved to the cathedral treasury. See E. Santamaría, 'Cathedral Cloisters', 94. Something similar clearly happened at Salamanca. The greatest example of the former is the chapter-house at Pamplona Cathedral, dominated by the mid-14th-century tomb and effigy of its founder, Bishop Arnaldo de Barbazàn (d. 1356). Burial in monastic cloisters may not develop quite in tandem with chapter-house burial, and it is something

that is recorded in the 10th century, as in the celebrated colophon written alongside the representation of the tower and scriptorium of the monastery of Tábara in a manuscript now in Madrid [Archivo Histórico Nacional, Cod. 1097B]. The relevant section of the colophon has been translated by John Williams as 'O truly blessed man, whose body lies in a coffin in the cloister and who wished to see the book brought to completion and bound. This was Magius, priest and monk, the worthy master painter. He gave up the work he began when he went eternally to Christ on the feast of Saint Faustus, the third day before the ides [13 October]. The calends of November had their third day before he departed out of time, era 1006 [30 October 968]'. Emeterius went on to complete the manuscript in August 970, when he wrote the colophon. See J. P. O'Neill ed., *The Art of Medieval Spain AD500–1200* (New York 1993), 155–156.

19. F. Behn, *Die Karolingische Klosterkirche von Lorsch an der Bergstraße. Nach den Ausgrabungen von 1927–1928 und 1932–1933* (Berlin and Leipzig) 1934. More accessible reproductions of Behn's plans can be found in Horn, 'Origins', fig. 41 and, for the main monastic church of St Nazarius and associated cloister, now thought to have been constructed after 805, fig. 43.

20. For a selection of the more recent literature on the origins of the monastic cloister, see note 1.

21. The only cloister arcades to survive *in situ* prior to Westminster Abbey and Salisbury Cathedral are a section of the east arcade of the mid-12th-century Infirmary cloister at Christchurch priory, Canterbury, and the early-13th-century south cloister arcade at West Malling Abbey, though even West Malling cloister walk was dismantled, modified and re-erected *c.* 1500. For the Canterbury Infirmary cloister, see the article by Tim Tatton-Brown in this volume. For West Malling, see T. Tatton-Brown, 'The Buildings of West Malling Abbey', *Architectural History*, 44 (2001), 184–86, and figs 4, 5 and 7.

22. In addition to the material surveyed by Stuart Harrison and David Robinson elsewhere in this volume, there are important ensembles of 12th-century cloister capitals surviving from Westminster Abbey, Reading Abbey, Norwich Cathedral Priory, Hyde Abbey, Glastonbury Abbey and Winchester Cathedral Priory — for which see G. Zarnecki, J. Holt and T. Holland ed., *English Romanesque Art 1066–1200* (London 1984), 146–48, 158, 159, 167–75, 184–85, and 186; R. Baxter and S. Harrison, 'The Decoration of the Cloister at Reading Abbey', in *Windsor: Medieval Archaeology, Art and Architecture of the Thames Valley*, ed. L. Keen and E. Scarff, *BAA Trans.*, xxv (Leeds 2002), 302–12; J. Franklin, 'The Romanesque Cloister Sculpture at Norwich Cathedral Priory', in *Studies in Medieval Sculpture*, ed. F. H. Thompson (London 1983), 56–70; and J. Hardacre, *Winchester Cathedral Triforium Gallery: Catalogue* (Winchester 1989), 7–11.

23. For Brindisi and Conversano, see T. Garton, *Early Romanesque Sculpture in Apulia* (New York 1984), 136–48 and pls 86–90 and 113–15. For Nieul-sur-l'Autize, see M. Dillange, *Églises et abbayes romanes en Vendée* (Marseille 1983), 142–47; and A. Tcherikover, *High Romanesque Sculpture in the Duchy of Aquitaine c.1090–1140* (Oxford 1997), 26–29. The literature on Moissac is enormous, but the classic account in English remains that of Meyer Schapiro, most conveniently reprinted, with new photographs, in M. Schapiro, *The Sculpture of Moissac* (London 1985).

24. Although undated, the cloister attached to St-Trophime clearly postdates the existing nave and west front. Topographically, and liturgically, it is the most unusual cloister to survive from 12th-century Europe, and confers considerable insight into the potential flexibility of cloister design. Given the existence of the archbishop's courtyard and palace to the south of the nave, it was necessary to construct the cloister to the south-east of the cathedral apse. However, the underlying ground level slopes steeply downwards from east to west, and so as to keep the walks and garth level a basement had to be constructed beneath the west range, while the garth was almost certainly levelled upwards. As the cloister is not only east of the ritual choir (ruling out entry to the church from the east walk), but above it, entry to the church was via a steep ramp staircase towards the west end of the north range. And the somewhat unexpected appearance of a north range in a southern cloister was made possible by the designer's realisation that if the cloister was to be above and to the east of its church, it may as well be detached in all dimensions, and so displaced it by around 30 feet from the line of the south nave aisle. As such, the conventional arrangement of buildings around the cloister could be reordered, so that the dormitory occupies the east range, and the refectory the west (with a kitchen at its southern end extending into the western third of the area to the south of the south walk). Most importantly, the chapter-house occupies the north range, open to the north cloister walk for the whole of its length through high-silled single arches, and connected directly to the church via the stair. The sequencing of the sculpture on the garth side of the north walk, opening with the figure of Saint Trophime between Saints Peter and Paul (and the reliefs foreshadowing the news of Christ's Resurrection — i.e. the empty tomb and the women buying aromatic oil) needs to be understood in the context of this ingenious re-interpretation of a conventional cloister plan. The above description simplifies the phasing and archaeology of a set of conventual buildings it is agreed were built slowly — and from west to east — but there is no evidence at Arles to suggest that once the major elements of the design had been decided on there was any change in the shape or disposition of elements. See J. Thirion, 'Saint-Trophime d'Arles', *Congrès Archéologique*, CXXXIV (1976), 402–45 (the chapter entitled 'le cloître'); and A. Hartmann-Virnich, 'Les galeries romanes du cloître de

Saint-Trophime d'Arles', in *Der Mittelalterliche Kreuzgang*, ed. P. Klein (Regensburg 2004), 285–316. There is, as it happens, a discernible tendency in the design of cloisters attached to cathedrals whose chapters were Augustinian to position the chapter-house between a cloister walk and the church — and therefore slightly detach the cloister. This was the certainly the case at Gérona Cathedral, and is arguable at Aix-en-Provence. See P. Klein, 'Topographie fonctions et programmes iconographiques des cloîtres', in *Der Mittelalterliche Kreuzgang*, ed. P. Klein (Regensburg 2004), 129–40. The plan of Santa María la Mayor at Tudela, another late-12th-century Augustinian house, also suggests the existence of a claustral range between itself and the church.

25. See E. Galasso, *Il Chiostro allo Specchio* (Benevento 1991); and D. Glass, *Romanesque Sculpture in Campania* (University Park 1991), 37–40.

26. See M. Pladelesala and E. Riu-Barrera, 'Sant Pere de Rodes', 238 for a plan. This list is confined to 'great' cloisters and is by means exhaustive. Zdeněk Dragoun has even pointed out to me the evidence for a 12th-century cloister abutting the Romanesque cathedral at Prague whose east walk lay east of the cathedral apse, though there is some doubt as to whether there was also an east range. Personal communication.

27. For Old Sarum, see the article by John Montague in this volume. For the problems associated with the planning of the cloister at Rochester, see J. McNeill, 'The East Cloister Range of Rochester Cathedral Priory', in *Medieval Art, Architecture and Archaeology at Rochester*, ed. T. Ayers and T. Tatton-Brown, *BAA Trans.*, XXVIII (Leeds 2006), 181–86.

28. See the entry on Serrabone in M. Durliat, *Roussillon Roman* (La Pierre-qui-Vire 1975), 150–85.

29. Santa Maria di Cerrate is undated, though the west portal of the monastic church is stylistically related to the architectural sculpture at Santi Nicolò e Cataldo in Lecce, founded in 1180 by Tancred, Count of Lecce. The loggia has been extensively restored, and five of the columns and capitals around the opening in the stylobate were replaced in the restoration of 1971–83. None the less, most of the sculpture is original and though it differs from the west portal in certain particulars, it has enough in common with the portal capitals and rather stiff drilled foliage of the jambs for the loggia to by a workshop which followed on quite quickly, perhaps taking one of the portal sculptors with it. As such a date around 1200 seems plausible. There is no detailed study of the monastery, but there is a summary account in R. Barletta, *Santa Maria di Cerrate* (Lecce 2003).

30. J. Le Maho, 'Autour de la fondation de l'abbaye de Boscherville (début du XIIe s.), quelques observations historiques et archéologiques', *Bulletin de la commission départementale des Antiquités de la Seine-Maritime*, XLIII (1995), 129–42.

31. See K. Horste, *Cloister Design and Monastic Reform in Toulouse* (Oxford 1992), and for the relationship between the reconstruction of the cathedral, and its precincts, see Q. Cazes, 'Le cloître disparu', particularly 269–72 and 282–84.

32. Burgos Cathedral, which is not strictly speaking a reconstruction, and Barcelona Cathedral, which is, are examples of complete cathedral-and-precinct building campaigns in 13th- and 14th-century Spain. The most extraordinary, and unusual, was Segovia, where a new cathedral and precinct were built on a new site, following the damage caused to the predecessor cathedral in the *communeros* uprising of 1520. The earlier cathedral had stood immediately beneath the castle, towards the angle in the cliffs that marks the western edge of the city, and in a politically motivated burst of activity the old site was cleared and a new cathedral planned adjacent to the plaza major, the late-15th-century cloister arcades being dismantled and then re-erected as part of the new conventual precinct. The situation in France is rather different, as the majority of cathedral cloisters were anyway established relatively late, and were either shoehorned into existing precincts or involved the acquisition of new land. Early instances of cathedral cloisters in France are listed above, in note 12. Otherwise, the largely Augustinian chapters of Provence began to acquire conventual precincts in the second half of the 12th century — at Vaison, Carpentras, Arles, Aix, Viviers and Cavaillon, while the earliest cloister in the north is the truncated, and unfinished, gallery at Laon Cathedral of *c.* 1190. The best preserved is that of Noyon Cathedral, of *c.* 1240. Neither of these, however, seem to have been anticipated when their respective cathedrals were begun. For an excellent short account, see Y. Esquieu, 'La place du cloître', 80–88.

33. At least this seems to have been the intention at Saint-Jean-des-Vignes when one looks at what Sheila Bonde and Clark Maines describe as Phase D (First Gothic Phase of *c.* 1215–30), which involved the laying out of a new east elevation for the Augustinian church, and a new west front and west cloister range. In the event, the new church and conventual precincts were not completed until the second half of the 14th century. See S. Bonde and C. Maines, '*Ne aliquis extraneus claustrum intret*: Entry and Access at the Augustinian Abbey of Saint-Jean-des-Vignes, Soissons', in *Perspectives for an Architecture of Solitude*, ed. T. Kinder (Turnhout 2004), 185. The documentary history of St-Nicaise at Reims, along with a catalogue of drawings, is given in M. Bideault and C. Lautrier, 'Saint-Nicaise de Reims. Chronologie et Nouvelles Rémarques sur l'Architecture', *Bull. mon.*, 135 (1977), 295–300.

34. In contrast to the remains of the monastic church, little has been published on the surviving conventual buildings at Charroux. On the dating of the main 11th-century construction campaigns see M.-T. Camus,

Sculpture Romane du Poitou: Les Grands Chantiers du XIe Siècle (Paris 1992), 174–78. See also F. Eygun, 'L'abbaye de Charroux, les grandes lignes de son histoire et de ses constructions', *Bulletin de la Société des Antiquaires de l'Ouest*, 4e séries, X (1969/70), 11–23. The capital mentioned in the main text is designed for paired columns and depicts evangelist symbols. It is likely to have come from a cloister arcade, suggesting that one or more of the cloister walks were reconstructed towards the middle of the 12th century.

35. For a drawing showing how vaults replaced the earlier wooden roof over the east walk of the cloister of St-Aubin at Angers, see J. McNeill, 'The East Cloister Walk of Saint-Aubin at Angers: Sculpture and Archeology', in *Anjou: Medieval Art, Architecture and Archaeology*, ed. J. McNeill and D. Prigent, *BAA Trans.*, XXVI (2003), 114 (Fig. 1). The style of the figures and foliage carved on the deep bracket corbels used to support the vault where it cuts across the inner orders of the chapter-house portal suggests the east walk was vaulted in the 15th century. For Cadouin, where the cloister walks were vaulted *c.* 1490, see J. Gardelles, 'L'abbaye de Cadouin', *Congrès Archéologique*, CXXXVII (1979), 146–78. Both examples illustrate the difficulties of co-ordinating openings in traceried cloister arcades with pre-existing chapter-house façades, and arise out of a desire to extend the rhythm of the traceried arcades across the vault. They are effectively a function of conventional rib vaulting in that the ribs spring at the same level as the tracery lights, and the alternative — lunettes or relieving arches above the arcades — is impractical given the two-storey nature of most east ranges. With a simple wooden pentice, or indeed a barrel vault, the elevations of the cloister arcade and inner range remain comfortably autonomous.

36. Meyvaert, 'Monastic Gardens', 52.

37. ibid., 52.

38. Hugh of Fouilloy, *De Claustro Animae*, columns 1172–73 in J. P. Migne, *Patrologia Latina*, 176.

39. J. Thorpe, *Registrum Roffense* (London 1769), 122.

40. For summary accounts of the documentation and main 12th and 13th-century building phases at Poblet and Santes Creus, see N. de Dalmases and A. Pitarch, *Història de l'Art Català, Vol II: L'Època del Cister* (Barcelona 1985), 59–70. The lavabo projecting into the cloister garth at San Zeno, Verona, has been completely rebuilt, but all three examples are exactly the type of arcaded pavilion sheltering a water basin (and positioned opposite the refectory) that is illustrated in the Waterworks plan of Christchurch Cathedral Priory. See Fig. 4 of the article by T. Tatton-Brown in this volume. Later medieval lavabo enclosures survive in greater numbers, good examples surviving at Maulbronn and the cathedrals of Pamplona and Santo Domingo de la Calzada, these being of a broadly similar type to the early-16th-century traceried lavabo pavilion from Sherborne Abbey, subsequently re-erected in the Parade at Sherborne. The situation in the British Isles has been most recently surveyed in J. Bond, 'Monastic Water Management in Great Britain', in *Monastic Archaeology*, ed. G. Keevil, M. Aston and T. Hall (Oxford 2001), 88–136, particularly 115–18.

41. The *Horologium Stellare Monasticum* also speaks of there being a clock, or sundial, in the cloister, which must have been in the garth. See G. Constable ed., *Corpus Consuetudinum Monasticarum*, VI (Siegburg 1975), 1–18. Bernard of Cluny mentions a water clock at Cluny. How common either water clocks or sundials might have been as objects in garths is unknown, though Neil Stratford has recently suggested the carved Romanesque pillar at Souvigny would originally have supported a gnomon in the garth at Souvigny, and points to the survival of a magnificent 12th-century cloister sundial from St Emmeram at Regensburg. See N. Stratford, *Chronos et Cosmos: Le pilier roman de Souvigny* (Souvigny 2005), 75–82. I am enormously grateful to the author for sending me a copy of this.

42. For a masterful short account of 'the cloister as a wash place', see P. Meyvaert, 'Medieval Monastic Claustrum', 55–56.

43. Thierry of Fleury was also exercised over the provision of towels in the cloister, distinguishing the towels used by the choir monks from those of the oblates and those used for the weekly washing of feet, and stating it was the duty of the cellarer to provide clean towels each Sunday. See A. Davril and L. Donnant ed., *Corpus Consuetudinum Monasticarum*, VII/3 (1984), 56–57.

44. One needs to distinguish between the *mandatum fratrum*, the weekly washing of the feet of the monks, and the *mandatum pauperum*, the washing of the feet of the poor on Maundy Thursday. In Cluniac houses, the *mandatum fratrum* took place in the chapter-house, the oblates bringing bowls of warm water from the kitchen, which they left outside the chapter-house door. The abbot then supervised the ritual within the chapter-house. See L. Späling ed., *Corpus Consuetudinum Monasticarum*, XII/1 (1985), 99. At Cluny, the *mandatum pauperum* took place in the cloister walk adjacent to the church. See P. Dinter ed., *Corpus Consuetudinum Monasticarum*, X (1980), 75–76. Whether this was true of other Cluniac houses is unknown, and Peter Klein has suggested that the capital showing Christ washing the feet of the apostles with the inscription MANDATUM in the east cloister walk at Moissac (approximately half way between the pier opposite the chapter-house entrance and the south-east angle), indicates the position of the Moissac *Mandatum pauperum*. See P. Klein, 'Topographie, fonctions et programmes iconographiques', 124. He attaches the same significance to the placement of a capital depicting the washing of feet (opposite the chapter-house entrance) at Sant Cugat del Vallès of *c.* 1200 (ibid., 124 and 140–44). Cistercians simply used the walk adjacent to the monastic church for their *mandatum*.

45. Meyvaert, 'Medieval Monastic Claustrum', 56.

46. M. Herrgott ed., *Vetus Disciplina monastica: Ordo Cluniacensis per Bernardum* (Paris 1726), 214 (hereafter cited as 'Bernard').

47. 'Bernard', 204.

48. 'Bernard', 214–15.

49. A. Gransden ed., *Corpus Consuetudinum Monasticarum*, II (1963), 118, and A. Davril, 'Fonction des cloîtres', 25.

50. Hence the stone bench that frequently survives in Cistercian monasteries between the monastic and conversi entries to the nave. Occasionally, evidence even survives for the reader's lectern and abbot's throne, most spectacularly at Cadouin, and frequently encountered in the British Isles. See R. Gilyard-Beer, 'Boxley Abbey and the 'Pulpitum Collationis', in *Collectanea Historica. Essays in Memory of Stuart Rigold*, ed. A Detsicas (Maidstone 1981), 123–31, and A. Hamlin, 'Collation Seats in Irish Cistercian Houses', *Med. Archaeol.*, XXVII (1983), 156–58 and pl. XIII A-E.

51. See P. Klein, 'Topographie, fonctions et programmes iconographiques', 123–24. Not only is this the walk usually favoured for carrels, but it also accords with the much quoted remark of Peter of Blois, '*In latere claustri occidentali est scholaris subjectio; in eo quod contigit ecclesiam, lectio moralis; in ipsa ecclesia meditatio spiritualis; ad orientem in capitulo, correctio materialis*'. E. Martène, *De Antiquis Ecclesiae Ritibus*, I (Venice 1763), 18.

52. A fairly elaborate sign language was developed to enable monks to communicate during periods of silence, which, by the 10th century, had come to encompass 118 hand signs. Identical copies of this were included by Bernard of Cluny and Ulrich of Zell in their monastic customaries. See S. Bruce, 'Monastic Sign Language in the Cluniac Customaries', in *From Dead of Night to End of Day: The Medieval Customs of Cluny*, ed. S. Boynton and I. Cochelin (Turnhout 2005), 273–86.

53. The arrangement shown on the St Gall plan, which implies an opening in the centre of each walk, is not, as far as I am aware, replicated in any surviving medieval cloister. The question is obviously complicated by the ease with which openings might be cut into a stylobate retrospectively — as frequently happened and which can create an illusion off extreme porousness, as at Fontenay. The majority of cloisters have between one and four openings, though their distribution between walks is such to make it clear that this is an area of considerable freedom in cloister design. There are even a group of cloisters in the Pyrenees, mostly Augustinian, where the stylobate appears to be original and where there is no opening at all between the walks and the garth. The most impressive example is that at Elne Cathedral, but other examples include Sant Pere de Galligants at Gérona and Sant Joan de les Abadesses. As reconstructed in the later Middle Ages, the cloister at Pamplona Cathedral is also like this, though, prior to the modern reconstruction of the north-east angles of the lavabo enclosure, entry to the garth was presumably here. The only opening visible now, opposite the chapter-house, is a later incision cut through the stylobate.

54. See L. Delisle, *Inventaire des manuscrits de la Bibliotheque National: Fonds de Cluny* (Paris 1884), 337–73.

55. Virtually all surviving 12th-century Provençal cloisters are vaulted and employ intermediate piers within the arcades. The main variants seem to be whether paired columns are grouped beneath broad relieving arches, as at Sénaque, St-Paul-de-Mausolée, Vaison et al., whether there is a tighter arrangement of arches subdivided just the once, as at Silvacane, or whether relieving arches are dispensed with all together, and intermediate pier buttresses are employed instead, as at St-Trophime, Arles.

56. See, for example, the two surviving cloisters in Gérona, at Sant Pere de Galligants and the cathedral, both of which employ quadrant vaults, rising from the arcades to the backs of the walks.

57. See D. Cazes and M. Durliat, 'Découverte de l'effigie de l'abbé Grégoire, créateur du cloître de Saint-Michel de Cuxa', *Bull. mon.*, 145 (1987), 7–14; and on the dismantling of the cloister, see M. Durliat, 'La fin du cloître de Saint-Michel de Cuxa', *Cahiers de Saint-Michel de Cuxa*, 2 (1971), 9–16. On Roda de Isábena, see J. Pesqué ed., *Signos: Arte y cultura en el Alto Aragón Medieval* (Huesca 1993), 72.

58. For a discussion of the sequencing of cloister arcade supports, see K. Horste, *Cloister Design*, 184–85.

59. The list is Horste's (as above), though the only examples still standing are St-Lizier and San Juan de la Peña, and even this last has been reconstructed. The problem is that in the absence of antiquarian records, it is impossible to determine precisely where *ex-situ* cloister capitals were originally placed, though if single and double capitals of similar style survive it is likely there was some sort of alternation in the cloister walks. Both single and double capitals from the cloister of St-Volusien at Foix survive, for example, which are stylistically related to the later capitals from the cloister of La Daurade in Toulouse, and which I would add to Horste's Languedoc-and-Pyrenean list. A particularly unusual variation — an intensification really — is to be found at the Augustinian house of Santa María la Mayor at Tudela, where the cloister was begun *c.* 1186 and alternates double and triple columns and capitals. See P. Patton, 'The Cloister as Cultural Mirror: Anti-Jewish Imagery at Santa María la Mayor in Tudela', in *Der Mittelalterliche Kreuzgang*, ed. P. Klein (Regensburg 2004), 317–32. Horste is right to draw attention to this regional concentration, though the level

of losses of 12th-century cloisters in other areas of Latin Europe cautions against attaching great significance to it, other than the point she does make, that with the exception of San Juan de la Peña all the examples in south-western France are closely related, and form a family of cloisters. In a very different style, there are other 12th-century examples of single-double column alternation, as with the fragments of cloister arcade from the former abbey of Eschau, now displayed in the Musée de l'Œuvre Notre-Dame at Strasbourg, and dated to *c.* 1130. Moreover, the evidence of what is usually described as the *ancien promenoir roman* built by Bishop Hugues de Montaigu (1115–36) at Auxerre, where the columns and capitals are also alternately single and double, suggests that the system could have been used in the lost early-12th-century cloisters of Burgundy — a point made by Neil Stratford. See L. Saulnier and N. Stratford, *La Sculpture Oubliée de Vézelay* (Geneva 1984), 170. In England the cloisters at Glastonbury, Waverley and Winchester Cathedral priory seem to have deployed some sort of combination of single and paired columns, though the evidence of the Infirmary cloister at Canterbury makes clear these were not necessarily arranged in simple iambic alternation.

60. The exact date of the construction of the cloister at Santa Sabina is unknown, though a good case can be made for it being Dominican and of the 1220s. By this date, single and paired columns had already been used in a Roman cloister walk, at San Lorenzo fuori le mura, though in a manner appreciably less regular than that of Santa Sabina. See R. Krautheimer, *Rome: Profile of a City, 312–1308* (Princeton 1980), 175–76.

61. Châlons-sur-Marne is discussed more fully below. Léon Pressouyre has dated the cloister to *c.* 1170–1180. See L. Pressouyre, 'Les fouilles du cloître de Notre-Dame-en-Vaux de Châlons-sur-Marne', *Bulletin de la Société nationale des Antiquaires de France* (1964), 23–38; and L. Presssouyre, 'Le cloître de Notre-Dame-en-Vaux de Châlons-sur-Marne', *Congrès Archéologique*, CXXXV (1977), 298–306.

62. Figures carved in relief obviously appear on the angle, and one of the intermediate, piers at Moissac, and substantial figures of the apostles were a feature of the cloister at St-Etienne, Toulouse also. The Toulouse figures did not belong to a cloister arcade, however, since their blocking out indicates they were originally organised as part of a wall, most probably acting as a portal. The column figures at Notre-Dame-en-Vaux are exactly that — carved integrally with a columnar support, and were set within the cloister arcade. See the articles by Pressouyre above. St-Denis was probably the site of the first cloister to employ column figures in the walks, though the precise date of this is unknown. Montfaucon illustrates three column figures from the St-Denis cloister, one of which perhaps survives in the Metropolitan Museum of Art, New York (Inventory 20.157). See B. de Montfaucon, *Les Monuments de la monarchie françoise* (Paris 1729), I, pl. 10, and L. Pressouyre, 'Did Suger build the cloister at Saint-Denis?', in *Abbot Suger and Saint-Denis*, ed. P. Gerson (New York 1986), 229–44.

63. See L. Pressouyre, 'Deux inscriptions ravennates et le cloître de Saint-Vital', *Bulletin de la Société nationale des Antiquaires de France* (1968), 140–53. Other Italian sites published by Léon Pressouyre include Sant' Ellero at Galatea and Ancona. See L. Pressouyre, 'St. Bernard to St. Francis: Monastic Ideals and Iconographic Programs in the Cloister', *Gesta*, XII (1973), 76 and 88 (n.64).

64. R. Krautheimer, *Rome: Profile of a City*, 175–76.

65. Seventeenth-century bird's-eye perspective engravings of the cloisters at Saint-Pierre-sur-Dives, Saint-Evroult and Saint-Vigor at Bayeux make it clear that these also were built with the same type of syncopated cloister arcades as at Mont-Saint-Michel. See M. Déceneux, *Mont-St-Michel Stone by Stone* (Rennes 1996), 53–54, for convenient illustrations.

66. Dark polished marble columns survive from the cloister of Notre-Dame-des-Doms at Avignon, and a lighter, grey polished marble was used for octagonal columns in the cloister attached to Carpentras Cathedral. Fragments from both are now kept at the Musée du Petit-Palais in Avignon. The cathedral cloister at Aix-en-Provence also employs some similarly polished light grey octagonal shafts — used in asymmetrical pairs with octagons towards the walk and cylinders towards the garth. Carpentras is probably the earliest of these cloisters, of perhaps *c.* 1170–80. On the probable dating of this group, see Y. Esquieu, 'La place du cloître', 81–82. In England, coloured and polished stone appears in cloisters slightly earlier than this, around 1150, in the chapter-house vestibule of St Augustine's, Bristol, in the cloister arcade at Glastonbury Abbey, facing on to the east walk at Rochester Cathedral Priory, and perhaps at St Augustine's Abbey, Canterbury. For its use at Christchurch Cathedral Priory, see the article by T. Tatton-Brown in this volume.

67. The finest are those discovered in the late-19th-century buried in a wall of the chapter-house of Saint-Nicolas at Angers. Short lengths of six different columns survive, which may have come from the chapter-house façade, and which are likely to date to *c.* 1150–60. See J. Mallet, *L'art roman de l'ancien Anjou* (Paris 1984), 156–57.

68. These last have been drastically rebuilt.

69. See J. Hayward, 'Glazed Cloisters and their Development in the Houses of the Cistercian Order', *Gesta*, XII (1973), 95–99.

70. P. Marchegay and E. Mabille ed., *Chroniques des églises d'Anjou* (Paris 1869), 257 and 270–71.

71. V. Mortet, *Recueil de textes relatifs à l'histoire de l'architecture et à la condition des architectes en France au Moyen Age. XIe-XIIe siècles* (Paris 1911), 118–19.

72. There are some historiated capitals surviving from the cloister of St-Foi at Conques, constructed during the abbacy of Begon (1087–1107) which could just pre-date Moissac, though this does seem unlikely.

73. The date of 1100 is given in the inscription cut into the central pier of the west walk. *ANNO INCARNATIONE AETERNI PRINCIPIS MILLESIMO CENTESIMO FACTUM EST CLAUSTRUM ISTUD TEMPORE DOMINI ANSQITILII ABBATIS AMEN*. Ansquitil was abbot from 1085 to 1105. The most accessible, and best illustrated, general study of the Moissac cloister in English is M. Schapiro, *The Sculpture of Moissac* (London 1985), 1–76, which is a reprint (with a few minor changes) of two articles first published in *Art Bulletin*, XIII (1931), 248–351 and 464–531. See also R. Rey, 'Les cloîtres historiés du midi dans l'art roman (Étude iconographique)', *Mémoires de la Société Archéologique du Midi de la France*, XXIII (1955), 7–174; M. Durliat, 'L'église abbatiale de Moissac des origines à la fin du XIe siècle', *Cahiers Archéologiques*, XV (1965), 155–77; K. Horste, *Cloister Design*, particularly 95–121; P. Klein, 'Topographie, fonctions et programmes iconographiques', 107–16; L. Rutchick, 'Visual Memory and Historiated Sculpture in the Moissac Cloister', in *Der Mittelalterliche Kreuzgang*, ed. P. Klein (Regensburg 2004), 190–211; and M. Pereira, 'Syntaxe et place des images dans le cloître de Moissac', in *Der Mittelalterliche Kreuzgang*, 212–19.

74. This is not to say the placement of capitals is arbitrary. In many cases it clearly is not. The break in the stylobate at the south end of the east walk, the route that connects the garth to the choir (what an extravagant exegetist, such as Honorius of Autun, might have characterised as the route from the Garden of Eden to the New Jerusalem), is flanked on one side by the reliefs of Peter and Paul, and on the other by a capital devoted to the martyrdoms of Peter and Paul, a capital moreover which contained a relic and therefore acted as cloister shrine. See L. Rutchick, 'A Reliquary Capital at Moissac: Liturgy and Ceremonial Thinking in the Cloister', in *Decorations for the Holy Dead. Visual Embellishments on Tombs and Shrines of Saints*, ed. E. Valdez del Alamo (Turnhout 2002), 129–50. There is nothing random about the placing of the capital showing Christ washing the feet of the disciples half way between here and the chapter-house entrance, or that Durandus, abbot at the time of the Cluniac reform, stands opposite the chapter-house portal. Comparable points can be made about the positions of other specific images. Various authors have also noted suggestive rhythms or thematic concentrations. For Peter Klein, the western half of the south walk hints at an a-b-c (New Testament — Ornamental — Old Testament) rhythm in an area rich in Apocalyptic imagery. See P. Klein, 'Topographie, fonctions et programmes iconographiques', 112–16. Maria Christina Pereira identifies a system of triangulation in the cloister, linking groups of Christological material and connecting the apostles diagonally across the garth. See C. Pereira, 'Syntaxe', 214–16. Benedict Forndron has identified zodiacal motifs organised clockwise so as to run from Aquarius at the west end of the north walk to Capricorn at the north end of the west walk. If one were to then interrogate the capitals and reliefs as a calendar, around half which can be associated with feasts are roughly where one would anticipate finding them — more than would be expected through random placement, though the feasts in question may not be the principal feasts. The capital devoted to Saint-Sernin, for instance, the festival of whose martyrdom is 29 November, is in the compass of Gemini, which would only fit if one were marking the consecration of the high altar of Saint-Sernin, Toulouse on 24 May 1096. See B. Forndron, 'Die Kapitellverteilung des Kreuzgangs von Moissac. Disposition und Funktion der Skulptur eines kluniazenischen Kreuzgangs' (unpublished doctoral dissertation, University of Bonn, 1997). There almost certainly is a level at which the Moissac cloister could be understood as a sequence of feasts, but it is not one in which there is a consistent equivalence between space and time, between where you stand in the cloister and the liturgical calendar, and for every subject that does correspond with the right date, there is one that does not. I am extremely grateful to Dr Tara O'Connor for sharing with me her own calendrical diagrams of the Moissac cloister. Scholars have also suggested particular capitals are musical prompts, or have a musical counterpart. For example, the Moissac Troper includes an introit to be used on the feasts of Saint Peter's martyrdom and deliverance from prison — *natali petri et ad vincula* — the initial letters of whose opening phrase — *Nunc Scio Vere Quia Misit Dominus Angelum Suum Et Eruptit Me De Manu Herodis* — appear on the scroll held by Peter on the Deliverance capital. See L. Rutchick, 'A Reliquary Capital'. Alternatively, and at a slightly different level, the capital showing Daniel in the Lion's Den in the north walk supports an abacus showing beasts tearing a man apart. The abacus serves as a comment on the natural order of things — in contrast to the indemnity provided to Daniel which turns him into a type for Christ — and is a simple reminder of what would happen to the human soul were it not for the salvation made possible by Christ's sacrifice. One might take the Daniel capital as the prose, and the abacus as the antiphon. What is at issue is not whether the position of certain images was carefully chosen, but what in the first instance, motivated such choices and what, in the second, did the monks make of it? How many choices were made, and at what stage? It is easy to see loose groupings and associations at various different levels at Moissac, creating the potential for a lifetime of monkish rumination, but difficult to see a single overarching *schema*, a controlling discipline that makes sense of each and every element. One might argue that Moissac's potential is enormously increased by this, that it was

intended to be neither comprehensive, nor exclusive. Some things are connected, some things may be connected, and some things are not connected. In terms of the actual deployment of imagery, Moissac is reminiscent, on a vastly more ambitious and spatially diffuse scale, of the overlapping elements of ornament, narrative and parallelism one associates with 4th-century Christian sarcophagi.

75. K. Horste, 'Cloister Design', 96–97.

76. ibid., 111–17.

77. Kathryn Horste has pointed to the stylistic similarities between the historiated capitals at Moissac and those of St-Caprais d'Agen, Moirax and, most importantly, St-Michel de Lescure, ibid., 118–19. See also M. Durliat, 'Aux origines de la sculpture romane languedocienne', *Cahiers de Civilisation Médiévale*, 5 (1962), 411–18. There is one further complication, however. The foliate capitals at Moissac do not relate to this group of buildings. Rather they develop out of the repertoire established in the eastern parts of St-Sernin, Toulouse.

78. L. Rutchick, 'Visual Memory', 197–204.

79. M. Schapiro, *The Sculpture of Moissac*, 26.

80. Only one half-walk, the eastern section of the walk adjacent to the church, has no foliate or animate capitals. Across the rest of the cloister they seem as if liberally scattered, and it is this relatively free distribution that is striking, seeming to act as a series of pauses — or punctuation marks — among the narrative forms on the one hand, and introducing the imagery of the garden to the walks on the other.

81. On the early-12th-century capitals from La Daurade now in the Musée des Augustins, Toulouse, see K. Horste, *Cloister Design*, particularly 45–102, that is the chapters dealing with the architectural context of the cloister and the relationship between the first series of La Daurade capitals and Moissac. The first inventory of the Musée des Augustins, the *Notice des Tableaux*, was compiled by Alexandre du Mège in 1818–19, where the *tableaux de la vie domestique* (now M.111) is No. 167 and the *toilette du prince* (now M.105) is No. 166.

82. The stark contrast was the interpretation preferred by M. Camille, *Image on the Edge* (London 1992), 56–61.

83. K. Horste, *Cloister Design*, 122–56.

84. The Inventory numbers now used by the Musée des Augustins for these capitals are M.114 (First Workshop: Arrest of Christ, Entry into Jerusalem — double capital), M.131 (Second Workshop: Arrest of Christ, Flagellation, Christ before Pilate, Way to Calvary — triple capital), and M.157 (Second Workshop: Four Rivers of Paradise — double capital).

85. Respectively catalogued as M.28 and M.33. See also Q. Cazes, 'Le cloître disparu', 275–84. Horste dates this work at the cathedral to *c.* 1125–35, very slightly later than the work of the Second Daurade workshop, who she argues probably restarted work at La Daurade *c.* 1123. Marcel Durliat dated most of this sculpture around a decade later, *c.* 1135–40. See M. Durliat, *Haut Languedoc Roman* (La Pierre-qui-Vire 1978), 205.

86. A total of 19 single column capitals survive from the cloister of Saint-Sernin, all now in the collections of the Musée des Augustins. Stylistically they are likely to date from some time between *c.* 1120 and *c.* 1140.

87. The finest of these are the double capitals M.172 and M.174, but La Daurade even ran to sub-bases decorated with fish and birds.

88. S. Simon, 'David et ses musiciens. Iconographie d'un chapiteau de Jaca', *Cahiers de Saint-Michel de Cuxa*, 11 (1980), 239–48.

89. On the capitals from the 12th-century cloister at Pamplona, see D. Simon, 'Late Romanesque Art in Spain', in *The Art of Medieval Spain ad 500–1200*, ed. J. O'Neill (New York 1993), 199 and 216–18. One final comment on the influence of Moissac is that its adoption of figural reliefs on the angle piers inspired a comparable arrangement in the cloister at Santo Domingo de Silos. The reliefs at Silos, however, were narrative — indeed dramatic — and its concentration of Christological imagery in scenic groupings at the angles of the walks inspired later cloister designers in Spain. Chris Welander has pointed out that it was Silos that lay behind the life-size figures at the angles of the late-13th-century cloister at Burgos Cathedral. See C. Welander, 'The Architecture of the Cloister of Burgos Cathedral', in *Medieval Architecture and its Intellectual Context*, ed. E. Fernie and P. Crossley (London 1990), 159–68. Indeed, it endures in Spain for a very long time indeed, and one even finds large figural groups deployed at the angles of the mid-16th-century great cloister of the Dominican house of San Esteban at Salamanca.

90. P. Patton, 'The Capitals of San Juan de la Peña. Narrative Sequences and Monastic Spirituality in the Romanesque Cloister', *Studies in Iconography*, XX (1999), 51–100.

91. P. Patton, 'The Cloister as Cultural Mirror', 317–32, but see especially the plan on 320 and list of subjects on 332.

92. See, in particular, Peter Klein's sensitive interpretation of Sant Cugat. P. Klein, 'Topographie, fonctions et programmes iconographiques', 140–45.

93. See L. Pressouyre, 'Les fouilles du cloître de Notre-Dame-en-Vaux de Châlons-sur-Marne', *Bulletin de la Société nationale des Antiquaires de France* (1964), 23–38; and L. Presssouyre, 'Le cloître de Notre-Dame-en-Vaux de Châlons-sur-Marne', *Congrès Archéologique*, CXXXV (1977), 298–306.

94. In addition to the above, for a discussion of the subjects found in the cloister, see the excellent short catalogue of the museum constructed just to the north of the site of the former cloister specifically to house its stonework. S. and L. Pressouyre, *Le cloître de Notre-Dame-en-Vaux* (Paris nd), 1–15.

95. L Pressouyre, 'St. Bernard to St. Francis', 76–77.

96. ibid., 75.

97. These are now displayed in the Musée des Augustins in Toulouse. Until the end of the 19th century the bases of the figures of St Andrew and St Thomas carried inscriptions giving the name of one of the sculptors: VIR NON INCERTUS ME CELAVIT GILABERTUS and GILABERTUS ME FECIT. For plans of the cloister and conventual precincts of St-Etienne, see Q. Cazes, 'Le cloître disparu', 270–71.

98. For a summary of the various claims made by du Mège as to the Apostles, see K. Horste, *Cloister Design*, 194. For a short account of Alexandre du Mège's career as a faker of medieval tomb slabs, see the exhibition catalogue, *Toulouse et l'art médiéval de 1830 à 1870* (Toulouse 1982), 65–69.

99. Q. Cazes, 'Le cloître disparu', 269.

100. L. Seidl, 'A Romantic Forgery', *Art Bulletin*, 50 (1968), 33–44.

101. Kathryn Horste tentatively suggests apostles may have been incorporated into the cloister piers, though this seems extremely unlikely, especially since it is known from 16th- and 17th-century accounts that images of Saints Sernin and Peter occupied the north-west angle pier, and Saint-Exupère was paired with a deacon at the north-east angle. See Q. Cazes, 'Le cloître disparu', 276. Quitterie Cazes herself is in no doubt the apostles constituted the chapter-house portal (ibid., 280), a view I share, but quite how they were physically arranged remains problematic.

102. K. Horste, *Cloister Design*, 58–61.

103. S. Moralejo, 'La Fachada de la sala capitular de la Daurade de Toulouse:datos iconograficos para su reconstrucción', *Anuario de estudios medievales*, 13 (1983), 179–204.

104. K. Horste, *Cloister Design*, 213–21.

105. The column figures of La Daurade are in a line of descent from the Portail Royal at Chartres, their breadth and concern for a sense of very slight movement having, perhaps, most in common with the west portal of Angers Cathedral. There are also very clear similarities between the Daurade Virgin and Child and that of the Saint Anne portal of Notre-Dame, Paris. The chapter-house façade of La Daurade was not specifically modelled on any one northern French portal scheme, nor indeed could it be. There are no tympana at La Daurade, it was smaller in scale than a church portal, and its proportions were different. Nonetheless, an early Gothic northern French portal scheme was the suggestive basis for its design, though the extent to which the motivation was formal, or iconographic, is debatable. For a fairly exhaustive account of the relationships between the portal sculpture of northern France, Spain and La Daurade, as well as an extended analysis of the iconography of La Daraude, see K. Horste, *Cloister Design*, 198–231.

106. The same phenomenon has been observed with regard to the way imagery was applied to chapter-house interiors, for an extended consideration of which see H. Stein-Kecks, '"Claustrum" and "Capitulum"', particularly 173–89. Stein-Kecks makes the point that other than a representation of the cross, which was standard, the internal embellishment of chapter-houses was astonishingly varied, unlike refectories. 'In fact, of all preserved chapter-houses known to us, none of them has an interior decoration identical with any of the others' (ibid., 173–74). Given the number of chapter-houses that have been lost, one should not be too categorical about applying Stein-Kecks' findings to their façades. Most chapter-houses seem to have carried no imagery around their entrances, and at a very simple level — chapter-house façades with just one or two figurative reliefs or capitals — there is a certain consistency. Images of the Virgin and Child, or Annunciation, are definitely favoured over other types of image. But when it comes to more ambitious iconographical schemes, exteriors do seem to be as varied as interiors. In England, for example, one might compare the interiors of the chapter-houses at Worcester, Westminster, Salisbury, Wells and York — or the exteriors of Rochester and Salisbury. For a fuller and more interesting appraisal of this, see T. A. Heslop, 'Worcester Cathedral Chapterhouse and the Harmony of the Testaments', in *New Offerings, Ancient Treasures: Studies in Medieval Art for George Henderson*, ed. P. Binski and W. Noel (Stroud 2001), 280–311; P. Binski, *Westminster Abbey and the Plantagenets* (New Haven and London 1995), 185–92; and S. Brown, 'The Thirteenth-Century Stained Glass of the Salisbury Cathedral Chapter House', *Wiltshire Archaeological and Natural History Magazine*, 94 (2001), 118–38, particularly 135–36.

107. See J. McNeill, 'The East Cloister Walk of Saint-Aubin at Angers: Sculpture and Archaeology', in *Anjou: Medieval Art, Architecture and Archaeology*, ed. J. McNeill and D. Prigent, *BAA Trans.*, XXVI (2003), 111–37.

108. I realise I am out on a limb in suggesting the paintings beneath the Virgin and Child were not anticipated when the chapter-house façade was first planned. Both Christian Davy and Eric Palazzo have

recently published important studies which argue that painting and sculpture are contemporary. See C. Davy, *La peinture murale romane dans les pays de la Loire* (Laval 1999), 156–61, and E. Palazzo, 'Exégèse, liturgie et politique dans l'iconographie du cloître de Saint-Aubin d'Angers', in *Der Mittelalterliche Kreuzgang*, ed. P. Klein (Regensburg 2004), 220–40. My initial apprehension that the paintings were added beneath the carved image of the Virgin and Child retrospectively was based on their respective figure styles. Subsequently, I began to feel the iconography of the south arcades was perfectly coherent without the paintings of the Adoration of the Magi and Massacre of the Innocents. Sheila Connolly clearly felt similarly; 'how crucial are the paintings to the symbolism of the programme? It is essentially complete without the addition of the scenes of the Magi and the Massacre. In fact, the concept of the Virgin as intercessor has little to do with the painted scenes', though Connolly felt the painting was probably an afterthought and both it and the sculpture could still be contemporary. See S. R. Connolly, 'The Cloister Sculpture of Saint-Aubin in Angers' (unpublished Ph.D. thesis, Harvard, 1979), 182.

109. See A. Grabar, 'The Virgin in a Mandorla of Light', in *Late Classical and Medieval Studies in Honor of Albert Mathias Friend, Jr.* (Princeton 1955), 305–11.

110. J. Migne ed., *Patrologiae Cursus Completus, Series Latina*, Vol. 189 (Paris 1844–1904), 1018.

111. J. McNeill, 'East Cloister Walk', 126.

112. It seems particularly appropriate in the context of the *capitulum culparum*, or chapter of faults; that part of the chapter meeting in which any monk who had committed a fault was required to announce it publicly, and ask forgiveness. The chapter-house as a place of discipline and punishment is most famously alluded to in the façade of the chapter-house of Saint-Georges-de-Boscherville. See L. Pressouyre, 'St. Bernard to St. Francis', 78–81, and K. Morrison, 'The Figural Capitals of the Chapterhouse of Saint-Georges-de-Boscherville', in *Medieval Art, Architecture and Archaeology at Rouen*, ed. J. Stratford, *BAA Trans.*, XII (Leeds 1993), 46–50.

113. The positioning of the St-Aubin Virgin and Child chimes with the great Marian homilies of the late 11th and early 12th century — Anselm's representation of the Virgin as *porta coeli, januas paradisi* — but perhaps most striking in this respect is the text of a sermon for the feast of the Assumption written by Hildebert de Lavardin, and known from a collection of Hildebert's sermons kept in the monastic library at St-Aubin (now in the Bibliothèque Municipal, Angers). The sermon is a commentary on Ezekiel's description of the New Temple — whose *porta haec clausa* — had been recognised since the 4th century as indicating Mary's virginity remained intact after the birth of Christ. The most interesting passage for our purposes is where Hildebert distinguishes between the inner and outer gates. *Sanctuarium itaque interius est verbum in principio apud Patrem, portans omnia verbo virtutis suae. Sanctuarium exterius Verbum caro factum in tempore, purgationem faciens infirmitatis nostrae. Interioris porta est Deus Pater .... Exterioris porta est beata Virgo, per quam in nostram deus humanitas ingressus est civitatem.* Angers, Bib. Mun., MS. 330, fol. 41v. In other words, the outer gate is the Virgin Mary, through whom we accomplish the forgiveness of sins, thanks to the mystery of the Incarnation. I am enormously grateful to Eric Palazzo for bringing this to my attention, and for generously sending me a copy of his article on the iconography of the St-Aubin chapter-house prior to publication. See E. Palazzo, 'Exégèse, liturgie et politique', 232–34. If the interpretation of the St-Aubin Virgin as a mediatrix is accepted, she takes a place within a diversified range of images of the Virgin which testify to a pictorial revalorisation of her cult during the second quarter of the 12th century. The most striking example of this within the vicinity of Angers was the transformation wrought to the west front of Saint-Jouin-de-Marnes which, as Anat Tcherikover has demonstrated, started out as a straightforward vision of the Second Coming as described in St Matthew's Gospel. It was initially completed *c.* 1110–20, yet within a generation of this, perhaps around 1150, its meaning was transformed in a wholly startling way, and the people from far and wise who originally gathered at the feet of Christ, instead present themselves to the figure of the Virgin — inserted there as an intermediary. See A. Tcherikover, *High Romanesque Sculpture*, 82–82, 162–64.

114. See V. Godard-Faultrier, *L'Anjou et ses Monuments* (Angers 1839), 381. The 12th-century chapter-house façade had only been rediscovered in 1836.

115. For a perceptive and enlightening discussion of this, see S. R. Connolly, 'Cloister Sculpture', 176–78.

116. See L. Labande, 'Nouvelles remarques sur la même inscription', *Bull. Mon.* (1905), 466–68. This follows on from his long article, 'La cathédrale de Vaison' in the same volume, 253–321.

117. M. Rambaud, 'Le Quatrain mystique de Vaison-la-Romaine', *Bull. Mon.* (1951), 157–74.

118. L. Pressouyre, 'St Bernard to St Francis', 72–72.

119. *Perpetuis Annis/ Stat Quarti Fama Iohannis/ Per Quem Pastorem/ Hunc Habet Ista Decorem.* 'For years without end the good name of John the Fourth abides. It is to him as shepherd this house owes its beauty'. See E. Galasso, *Il Chistro allo Specchio*, 26. My thanks to Nigel Jaques for improvising an on-the-spot translation of this in March, 2005.

120. Michael Camille produced a short survey of what might be described as the margin in context — an attempt to look at the relationship between images at the margin and the centre, taken across a variety of

media and within different sorts of space. M. Camille, *Image on the Edge* (London 1992). As far as I am aware, other explorations of the theme, of which there are many, tend to be case studies, or focus on a particular vehicle, like manuscripts, or the corbel.

121. This debate is usually conducted within reach of a copy of the celebrated *Apologia ad Guillelmum Abbatem* of Bernard of Clairvaux. For some of the issues this raises, see C. Rudolph, *Artistic Change at Saint-Denis: Abbot Suger's Programme and the Early Twelfth-Century Controversy over Art* (Princeton 1990), 8–18.

122. T. Dale, 'Monsters, Corporeal Deformities, and Phantasms in the Cloister of St-Michel-de-Cuxa', *Art Bulletin* (2001), 402–36.

123. P. Ponsich, 'Chronologie et typologie des cloîtres romans roussillonais', *Cahiers de Saint-Michel de Cuxa*, 7 (1976), 75–97.

124. N. de Dalmases and A. Pitarch, *Història de l'Art Català, Vol III: L'Art Gòtic* (Barcelona 1984), 114–19.

125. Glazed cloisters could be very highly charged indeed. Symon Gunton reports that at Peterborough Abbey the cloister glass contained Old Testament imagery in the south walk, New Testament imagery in the east walk, English kings in the north walk and a history of the monastery in the west walk, all of it accompanied by verse inscriptions. S. Gunton, *The History of the Church of Peterborough* (London 1686), 103. Cloister glass may have lent itself to saying something about the origins of a community, much as it was not unusual for Romanesque cloisters to carry an image of a founding or reforming abbot. St Peter's at Gloucester apparently carried twenty-two Latin verses on the history of the monastery in its cloister glass. See R. Marks, *Stained Glass in England during the Middle Ages* (London 1993), 90.

126. The plaques at Elne extend around two walks of the cloister, and are the sort of discrete images arranged at regular intervals that were to be used in the following century for the dramatic narrative of the Stations of the Cross. For an account of their archaeology and date, see M. Durliat, 'Un cycle gothique de la passion et de la résurrection du Christ au cloître d'Elne', *Cahiers ligures de préhistoire et d'archéologie*, 18 (1969), 71–78. However, in the later Middle Ages it was more usual for the rear walls of cloisters to be embellished with paintings. This seems to have been most common in Italy, but is also to be found in Spain, at León Cathedral or Santa María de Pedralbes in Barcelona, for example. Just how important paintings could become might be obliquely gauged at the cloister of the Emmaus monastery in Prague, where the initial entrance to the chapter-house was blocked so as to make available the largest possible surface area for painting on the rear wall of the east walk. The south walk rear wall was also modified. The result was a quite spectacular series of largely typological paintings around all four walks, and a loss of that sense of architectural permeability that had been a cornerstone of chapter-house design since the late 10th century. Indeed, the resulting chapter-house portal at the Emmaus monastery must be one of the most unobtrusive of medieval Europe. See Z. Opačić, 'Charles IV and the Emmaus Monastery: Slavonic Tradition and Imperial Ideology in Fourteenth-Century Prague' (unpublished Ph.D thesis, University of London, 2003).

127. The height of the east walk at Gloucester is 4.72 m (15 ft 6 in.). The heights of the cloister walks at Westminster Abbey vary, but that of the east walk is 7.4 m from pavement to ridge (24 ft 3 in.). The south walk is around 1 m lower. As far as the evidence allows, Westminster had far and away the tallest cloister walks to be built in England and Wales. Gloucester is very much more typical. I am enormously grateful to Carolyn Heighway for sending me details of the Gloucester cloister, and to Christine Reynolds, Tim Tatton-Brown and Warwick Rodwell for putting me right on the height of Westminster's various walks.

128. The cloister at Pamplona was begun some time after the Romanesque cathedral was damaged by French troops during the war of the Navarrería in 1276–77. The cathedral was subsequently repaired, but the precise date when work began on a new cloister to the east of the earlier, 12th-century, cloister is unknown. A donation is recorded on the part of Sancho Martínez de Izu, cellarer, who gave 300 soldi specifically for work on the cloister of Santa Maria de Pamplona in 1291 — and the cloister is described as being under construction in 1311. See J. Goñi Gaztambide, 'Nuevos documentos sobre la Catedral de Pamplona', *Príncipe de Viana*, 16 (1955), 134. Progress was slow, however, and most of the work was done while Cardinal Arnaldo de Barbazán was bishop (1317–56). The principal processional portal connecting the south-west angle of the cloister with the church, the Puerta del Amparo, can be dated to c. 1330–40, and a wall-painting, formerly in the canons' refectory, is inscribed with the date 1330. See also P. Frankl, *Gothic Architecture*, rev. P. Crossley (New Haven 2000), 279–80.

129. E. Santamaría, 'La Mezquita Major, Santa María l'Antiga y la canónica de la Seu Vella de Lleida: historia de una confusión', *Actas del XIII Congreso del CEHA* (Granada 2000), 65–74.

130. The dating, topography and function of the cloister at Lérida are controversial. The earliest document specifically mentioning work on the cloister dates from 1317, though the sculpture of the east walk arcade relates to that of the west font of the cathedral (consecrated in 1278) and is usually dated stylistically to the late 13th-century. The north and west walks are recorded as being in building during the episcopacy of

Ferrer Colom (1334–40), and the cloister was certainly complete by 1378. See F. Español, 'El claustro gótico de la catedral de Lérida: forma y función', in *Der Mittelalterliche Kreuzgang*, ed. P. Klein (Regensburg 2004), 357–60. There is uncertainty over the relationship between the plan of the 13th-century cathedral, the pre-1149 mosque and structures abutting the north walk of the cloister, however. The mosque was converted to Christian use on 30 October 1149, and a chapter of Augustinian canons was introduced in 1168. Elements of what is probably a 12th-century dormitory and refectory, subsequently referred to as Santa Maria l'Antiga, survive off the north cloister walk. By 1186 there is mention of a burial *in claustro*, and there are further records of burials in what is described as a cloister in 1214, 1229 and 1266. The most widely favoured hypothesis holds that the site of the present cloister overlaps that of the patio of the mosque, and that it was used for burial from the second half of the 12th century. After the new cathedral was completed a new cloister was gradually created, significant landmarks being the effective restriction of burials within the cathedral to private chapels in 1318, and the promulgation of an order regulating burials in the cloister by Bishop Jaume Sitjó in 1343. Thereafter the cloister became a high status urban cemetery. See F. Español, 'Espais de la Mort, Espais de Poder, Fundaciones i Capelles', in *Seu Vella: l'Esplendor Retrobada* (Lérida 2003), 130–47. But it was always much more than this. It was a major processional space, and the walks were used by the chapter. Indeed in 1406, the cathedral chapter asked for stone benches to be provided in the south walk for their summer meetings. See E. Santamaría, 'Cathedral Cloisters in the Kingdoms of León and Galicia', 94.

131. F. Vilà, 'L'Au Fènix: De L'Esfondrada a la Nova Integració de la Seu Vella en la ciutat contemporània', *Seu Vella: L'Esplendor Retrobada* (Lleida 2003), 159–74.

The Cloister and Bishop's Palace at Old Sarum with Some Thoughts on the Origins and Meaning of Secular Cathedral Cloisters

JOHN MONTAGUE

Between 1909 and 1915 the Society of Antiquaries of London sponsored the excavation of the Iron-Age, Roman and medieval levels of Old Sarum. Progress was halted in the latter year because the demands of the First World War had created a shortage of man-power. Nevertheless, by 1915 most of the site had been examined in some form or other. Annual interim reports were delivered to the Society of Antiquaries, but the comprehensive appraisal of the site that was intended was never written as a result of the untimely death of the principal director of excavations, Sir William St John Hope. This has resulted in confusion over the sequence and chronology of construction at Old Sarum, particularly as regards those buildings to the north and east of the cathedral church. The following article is a reappraisal of the evidence, especially as it pertains to the cloister and the bishop's palace, and proposes a new interpretation of the chronology of the buildings in this sector of the cathedral close. Certain implications, including those that apply to our understanding of early secular cathedral communities after the Norman Conquest, are considered in the light of this new appraisal.

NOT enough is known about secular cathedral cloisters as a group. Cloisters — the very word is suggestive of the enclosed nature of monastic life — might appear better associated with the setting of the great monastic churches. It is tempting to believe cathedrals run by secular canons, in holy orders but 'of the world', should have had no need for cloisters. However of the nine secular cathedrals in England, seven — Chichester, Exeter, Hereford, Lincoln, London, Salisbury, and Wells — were to build cloisters before the close of the Middle Ages. Only Lichfield and York did not.

A comparison between a monastic plan and that of a secular cathedral (Figs 1 and 2), quickly reveals the extent to which their cloisters differed. The monastic cloister was set at the heart of a complex of conventual buildings which included the refectory, dormitory and chapter-house, and gave onto the great church itself. Besides its liturgical functions, the cloister was the means by which buildings of disparate plans and elevations were integrated, and that circulation from one area to another was facilitated. The cloister at a secular cathedral such as Lincoln, on the other hand, was a stand-alone enclosure, encased by a single wall. The monastic chapter-house was integrated amongst the other buildings, very often with the dormitory above; at the secular cathedral the chapter-house stood isolated from the cloister, separated by a passageway or some sort of vestibular space. In later years at

JBAA, vol. 159 (2006), 48–70
© British Archaeological Association 2006
DOI: 10.1179/174767006X132961

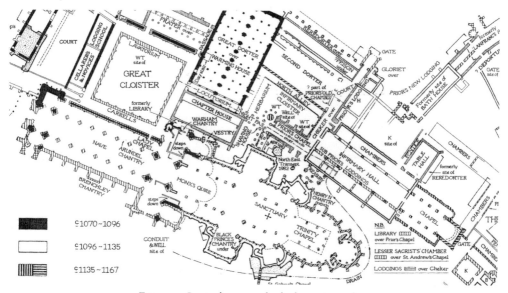

FIG. 1.   Canterbury: cathedral precinct plan

Jill Atherton: reproduced by permission of Canterbury Archaeological Trust

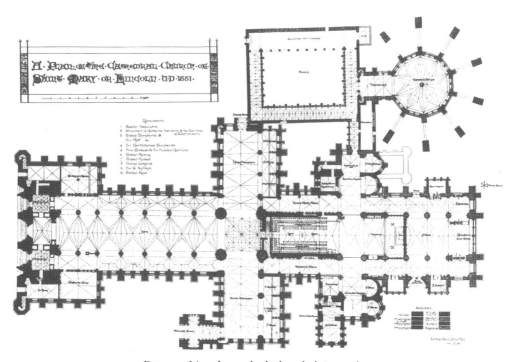

FIG. 2.   Lincoln: cathedral and cloister plan

Arthur Beresford Pite in The Builder *(1881)*

least, there were no refectories or dormitories at the secular cathedrals, and as most canons had their own house and most likely their own outlying manor, as part of their prebendary possessions, residential facilities seem on first sight to have been superfluous.

The apparently anomalous nature of the secular cathedral cloister is perhaps reflected by its haphazard development in England. Although seven cloisters were eventually completed by the end of the 15th century, only three secular cathedrals constructed cloisters before 1300 — Wells, Salisbury (and its predecessor Old Sarum) and Lincoln. In other words, from the Conquest until 1300, six of the secular cathedral chapters could find no pressing reason to build a cloister. By contrast, the cloister was seen as a prerequisite at any monastic great church, including the monastic cathedrals. The European position seems to have been no different. A recent survey of French cathedral cloisters indicated that, just as in England, the majority of cloisters at secular cathedrals were not built until between *c.* 1300 and *c.* 1500.[1]

The great cloister at Salisbury, built in the 1260s, survives as one of the showpiece cathedral cloisters of the Middle Ages, and remains more or less in its original form. While all questions are far from answered, the background and history of Salisbury and the related and slightly earlier cloister at Wells have been well researched.[2] So too has the history of secular cathedral chapters from the second half of the 12th century onwards. Built upon the rights and privileges of a secular clergy, the chapter of canons was headed by a dean, whose authority often rivalled that of the bishop. However, the so-called four-square hierarchy of the chapter — dean, precentor, chancellor and treasurer — and the dignities and rights which they represented, were a development of the mid-12th century and beyond, rather than a practice of secular cathedrals from the start.[3] Our knowledge of how secular cathedral chapters were organised before this, during their crucial formative stages, is for the most part vague. The built environment in which they lived out their everyday lives is likewise also largely unknown.

It is these issues of socio-architectural history that this article aims to address. For the most part it is not concerned with stylistic development, as the evidence which survives for earlier cloisters is often in plan form only. Nor is it the object of this work to determine a precise chronology, nor indeed a genealogy of secular cathedral cloisters.[4] Rather, the intention is to look closely at Old Sarum, while in conclusion, to consider one or two other early secular cathedral cloisters to the extent that they might shed light on the meaning and origins of early cathedral communities and their buildings.

THE CLOISTER AND BISHOP'S PALACE AT OLD SARUM

OLD SARUM is clearly the critical monument for understanding English secular cathedral practice.[5] It was at Old Sarum that the so-called Use of Sarum evolved, and while it is now accepted that its codification in the *Institutio* of St Osmund probably dates to the mid-12th century rather than the late 11th, we can be sure that it was here that a good deal of the normative practice for English secular cathedrals was first developed.[6] While much has been written about Old Sarum, a definitive chronology of the buildings to the north of the cathedral has not been agreed.[7] The key to understanding their chronology must be the misaligned cloister (Fig. 3). The lengths of its four sides all differed and critically the north and south walks were not parallel.[8] The lines of the presbytery and of the north transept of the cathedral dictated the southern and western lines of the cloister respectively and so it follows that the cloister must

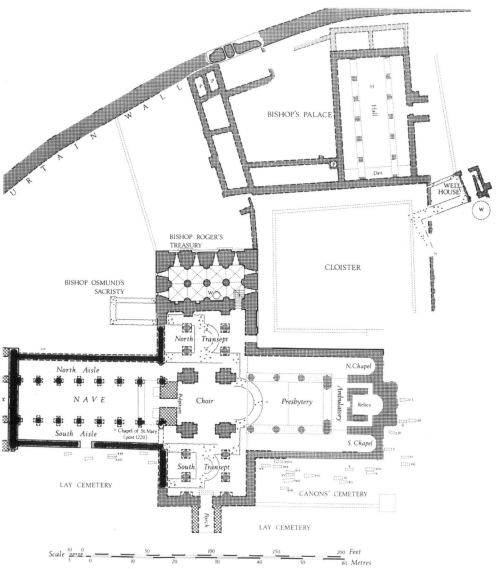

FIG. 3.   Old Sarum: plan of the cathedral, cloister and palace
© *Crown copyright. NMR*

at least have been built after, or be contemporary with, the extension of the east end of the cathedral. However, the skewed northern boundary of the cloister must surely have been dictated by the line of the palace, which consequently must predate the cloister. The obtuse angle of the eastern cloister boundary may also suggest some previous structures on this side, although there was no archaeological evidence to confirm this one way or another.[9]

It may be impossible to arrive at a certain date for the cloister on the basis of a constructional sequence, as the documentary evidence for the extension of the church, which we are confident was carried out by Bishop Roger (1102/7–39) mentions no dates.[10] Roger Stalley, among others, has leaned in the direction of the evidence posited in the *Gesta Stephani*, that at the end of his life a small portion of the money and treasure left by Bishop Roger was returned to the canons by King Stephen for roofing the church — '*ecclesiam cooperiendam*'.[11] This would imply a period late in Roger's career if the church still remained to be roofed at the time of his death. In the *Historia Novella*, William of Malmesbury at first seems to confirm this picture when he tells us that Roger himself stipulated that the treasure and money which he left on the altar was to be used for the completion of the church.[12] However, it can be deduced from the scale and positioning of the crossing piers that a new nave must also have been planned, and it is as reasonable to infer that it was to the nave that Roger was referring, rather than to an incomplete east end.

The most important evidence for an earlier date, that the new east end, including transepts, choir and presbytery, were constructed, or at least largely completed, well before Roger's death, comes from William of Malmesbury's *Gesta Regum Anglorum*. Having described the expense of the building, and famously the quality of its ashlar — 'that the joints defy inspection and give the whole wall the appearance of a single rock face' — William tells us that: '[Roger] made the new church at Salisbury and adorned it with furnishings so that it yielded place to no others in England, but surpassed many.'[13] The 19th-century translator of this passage suggested that William of Malmesbury was writing around the year 1125.[14] This date has been accepted by some as a reasonable *terminus ante quem* for the construction of Roger's east end.[15] But the *Gesta Stephani* evidence regarding the roof, and the interpretation that Roger's bequest to complete the church was referring to the east end, has cast a shadow over this earlier dating of William's quote in the *Gesta Regum*. Despite this, the most recent scholarly translation of the *Gesta Regum* comes out strongly in favour of Stubbs' early date.[16] The passage in which William describes Roger's building the new (or building anew) the church at Salisbury appears in chapter 408, part of a second version of William's first draft of the *Gesta*, which Thomson argues convincingly was completed between the years 1124 and 1126.[17]

If Roger completed his eastern extension to Osmund's church by *c.* 1125, then it is reasonable to wonder whether he might have begun the cloister at some point over the next fourteen years. Some aspects of the management of the ground levels in this area imply that the cloister was at least planned in conjunction with the construction of Roger's new building. The early-20th-century excavations revealed a complex succession of steps rising west to east within the church. Although this is not unusual, it also neatly followed the underlying ground upon which Roger's eastern building was constructed. Throughout the whole site the ground slopes upwards from the outer ramparts towards the centre where the motte or inner bailey was built by King William in the early years after the conquest.[18] This slope is particularly marked along a radial line which runs from the north-west angle of the treasury to the south-east angle of the new presbytery and continues in this direction towards the centre of the motte (Fig. 4). Consequently we find that the eastern aisle of the transepts was a step higher than the central and western transept aisles; the choir and the side aisles of the presbytery were a step up from the transept aisles; the presbytery was a step up again, as was the high altar beyond it, and so on continuing in this fashion as far as the step up to the altars of the eastern chapels. The area of the cloister, however, remains level

FIG. 4. Aerial view of Old Sarum
© Crown copyright. NMR

throughout with that of the entrance into the crypt of the treasury/vestry building
north of the north transept. Maintaining this level appears to have been achieved by
excavating the southern and eastern parts of the area to be occupied by the cloister,
which consequently is seated below the natural slope of the hill. The latter can be seen
in the ground immediately east of the claustral precinct which continues to climb
towards the south (Fig. 5).

A section of undamaged ashlar masonry — part of a chamfered plinth — was
uncovered during the original excavations in the angle between the north transept and
the eastern arm of the church (Fig. 6).[19] This gave onto the west walk of the cloister,
and demonstrates that the area of the future cloister was cleared when the new

53

FIG. 5.   Recent view of Old Sarum cloister area excavated by its builders contemporaneously with the eastern extension of the cathedral

John Montague

FIG. 6.   Old Sarum: photograph taken in 1913 of the recently excavated steps leading into the cloister. These appear not to have been integral to the chamfered east wall of the north transept

© *Salisbury and South Wiltshire Museum*

presbytery was being built. The exterior base levels, on the southern and eastern sides of the presbytery, in contrast, are level with the ground level on the interior of the church, all of which followed the slope of the hill. If a cloister space had not been at least planned, the interior and exterior of the northern side of the presbytery would also have been level, and would have saved on the considerable earth moving that the cloister space implies must have taken place. However, a 1913 photograph of the steps connecting the eastern aisle of the north transept with the cloister appears to show that they were inserted into the external plinth. This suggests that the cloister was not built immediately, even if its precinct was excavated at the same time as the eastern extension was being built. As such, the cloister may well have been built by Roger's successor Bishop Jocelyn (1142–84), though an earlier completion date, in the latter stages of Roger's episcopacy, remains possible. Notwithstanding uncertainty over a completion date for the cloister, progress may still be made on the chronology of the bishop's palace to the north.

For this we must return to the north walk of the cloister, whose misalignment convincingly suggests it had to abut a pre-existing structure, namely the bishop's palace (Fig. 3). The west and south walks of the cloister were evidently dependent upon the lines of the north and east arms of Roger's extension to the church, as mentioned already, and consequently are at right angles to one another. The boundary line of the north walk, in contrast, was clearly dictated by the southern boundary of the bishop's palace. Nor was the external boundary line of the east walk parallel to the line formed by the north transept on the opposite side of the cloister. It is inconceivable in this age that a cloister, whose ideal had long been square, should have been built so far off true. The bishop's palace therefore must have been built even before the east end of the cathedral had been extended (the outline of Osmund's earlier cathedral is indicated in Fig. 3). Indeed, as the bishop's palace was built at some distance from Osmund's presbytery, there was no need for it to be aligned with an east end *en echelon*, particularly since this did not present it with a continuous straight line. Thus the southern perimeter of the palace — neither parallel to the outer perimeter of the castle, nor to the early-12th-century cathedral extension — must pre-date the cloister. This seems the only explanation for the latter's off-square plan. Roger's masons had no problems maintaining right angles throughout the east-end extension and indeed in his later house at Sherborne, and we have no reason to doubt the ability of later builders should the cloister date to Roger's successor Jocelyn.

There were two bishops at Salisbury before Roger, Hereman who ended his long episcopate of the combined sees of Sherborne and Ramsbury at Sarum during the years 1075–78, and Osmund, the founder of the chapter of canons at Old Sarum and bishop of Salisbury from 1078 to 1099. Either of these, along with Roger, could theoretically have been responsible for establishing the bishop's palace. However, once again, the off-square nature of this enclosure — with three definite ranges, west, south and an eastern hall range, and a possible fourth along the northern perimeter wall — is disquieting.[20] Why might Roger, who was most probably responsible for the intricate discipline of the quadrangular enclosure of the courtyard house in the inner bailey, and for the equivalent and even more exceptional house at Sherborne Castle, be satisfied with such an irregular bishop's palace? A part explanation for the irregularity of this space was arrived at by an insight John Blair brought to bear in his important article on English domestic planning from AD 1000–1250.[21]

As an illustration to his article, Blair included a phased diagram of the bishop's palace which assigned the west range to *c.* 1130, that is, in the latter part of

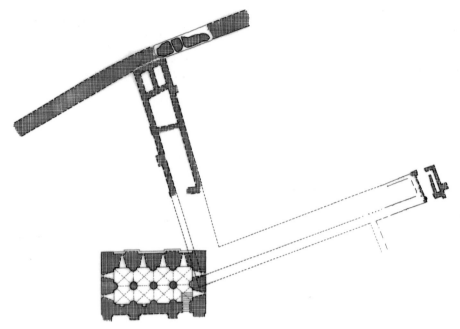

FIG. 7. Old Sarum: John Blair's 1993 conjectural plan of the bishop's palace reconsidered in relation to the treasury/vestry building, north of the north transept

Caitríona Harvey (Shaffrey Associates Architects, Dublin) based on the author's original drawing

Roger's episcopacy, and the hall, which makes up the east range, to Jocelin de Bohun (1142–84), in the later years of his pontificate, that is, *c.* 1180.[22] In a diagram which illustrated the earlier phase only, Blair made a connection between the remains of a building (crossing the north-east corner of the cloister) and the western wing of the later palace.[23] These Blair joined along a plausible right angle, which very sensibly suggested an earlier complex of ranges around a square plan.[24] However, what he failed to include, and indeed his upturned plan may explain the omission, was the plan of the treasury/vestry building north of the north transept, which Hope had demonstrated pre-dated Roger's extension.[25] If the buildings were joined by Bishop Roger in the manner suggested by Blair, the lines of the buildings would collide with the treasury (Fig. 7).[26] The square alignment must therefore belong to a group of buildings constructed before the treasury building. Indeed, in order for the treasury to have been built, the earlier ranges of the bishop's palace must have been demolished and replaced by the layout which was found by the excavators, as is shown on the site plan. The construction of the new south and west ranges of a new bishop's palace must therefore have been carried out before *c.* 1110–25.[27]

Hope's description of what remained of the building at the north-east corner of the cloister, based on three seasons of excavation on site, confirms this interpretation. He makes it clear that the building which diagonally crossed the line of the cloister here, and which must have pre-dated it, could not have belonged to anything within Roger's *œuvre*: 'The ashlar work at its east end is quite unlike any other masonry yet laid open at Old Sarum, being built of larger and deeper stones than the twelfth-century walls of the castle [for which Roger is known to be responsible], and with different tooling.' On the other hand, it was also concluded that the chamfered edge and the use of ashlar precluded a pre-11th-century date.[28] As for the remains of the west range, which appeared to form part of this earlier enclosure, Hawley described its masonry as 'of flint rubble and poorly-made white mortar'.[29] This contrasts with all that was reported in the Middle Ages about the splendour of Roger's work, as well as the standing evidence of fine ashlar work at his palace in the Inner Bailey at Sarum.[30] The fact that the final bishop's palace was the result of two phases of construction explains the trapezoidal shape of the combined enclosure found by the excavators. Its unusual shape and reduced area must have been accepted with the development of a cloister (and, perhaps, claustral ranges) in mind. The new south and west ranges of the bishop's palace were extremely likely to have been built before the treasury, therefore, and are most likely to have been Roger's work, although we cannot rule out the possibility that the change took place before he became bishop. What is certain is that the hall dates to before *c.* 1110–25, and that the preceding palace enclosure was constructed by one of Roger's predecessors, probably Bishop Osmund (1078–99).

A late-11th-century bishop's palace enclosure and an early-12th-century aisled hall: comparative evidence

A rectangular enclosure of high-status domestic buildings at the end of the 11th century appears to have been almost unique, but may be profitably compared to a number of other bishop's palaces dated for the most part to the first half of the 12th century. The plan type, however, was not found amongst secular buildings at this time, but rather only in high status complexes associated with ecclesiastical dwellings.[31] This leads one to speculate whether the example of a monastic enclosure was part of the inspiration behind Osmund's palace, and whether this in turn influenced Roger in his later palace buildings. The latter included the bishop's palace as it was built over Osmund's earlier enclosure, the refined complex with a cloister at Roger's castle in Sherborne and the courtyard house in the inner bailey at Sarum, where the idea received considerable development and was to be profoundly influential on high status secular buildings in turn.[32] An important element in Blair's chronology of the development of the English hall is his contention that the hall in the bishop's palace at Sarum was built by Jocelin de Bohun *c.* 1160–80. However, although it is aisled, it lacked certain other elements associated with the classic hall. Most pertinently, it was entered through a doorway in the middle of its east wall (along the flank of the building), rather than at the lower end where services were usually located. As Blair acknowledges, the services at Old Sarum (at the northern end) are a later addition.[33] It is to the possible comparisons with this aisled hall that we will first turn.

The archaeological evidence for the building of aisled halls in England in the late 11th and early 12th century is fairly limited but not absent completely. The most dramatic example, rivalling in scale halls built for centuries to come, was that built by William Rufus at Westminster at some point between 1087–1100.[34] The extreme dimensions of this hall, 72 m × 20 m approx.,[35] would suggest that despite the lack of surviving evidence for post holes or for foundations for an arcade, the building could not have been roofed, given contemporary timber technology, without the use of arcades.[36] If we remember that Osmund had been chancellor to William the

Conqueror, was Norman by origin and a contemporary of William II, it is not impossible that he should also seek to build an aisled hall, even if the balance of the evidence suggests the bishop's hall excavated at Old Sarum dates to the first two decades of the 12th century. Another slightly later example of the type is Henry I's hall at Cheddar, built in the first quarter of the 12th century and also known to have been aisled. Rahtz's excavations also revealed that Henry's hall had been preceded by an earlier aisled building of the late 11th century.[37]

Nor should we allow the limited archaeological record to dictate our perception of aisled halls at this time. Another source for the kinds of buildings possible and indeed common within late-11th-century royal or seigneurial contexts is the Bayeux Tapestry, commonly believed to have been commissioned by Bishop Odo of Bayeux between c. 1070 and 1082.[38] Represented here are a number of secular buildings, including what may be a chamber block at Bosham and William's great hall in Rouen. Commissioned by a Norman prelate, but perhaps designed by an Anglo-Saxon artist, the architecture depicted may be representative of building practices on both sides of the channel.[39] The Bayeux Tapestry illustrates a number of secular aisled buildings — churches seem all to be distinguished by having crosses for roof finials. The chamber building at Bosham where Earl Harold feasted before his fateful voyage to France, shows aisles at lower floor level apparently representing a vaulted undercroft. There are also two other significant buildings depicted that are unnamed. The first could be interpreted as an arcaded hall, with a curved roof (Fig. 8). This was located somewhere between William's camp at Rouen in Normandy and Guy, count of Ponthieu's base at Beaurain. It was in fact a basilical building with a wider central vessel and quasi-quadrant arches over the aisles.[40] Another slightly less impressive, but similar building (Fig. 9) had three aisles of equal height and was located near the shore where William's men are shown making preparations for his invasion of England.[41]

William's hall at Rouen is itself worth considering. While there remains no clear archaeological evidence for the ducal residence at Rouen, we know it was a once extensive and impressive complex.[42] It would have been with Rouen — then in the hands of Robert Curthose — that William Rufus sought to compete when he went about building Westminster Hall. Both Osmund and Roger, who held important positions in the courts of William and Henry I respectively, and who both hailed from Normandy, would have been familiar with the buildings at Rouen and Westminster and would certainly have been aware of their significance as centres of seigneurial power. In the tapestry William is depicted enthroned in his hall at Rouen (Fig. 10), receiving the compromised Harold. The grandest building on the tapestry, save for Westminster Abbey, it gives the impression of tremendous and ample space. The Bayeux tapestry does not make the section of the building clear, though the arcade represented towards the top of the image might be interpreted (at a stretch) as an attempt to manage the perspective of an aisle arcade to the rear of the seated figures.

The aisled hall, or basilica, had been the very essence of political power in ancient Rome. It was in the basilica that legal and political decisions were made in assembly. The type was adopted in the early Christian era to serve a function which was religious but still involved mass assembly. While the significance of its ancient authority was carried by the Church, its practicality was also part of the reason for its first adoption. It may have been for similarly practical reason that the form was adapted in monastic buildings other than churches in the course of the 11th century. It is to monastic buildings of this kind that we must now turn to complete the background to the hall that Osmund may have built at the end of the same century.

FIG. 8. Detail of the Bayeux
Tapestry — 11th century: arcaded
hall with curved roof

By special permission of the City of Bayeux

FIG. 9. Detail of the Bayeux
Tapestry — 11th century: arcaded
hall with aisles of equal height

By special permission of the City of Bayeux

FIG. 10. Detail of the Bayeux Tapestry — 11th century: William enthroned at Rouen

By special permission of the City of Bayeux

In terms of form and function, the similarity between the secular domestic hall and the monastic refectory is striking.[43] Not only was each the location of communal eating, but the refectory was often divided into aisles by arcades held aloft by columns or piers. According to Conant's reconstruction, the refectory at Cluny II (c. 1043) was on the ground floor and had three aisles separated by arcades supported on stone columns. The entrance was at the 'lower' western end and from the west wall of the refectory two doors led into the pantry and the kitchen, with the cellar just to the north.[44] The refectory at Lewes Priory, the first Cluniac monastery in England, and therefore potentially influenced by the architecture at Cluny, is notoriously ambiguous archaeologically.[45] The second phase of conventual building appeared to include a first-floor refectory over a vaulted undercroft supported by an axial arcade. We are on firmer ground when it comes to the refectory at Thetford Priory, Norfolk 1120–40 (Fig. 11),[46] also Cluniac, which clearly embodies many of the features associated with the classic medieval hall. There is evidence of a privileged east end, raised on a dais, with a west entrance beside the buttery and kitchen. It is less clear whether the refectory was ever aisled, and its lateral span suggests it may well have been aisleless. However, one last example of an 'aisled hall' in a late-11th-century/early-12th-century English monastery may serve to highlight the potential for borrowing across building types. While the infirmary at Christ Church Priory, Canterbury, fulfilled a different function to that of the refectory or indeed the seigneurial hall, it none the less indicates that in the period around 1100 an aisled hall within the context of a religious community was possible.[47]

The existence of an enclosed bishop's palace during Osmund's episcopate is perhaps even more significant than the early date (before c. 1110–25) for the hall on the eastern range. As already noted this arrangement is suggestive of the enclosed or cloistered monastic plan. In terms of domestic planning around 1100, the enclosed form was unique to bishops' houses. It was also to appear in the first half of the 12th century at the bishop of Winchester's palace at Wolvesey.[48] A scheme such as this suggests a conscious emulation of monastic enclosure, and, to the extent that the analogy holds, the hall acted in place of the refectory. Certainly it would have been here that the bishop held court with his *familia*, which in the case of Wolvesey were the *clerici* who served the bishop, rather the Benedictines of the cathedral priory. The fact that the complex was enclosed added to the sense of its serving a regular community. Purely secular palaces at this time, in contrast, tended to be built along a linear axis, with free-standing chamber blocks standing end-to-end with free-standing halls.[49] According to the chronology proposed here, the bishop's palace at Sarum rather than Wolvesey, becomes the earliest known example of the type. As we know so little about these early post-conquest secular foundations and how the lives of the canons were organised, their built environment is especially important. A consideration of Osmund's community, as the limited documentation allows us to understand it, will serve to amplify this point.

Osmund's enclosed palace: the historical evidence

CONTRARY to long-held understanding, Osmund was not the source for the constitution and liturgical practices known as the 'Use of Sarum'. What is known as the *Institutio* of St Osmund, which lays out the rights and dignities of the chapter of Old Sarum, has been shown by Diana Greenway to have been variously compiled between c. 1150 and c. 1200.[50] The customs of Osmund's community may be contrasted with

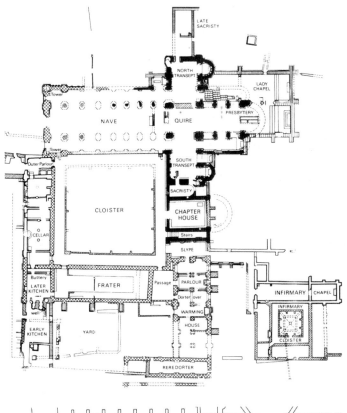

FIG. 11. Thetford Priory plan
English Heritage

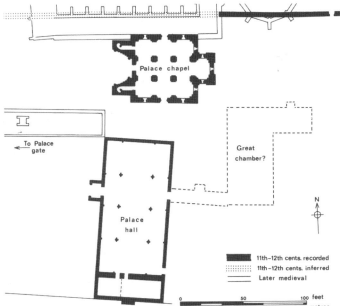

FIG. 12. Hereford bishop's palace, conjectural plan
By kind permission of John Blair

the independence from episcopal intervention which characterised later chapters, and which indeed found early articulation at Sarum in later years. In contrast, all that we know of Osmund's community is characterised by close co-operation between bishop and chapter.

Secular cathedral chapters were formed at a time when there was considerable pressure in England for cathedral communities to adopt a rule. On the one hand there was the widely advocated example of Lanfranc's Benedictine community at Christ Church, Canterbury, parallel to which were those cathedral communities that lived according to some variant of the 8th-century Rule of Chrodegang, which insisted that cathedral canons should lead a regular and communal life. Prominent supporters of the latter included a group of five bishops from, or trained in, Lotharingia, that is, Leofric of Exeter (1046–72), Ealdred of York (1061–69), Giso of Wells (1061–88), Robert of Hereford (1079–95), and Walcher of Durham (1071–80).[51]

Osmund's community must have followed a practice which lay somewhere between the relative independence of the community which developed at Sarum after *c.* 1150 and that of the regular Lotharingians and monastic cathedral chapters. There is little by way of documentary description of Osmund's community. William of Malmesbury commented that under Bishop Osmund 'priests famed for their learning came [to Old Sarum] from all sides. Not only did they find a warm welcome, but they were even treated with generosity to make them stay. In the end, more than anywhere else, Salisbury was a beacon for the fame of its canons, who were equally adept in music and literature. A supply of books was collected, since the bishop himself was never tired of writing them, or binding them when they were written'.[52] This suggests Osmund fostered a studious, if not contemplative, atmosphere reminiscent of houses under a monastic rule. While William of Malmesbury's description is isolated, something of the nature of the community has been gleaned from the content of the manuscripts themselves by Teresa Webber.[53] Webber has identified at least seventeen different hands and up to fifty manuscripts produced at Old Sarum during the twenty years of Osmund's episcopate.[54] The primary interests of the community were represented by the choices of manuscripts copied. For the most part these were very similar to other monastic and semi-monastic communities of the time, and a good deal of them consisted of copies of the early fathers.[55] Of particular interest is the work of the scribe who assigned the initials D.M. — *dignum memoria* — to selected passages in manuscripts dating to this period in the collection. This annotator, possibly Osmund himself, Webber has called 'scribe I', and was responsible for proofing many of the manuscripts. The content of the passages which he considered worthy of memory — and by implication committing to memory and practice — 'point to an underlying similarity with the spirituality of the regular orders in this period'.[56] The fact that in some volumes up to five different hands worked on a single page suggest the canons at Old Sarum were living and working in very close proximity to each other. This unusually close co-operation enabled a book, which may have been on short loan to the community, to be copied at speed.

Amongst the texts copied by 'scribe I' was Amalarius' *Liber Officialis*, and it is possible, as Greenway has suggested, that its description of the common life was followed in part by the canons at Sarum during this time.[57] As late as *c.* 1120 we find cantor Godwin quoting Amalarius, when he made some tentative remarks in support of the idea of canons holding property individually, claiming that this would not render them irregular provided they used their resources for the needs of the church. On the other hand the foundation charter of 1091 also referred to 'houses and gardens of the canons, "before", that is outside, the gate at Old Sarum', which implied that some limited individualism alongside the organised *communa* was already tolerated during Osmund's episcopacy.[58] Godwin's speculations upon the meaning of the word canon, that is, 'that canon meant rule, and that therefore a canon was one who lived according to a rule' is, however, instructive.[59] As Greenway has noted, Osmund's 1091 charter talks of the canons '*viventibus canonice*' and that the 'goods of the church [were] possessed "*ut exigit regularis censura canonice*"'.[60] The word canon in both of these cases seemed to have a compacted meaning — a cathedral clerk in its normal sense, but also implying a life under some kind of 'canonical' rule. One aspect of this late-11th-century conception of cathedral canons living in community or under some semi-monastic rule, was the central, paternal, or semi-abbatial, role played by the bishop in these communities. Osmund's preparedness to carve an endowment for the chapter out of his own episcopal property, the wording of his charter, and the role he played in the creation of Sarum's considerable library as described above, implies a very close relationship between the bishop and his *familia* at Old Sarum. We should not be surprised to find this reflected in the architecture.

So what do we know of the building activities of the Lotharingian bishops and their immediate successors? We are given to believe that Bishop Giso established a cloister and conventual buildings at Wells, which were subsequently destroyed by his successor John de Villula (1088–1122).[61] Bishop Walcher (1071–80) whose secular chapter would in later years adopt a Benedictine constitution, built '*monachorum habiticula*' for his canons at Durham.[62] Archbishop Ealdred of York, we are told, had established a dormitory and refectory which was destroyed by William I during his 'harrying of the north'. What is interesting about this case is that Ealdred's Norman successor, Thomas of Bayeux, rebuilt Ealdred's conventual buildings for the secular community he formed there at the end of the 11th century.[63] Thomas, along with Remigius of Lincoln and Maurice of London, was present at the inauguration of Osmund's chapter at Salisbury, and like them was a signatory to its foundation charter.[64] From this we can see that Osmund's closest peers, the bishops who operated under a variation of the rule of Chrodegang, all considered it necessary to provide some communal buildings for their secular cathedral communities.

Old Sarum: Conclusion

WHAT I have argued regarding the archaeology and chronology of Old Sarum is that the bishop's enclosure, on the northernmost part of the site, pre-dated the building of the cathedral cloister — and that the southern boundary of the palace established the outer northern limit of this cloister. Unfortunately we cannot be certain about the dating of the cloister itself, other than that it must have post-dated the completion of Roger's east end, the most important contemporary documentary sources are in conflict. The first draft of William of Malmesbury's *Gesta Regum*, currently dated to 1124–26, implies that Roger's new presbytery was more or less complete when William described it. The *Gesta Stephani* makes reference to the need for constructing a roof there, some thirteen years later. Nevertheless the bishop's palace must have been laid out in its final form, before the construction of the treasury/vestry building, which Roger probably built early in his career as bishop of Salisbury. This means that the aisled hall of the palace, dates to before *c.* 1110–25 and that an earlier enclosure of regular form, and on a larger scale than that replaced by Roger, was constructed before that, most likely by his immediate predecessor, Osmund. We should neither be surprised that such an aisled hall was constructed during the first decades of the 12th century, nor to find an extensive bishop's palace enclosed within a quadrangle in a form which brings to mind a monastic cloister. One may have followed the other, but both were created at a time when the nature of communal life in secular cathedrals was still in flux. Two final examples of possible early pre-claustral arrangements at secular cathedrals will hopefully complete this tentative picture.

THE BISHOP'S PALACE AND CLOISTER AT HEREFORD

THE case of Hereford offers an interesting parallel to Old Sarum. Here the bishop's palace impinged closely upon the south side of the cathedral (Fig. 12). Built long before the late-14th-century cloister, the late-11th or early-12th-century wall which was the northern perimeter of the bishop's enclosure would later form the basis for the garth wall of the cloister.[65] In the same way, the south wall of the cloister still contains masonry from the palace chapel to whose northern wall it was joined in the 14th century.[66] Just as at Old Sarum, the lines of the bishop's enclosure resulted in an eccentric cloister plan. Bishop Robert de Losinga, who was arguably responsible for the initial arrangement of the palace and for the establishment of the first secular cathedral community, was, unlike his other Lotharingian brethren, quick to establish a system of relatively independent prebendaries, rather than any kind of semi-monastic chapter. However, property was only leased to the canons by the bishop and it was not intended that it should be under the perpetual control of the chapter.[67] The fact that the western line of the late medieval cloister of the vicars choral was also skewed, has suggested to Blair the possibility that this is a line contemporary with Bishop Robert's first settlement, and may indicate the location of the first canons' houses, which were thus in close proximity to the bishop's, in a way which might resonate with the early secular community at Old Sarum.[68]

PRE-CLAUSTRAL ACCOMMODATION AT LINCOLN

AT Lincoln the close and sometimes ambiguous relationship between bishop and chapter is also worth noting. In a similar fashion to Bishop Roger at Old Sarum, Bishop Hugh of Avalon (1186–1200) managed to combine the office of bishop with that of presiding over meetings of the cathedral chapter, while presenting himself as a staunch defender of the independence as well as the rights and dignities of the cathedral chapter.[69] The latter was expressed in architectural terms by his role in initiating the construction of the chapter-house, completed during the episcopacy of his successor Hugh of Wells (1200–35). This is implied in the *Metrical Life*: 'If the completion of the work remains to be done, the work of Hugh the first will be completed under Hugh the second', and is confirmed by the archaeological evidence outlined by Jenny Alexander elsewhere in this volume.[70] The eventual construction of the cloister almost a century later was also undertaken, Canon John de Schalby tells us, by Bishop Oliver Sutton.[71] By this date, application had already been made (1285) to Edward I for a license to 'enclose the buildings surrounding the church with a wall of a certain height, along with the lanes in between them, for the security of the canons and other ministers of the said church who at that period went at midnight to the same church to say matins'.[72] It is significant that nearly all of the secular cathedrals made applications to enclose their precincts with high protective walls around this time.[73]

The building of protective walls seems to have preceded the construction of the present cloister at Lincoln — but was there any sort of conventual precinct on the site previously? Despite the assignment of grounds and the building of houses in the minster yard for prebendaries, there is evidence that at least some of the Lincoln canons lived a partially common life. Chief amongst these is the reference in an agreement regarding his prebendal holding made by Canon Samson at some date before 1187. In this agreement Samson acknowledges that should the need arise for the construction of a cloister here 'or to alter or enlarge the *bedern* or the atrium of the *bedern*' he would return this ground for such a purpose.[74] Amongst other things this tells us that as early as the episcopacy of St Hugh, and perhaps before, a cloister was considered. We may also assume, given the proximity of the south transept to the northern perimeter wall of the bishop's palace, that a cloister would only be possible in its present position north of the cathedral, and this consequently suggests that the bedern and Canon Samson's holding were on the north side also.[75] More importantly, Samson's charter referred to a bedern with an *atrium*, a word which we might infer was applied to some kind of enclosed structure.

Some sense of what this word signified might be gleaned for example by its later use for conventual buildings occupied by the vicars choral at Lincoln, or in reference to the recently excavated bedern at Beverley Minster.[76] Although the archbishop had a palace north of the cathedral at York, in later years at least, he seemed to prefer to spend more of his time out of York at his various manor houses.[77] A particular favourite seemed to have been his collegiate minster at Beverley, where a college of canons was in residence. Their accommodation in the Bedern was south of the church, and was intimately associated with the bishop's moated manor house there, known as the Hall Garth. The enclosed courtyard complex of buildings included a 12th-century aisled hall built along the same dimensions as an earlier timber-framed hall.[78] This familiar arrangement indicates a type of relationship we have seen at Sarum and at Hereford (at Lincoln the bishop's house was on the opposite side of the cathedral).

CONCLUSION

IN some ways the most interesting phase in the development of cloisters at secular cathedrals is that in which most of the cloisters had still to be built. It is by considering their absence, surely the more prevalent condition in the first two centuries after the Conquest, that we might form a view as to why so many were created later in the Middle Ages. By 1100 the only secular cathedral cloister for which there is evidence is the cloister constructed by Giso of Wells and destroyed by his successor John de Villula. By 1200 the only certain secular cathedral cloisters were those built by Robert of Lewes at Wells in the mid-12th century and that built at Old Sarum by either Roger of Salisbury, or his successor Jocelyn. In the 13th century, grand cloisters to rival those at the monastic cathedrals would be built at Wells and the new cathedral of Salisbury. The next cloister does not seem to arrive until *c.* 1290, at Lincoln. In this regard Lincoln's position was far from exceptional, and must reflect a sense of what is appropriate to a chapter of canons shared by the other six cathedrals still to build a cloister.

However, despite the absence of a cloister *per se* at Old Sarum until some time during the first half of the 12th century or later, an extremely interesting iconographical statement of *communa* seems to have been made at the earliest opportunity by a strong bishop (Osmund), whose life and works exemplified ideals otherwise expressed by the cloister. The enclosed bishop's palace Osmund built was reduced in scale by Bishop Roger with the construction of a proper cloister in mind, even if the cloister itself may not have been built during his episcopacy. His new, and slightly compromised trapezoidal palace, included an aisled hall, was both integral to the palace enclosure and, in the manner of a Cistercian refectory set perpendicular to the axis of the church, integral to the cloister that followed. The chronology for Old Sarum proposed here highlights the unique architectural expression given to the working-out of secular community by Bishop Osmund in the late 11th century. This was picked up by Bishop Roger when he rebuilt an abbreviated bishop's palace in the same location, in order to accommodate a new treasury building and intended cloister. Roger, however, then employed the principle of an enclosed palace, otherwise unrepresented in secular high status house design, for the courtyard house in the inner bailey at Sarum, and at the related house, perhaps with cloister, at Sherborne.[79] The cloister itself, of course, was the location for much of the outdoor ceremonial in the *Use of Sarum*, and was doubtless complicit in the construction of the cloister at the new cathedral and, indeed, many of the later medieval cathedral cloisters which also adhered to Sarum Use.[80] While the cloister at Old Sarum requires re-excavation to arrive at a final dating, much of its meaning and the source for its construction can be said to have come from the enclosed bishop's palace built to its north, by Bishop Osmund in the closing decades of the 11th century.

ACKNOWLEDGEMENTS

This paper is based in part on my master's dissertation: 'The impact of some secular cathedral cloisters and their patrons on developments in English architecture before 1300.' This was completed in September 2000, under the generous supervision of Richard Morris at Warwick University, and I am greatly indebted to him for the breadth of his knowledge, as well as his relentless encouragement and assistance then and since. Duncan Givans, a fellow-student, accompanied me on a number of field trips to some of the buildings discussed above, and took some valuable photographs for me at Old Sarum. I am also grateful to Caitríona Harvey (now Noonan) of Shaffrey Associates Architects in Dublin, for creating a clean version of my initial sketch plan for Figure 7. My understanding of medieval archaeology and architectural history was greatly enhanced by my attendance at the BAA conference in Angers in 2000 (as well as others since) for which I was granted a student bursary. It was at the Angers conference that I made the acquaintance of a host of people who gave me advice and suggestions about my thesis, some of which have survived into this paper. These included Jeremy Ashbee, Stephen Brindle, Sarah Brown, Antje Fehrmann, Eric Fernie, Lindy Grant, Alexandra Gajewski, Matthew Palmer, Richard Plant, Abigail Wheatley and Christopher Wilson. Roger Stalley, my undergraduate supervisor at Trinity College, Dublin, and an authority on the buildings of Roger of Salisbury, made a number of valuable suggestions during a bus ride to Saumur, and subsequently. Also as a result of attending the conference, Tim Tatton-Brown generously met me at Salisbury and shared with me his views on the Salisbury cloister as well as the palace and cathedral at Old Sarum, while Jenny Alexander invited me to stay with her in Nottingham, from whence we travelled to Lincoln and Southwell where she gave generously of her knowledge and expertise. Since then I have discussed aspects of this paper with David Stocker who has been particularly helpful, and with John McNeill who was happy to share his extensive knowledge of Old Sarum, and was deeply encouraging when my nerve began to flag. It goes without saying, however, that all interpretations as well as any errors are my own.

NOTES

1. Y. Esquieu, 'La place du cloître dans l'organisation du quartier cathédral', in *Der Mittelalterliche Kreuzgang*, ed. P. Klein, 80–88. I am very grateful to Antje Fehrmann of the University of Marburg, who kindly provided me with a copy of the Kunstchronik synopsis of this article which preceded its full publication, along with her own translations into English of the same.

2. On the cloister at Salisbury, see T. Tatton-Brown, 'The cloisters of Salisbury Cathedral', *Spire: Report of the Friends of Salisbury Cathedral*, 65 (1995), 6–10; and for an alternative interpretation P. Z. Blum, 'The Sequence of the Building Campaigns at Salisbury', *Art Bulletin*, 73, March 1991, 6–38. For the cloister at Wells, see W. Rodwell ed., *Wells Cathedral: Excavations and Structural Studies, 1978–93* (London 2001), passim; and W. Rodwell, 'The Anglo-Saxon and Norman Churches at Wells', in L. S. Colchester ed., *Wells Cathedral: A History* (Wells 1982), 1–23.

3. D. E. Greenway, 'The false *Institutio* of St Osmund', in *Tradition and Change: Essays in Honour of Marjorie Chibnall*, ed. D. Greenway, C. Holdsworth and J. Sayers (Cambridge 1985), 77–101.

4. J. H. Harvey, *Cathedrals of England and Wales*, 3rd edn (London 1974), 251, has constructed just such a genealogy for cathedral cloisters in general. However, he included only those for which physical evidence had remained and failed to consider the influence other cloisters, such as the 12th-century cloister at Old Sarum, must have had on those which are still standing.

5. An earlier secular cathedral cloister, which predated the cloister at Sarum, is that thought to have been built by Bishop Giso (1061–88) at Wells. While it is the earliest recorded post-conquest secular cathedral cloister, the archaeological evidence for the structure, which was found north of the Saxo-Norman chapel of St Mary's at Wells, was not substantial nor altogether certain. Rodwell, *Wells: Excavations and Structural Studies*, 99–101, 104.

6. Greenway, *Institutio* (1985), passim.

7. The most recent English Heritage Guide, J. McNeill, *Old Sarum* (London 2006), assigns the hall of the bishop's palace to Roger of Salisbury and the cloister to Jocelin de Bohun (1142–84) his successor. The RCHME report *Ancient and Historical Monuments in the City of Salisbury*, 1 (London 1980), 15, assigns both palace and cloister to Roger. However, both M. Thompson, *Medieval Bishop's Houses in England and Wales* (Aldershot 1998), 47, and K. Edwards, 'The Cathedral of Salisbury', in R. B. Pugh and E. Crittal ed., *VCH Wiltshire*, 3 (London 1956), 161, suggest that the palace was built by Osmund. J. Blair, 'Hall and Chamber: English Domestic Planning 1000–1250', in *Manorial Domestic Buildings in England and Northern France*, ed. G. Meirion-Jones and M. Jones (London 1993), 13, ascribes the hall to Jocelin de Bohun, with a date 'c. 1160–80', a critical interpretation in terms of the evolution of my own understanding of the site.

8. 'It cannot be called square, since its sides are all unequal, and it may not be described as rectangular, since none of its angles is a right angle'; W. H. St John Hope, 'Report on the excavation of the cathedral church of Old Sarum in 1913', *Proceedings of the Society of Antiquaries of London*, 2nd series, 26 (1914), 103.

9. Old Sarum was first systematically excavated by W. H. St John Hope from 1909 until the pressures of the First World War forced an end to progress on site in November 1915. The whole enclosure — its ramparts, the inner bailey or motte as well as the cathedral and its related buildings — was investigated. The outline of an off-square cloister, formed by the remains of the foundations of a garth wall on all four sides, emerged. 'The south side measures 137 ft., the north 133 ½ ft., the east 125 ½ ft., and the west 113 ½ ft ... [The] alleys were 12 ft. wide on three sides, but the south alley was 13 ft. wide. The wall towards the garth that carried the pentice roof could be traced all round and was 2 ft. thick, but only more or less of its foundation remained, and there was nothing to suggest what had stood upon it. From the large number of fragments found the pentice seems to have been roofed with tiles.' Hope, 'Old Sarum in 1913', 103–04, 114.

10. William of Malmesbury, *Gesta Regum Anglorum*, I, ed. and trans. R. A. B. Mynors, R. M. Thomson and M. Winterbottom (Oxford 1998), ch. 408, 736–39. The dating and other aspects of this are considered below.

11. R. A. Stalley, 'A Twelfth-Century Patron of Architecture: A Study of the Buildings Erected by Roger, Bishop of Salisbury 1102–1139', *JBAA*, 124 (1971), 71, fn. 8, referring to K. R. Potter trans. and ed., *Gesta Stephani* (London 1955), 65; John of Worcester, *The Chronicle of John of Worcester*, ed. P. McGurk (Oxford 1995), 278, uses the same Latin expression, '*ecclesiam cooperiendam*', to describe the event, which suggests some correspondence between the two volumes on this issue at least.

12. K. R. Potter trans. and ed., *The Historia Novella by William of Malmesbury* (London 1955), 39.

13. William of Malmesbury, *Gesta Regum Anglorum*, I, ch. 408, 738–39; the second part of the quote is a more telling translation of '*Aecclesiam Salesberiensem et nouam fecit*' from W. Stubbs ed., *Willelmi Malmesbiriensis Monachi: de Gestis Regum Anglorum* (Rolls Series, XC, 1887–89), ii, 484.

14. Stubbs, *De Gestis Regum Anglorum*, I, xix–xx; xliii–lii.

15. RCHME, *City of Salisbury*, 15.

16. Mynors, Thomson and Winterbottom, *Gesta Regum Anglorum*, I, xxxii–xxxiii; Stubbs, *De Gestis Regum Anglorum*, I, xvii–xviii.

17. Mynors, Thomson and Winterbottom, *Gesta Regum Anglorum*, II, xvii–xviii, notes that in a pair of appended letters to these first two editions of the book, authority for the book was sought from King David of Scotland (who had succeeded to the throne in 1124) and also that he might pass on the volume to his sister Matilda: the known movements of these two suggesting a strong likelihood that this must have taken place in the two years after his accession; the reference to the capture of Baldwin II of Jerusalem 'last year' and a report of his release, both of which happened on April 1123 and August 1124 consecutively; and perhaps the most convincing is the description of all of these events as being 'before 60 years had passed [since the conquest]', i.e. before the year 1126.

18. RCHME, *City of Salisbury*, 2.

19. Hope, 'Old Sarum in 1913', 105.

20. William Hawley, 'Report on the Excavations at Old Sarum in 1914', *Proceedings of the Society of Antiquaries*, 27 (1915), 232.

21. Blair, 'Hall and Chamber', 11–13.

22. Blair, 'Hall and Chamber', fig. 6.

23. This group of buildings, including what was called a well house, cross the north-east angle of the cloister. They are also recorded in the RCHME plan of the cloister area (Fig. 3). They were uncovered during the last season of work on site. St John Hope, 'Report on Excavations on the Site of Old Sarum in 1915', *Proceedings of the Society of Antiquaries*, 28 (1916), 180.

24. Blair, 'Hall and Chamber', 1993, fig. 6.

25. Hope, 'Old Sarum in 1913', 104. Compare Blair's fig. 6 with Fig. 3 in this article.

26. I am grateful to Caitriona Harvey (now Noonan) of Shaffrey Associates Architects, Dublin, who drafted this diagram, based on my original drawing.

27. The approximate and plausible date bracket given by the RCHME for the treasury/vestry building and the eastern extension to the cathedral is *c.* 1110–1125. RCHME, *City of Salisbury*, 17. However, based on the existence of pilasters on the southern exterior wall of the treasury/vestry building, Hope concluded that this structure predated the cathedral extension itself, suggesting that it was built early in the period indicated above. Hope, 'Old Sarum in 1913', 104–05.

28. Hawley, 'Old Sarum in 1915', 180. For Roger's role in the construction of a boundary wall along certain portions of the external ramparts of the site, see Philip A. Rahtz and John W. G. Musty, 'Excavations at Old Sarum, 1957', *The Wiltshire Archaeological and Natural History Magazine*, 57 (1960), 352–70.

29. Hope, 'Old Sarum in 1914', 232.

30. Stalley, 'A Twelfth-Century Patron', 65, fn. 1 cites the *Gesta Stephani* which referring to Roger's buildings speaks of '*castella sua, quae ornatissime construxerat*'; William of Malmesbury stated that Roger 'made new the church of Salisbury and adorned it with ornaments, so that it is inferior to none in England but surpasses many', quoted from Stubbs, *De Gestis Regum Anglorum* (Rolls Series, XC), ii, 484, in Hope, 'Old Sarum in 1913', 103.

31. Blair, 'Hall and Chamber', 10–13.

32. I have developed this point with reference to the enclosed buildings in the upper bailey at Windsor in J. Montague, 'The impact of some secular cathedral cloisters and their patrons on developments in English architecture before 1300' (unpublished M.A. thesis, Warwick University, 2000), 36–43, based on the possibility, as suggested by Steven Brindle, that Henry I was responsible for the courtyard enclosure in the Upper Bailey known as the 'king's houses'. See S. Brindle and S. Priestley, 'A history of Windsor castle: draft historical text. Part one: from Saxon times to 1216' (unpublished draft report for English Heritage, 2000), 14. Brindle had also noted the parallel between this enclosed domestic structure, and the buildings at Old Sarum and Sherborne of Roger of Salisbury, Henry's justiciar. For a recent assessment of the courtyard house at Old Sarum and Roger's work at Sherborne, see the article by Jeremy Ashbee, 'Cloisters in English Palaces in the Twelfth and Thirteenth Centuries', in this volume.

33. The plan in Hope, 'Old Sarum in 1914', facing p. 232, and the discussion of the building on p. 234, make clear that this is an addition of a later date.

34. W. R. Lethaby, 'The Palace of Westminster in the Eleventh and Twelfth Centuries', *Archaeologia*, 60 (1907), 131.

35. The measurements given by the RCHME are 239 ft 6 in. by 67 ft 6 in. (approx 72 m by 20 m). RCHME, *An inventory of the Historical Monuments in London, vol. 2, West London* (London 1925), 121.

36. L. T. Courtenay, 'The Westminster Hall Roof and its 14th-Century Sources', *Journal of the Society of Architectural Historians*, 43 (1984), 295.

37. P. Rahtz, *Saxon and Medieval Palaces at Cheddar, Excavations 1960–62* (London 1979), 53–62.

38. F. Wormold, 'Style and Design', in F. Stenton ed., *The Bayeux Tapestry: A Comprehensive Survey*, 2nd edn (London 1965), 3.

doesn't cite recent h.y.

39. Wormold, 'Style and Design', 28–33, suggests that the style of the figures as much as the circumstances of its creation point to the probability that an English artist was responsible for the design of the tapestry. Hence we might presume the buildings depicted would reflect those constructed by the Normans in England directly after the conquest.

40. D. M. Wilson ed., *The Bayeux Tapestry* (London 1985), fig. 12.

41. Wilson, *Bayeux Tapestry*, fig. 37.

42. B. Bauthiez, 'Hypotheses sur la fortification de Rouen au onzième siecle. Le donjon, la tour de Richard II et l'enceinte de Guillaume', *Anglo-Norman Studies*, 14 (1992), 61–76.

43. See, in particular, M. Thompson, *The Medieval Hall: the Basis of Secular Domestic Life 1000–1600 AD* (Aldershot 1995), 51ff.

44. K. J. Conant, *Cluny: les églises et la maison du chef d'ordre* (Cambridge, Mass. 1968), fig. 47. The evidence however for the functions of the buildings to the west is not altogether reliable, and there may be a certain circularity in the functions ascribed to them by Conant.

45. *VCH Sussex vol 8*, plan opposite p. 47.

46. F. J. E. Raby and P. K. Baillie Reynolds, *Thetford Priory Norfolk* (London 1979), 10–11.

47. There is no definitive archaeological or historical evidence for the construction of the infirmary at Canterbury, although it seems certain to have followed closely upon the extension of the eastern arm of the cathedral between *c.* 1096 and *c.* 1120. Tim Tatton-Brown, pers. comm.

48. T. B. James, *The Palaces of Medieval England c.1050–1550: Royalty, Nobility, the Episcopate and their Residences from Edward the Confessor to Henry VIII* (London 1990), 46–47 and fig. 22; Martin Biddle, 'Excavations at Winchester, 1970: ninth interim report', *Antiq. J.*, 52 (1972), 93–131.

49. Blair, 'Hall and Chamber', 5–7.

50. Greenway, 'False *Institutio*', passim.

51. K. Edwards, *The English Secular Cathedrals in the Middle Ages: a Constitutional Study with Special Reference to the Fourteenth-Century* (Manchester 1967), 3 and 19, for the first four listed bishops. Regarding Walcher, see note 62 below.

52. William of Malmesbury, *The Deeds of the Bishops of England*, trans. D. Preest (Woodbridge, 2002), 122.

53. T. Webber, *Scribes and Scholars at Salisbury Cathedral c.1075–c.1125* (Oxford 1992).

54. Webber, *Scribes and Scholars*, 11–17.

55. ibid., 31.

56. ibid., 139.

57. N. R. Ker, 'The Beginnings of Salisbury Cathedral Library', in J. J. G. Alexander and M. T. Gibson ed., *Medieval Learning and Literature: Essays Presented to Richard William Hunt* (Oxford 1976), 38; John le Neve, *Fasti Ecclesiae Anglicanae 1066–1300: IV Salisbury*, compiled by Diana E. Greenway (London 1991), xxiv.

58. *Fasti*, xxiv & fn. 6 referring to Oxford, Bodleian Library, MS Digby 96, esp. fols 20v–22v; Greenway, '1091, St Osmund and the constitution of the cathedral', in *Medieval Art and Architecture at Salisbury Cathedral*, ed. L. Keene and T. Cocke, *BAA Trans.*, XVII (Leeds 1996), 4.

59. Edwards, *English Secular Cathedrals*, 47 fn. 4.

60. *Fasti*, xxiv.

61. *English Secular Cathedrals*, 19 and n. 3: quoting from *Historiola de primordiis episcopatus Somersetensis*, 22; Rodwell, 'Anglo-Saxon and Norman Churches at Wells', 10.

62. J. Barrow, 'English Cathedral Communities and Reform in the Late Tenth and the Eleventh Centuries', in *Anglo-Norman Durham 1093–1193*, ed. D. Rollason, M. Harvey and M. Prestwick (Woodbridge 1994), 33. I am grateful to Eric Fernie who brought this secular phase of Durham's history, and Bishop Walcher's building work there, to my attention.

63. D. Phillips, *The Cathedral of Archbishop Thomas of Bayeux: Excavations at York Minster: Vol. II* (London 1985), 3; Eric A. Gee, 'Architectural History until 1290', in *A History of York* Minster, ed. G. E. Aylmer and R. Cant (Oxford 1977), 114 & fn. 20, quoting from Hugh the Chanter in *Hists. York*, ii, 108, 362.

64. Edwards, *English Secular Cathedrals*, 12–13, & 13 fn. 1, referring to *Statuta et Consuetudines Ecclesiae Cathedralis Beatae Mariae Virginis Sarisberiensis*, ed. C. Wordsworth and D. Macleane, 22–23, 32–33.

65. R. K. Morris, 'The Architectural History of the Medieval Cathedral Church', in G. Aylmer and J. Tiller, *Hereford Cathedral, A History* (London 2000), 229.

66. J. Blair, 'The 12th-Century Bishop's Palace at Hereford', *Med. Archaeol.*, 31 (1987), 69.

67. J. Barrow, 'A Lotharingian in Hereford: Bishop Robert's Reorganisation of the Church of Hereford 1079–1095', in *Medieval Art, Architecture and Archaeology at Hereford*, ed. D. Whitehead, *BAA Trans.*, XV (Leeds 1995), 35 and passim.

68. Blair, 'Hereford Bishop's Palace', 67.

69. E. U. Crosby, *Bishop and Chapter in Twelfth-Century England: A Study of* Mensa Episcopalis (Cambridge, 1994), 306–09; D. Owen, 'Historical Survey, 1091–1450', in *A History of Lincoln Minster*, ed. D. Owen (Cambridge 1994), 130–31.

70. '*Si quorum vero perfectio restat, Hugonis/Perficietur opus primi sub Hugone secundo*', in *The metrical life of Saint Hugh*, ed. and trans. Charles Garton (Lincoln 1986), 60–61; see also the article by J. Alexander, 'Lincoln Cathedral Cloister' in this volume. I am grateful to Jenny Alexander for first bringing to my attention Hugh's role in the construction of the chapter-house when she generously brought me on a visit to Lincoln Cathedral in the summer of 2000.

71. J. H. Strawley ed. and trans., *The Book of John de Schalby, Canon of Lincoln 1299–1333: Concerning the Bishops of Lincoln and their Acts* (Lincoln 1966), 15.

72. *John de Schalby*, 15.

73. According to C. Coulson, 'Hierarchism in Conventual Crenellation: An Essay in the Sociology and Metaphysics of Medieval Fortification', *Med. Archaeol.*, 26 (1982), 72–81, the following made applications to build walls to enclose their cathedral precincts at the following dates: Lincoln, London and York, 1285; Wells and Exeter 1286; Lichfield 1299; Salisbury Cathedral was to enter into a long-running dispute at the beginning of the 14th century with the town over the extent of its enclosure plans; Hereford 1389.

74. Charles Foster and Kathleen Major ed., *Registrum Antiquissimum of the Cathedral Church of Lincoln*, IX (1968), no. 2603: '. . . *si ex consilio episcopi vel capituli neccessitas ecclesie predictam terram postulauret ad claustrum faciendum vel Beddernam vel atrium Bedderne innouande ampliandum. ex pacto teneor ad cedendum.*'

75. *Reg. Antiq.*, 336 (in a possibly post-medieval marginal note) refers to a *bedern* on the south side of the cathedral. David Stocker has suggested (pers. comm.) that this more likely referred instead to the buildings reserved for the vicars choral established in the second half of the 13th century. I am grateful to David Stocker for, amongst other things, his lead on this and his help in the interpretation of *Reg. Antiq.*, no. 2603, referred to above.

76. David Stocker, 'The Development of the College of the Vicars Choral at Lincoln Minster', in Richard Hall and David Stocker ed., *Vicars Choral at English Cathedrals: Cantate Domino: History, Architecture and Archaeology* (Oxford 2005), 76–97; P. Armstrong, 'Beverley, Lurk Lane: Excavations', *Med. Archaeol.*, 25 (1981), 171, 188–89.

77. This is the case at least from the 14th century where more is known about the palace from the visits of the king than by any records associated with the bishop; R. M. Butler, 'Notes on the Minster Close at York', *York Historian*, 14 (1997), 13, though there is no reason to doubt that relations between York and Beverley were not close in the 12th and 13th centuries.

78. Armstrong, 'Beverley Excavations', 188–89.

79. The aisle walks of the cloister at Sherborne Castle were rebuilt in the 16th century, although fragments of roof tiles from an earlier work also survived; Stalley, 'Twelfth-Century patron', 66; P. White, 'Sherborne Old Castle', *Archaeol. J.*, 140 (1983), 67–70. However, the excavated garth revealed foundations for an aisle walk of greater depth than the one of the 16th century, with a dwarf-wall of sufficient girth to support an arcade of double columns set laterally to the wall, in the style of the 12th and 13th centuries; Peter White, pers. comm., December 2002. This suggests that an arcaded cloister was included as part of the first design and construction of Roger's courtyard castle.

80. *The Use of Sarum I: the Sarum Customs as Set Forth in the Consuetudinary and Customary*, ed. Walter Howard Frere (Cambridge 1898), 59–61, 131.

Cloisters in English Palaces in the Twelfth and Thirteenth Centuries

JEREMY ASHBEE

Between the early 12th and late 13th centuries, a number of royal and episcopal residences incorporated or were planned around covered walkways, for which the word 'cloister' was sometimes used. The form may have originated in monastic planning conventions, although the two earliest survivals, the 12th-century episcopal palaces at Sherborne and Old Sarum, were configured differently to each other. By the mid-12th-century, cloisters had also been adopted for entirely secular palaces, including the royal retreat at Everswell, for which alternative prototypes in Islamic architecture have also been suggested. 13th-century documents indicate that several cloisters were associated with queens, and suggest that cloisters had come to be regarded as adjuncts of the garden and the chamber rather than the church or domestic chapel.

OF all the hundreds of descriptions of royal ceremonies in medieval chronicles, one of the most enigmatic must be the account written by the Seigneur de Joinville in his Life of Saint Louis, describing a banquet at Saumur in 1241. This was probably the young Jean de Joinville's first sight of the king to whose service he would devote much of his life, and his memories of the event, only written down many decades later, show a preoccupation with the sort of details a young nobleman might be expected to recall: the names of the greatest figures present, the sheer numbers of the whole company, and the expensive clothes they all wore. However, to modern architectural historians, these elements have been eclipsed by Joinville's observations about the setting:[1]

Le roy tint cele feste es hales de Saumur, et disoit l'en que le grant roy Henri d'Angleterre les avoit faites pour ses grans festes tenir; et les hales sont faites a la guise des cloitres de ces moinnes blans, mes je croi que de trop in n'en soit nul si grant. Et vous dirai pour quoy il me semble, car a la paroy du cloistre ou le roy mangoit, qui estoit environne de chevaliers et de serjans qui tenoient grant espace, mangoient a une table xx que evesques que arcevesques; et encore apres les evesques et les arcevesques mangoit encoste cele table la royne Blanche, sa mere, au chief du cloistre, de celle part la ou le roy ne mangoit pas. Et si servoit a la royne le conte de Bouloingne, qui puis fu roy de Portingal, et le bon conte Huel de Saint Pol et un Alemant de l'age de xviii ans que en disoit que il avoit este filz Saint Helizabeth de Thuringe, dont l'en disoit que la royne Blanche le besoit ou front par devocion pour ce que ele entendoit que sa mere l'i avoit maintes foiz besie. Au chief du cloistre d'autre part estoient les cuisines, les bouteilleries, les paneteries et les despenses. De celi chef servoient devant le roy et devant la royne de char, de vin et de pain. Et en toutes les autres elez et au prael d'en milieu mangoient de chevaliers si grant foison que je ne sce le nombre. Et dient moult de gent que il ne avoient onques veu autant de seurcoz ne d'autres garnemens de drap d'or et de soye a une feste comme il ot la, et dient que il y or bien mmm chevaliers.[2]

The king held this feast in the *hales* of Saumur, said to have been built by the great King Henry of England for holding his great feasts. The *hales* were built in the likeness of a cloister of the White

DOI: 10.1179/174767006X132970

Monks, though I think there were none as big. I shall explain why I think not. On the side of the cloister where the king was eating, surrounded by a great body of knights and serjeants, there also stood a table of twenty bishops and archbishops. At the head of the cloister sat Queen Blanche, the king's mother, on the opposite side of the table of the bishops and archbishops from where the king was dining. The queen was served by the Count of Boulogne, who was later king of Portugal, and the Count of Saint Pol, and a German youth of eighteen, apparently the son of Saint Elizabeth of Thuringia; I heard that Queen Blanche kissed him on the forehead because she thought that his mother had often kissed him there. At the head of the cloister on the other side were the kitchens, butteries, pantries and dispensary, from which the king and queen were served with meat, wine and bread. And in all the other passages, and in the garth in the centre, there dined such a crowd of knights that I cannot number them; many people said that they had never seen so many surcoats, silks and cloth of gold at a banquet as they saw there, at least three thousand knights.

By the time he recorded his reminiscences, Joinville had become very familiar with both palaces and monasteries and his observations on this *al fresco* banquet are still likely to command respect, if not complete credibility. The building he saw, with its walkways (*elez*) and central garth (*prael*) conformed in its overall shape to a monastic cloister. Given this layout, it is understandable that Joinville should make the comparison, although his specific point about Cistercian cloisters (*cloitres de ces moinnes blans*) is less easy to fathom. Perhaps, given that the building evidently stood in a town, Joinville wished to stress that it surpassed in size even the spacious cloisters of the most successful rural monastic order. Still more difficult is his use of the term '*les hales*' rather than 'great hall', 'palace', or 'castle.' As has been pointed out, *les hales* is now associated with covered markets, and it has even been suggested that King Louis held the banquet in the town's actual market-place.[3] Whether or not this was where the building stood, Joinville's informant told him that it had been constructed specifically for the hosting of great feasts: it cannot simply be dismissed as a converted market building. An alternative reading might be that *les hales* specifically denoted a wooden building, as seems to be the import of the cognate word *hala* in later English documents for the temporary banqueting houses for Edward II's coronation in 1308 or a short-lived court-house in York Castle in 1298.[4] However, the building at Saumur was clearly not temporary, whether intentionally or not, since the final piece of information indicates that it was at least fifty years old. Joinville identified the builder of the palace as 'the great King Henry of England', Henry II (1154–89).

Though Joinville may not have been aware of the fact, Henry II's building at Saumur lay within a wider tradition of palace-design in which cloisters played a central role. This paper aims to discuss the details of several sites critical to the development of this feature and attempts to trace the later development of 'claustral' palaces through the 13th century. This motif appears on present knowledge to have a particular association with England and to have a fairly restricted chronological range, from the early 12th to the late 13th century. Thereafter, though cloisters continued to appear in non-monastic contexts, they were, with notable exceptions, associated less with the palace and more with the college.

The planning of a palace around a cloister immediately invokes a contrast with the mainstream of medieval English palace architecture, at least as it is generally perceived. Cloisters necessarily injected an element of regularity: at the very least they entailed the arrangement of buildings roughly parallel or at right angles to one another, and at the most, a rigid plan governed by a unified system of proportion or dimensions. By contrast, palaces built before the 14th century and even afterwards are often characterised as informal or 'rambling' in plan, with detached structures disposed apparently without reference to each other. Because of the very limited *corpus* of surviving architecture, this review touches on several issues concerning the planning and layout of royal or episcopal residence in the period. Were the relationships between halls, chambers, chapels and gardens managed according to any rationale, or were they randomly disposed according to local circumstances? How should the word '*claustrum*' be translated when it occurs in a document of the 12th or 13th century? And finally, were cloisters in secular palaces inevitably derived from a monastic prototype?

THE ORIGINS OF CLAUSTRAL HOUSES AND THE PALACES OF BISHOP ROGER OF SARUM

THE best known early examples of cloistered palaces in England are Sherborne Old Castle in Dorset and Old Sarum in Wiltshire (Figs 1 and 2).[5] Both of them have been attributed to Bishop Roger of Sarum (d. 1139), Chief Minister and leading light in the Exchequer and Council under Henry I (1100–35), and famously described as 'Viceroy of England' in the most detailed biography of Roger published to date.[6] Sherborne was evidently built as a rural palace for the bishop himself, set in a large park carved out from the estates of the Benedictine priory, later abbey. The circumstances behind the establishment of Old Sarum were slightly different. Here, the palace was built, perhaps still for the bishop's own use, inside the rampart of a pre-existing royal castle, itself planted within the ramparts of a massive prehistoric hill-fort. The conditions in which the monuments come to us are also very different, with substantial upstanding masonry at Sherborne, but only excavated footings at Old Sarum. Nevertheless there are several convincing points of similarity, not least the feature most relevant to this discussion: that both houses were built in a single campaign to a coherent design which positioned an open courtyard at the centre of the architectural complex.

John Blair has argued that sites like Sherborne and Sarum sprang from the context of functionally hybrid buildings of the 11th century, characterised by regularity in planning and close institutional ties to the Church but which lay significantly outside the strict confines of regular monasticism. None of these structures has survived and only a few, such as the monastic grange at Minster Court on the Isle of Thanet, have been excavated.[7] In their absence, some of the most evocative evidence comes from documentary sources. For example, the chronicle of Abingdon contains a reference to a church built around 1050 by a priest Blacheman, 'with cloister sides to right and left after the fashion of conventual buildings (*in lateribus dextrorsum et sinistrorsum claustralibus ad monachorum formam habitaculorum*), with buildings for eating, cooking and sleeping, and other necessary offices wonderfully equipped for the converse of men'.[8] It is notable that this quotation makes it clear that the inspiration for the building was monastic and that the new houses were intended to serve a community (*conversationi virorum necessarii . . . coaptatis*) rather than a single man. From here to the residence of a magnate and his subordinate household requires a functional leap.

In the standard survey of Bishop Roger's architectural patronage, Sherborne Castle is presented as earlier than Old Sarum, and its construction is generally dated to the 1120s and 1130s.[9] Previous studies have tended to make more reference to the military capacity of the castle than would now be fashionable, for example pointing out that the large surviving windows in the ranges are only made possible because the

FIG. 1.   Sherborne Old Castle, Dorset, showing a view north across the site of
the great hall (foreground) to the cloister courtyard beyond. Note the remains of
interlaced blind arcading at first-floor level, marking the exterior of the upper chapel

Jeremy Ashbee

FIG. 2.   Old Sarum Castle, Wiltshire, showing a view north across the ruins of the
courtyard house. The range in the foreground contained chapels on two levels, the
lower chapel set well below the level of the courtyard beyond

Jeremy Ashbee

buildings are set well back from the curtain wall.[10] It has also been stated that the tall tower at the south-west corner of the inner complex, though designed integrally with the other buildings, is worthy of comparison with many other Norman great towers. Of the other elements of the central complex, the south range, now reduced to footings and a western gable wall, has been shown to have contained only one storey, open to the roof, rather than the two which were once supposed.[11] This is evident from the chevron-moulded string-course running along the inner face of the gable wall at the level where an upper floor might be expected, making it clear the room was originally a ground-floor hall, open to the rafters.

It is also clear that the north range, parallel to the hall, was a two-storey structure, with evidence for vaulting surviving at both levels.[12] John Blair has tried to revise the standard interpretation of this range as consisting of upper and lower chapels, and re-interpret the first-floor room as a great chamber.[13] However, the presence of vaults (groins below with what were almost certainly rib vaults with beak-head profiles above) and the apparent absence of fireplaces or garderobes serving either storey argues in favour of the upper room as a chapel. Moreover, this range was distinguished by its architectural detailing, principally on the side facing into the courtyard. Surviving fabric to east and west suggests that the interlaced arcading was used on this range alone and did not continue along the corresponding elevations of the east and west ranges. The particular form of interlaced blind arcading is very similar to surviving traces in Roger's contemporary Sherborne Abbey church, now visible inside the vestry (commonly known as Bishop Roger's chapel) but formerly on the exterior of the north choir aisle.[14] Examples such as the cloister of Castle Acre Priory, where the negatives of blind arcading can still be seen in the flintwork of the dormitory range above the line of the former walkway roofs, demonstrate that buildings other than churches or chapels could bear external decoration of this kind, but at Sherborne, the programme is quite specific in highlighting the north range and the identification as a chapel seems credible.

As to the courtyard between the ranges, this has undergone many alterations, but the archaeological evidence strongly suggests that an arcaded walkway around the perimeter was always part of the plan. The chamfered footing visible around the central lawn is post-medieval, having been found in excavation to sit over a layer of rubbish that included medieval roof tiles, but underlying this is a broad stone sleeper wall, identified on all sides of the courtyard.[15] Enough of the ground-floor masonry of the ranges survives to show that the walks were covered by a steeply pitched lean-to timber roof resting against the outer walls.[16] As far as is known, none of the architectural fragments recovered from the site originated in the cloister, and it is possible that the original arcade was in timber. Nevertheless, the similarity between this layout and that of a monastic site is extremely suggestive: the chapel sits to the north, the hall faces it across a cloister garth, and the chambers for the bishop, probably centering on a solar tower in the south-west corner, occupy the west range. It is principally in the east range that the differences between the two types of site manifest themselves: a bishop's house was obviously a community of a kind, but it needed no meeting room like a chapter house, and while the servants may have lived in the upper chamber of the east range, like a dormitory, the analogy can be taken too far.

Also attributed to Bishop Roger is the courtyard palace in the royal castle at Old Sarum. This was excavated between 1909 and 1911, having been completely buried, and as a consequence, only survives as low walls of robbed-out rubble with none of the architectural detailing of Sherborne still *in situ*.[17] The circumstances whereby

75

FIG. 3.   Reconstruction by Peter Dunn of the courtyard house at Old Sarum facing east, with the hall shown cut away in the foreground

English Heritage

Roger had this complex built within the royal castle are unclear, not least because he himself is thought to have possessed a very large hall complex of his own in the outer bailey to the north of the cathedral.[18] His work in the inner ward seems to be part of a wider phenomenon in the 1130s in which senior ecclesiastics came to occupy royal castles: the type-site for this is the keep of Rochester Castle, built under royal licence by the Archbishop of Canterbury at almost exactly the same date. Roger clearly had not acquired Sarum castle by 1129, when the sheriff of Wiltshire was building there, but probably took possession soon afterward.[19] The much cruder jointing of the masonry than that at Sherborne has led at least one interpreter to suggest that the buildings date to the earlier 12th century, perhaps still built by Bishop Roger, but for the use of Henry I.[20] The most curious detail however is the way in which the ground levels vary between different parts of the palace, most of the masonry surviving from undercrofts revetted against two sides of a courtyard, with the upper levels lost. The courtyard itself was evidently set much higher than the ground to the south and east outside the ranges, reflecting the need of Roger's builder to adapt his design to a site which already sloped up to an earlier Norman rampart.

Even if one accepts the burden of the documentary evidence, that it is later than Sherborne, the constraints of the site seem to have made Sarum the less coherent of the two courtyard plans (Fig. 3). The location of the chapels is fixed in all reconstructions by the desire for orientation: they must have occupied the south range (the east end of the north range is occupied by garderobes), with St Margaret's chapel at the lower level, still partially surviving with a stone *mensa*, and St Nicholas's above it at courtyard level. Thereafter nothing in the layout is entirely clear, but there is general acceptance that the Great Hall ran north-south in the west range. The most detailed evidence for the remainder of the complex is the set of writs for repairs and building works surviving from the 13th century, by which time the palace was firmly in the royal rather than the episcopal estate, and a 14th-century dilapidation survey and repair contract from the last period of the castle's occupation. In July 1246, a list of buildings needing repairs includes a crucial reference to 'a cloister between the hall and the great chamber'.[21] The same writ continues to state that the chamber lay in a building of at least two storeys, with the chamber 'above the king's wardrobe'. This entry, combined with the evidence from the 1366 repair contract that beside Herlewin's Tower (near the north-west corner) was a room variously called 'great chamber' and 'high chamber', places the principal chamber in the north range, perhaps with views outwards towards the cathedral below the adjacent rampart.[22] It was along this side of the courtyard that the documented 'cloister' covered walkway was rebuilt in 1246. Such a reconstruction is architecturally problematic, giving a two-storeyed north range with its roof almost certainly higher than the remainder of the claustral complex (which had undercrofts below courtyard level), but represents the best of the possible alternative identification of rooms within the complex.

When comparing the two palaces, Sarum seems very much further removed from monastic plans than Sherborne, with its cloister walkways and 'day stairs' leading up into the ranges. At Sarum the two-storey chapel and hall stood at right angles, rather than parallel to one another (as church and refectory), and two sets of chambers filled the other two sides. As far was can be ascertained from very limited evidence, there was nothing like either of them at Roger's other two castles, Devizes and Malmesbury. Devizes in particular was famous for its imposing great tower, and a writer such as William of Malmesbury, who described several of Roger's buildings, was evidently more impressed by the fine jointing of the stonework than by their clever planning.[23]

It may be argued that the differences between Sherborne and Old Sarum are just as significant as their similarities. The varying degrees of regimentation in the two plans might be considered the difference between working on a virgin site at Sherborne and in an existing earlier castle at Old Sarum, or between a purely ecclesiastical palace at the former and a secular complex at the latter. It should also be remembered that Roger's own origins were not monastic; he had been a parish priest in Avranches, tying his fortunes to the future Henry I and eventually making himself indispensable in the circles of the court.[24] For a long time, historians actually saw him as an enemy of monastic churchmen, and though this judgement has softened with time, an active sympathy for the monastic world is still difficult to detect.[25] It is also ironic that architectural historians have seen a monastic connection in these palaces built for a secular churchman, but not in the residences of genuinely monastic patrons, such as the Cluniac Henry of Blois, who developed Wolvesey in Winchester in the second quarter of the 12th century, or the Carthusian Hugh of Lincoln later in the same century. The palaces of these figures have courtyards, but there is no suggestion of connecting walkways or such a careful management of the relationship between the different buildings.

FIG. 4.   Stone-lined pool known as 'Rosamond's Well', the principal surviving feature from the complex known as Everswell, now in the grounds of Blenheim Palace, Oxfordshire

Jeremy Ashbee

EVERSWELL AND THE THEORY OF ISLAMIC INFLUENCE

IT has already been mentioned that Bishop Roger's palaces passed into royal hands around the time of the outbreak of civil war between Stephen and Matilda, and were part of the royal estate at the time the next generation of claustral palaces were built in England. However, their relationship with the first of these — Everswell — is debatable. Everswell, sometimes known as 'Rosamond's Well' (in the grounds of Woodstock manor in Oxfordshire, now Blenheim Palace), first appears in the documentary record in 1165, in a Pipe Roll entry for £26 9 shillings on 'works to the well'; well being the standard term to distinguish works here from anything at the principal manor house of Woodstock (Fig. 4).[26] The complex at Everswell lies in a deep hollow, only 100 yards or so from the manor house. Because it is out of sight, and because of the occurrences of the name 'Rosamond', which first appear in the 13th century, it is often claimed that Henry II had built the palace for his mistress, Rosamond Clifford, with whom he began a liaison about this time.[27] In such profane circumstances, there is a clear preconception that the palace has nothing to do with monasticism. Nonetheless, it also appears from slightly later documentary evidence that cloisters were central to the design.

The reconstruction of Everswell rests on three pieces of evidence: one surviving rectangular pool, a set of writs for building works and staffing, almost all from the 13th century and later, and two 17th-century sketch surveys drawn up by John

Aubrey, when the site was clearly already in ruin.[28] What Aubrey recorded was an arrangement of two courtyards, one inside the other, entered from a 'noble gatehouse' at the top right-hand corner of his plan. The inner courtyard contained a line of three rectangular pools running down from the spring at the north end to the original river at the south: he annotates them as 'three baths in trayne' with the single surviving pool presumably the uppermost in the plan. This would place the other two either on the shore-line or actually under the lake, created by Capability Brown in the late 18th century. Aubrey shows that further along, the inner courtyard contained niches or perhaps seats in the wall. Some of the other details are intriguing but cannot presently be checked, including 'a free stone vault which leads from hence under ground to Combe church, near a mile distant, and I believe that there were other vaults besides which G as also (sic) the forme of the Labyrinth.' He also points out that between the chain of pools and the main gate, there was another rectangular basin, described as a pond in the court.

Since the publication of *History of the King's Works* in 1963, the standard, if hypothetical, interpretation of Everswell has been that it represents an adaptation of an architectural form from the Islamic world.[29] There is nothing unusual about elaborate water-features in late-12th-century English design: Henry II's keep at Dover has very sophisticated internal piping which took water from the well-head, and the famous water-system of Canterbury Cathedral priory also fed a series of open channels running around the area of the cloister garth. However, a ladder of rectangular basins with connecting water channels is seen as particularly diagnostic of certain strands of eastern architecture and is apparently without exact parallel in medieval western Europe.

The prototype suggested by Howard Colvin for Everswell was a palace in Palermo, Sicily, built under the Norman kings William I and William II in the 1160s, but essentially a cultural product of Fatimid north Africa.[30] The Sicilian palace which Colvin highlighted, *la Zisa*, does contain a distinctive 'train' of basins, smaller than the pools at Everswell, but linked by water channels in much the same way (Fig. 5). However, the parallel is less useful than it initially appears: the *Sala regia*, containing the water features, was in fact covered with a stone vault rather than an open cloister. Two storeys above this there was a courtyard open to the sky, but with only a single basin at its centre to catch the rainfall. Notwithstanding this, *la Zisa* has a slightly smaller copy a few hundred yards away, *la Cuba*, which is now accepted as having contained a central courtyard, with water-channels and a basin, rather than a grandiose dome as was once supposed.[31] Moreover, the surviving fabric here shows the springings for arches running to four columns around the courtyard, creating a circuit of covered walkways and providing some measure of shade. Arguably this could have struck a European observer as similar to a cloister.

One other detail is the repeated mention of the word *claustrum* in the documents for Everswell, though it should be noted that the fullest documentary record comes not from Henry II's reign but that of his grandson, Henry III (1216–72) between the 1220s and 1250s. Several of Henry III's writs describe the works as something new, rather than their being repairs to 12th-century buildings, and it is only in this 13th-century phase that the references to 'cloisters' appear. There were a 'greater pool' and a 'small pool', the 'greater pool' being surrounded by a 'great cloister.'[32] But this sort of arrangement was not confined to the single pool on the right-hand side of Aubrey's plan, because in 1244, a writ was issued for the paving and wainscotting of 'the cloisters around the pools', both in the plural.[33] A 'small pool' was surrounded by

FIG. 5. The *Sala Regia* of the palace called *la Zisa*, built *c.* 1165 outside Palermo, Sicily. The water channels are similar in inspiration to the 'three baths in trayne' built at Everswell at exactly the same time

Jeremy Ashbee

turf benches,[34] and certainly there was a covered walkway, a 'pentice around the pools', repaired in the 1250s.[35] At least one of these cloistered pools was overlooked by two-storey chamber blocks. The king certainly lived on an upper floor, in 'the king's high chamber by the pool'[36] and since in 1237, a walkway (*aleia*) was built to link it to the queen's chamber, there may have been a covered gallery on the upper level as well as by the pool.[37] Around one of the pools was a garden[38] and in the 1250s another garden was planted with 100 pear trees.[39] With references to such architectural details, it is perhaps justifiable that architectural historians should invoke formal analogy with Islamic buildings more immediately legible than the palaces of Sicily: 14th-century buildings in Al-Andalus, such as the Courtyard of Comares in the Alhambra, or the *Generalife* close by, featuring ensembles of water-filled pools, planting and arcaded ranges of buildings (Fig. 6).

The connection with Arab-Norman Sicily is anyway open to criticism. Both *la Zisa* and *la Cuba* are too late to have directly influenced the design of Everswell, being contemporary or later than the English palace, but they may all draw on a common source, now lost. Furthermore, as the late John Harvey pointed out, while Henry II's daughter Joan was indeed married to the king of Sicily, the marriage did not take place until five years after works began to the complex at Everswell.[40] Certain

FIG. 6.   *Generalife*, the garden palace adjacent to the Alhambra, Granada, built from the late
13th to the early 14th century. This gives an impression of the form of the complex at
Everswell, though doubtless with more exotic architecture

Jeremy Ashbee

other linkages between the two kingdoms are open to question. Thomas Brown, for instance, a former royal chaplain to Roger II of Sicily (1130–54) is described in *Dialogus de Scaccario* as an official at the Exchequer of Henry II, but had left Sicily in difficult circumstances ('because a new king arose who did not know him').[41] Similarly Henry II's tutor, Peter of Blois, another refugee to the Angevin court from the court of Palermo, wrote scathing letters back to Sicily and was evidently glad to have escaped.[42] Nonetheless. it is a pity that Harvey raised these objections, because such 12th-century courtiers in Palermo would have known several other royal palaces built after an eastern model, in which conventional arcaded courtyards were the dominant feature, and which were standing in the reign of Roger II long before the start of work at Everswell.[43] These included the suburban *la Favara* and *Altofonte* in the hills above the city, a fragment of which survives, built into a house in the present town (Figs 7 and 8). Surviving fabric demonstrates that both of these had central courtyards ringed by colonnaded walkways with groined vaulting, and are conventionally linked to oriental architecture, particularly the *Ribat* fortresses of the Levant and North Africa. They are also entirely in keeping with the orientalism of the Sicilian court, as portrayed in chronicle sources, notably the initiatives of George of Antioch, Roger's '*Emir of emirs*', to present the king as a Moslem ruler and withdraw him entirely from view into these private pleasure palaces.[44]

In summary, scholars have identified an alternative source for claustral plans, in the architecture of the Islamic world, transmitted from North Africa via Sicily and the

FIG. 7.   Remains of *la Favara*, a suburban retreat built outside Palermo for Roger II.
A stub of groined vaulting survives in the angle between the two ranges, part of an
arcaded walkway around a central courtyard

Jeremy Ashbee

FIG. 8.   Surviving bays of an arcaded cloister walkway of the royal summer palace at
Altofonte in the hills above Palermo. The spandrels are decorated with roundels of
sandstone and lava

Jeremy Ashbee

Iberian peninsula. The case may have been overstated, and the means of transmission remains elusive, but from what we know of Everswell, the architectural analogy of chains of pools is wholly specific. In spite of objections to individual points of interpretation, Everswell is conventionally viewed as a rural pleasure-palace after the oriental model. Should it ever be possible to drag the lake and undertake an excavation, some of the above may be testable archaeologically.

THE PALACES OF HENRY II AND HIS SONS

IF the best architectural information for Everswell comes not from Henry II's reign, but from Henry III's, there are at least other indications, archaeological and documentary, that the claustral model was adopted by the planners of royal palaces in the twelfth century. For example, in 1998, the former Royal Commission on Historical Monuments undertook a resistivity and magnetometry survey of the Inner Ward at Scarborough Castle, and recovered traces of a possible regular layout of buildings to the south of Henry II's great tower.[45] As with the earlier complex at Sherborne, these seemed to follow the alignment of the tower itself, although it has since been suggested that they actually pre-date the construction of the tower in the late 1150s. This would make such a complex either a very early work of Henry II, or a survival from William le Gros, the previous owner of the site.[46] Likewise, excavations in the Inmost Ward at the Tower of London revealed only one surviving medieval footing incorporating a pilaster buttress on its western face, lying in the middle of the space later occupied by Henry III's Great Hall, but defining a right angle to the south wall of the White Tower on the opposite side of the palace enclosure.[47] The idea that the 12th-century royal lodgings were set out on a regular plan finds some support in documentary sources: the Pipe Roll of 1185–86 recorded payment for 'building a chamber in the cloister which lies between the chambers (*camera in claustro quod est inter cameras*).'[48] Beaumont Palace, the royal residence in Oxford lying east of the site later occupied by Worcester College, contained a cloister, probably running across the southern end of Saint John's Street. This cloister, which needed repairs in 1246,[49] originated in the 12th century, as the Pipe Roll of 1196–97 included an item for 'roofing the cloister there' using shingles.[50] A recent excavation of part of the site found no trace of the cloister, though it did reveal traces of regular early tree-plantation, evoking comparison with the orchard garden at Everswell nearby.[51]

The most impressive adoption of the claustral plan in palace-design is however Windsor Castle, a site in which the motif appeared in two separate locations. While remaining in continuous occupation from the 12th century to the present, the upper ward at Windsor has undergone some of the most radical alterations of any site in the country, from Edward III's reconstruction of the mid-14th century, through Hugh May's re-casting for Charles II and Wyattville's new designs for George IV to recent reconstruction after the fire of 1992. Though these last works were preceded and accompanied by the most intensive archaeological examination in Windsor's history, relatively little fabric was found upstanding from the earlier phases. However, the documentary record is usually taken to support the idea that from Henry II's reign onwards, the upper ward contained a residential complex for the king, known by the generic term 'the king's houses.' In 1195–96, the Pipe Roll contains a payment for 'repairing the king's cloister'[52] and though this document of Richard I marks the first occurrence of the term, this almost certainly represents a work begun in Henry II's reign. The location of this cloister has generally been accepted as on the same footprint as the second courtyard, shown in the famous Hollar aerial view. Clearly it survived until Edward III's reconstruction works of the 1360s: there are sporadic references to it in documents, such as a payment in 1320 for 'making a garden in the upper ward inside the cloister of the queen's chambers.'[53]

THE PALACES OF HENRY III AND EDWARD I

IN addition to the documented complex in the upper ward, Windsor subsequently contained a second royal residence in the lower ward, to the north and east of the site now occupied by Saint George's Chapel, recently elucidated in the researches of Dr Steven Brindle and, particularly, Tim Tatton-Brown.[54] It is now clear that from the late 12th century, a great hall in the lower ward ran east-west, rather than north-south as had hitherto been supposed, greatly facilitating an understanding of developments in this area under Henry III. The 12th-century hall was extensively repaired early in Henry III's reign, before the king turned his attention to the buildings of the castle's upper ward. However, in January 1240, he issued a writ for the creation of two new chambers for himself and Eleanor of Provence (c.1223–91) in the lower ward at the 'low' eastern end of the hall, to stand end-to-end under a single roof.[55] The writ went on to order the building of 'a chapel 40 feet long and 28 feet wide, in such a way that there is sufficient space between the said chambers and the said chapel to make a lawn (pratellum).' This new chapel occupied the footprint of the present Albert Memorial Chapel to the east of Saint George's, and the document set out some of the key dimensions for the Deanery Cloister, shown in John Norden's survey of the early 17th century. In 1243, the area occupied by this lawn was first referred to as a 'cloister' (Fig. 9).[56]

Tantalising elements of this cloister still survive, notably the blind arcade which forms the south walk of the cloister, or alternatively the external north wall of the chapel. In the writ of 1243, issued from Bordeaux, Henry III ordered 'a supply of marble to be sent from the Purbeck region to Windsor to build the cloister of the king's chapel there and have it ready by Whitsun,' though this writ was clearly not executed immediately. The lead roof for the cloister was only ordered in October 1248, and in 1263, some of the marble columns were said to be broken and in need of replacement. The walls of the cloister facing into the central garth were reconstructed in the 1350s for the new collegiate canons of Saint George, and it is not clear whether any of the documented marble columns were intended for an open arcade, or whether there was simply a wooden pentice and the columns were set as blind arcading around the outer walls (Fig. 10).[57] The moulding profiles of the surviving stretch of arcade are similar to those in Saint Faith's Chapel in Westminster Abbey, indicative of common design from master Henry of Reyns, who appears as master of the king's masons in a writ given at Windsor in 1243. Paul Binski has even suggested that certain details, such as the form of the floriate crocket capitals and the continuous plinth show a sign of French influence, and lend further support for the idea that the mason may have been French.[58] In 1251, the finished cloister was also to be decorated with wainscotting and with paintings of the Apostles, on the instruction of Henry himself and master William the Painter.[59] The head of a king, though not one of the apostles, has survived in the westernmost bay and gives some idea of the decoration. This area, visualised with a garden at its centre and with painted decoration, shut off from the outside world by wooden barriers, is as evocative as any of the surviving elements of his palaces, of the sophistication in palace-design to which Henry III aspired.

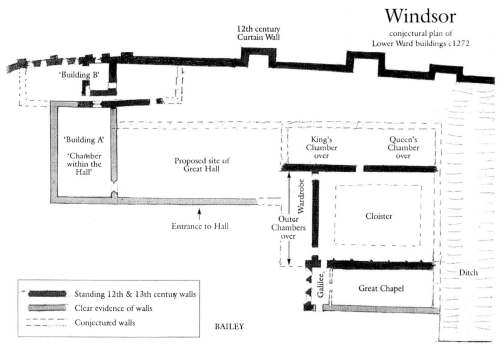

FIG. 9.   Reconstructed plan showing the claustral complex in the Lower Ward at Windsor
Castle

English Heritage

Study of the writs of Henry III reveals that palace-cloisters were not as rare in the
13th century as might be expected: as well as Windsor and Sherborne, Sarum and
Everswell, all of which remained in use within the royal estate, the word *claustrum* is
used in relation to several other sites. These include the entirely utilitarian 'cloister in
front of the kitchens' at Clarendon Palace, discovered during excavations to have been
an irregular rectangular courtyard with covered walkways around all sides,[60] Rochester Castle, where in a single reference of 1254, Henry III ordered a new stair to run up
into the first-floor chapel, 'not from the side of the cloister, but the other side',[61] and
an evidently ostentatious architectural scheme at Guildford where, in 1251, Henry III
ordered a garden to be created adjacent to the king's chamber.[62] To this, five years
later, he added a cloister,[63] paved and with benches,[64] and surrounded once again with
marble columns. Sadly no trace of such a cloister has been recovered at either
Guildford or Rochester.[65]

One final example which seems to have been built at the end of the 13th century is
the royal manor at King's Langley in Hertfordshire, a property since 1276 of Queen
Eleanor of Castile (1241–90), whose passion for gardening has been much commented
on by later biographers.[66] An account of the late 1270s and early 1280s contains details
of building and landscaping works around the manor, as well as mentioning chambers
intended for the king, the queen and their eldest son Alphonso. The account makes
it clear that the cloister was specifically for Eleanor herself. Unfortunately the only
detailed information is that the Queen's cloister, like her great chamber and 'middle

FIG. 10.   Surviving bays of blind arcading around the outer face of the south range of the cloister at Windsor Castle

John Goodall

chamber', was to be paved, almost certainly with tiles.[67] Once again, no trace of the cloister has been recovered in excavation. However, the context, a rural moated manor distinguished by its park, gardens and vineyards, suggests it was developed more for leisure than for the execution of royal business and that the cloister was conceived as a recreational feature.

With the exception of the one surviving wall at Windsor, the complete lack of standing fabric from these palace-cloisters presents something of a challenge to the modern historian. It is evident that 'cloister' was an umbrella term with a fairly wide range of meanings, though slightly more specific than merely a courtyard or enclosure.[68] Numerous references leave no doubt that the 'cloisters' were upstanding structures needing to be built or repaired, and with roofs. '*Claustrum*' may often be taken to refer to the covered walkway itself, the structure which is more commonly described as a '*pentice*', '*alura*' or '*tresaunce*', exemplified by the surviving 14th-century covered way along the western side of Green Court at Canterbury Cathedral Priory. The term *pentice* itself defines nothing more than its attachment to another building, without any specific functional connotation, and some documented examples of the 12th and 13th centuries were apparently fairly elaborate, with doors, windows, latrines and fireplaces.[69] But the significant thing about the palace *claustra*, in their 13th-century occurrences, is that the wording often speaks of the cloister as a passage leading somewhere, as in the reference in 1252 at Silverstone manor in Northamptonshire to 'a cloister from the door of the king's chamber to another hanging cloister (*claustrum pendens*) leading to the queen's chapel.'[70] This example, the kitchen cloister at Clarendon and the garden cloister at Guildford confirm that in the 13th century, *claustra* could be built without any relationship to chapels (nor even necessarily to courtyards): just as commonly, they belong to the world of the royal chamber.

CONCLUSION

THOUGH several of these 12th and 13th-century examples survived intact and in use, the development of new palace claustral complexes along these lines seems to tail off after Henry III's and Edward I's reigns, and it is fair to say that thereafter, the principal non-monastic examples are connected to secular cathedrals and colleges, even if on occasion, as at Westminster, they were built within the confines of a royal palace.[71] Some of the statements previously made in synthetic works, that cloisters-without-ranges were only built from the 14th century onwards,[72] are probably open to question: 13th-century Guildford, for example, may have stood in its garden without other buildings. More important though, is the suggestion that the form had become normalised by the end of the 13th century, to the extent that it did not always attract comment. So common are references to pentices linking the buildings of 13th-century palaces and castles, that there is no reason to invoke a monastic parallel for sites like Goodrich Castle, redeveloped for an almost-royal patron in the second half of the 13th century. Clearly the castle contained a covered walkway around a central courtyard,[73] but there must be doubt whether a late 13th-century visitor, on seeing it, would have made a connection with a monastic plan.

In architectural terms, the importance of a claustral layout was that it injected a measure of regularity into palace-planning. It has been a point of orthodoxy in the published literature that this is unusual, and that the majority of English palaces were informally or erratically planned, if they were planned at all. Sites like Clarendon may appear to a modern observer to wander randomly across the landscape, but in fact the ground plan was almost rectilinear, with the main buildings running east-west, terminating in the queen's chamber running north-south. It is the elevations which are most likely to have struck the contemporary observer as irregular, with offset wall-lines and roofs of different heights in different materials, and it is here that the effect of the pentices may have been to tie the disparate buildings together into a single ensemble. Likewise when Henry III introduced a new cloister into his existing garden at Guildford, it probably had the effect of unifying the complex of buildings to either side of it, both functionally and aesthetically. The earliest examples, such as Sherborne and Old Sarum, may have been created as unified and coherent entities, but the later palaces tend to be the products of additive development,

In terms of their function, it is hard to generalise about the cloisters mentioned above. The period of Roger of Salisbury is probably too distant to allow any point to be made as to whether a bishop's household bore a convincing resemblance to a monastery. Certainly at Sherborne, and possibly at Old Sarum, the layout of the cloister, and particularly the provision of 'day stairs' leading from the cloister to the upper storeys of the ranges is a fairly close analogue to a monastic cloister, but one of the most vital elements, easy access into the church or chapel, is missing, and the all-important stylobate on which monks could sit in study in their monastic cloisters cannot be confirmed as a feature in these or any other palace-cloister. Later on, the function of claustral palaces seems to be one of escape from duty, as in Henry II's rural retreat at Woodstock, or the gardens at Guildford or both the upper and lower ward cloisters at Windsor. They become adjuncts to the world of the chamber, and as such, privacy rather than ostentation is the most likely driver behind their development. It may be significant that several of them are connected to the person and household of the queen, as in the Upper Ward at Windsor (from the 13th century onwards), at Silverstone and at King's Langley. However, if the tide turned, palace-cloisters might be adapted to monastic use. When Edward II, fulfilling a vow made in his escape from Bannockburn, gave Beaumont Palace to the Carmelites, the friars were able to convert the palace into a friary quickly and apparently without major building works.[74] Likewise at King's Langley, the Dominicans, whom Edward II had installed in the nearby parish church, were briefly entrusted with the manor complex in the 1350s.[75] From 11th- and 12th-century beginnings in the houses of churchmen, the cloister was clearly adopted by the Plantagenets (and their queens) in entirely secular contexts of rural *solatia* and garden-palaces, only to be re-adopted by quasi-religious institutions such as colleges and episcopal households as the fourteenth century wore on.

But in fact the best account for the use of a palace cloister is the quotation with which this paper began: the Seigneur de Joinville puzzling over the building left from the reign of Henry II, and celebrating its fitness for grand royal ceremonial. This, it should be remembered, was the use for which Henry II had originally intended it, but which is otherwise undocumented on English sites. And certainly all of the specifics of the building itself, with its '*allée*' walkways in which diners were seated, or its lawn with its crowd of knights, refer to a cloister rather than a conventional hall. However unusual such a building appeared, its architectural context in England furnished it with ample precedent, and developments in the rest of the thirteenth century indicate that later English monarchs were receptive to the idea of palaces containing cloisters. The contention of this paper is that if Jean de Joinville had been able to see certain other palaces in England, he might have found Saumur less of a surprise.

NOTES

1. E. Impey, 'Seigneurial Domestic Architecture in Normandy 1050–1350', in *Manorial Domestic Buildings in England and Northern France*, ed. G. Meirion-Jones and M. Jones (London 1993), note 77; L. Grant, 'Le Patronage Architectural d'Henri II et son Entourage', *Cahiers de Civilisation Médiévale*, 37 (1994), 73–84; M. W. Thompson, *The Rise of the Castle* (Cambridge 1991), 44–46.

2. Jean de Joinville, *Vie de Saint Louis*, ed. J. Monfrin (Paris 1995), 48.

3. Dr Edward Impey, personal communication.

4. R. A. Brown, H. M. Colvin and A. J. Taylor, *The History of the King's Works: The Middle Ages*, ed. H. M. Colvin, I (London 1963), 1043, clause 35; National Archives, Public Record Office (PRO) E159/71 rot 114d. Note that this document also includes *aula* for a conventional hall, suggesting that *hala* was perceived as something different.

5. R. A. Stalley, 'A Twelfth-Century Patron of Architecture: A Study of the Buildings Erected by Roger Bishop of Salisbury', *JBAA*, 124 (1971), 62–83.

6. E. J. Kealey, *Roger of Salisbury, Viceroy of England* (Berkeley, Los Angeles and London 1972).

7. W. J. Blair, 'Hall and Chamber: English Domestic Planning 1000–1250', in Meirion-Jones and Jones, 1–21, especially 11. See particularly P.K. Kipps, 'Minster Court, Thanet', *Archaeol. J.*, 86 (1929), 213–23.

8. Abingdon Chronicle, *Chronicon Monasterii de Abingdon*, ed. J. Stevenson (Rolls Series, II, 1858), I, 474.

9. Stalley, 66.

10. ibid.

11. RCHME, *County of Dorset*, I (London 1962), 64–66.

12. P. White, 'Sherborne Old Castle', *Archaeol. J.*, 140 (1983), 67–70. White identifies the chapel primarily on the evidence of the ornate northern windows facing away from the courtyard.

13. Blair, 10–12 and note 36. Blair reiterates this view in T. G. Allen and J. Hiller, *The Excavation of a Medieval Manor House of the Bishops of Winchester at Mount House, Witney, Oxfordshire* (Oxford 2002), 229 but questions in fig. 72.

14. Stalley, 74. See also L. Keen and P. Ellis, *Sherborne Abbey and School: Excavations 1972–76 and 1990* (Dorchester 2005), 5.

15. Stalley, 66.

16. White, *passim*.

17. W. H. St John Hope, 'Report of the Committee for Excavations at Old Sarum during the Past Season', *Proceedings of the Society of Antiquaries*, 2nd Series, 23 (1909–11), 190–200, 501–518, and 24 (1912–1913), 52–65. Note that in the plan opposite p. 195 of volume 23, which preceded the excavation of the courtyard palace, it was provisionally interpreted as the 'great tower'.

18. See J. Montague, 'From Old Sarum to Lincoln: Thoughts on the Origins and Meaning of Secular Cathedral Cloisters', pp. 48–70, in this volume.

19. Stalley, 68.

20. RCHME, *City of Salisbury*, I (London 1980), 8–10.

21. *Calendar of the Liberate Rolls, 1245–1251* (London 1937), 65.

22. RCHME, *Salisbury*, 173–74. I am very grateful to John McNeill for suggesting this detail of the reconstruction, personal communication.

23. Stalley, 66.

24. Kealey, 16–17.

25. ibid., 118–45.

26. *The Pipe Roll 12 Henry II*, (London 1888), 116.

27. H. M. Colvin, 'Royal Gardens in Medieval England', reprinted in *Essays in English Architectural History* (New Haven and London 1999), 1–12, especially 9; J. Bond and K. Tiler, *Blenheim. Landscape for a Palace*, 2nd edition (Stroud 1997), 47.

28. Bodleian Library, MS Wood 176b fol 43v; J. Spooner, *Everswell; from Fantasy to Luxury*, unpublished MA Dissertation, (Courtauld Institute of Art, University of London, 1997). I am very grateful to Ms Spooner for allowing me to see a copy of her thesis.

29. *The King's Works*, II, 1015.

30. ibid. For the cultural context of the Sicilian palaces, see J. Johns, 'The Norman Kings of Sicily and the Fatimid Caliphate,' *Anglo-Norman Studies*, 15 (Woodbridge 1993), 133–159.

31. G Bellafiore, *Parchi e Giardini della Palermo Normanna* (Palermo 1996), 81–94.

32. *The King's Works*, II, 1014, citing Pipe Roll 19 Henry III rot 16.

33. *Calendar of the Liberate Rolls, 1240–1245* (London 1930), 219.

34. *The King's Works*, II, 1014, citing Pipe Roll 20 Henry III rot 14.

35. ibid., citing Pipe Roll 45 Henry III rot 20.

36. *Calendar of the Liberate Rolls, 1226–1240* (London 1916), 47.

37. ibid., 343.

38. ibid., 412.

39. *The King's Works*, II, 1015, citing Liberate Roll 49 Henry III m7.

40. J. Harvey, *Mediaeval Gardens* (London 1981) p 50.

41. D. Matthew, *The Norman Kingdom of Sicily* (Cambridge 1992), 211.

42. Peter of Blois, *Petri Blesensis Bathoniensis in Anglia Opera Omnia*, ed. S. Piget, (Paris 1667), 99.

43. Bellafiore, *passim*; V. Noto, 'I Palazzi e i Giardini Siciliani dei Re Normanni' in *Trésors Romans d'Italie du Sud et de Sicile*, ed. G. Coppola, (Milan 1995), 98–108.

44. This is implicit in the important newly-discovered biography of George of Antioch by al-Maqrīzī, discussed in J. Johns, *Arabic Administration in Norman Sicily* (Cambridge 2002), 80–82, 286–89; see also Romuald of Salerno, *The History of the Tyrants of Sicily by 'Hugo Falcandus' 1154–69*, ed. G. A. Loud and T. Wiedemann (Manchester and New York 1998), 237.

45. Historic Buildings and Monuments Commission for England, *Inner Bailey, Scarborough Castle, N Yorkshire. Results of Geophysical Survey, June 1998*, unpublished report, (English Heritage 1998).

46. University of York, *Scarborough Castle Conservation Plan,* unpublished report, (English Heritage 1999).

47. G. Parnell, 'The Roman and Medieval Defences and Later Development of the Inmost Ward, Tower of London: Excavations 1955–77', *Transactions of the London and Middlesex Archaeological Society,* 36 (1985), 37–43. The observation that this footing lies at right angles to the White Tower was first made by Beric Morley, personal communication.

48. *The Pipe Roll 32 Henry II* (London 1914), 49.

49. *Calendar of the Liberate Rolls, 1245–1251,* 69.

50. *The King's Works,* II, 986, n. 13 and 987 n. 1.

51. D. Poore and D. R. P. Wilkinson, *Beaumont Palace and the White Friars: Excavations at the Sackler Library, Beaumont Street, Oxford* (Oxford 2001), especially 30.

52. *The Pipe Roll 7 Richard I* (London 1929), 250.

53. PRO, E101 492/20 m5. I am grateful to Stephen Priestley for this reference.

54. T. Tatton-Brown, 'The Constructional Sequence and Topography of the Chapel and College Buildings at St George's', in *St George's Chapel, Windsor, in the Late Middle Ages,* ed. C. Richmond and E. Scarff (Windsor 2001), 3–38, especially 24–29 and fig. 1. The most detailed description of surviving fabric from this complex is P. E. Curnow, 'Royal Lodgings of the 13th Century in the Lower Ward at Windsor Castle: Some Recent Archaeological Discoveries', *Friends' Annual Report to 30th September, 1965* (1965), 218–28.

55. *Calendar of the Liberate Rolls, 1226–1240,* 439.

56. *The King's Works,* II, 869, n. 1.

57. Dr Richard Morris has pointed out that several Purbeck colonettes, conceivably salvaged from the thirteenth-century fabric, are incorporated into the fabric of the 1352–55 rebuilding of the inner walls, personal communication.

58. P. Binski, *Westminster Abbey and the Plantagenets. Kingship and the Representation of Power 1200–1400* (New Haven and London 1995), 35; V. Jansen, 'Henry III's Windsor: Castle-Building and Residences' in *Windsor. Medieval Archaeology, Art and Architecture of the Thames Valley* ed. L. Keen and E. Scarff, B.A.A. Trans., XXV (Leeds 2002), 95–109.

59. *Calendar of the Close Rolls, 1247–1251* (London 1922), 492.

60. *Calendar of the Liberate Rolls, 1240–1245,* 291; T. B. James and A. M. Robinson, *Clarendon Palace* (London 1988), 83–85.

61. *Calendar of the Close Rolls, 1253–1254* (London 1929), 285.

62. *Royal and other Historical Letters Illustrative of the Reign of Henry III,* ed. W. W. Shirley (Rolls Series, XXVII, 1866), II, 66–67.

63. *Calendar of the Liberate Rolls, 1251–1260* (London 1959), 289.

64. ibid., 525.

65. R. Poulton, *A Medieval Royal Complex at Guildford. Excavations at the Castle and Palace* (Guildford 2005).

66. J. C. Parsons, *Eleanor of Castile* (Basingstoke 1995) 53.

67. '*pavimento ad claustrum regine, magnam cameram et mediam cameram regine pavando ...*', PRO, E372/125 rot 2d. It should be noted that the gardens mentioned in this document were specifically the province of the king rather than the queen. Though little-mentioned, the cloister clearly survived redevelopments, and was re-roofed in the late 1380s, E101 473/5 m 11.

68. This observation is derived from a reading of the documents cited above. For a published discussion of the etymology and early use of the word *claustrum,* see P. Meyvaert, 'The Medieval Monastic Claustrum', *Gesta,* XII (1973), 53–59.

69. See for example *The Pipe Roll 21 Henry II* (London 1897), 188 for a reference of 1174–75 to a pentice (*appenticium*) in Winchester Castle 'where the young queen hears mass' and *Calendar of the Liberate Rolls, 1267–1272* (London 1964), 55 for a pentice with a fireplace at Guildford.

70. *Calendar of the Liberate Rolls, 1251–1260,* 23.

71. *The King's Works,* I, 526.

72. M. W. Thompson, *Medieval Bishops' Houses in England and Wales* (Aldershot and Brookfield 1998), 82.

73. A. Emery, *Greater Medieval Houses of England and Wales,* II (Cambridge 2000), 537; C. M. Woolgar, *The Great Household in Late Medieval England* (New Haven and London 1999), 50–59.

74. '... þe frere Carmes chirche þat Kyng Edward had geve ham, þe whiche cherch some tyme was þe Kyngus Halle', *The Brut or The Chronicles of England,* ed. F. W. D. Brie (London 1906), 208.

75. *The King's Works,* II, 974.

The Two Mid-Twelfth-Century Cloister Arcades at Canterbury Cathedral Priory

TIM TATTON-BROWN

Very few Romanesque cloister arcades have survived in Britain, in most cases because they were replaced in the later Middle Ages. Modern discoveries have, however, included some fine decorated capitals (particularly double capitals) and other carved stones, allowing a rough impression to be gained of at least some English Romanesque cloister arcades. Elements of one 12th-century cloister — the Infirmary Cloister at Christchurch, Canterbury — do survive in situ, *and it is with this, and certain mid-12th-century fragments that probably originated in the Great Cloister, that the following paper is concerned.*

THE survival rate of English Romanesque cloister arcades is low, and most of what is known about their appearance comes from loose or re-used stonework. For example, fragments have been found and published of the early-12th-century cloister arcades at Westminster Abbey, Hyde Abbey (Winchester) and Reading Abbey, while at Norwich Cathedral Priory, another Benedictine house, fragments of the double capitals from the mid-12th-century Romanesque cloister arcade were found in 1900 re-used in the early-14th-century buttresses of the south cloister walk.[1] Portions also survive of the 12th-century cloister arcading from Bridlington Priory, now reconstructed and displayed in the nave, and from the Cistercian monasteries of Rievaulx and Fountains, fragments of which have also been reconstructed as arcading.[2]

At what was the largest Benedictine priory in Britain, Christ Church Priory, Canterbury, there were two cloisters: the Great Cloister and the Infirmary Cloister. Six bays of the east walk of the mid-12th-century Infirmary Cloister arcade survive *in situ*, and fragments have also been found of what is probably the contemporary cloister arcade from the great cloister. Both of these cloisters are depicted in the waterworks plan (of *c.* 1160), and it is therefore surprising that they have not been discussed in detail before.

Canterbury Cathedral Priory was rebuilt in three main phases in the century following the arrival in England of Lanfranc as archbishop in 1070.[3] First the cathedral itself was rebuilt (1071–77), followed by the principal buildings around the Great Cloister (Chapter-House, *Dorter*, *Frater* and *Cellarium*). At this time, there were only timber arcades to the cloister. Before Lanfranc died in 1089, the decision had already been taken to greatly enlarge the monastery so that it could hold up to 150 monks (Fig. 1). A huge dormitory was being built in the 1080s and, following the construction of Archbishop Anselm's 'Glorious Choir' (1096–1107), a very large new reredorter and infirmary hall and chapel were built in the years soon after *c.* 1100. Other buildings around the Outer (Green) Court were also put up at this time, as well as a new stone wall around the extended eastern part of the Priory. Finally, during Wibert's

JBAA, vol. 159 (2006), 91–104
© British Archaeological Association 2006
DOI: 10.1179/174767006X132989

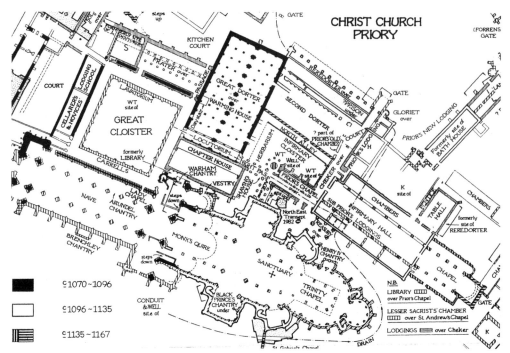

FIG. 1. Plan of the principal buildings of Christchurch Priory beside Canterbury Cathedral, showing the locations of the two cloisters

sub-priorate (*c.* 1140–52) and priorate (1152x54–67), the cathedral church was completed with various elaborately decorated turrets and a large crossing tower, while other fine buildings (particularly gateways) were erected in the precincts, including the *Vestiarium* or Treasury (with its double porch and gateways beneath) and the vast North Hall (or *Aula Nova*, as the Waterworks plan calls it) and its adjoining great gateway, the principal entrance into the priory (later called the Green Court gate).[4] Prior Wibert also installed the priory's aqueduct and piped-water system and built four water towers; those in the infirmary cloister and above the monumental staircase to the North Hall still survive, though their lead-lined cisterns were removed at the Dissolution. Wibert was also responsible for the large gateway in the wall between the monks' cemetery and the lay cemetery,[5] and for the elaborate *domus hospitum* (later the cellarer's hall) and its adjoining gateway into the kitchen court. All these buildings are clearly shown (and labelled) on the famous plan of the priory, which shows its sophisticated waterworks system.[6] This plan, made *c.* 1160, is now bound into the back of the Eadwine Psalter at Trinity College, Cambridge.[7] Earlier Norman builders at the Priory had used large quantities of fine Caen stone (and a little Quarr stone) for their buildings, but in Prior Wibert's time the Caen stone was often elaborately carved, and 'marble' was introduced for the first time. This was mostly Purbeck and onyx marble, but some black Tournai marble was also used. Similar marbles were also used around this date at Rochester Cathedral Priory, as well as by Henry of Blois (Bishop of Winchester 1129–71) in various buildings at Winchester.[8] Henry of Blois was also Abbot of Glastonbury (1126–71), in which capacity he used the local equivalent of Tournai marble, polished Blue Lias limestone, for the capitals (and probably the shafts and bases) in the cloister.[9] Nothing, however, has survived *in situ* of the Glastonbury cloister.

THE INFIRMARY CLOISTER AT CHRISTCHURCH PRIORY, CANTERBURY

ONLY six bays of the original arcading survive in the Infirmary Cloister (Fig. 2). These are at the north end of the east cloister walk (Fig. 3). This style of arcading probably continued all the way along the north cloister walk, but the west walk (against the south-east corner of the great dorter) was, according to the Waterworks plan, a timber pentice (Fig. 4). The south cloister walk is more complicated, as its first section (to the west) was an early-12th-century covered (and vaulted) passage, which still survives beneath the monks' night passage running from the dorter to the north-east transept of the cathedral. The east-west section of this passage, which is L-shaped in plan, was later used for part of the Infirmary Cloister, and on its north-east side Prior Wibert attached a round water-tower holding the main lead-lined cistern. East of this lies the early-13th-century undercroft of the Prior's chapel, which is double the width of the original cloister walk and replaced it and another water tower in the south-east corner of the Infirmary Cloister.[10] As originally built, this section of the cloister was presumably similar to the surviving section of the east cloister walk, as is perhaps confirmed by both the Waterworks plan, and by the fact that onyx marble shafts are re-used in the centre of the double openings in the north and south walls of the Prior's chapel undercroft. As we shall see, onyx marble shafting was almost certainly only brought into England for use in the mid-12th century. When it occurs, very rarely, in later structures at Canterbury, like the Prior's chapel undercroft and the chapter house façade, it is likely to have been re-used.

The 12th-century cloister arcading probably only survives here because Prior Henry of Eastry (1285–1331) built his counting house over this section of the east cloister walk in 1288–90, and, rather than replace the original arcading, he decided to spread the weight of the new west wall above it, over two wide relieving arches, on rectangular piers set into the east cloister arcading.[11] When Robert Willis wrote his classic account of the architectural history of Christ Church Priory in 1867, this fine building was still intact (Fig. 5).[12] It was to be demolished shortly afterwards, but luckily the Romanesque arcading was spared. The demolition work left the east cloister walk open to the sky, and for the first time, complete exposure to the weather. In 1964–66 a new brick building, the Wolfson Library, was erected over this cloister walk. The arcading itself is still dirty: apparently it was not cleaned and conserved in 1966.

The six surviving arches of the Romanesque arcade are each about 6 ft high internally (around 1.83 m) and have a bay-spacing of about 4 ft (around 1.22 m) (Fig. 2). However, as is usual with Romanesque architecture, much small-scale variation is found when exact measurements are taken.[13] The arches themselves are all made up of varying numbers of plain Caen stone voussoirs with a little ashlar work above and, on top of this, rubble flint walling with inset stone corbelling, presumably for the timber roof. To support the arches two different types of pier were used, either double and of Purbeck marble, or single and with fatter monolithic onyx marble shafts. These were clearly meant to alternate. At the north end of the arcade, however, they go out of step, presumably because the pier in the north-east corner was built last. This was

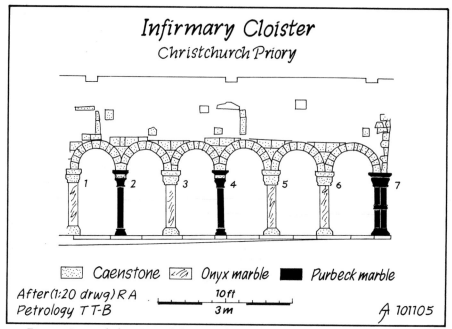

FIG. 2.   Internal elevation of the east cloister arcade of the infirmary cloister

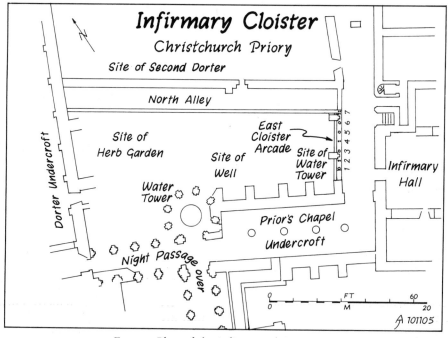

FIG. 3.   Plan of the infirmary cloister area

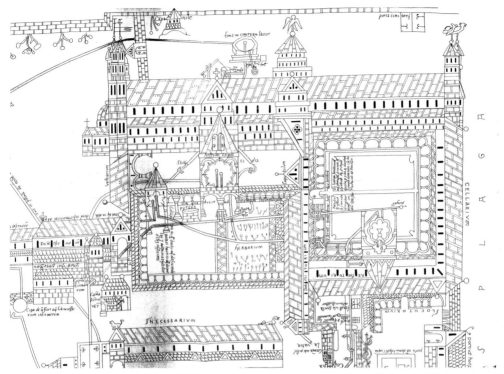

FIG. 4.   Detail of the buildings of Christchurch Priory in *c.* 1160, from Robert Willis' tracing of the Waterworks plan

to have quadruple shafts, although today only three Purbeck marble shafts survive sandwiched between quadruple capitals and bases.

The onyx marble piers have four main elements (Fig. 2); a Caen stone base (approximately 180 mm high by 370 mm square); an onyx marble shaft (around 960 mm high and between 200 and 230 mm in diameter); a squat scalloped Caen stone capital (approximately 180 mm high); and a Caen stone abacus block (around 110 mm high by 430 mm square). The Purbeck marble piers have five main elements; a double base with deeply undercut mouldings, but apparently no spurs (around 180 mm high and 370 by 250 mm in plan); spirally-cut shafts of various types (between 910 and 920 mm high with a diameter of 120 mm); a waterleaf capital (about 200 mm high); a plain Caen stone block (60 mm high); and an abacus (90 mm high and approximately 420 by 370 mm in plan). All these elements, except the plain block between the capital and the abacus (in itself a slightly strange 'filler') are made of Purbeck marble and the Christchurch Infirmary Cloister is among the first places in England where Purbeck marble is used monumentally.[14] However, under Prior Wibert, Purbeck marble was used in various other buildings within the conventual precincts, including the nearby water-tower, and was of course to be used on a colossal scale in the new cathedral choir, after 1175.

FIG. 5.   Robert Willis' drawing of the Checker building over the east walk of the infirmary
cloister in *c.* 1866

It is also worth noting here that three different types of 'marble' (i.e., a stone that could be polished) were used at this time in both Canterbury Cathedral Priory and at Rochester Cathedral Priory.[15] These are Purbeck marble, onyx marble and Tournai marble. At Canterbury, Tournai marble can only be seen *in situ* at one place: as a small octagonal pillar at the top of the northside of the 'Norman' staircase attached to the North Hall (see above).[16] All the other original shafts there are of Purbeck marble, with the capitals and bases of Caen stone.[17] Onyx marble, which is only used for *en délit* shafting (that is, with the beds of the stone set vertically), is also found at several other places in Canterbury Cathedral Priory, as well as on the façade of the east cloister range at Rochester Cathedral Priory, where it seems to have alternated with octagonal shafts of Caen stone on the outside west wall of the dorter.[18] Pairs of Tournai marble shafts are also used to flank the neighbouring doorways at Rochester.[19] One of a pair of shafts of onyx marble also survives in the outer order of the magnificent west doorway at Rochester Cathedral adjacent to the famous column figures. At Canterbury, onyx marble shafts also survive in the fine north doorway into the crypt from the north-west transept, and at the rear of the magnificent double doorway under the *vestiarium* (or Treasury).[20] Here four large shafts survive *in situ*, all of between 240 and 270 mm in diameter; these are the largest onyx marble shafts known to this author in Britain.

A pier with a quadruple capital and base closes the north end of the surviving arcade of the Infirmary Cloister. As we have already seen, this was planned to take four shafts of Purbeck marble, only three of which now survive; two 'barley sugar' shafts on the east, and a single plain shaft on the west, the latter set uncomfortably between a double base and capital. The quadruple base is 420 mm square, as is the abacus block. Above this pier there is a slight trace of the start of the arcade for the north cloister walk (Fig. 6).

This then is the only known surviving fragment *in situ* of a Romanesque cloister arcade in Britain. It is remarkable that it has not been accorded more recognition by earlier writers on Romanesque architecture.

THE ROMANESQUE GREAT CLOISTER

THE mid-12th-century Waterworks plan (Fig. 4) shows the Great Cloister with arcades on all four sides, and another (now destroyed) water-tower and laver to the south of the north cloister walk. All of the Great Cloister was rebuilt by Prior Thomas Chillenden at the very end of the 14th century and the beginning of the 15th century. No trace survives *in situ* of the earlier cloister arcades or stylobates, though some 12th-century work survives in the rear walls of the east and south cloister walks,[21] while the rear wall of the west walk (*cellarium*) dates from Lanfranc's time (*c.* 1080).

In plan the Great Cloister is almost a perfect square, with each of the four cloister arcades being about 100 ft long.[22] The exact dimensions of the Romanesque arcades, which anyway varied slightly in each walk, cannot be established without excavating beneath the present early-15th-century arcades. Is there, however, any other way that we can reconstruct, on paper, the earlier Romanesque arcades?

In the Canterbury Cathedral *lapidarium* are a series of very finely-carved Purbeck marble fragments which clearly come from an arcade with double capitals (Fig. 8).[23] There is a springing block, which also incorporates the abacus for the double capitals below, and one long voussoir block (along with a fragment of another) with chevron-flanked rolls on its underside, as well as along the faces. There is also a spurred double base, and various fragments of spiral shafts, all in Purbeck marble, which bear a marked resemblance to the *in situ* shafts in the infirmary cloister. Suprisingly, these important fragments have never been studied,[24] nor has their similarity to three more long Purbeck marble voussoir blocks been noticed. These three blocks are now built into the base of a spiral staircase that leads to the chamber over the so-called 'Prior Sellingate'.[25] They can just be seen on the south-east side of this gateway behind a bush, in the front garden of the Deanery.[26] Two of the blocks are badly damaged and weathered, but the third, despite being dirty and still subject to weathering, remains in fairly good condition. The three voussoir blocks are clearly not *in situ*, and must have been put here at some time after the Dissolution of the cathedral priory, perhaps in the early 19th century.[27]

Altogether, there are four nearly complete surviving voussoir blocks and a fragment of one more, and by lining up their plain outer faces one can see that they are meant to subtend an angle of 65 degrees at the centre. The one surviving springing block subtends on either side of an angle of 25 degrees, meaning that a voussoir block coupled with a springer would complete the right angle. There can be no doubt, there-fore, that each arch had two voussoir blocks sitting on the springing blocks, and the approximate internal diameter of these arches was 800 mm. This is similar in diameter to the surviving arches in the Infirmary Cloister arcade, though here only plain

Infirmary Cloister

Christchurch Priory

3 north

6

7

1 2 3 4 5 6 7

12 ins
30 cms
scale for details

2 east   4 east   7 east

A 101105

FIG. 6.   Architectural details of capitals and shafts at the north-east corner of the Infirmary
Cloister

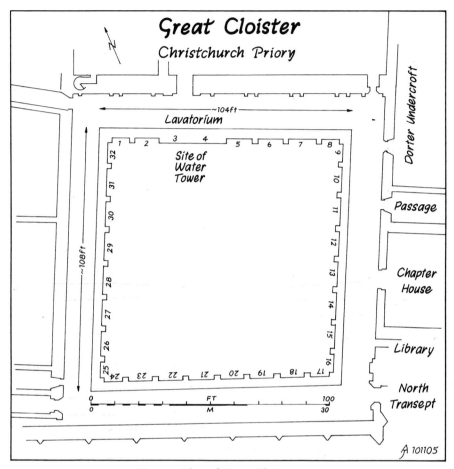

FIG. 7.   Plan of Great Cloister area

Caen stone blocks (usually eight voussoirs per arch) are used for the arcade. Below the arches, however, the Purbeck marble elements in the Infirmary Cloister are very similar to the surviving loose fragments.[28] The one surviving double base also has deeply undercut mouldings and trefoiled spurs. No complete loose shafts have survived, but there are several broken shaft fragments, all of which are cut with spiral patterns, again like the shafts in the Infirmary Cloister.

It is possible, then, that these more elaborate voussoir blocks were used for other arches in the Infirmary Cloister. However, as the voussoirs are so much more elaborate than the surviving Infirmary Cloister arches, on balance it seems more likely that they were used in the liturgically and processionally more important Great Cloister (Fig. 9).[29] As we have already seen, the Waterworks plan shows that by *c.* 1160 there were already arcades in the Great Cloister under sloping, lead-covered roofs,[30] and it seems most likely that some, if not all, of the arches themselves were made with these fine Purbeck marble voussoirs. Beneath the arches there was perhaps also an

99

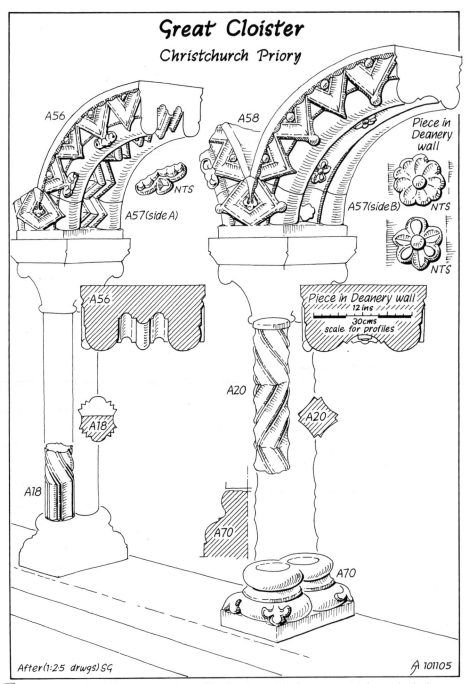

FIG. 8.   Partial reconstruction of Purbeck marble fragments in the cathedral
lapidarium, and in the Deanery garden (the numbers on the drawing are the numbers
in the *lapidarium* inventory)

FIG. 9.   Reconstruction drawings, by Jill Atherton, of the two cloister arcades at Canterbury cathedral priory

alternating system of single onyx marble, and double Purbeck marble piers mounted on a low stylobate.[31] If one accepts that the loose Purbeck voussoirs belong to the Great Cloister, the full width of each Romanesque bay would have been approximately 4 ft (around 1.22 m), as in the Infirmary Cloister. This would give rise to 24 or 25 arches in each of the four Great Cloister walks, assuming that each complete arcade was between 96 and 105 ft long. The later medieval cloister arcades are arranged at eight bays to the walk (Fig. 7), so, if the Perpendicular reconstruction reflected the earlier proportions, it is probable there were 24 arches to each arcade. Obviously, this is by no means a conclusive argument, as we do not know if the angles of the arcades were articulated by quadruple piers (as in the Infirmary Cloister), or by a completely different type of support, such as a solid pier. The north arcade also incorporated the water-tower and laver opposite the refectory door, while the east arcade may have had an opening into the garth near the chapter-house doorway, as in the later cloister. The water-tower was probably round like that in the Infirmary Cloister (it is shown thus in the Waterworks plan — Fig. 4), but was demolished in Prior Chillenden's time. It is likely that it was more elaborate than the main tower, but it too may have double capitals in its lower arcade. Some capitals and bases from a similar round tower were found at St Nicholas' Priory, Exeter (a cell of Battle Abbey) in 1913.[32] They too are also of Purbeck marble, and stylistically close to those in the Infirmary Cloister at Canterbury.

Finally, the style of the carving on the Purbeck marble voussoir-blocks compares with that used on Caen stone (e.g. in the use of chevron-flanked rolls) on other buildings erected in Prior Wibert's time (1140–67), that is the water-tower, *vestiarium*, *aula nova* and its monumental staircase), but it is exceptional for Purbeck marble to have been used and carved on such a scale at such an early date.[33] No other mid-12th-century building is known which employed Purbeck marble across arches, capitals, shafts and bases. The splendid Purbeck marble piers (with carved capitals, shaft rings and bases) in the rotunda of the Temple church in London, were, however, soon to follow,[34] and they in turn were followed by the building of the Galilee chapel at Durham Cathedral *c.* 1175.[35] Here only the shafts are of Purbeck marble, but the double waterleaf capitals and bases are stylistically similar to those in Canterbury.[36] The elaborate chevroned double arches at Durham also have some parallels with the Canterbury cloister work. It was at around this date, when the Durham Galilee Chapel was erected at the west end of the cathedral, that huge quantities of Purbeck marble began to be used in the magnificent rebuilding of the huge eastern arm of Canterbury Cathedral. Here Purbeck marble was being used for the first time in a fully-fledged French-inspired Gothic style, rather than with the Romanesque reminiscences of Durham, or the Lady Chapel at Glastonbury Abbey.

ACKNOWLEDGEMENTS

I am most grateful to Nigel Ramsay, Jill Atherton, Jeff West and Stuart Harrison for commenting most helpfully on earlier drafts of this paper, which was first written in 1995. The figures for this paper have been drawn by Jill Atherton (some of them based on earlier drawings by the late Miss Sheila Gibson and Rupert Austin), and I am most grateful to my wife Veronica, daughter Miranda and son Robert for word-processing the several versions of this paper, and to John McNeill who did much very useful editing.

NOTES

1. For all of these fragments see G. Zarnecki, J. Holt and T. Holland ed., *English Romanesque Art 1066–1200* (London 1984), 167–75. See also J. A. Franklin, 'The Romanesque cloister sculpture at Norwich Cathedral Priory', in F. H. Thompson ed., *Studies in Medieval Sculpture* (London 1983), 56–70.

2. At Fountains, it is really a 'narthex arcade'. At Rievaulx, there are fragments from both the Infirmary Cloister, and the main cloister. For recent drawings of these, see P. Fergusson and S. Harrison, *Rievaulx Abbey: Community, Architecture, Memory* (New Haven and London 1999), 116 and 137 (figs 81 and 100). See also the papers by S. Harrison and D. Robinson on Cistercian cloisters, and (for Bridlington) by S. Harrison on Augustinian cloisters in this volume.

3. For a fuller summary of this, see T. Tatton-Brown, 'Three Great Benedictine Houses in Kent: their buildings and topography', *Archaeologia Cantiana*, 100 (1984), 171–88.

4. See P. Fergusson, 'The Greencourt Gatehouse at the Cathedral Monastery of Christchurch, Canterbury', in *Das Bauwerk und die Stadt: aufsätz für Eduard Sekler*, ed. W. Böhm (Vienna 1994), 87–97; and P. Fergusson, 'Modernization and Mnemonics at Christchurch, Canterbury', *Journal of the Society of Architectural Historians*, 65 (2006), 50–67.

5. This gateway, which was later called the Middle Gate, was relocated 100 m further east in *c.* 1840.

6. For a detailed description of the plan (and a large-scale tracing of it), see R. Willis, 'The architectural history of the conventual buildings of the monastery of Christ Church in Canterbury,' *Archaeologia Cantiana*, VII (1868), 1–206 (esp. 158–83). For a recent account, see Klaus Grewe in *Die Wasserversorgung im Mittelalter* (1991), 229–36.

7. See F. Woodman, 'The Waterworks Drawings of the Eadwine Psalter', in M. Gibson, T. A. Heslop and R. W. Pfaff ed., *The Eadwine Psalter, Text, Image and Monastic Culture in Twelfth-Century Canterbury* (London 1992), 168–77.

8. On the Rochester cloister, see T. Tatton-Brown, 'The East Range of the Cloisters', *Friends of Rochester Cathedral: Report for 1988*, 4–8; idem, 'The Chapter House and Dormitory Façade at Rochester Cathedral Priory', *Friends of Rochester Cathedral: Report for 1993–94*, 20–28; J. McNeill, 'The East Cloister Range of Rochester Cathedral Priory', in *Medieval Art, Architecture and Archaeology at Rochester*, ed. T. Ayers and T. Tatton-Brown, *BAA Trans.*, XXVIII (Leeds 2006), 181–204.

9. Zarnecki et al., *English Romanesque*, 184–85. See also Y. Kusaba, 'Henry of Blois, Winchester, and the 12th century renaissance', in *Winchester Cathedral, Nine Hundred Years*, ed. J. Crook (Chichester 1993), 69–79. Blue Lias capitals, shafts, shaft rings and bases can also be seen *in situ* in the late-12th-century Lady Chapel at Glastonbury. See D. T. Donovan and P. D. Reid, 'The stone insets of Somerset Churches', *Proceedings of the Somerset Archaeological and Natural History Society*, 107 (1963), 60–71.

10. The chapel itself (along with the 1444 library above it) was demolished in the mid-17th century; Willis, 'Conventual Buildings', 65 and 73. See also figs 5 and 6.

11. ibid., 185.

12. ibid., 101 and fig. 16.

13. The imperial system is deliberately used here for overall measurements, as this seems a more rational way of giving these approximate dimensions. Feet and inches were no doubt used in the mid-12th century to set out the arcading. For the more exact smaller measurements, I have used the metric system.

14. One loose capital of similar date has, however, been found at the nearby Royal Abbey of Faversham. See Zarnecki et al., *English Romanesque*, 182, no. 146.

15. Marble, in its medieval (original) sense, was simply a stone that could be polished. Geologists now define marble as a metamorphosed limestone.

16. Other fragments of Tournai marble have been found in the cathedral precincts, as well as at Faversham Abbey. It is also worth noting that the much later tomb of Archbishop Meopham (d. 1333) is mostly of Tournai marble. See C. Wilson, 'The Medieval Monuments', in P. Collinson, N. Ramsay and M. Sparks ed., *A History of Canterbury Cathedral* (Oxford 1995), 466–67. This unique shrine-like structure may originally have been brought to the cathedral in the early 14th century to act as a new shrine for Anselm.

17. The doorway into the hall, however, has Wealden/Bethersden marble capitals, shafts and bases on its west side. This material, called by geologists 'Large Paludina limestone', is similar to Purbeck marble but contains much larger freshwater snail shells in it. It comes from the weald clays of Kent and Sussex. See B. C. Worssam and T. Tatton-Brown, 'Kentish Rag and other Kent building stones', *Archaeologia Cantiana*, 112 (1993), 107.

18. Some of the earlier literature wrongly calls these shafts jasper. It is also worth noting that this is onyx marble, which is different from onyx.

19. See T. Tatton-Brown, 'The Chapter House and Dormitory Façade at Rochester Cathedral Priory', *Friends of Rochester Cathedral Report for 1993/4*, 20–28. The date at which Tournai marble and onyx

marble were employed at Rochester post-dates a fire in 1137, and is almost certainly mid-12th century. Onyx marble is a hard crystalline variety of travertine. See B. Worssam, 'The Building Stones of Rochester Castle and Cathedral' , in *Medieval Art, Architecture and Archaeology at Rochester*, ed. T. Ayers and T. Tatton-Brown, *BAA Trans.*, XXVIII (Leeds 2006), 238–49.

20. The vaulted undercroft here acts as a monumental double gateway which led from the monks' cemetery to the infirmary. This is illustrated in D. Kahn, *Canterbury Cathedral and its Romanesque Sculpture* (London 1991), 107, and has most recently been treated by P. Fergusson in 'Modenization and Mnemonics' (54, fig. 4 for an illustration of the four onyx marble shafts on the west face of the *vestiarium*). The north entrance to the crypt is illustrated in Kahn, 116. Only one of the shafts survives here.

21. Some of the mid-12th-century refacing of the north wall of Lanfranc's nave survives above the vault in the south walk, while the mid-12th-century dormitory portal survives in a battered state in the east walk. There are also 12th-century doorways (infilled with later doorways) on either side of the chapter-house. The northern doorway leads to the mid-12th-century passage under the southern end of the dormitory, while the southern doorway probably led into the library (later Archbishop Warham's chantry chapel). Finally, part of the Norman tympanum above the processional doorway into the north transept of the cathedral survives above the vault (and above the roof).

22. It is, in fact, a parallelogram with the north walk slightly shifted to the east (see Fig. 7).

23. These are now kept at the Cathedral works department in Broad Oak Farm, Sturry. Unfortunately, their origin is unknown. For many years they were kept in the cathedral roofs. It is possible that they were fished out of the rubble infill in the later cloister arcades or vaults, while these were being restored in 1834, 1897, or in the major restoration carried out just after the Second World War (but not completed until the 1970s).

24. Kahn, *Canterbury Cathedral*, mentions them in passing at 135 and illustration 224.

25. The gateway into the Green Court was, in fact, built by Prior Thomas Chillenden (1391–1411), nearly a century earlier.

26. I am grateful to various Deans of Canterbury for allowing me access to examine them.

27. Possibly in the time of Dean Bagot (1827–45), whose wife, Lady Harriet, had a taste for 'ruins in landscape gardening'; Willis, 'Conventual Buildings', 122. See also M. Sparks, 'The Deanery, a House for Hospitality', *Canterbury Cathedral Chronicle*, 84 (1990), 18–25.

28. Unfortunately, no loose double capitals seem to have survived.

29. Rievaulx Abbey also had more elaborate arcades in the main cloister than those in the infirmary cloister. See Fergusson and Harrison, *Rievaulx*, 116, 137.

30. The waterworks plan, in its schematic way, shows nine arches in the south walk of the Great Cloister, and seven arches on the west side. The north and east walks are obscured by the Water Tower and other structures (Fig. 4).

31. The reuse of onyx marble shafts in Prior Henry of Eastry's late-13th-century chapter house façade suggests there may have been matching onyx marble columns in the cloister arcade.

32. See Harold Brakspear's note in *Proceedings of the Society of Antiquaries*, 2nd series, XVIII (1916), 245–50. The capitals taper towards one end, hence their suggested use in a circular building

33. See J. Blair, 'Purbeck Marble', in J. Blair and N. Ramsay ed., *English Medieval Industries* (1991), 48–49.

34. Currently dated by Dr Christopher Wilson to soon after 1161; pers. comm.

35. Given that the Purbeck marble columns were almost certainly first used in Bishop Hugh of Le Puiset's abortive attempt to build an eastern Lady Chapel, and were recycled into the western Galilee, it may be that they were cut and polished earlier than *c*. 1175.

36. R. Halsey, 'The Galilee Chapel', in *Medieval Art and Architecture at Durham Cathedral*, ed. N. Coldstream and P. Draper, *BAA Trans.*, III (Leeds 1980), 59–73. For this and a tentative reconstruction of the late-12th-century cloister arcade at Durham Cathedral, see S. Harrison, 'Observations on the Architecture of the Galilee Chapel', in *Anglo-Norman Durham*, ed. D. Rollason, M. Harvey and M. Prestwich, *1093–1193* (Woodbridge 1994), 213–34.

Benedictine and Augustinian Cloister Arcades of the Twelfth and Thirteenth Centuries in England, Wales and Scotland

STUART HARRISON

This paper and its companion on Cistercian cloister arcades brings together a number of reconstruction studies produced over many years of research. Each cloister is worthy of a paper in its own right, but lack of space here permits only a summary presentation in the form of a series of reconstruction drawings. A brief commentary is given on the form and detail of each reconstruction. Mention is also made of other surviving cloister fragments, but the paper is not exhaustive and some examples have doubtless escaped notice. The form of presentation adopted below does at least have the advantage of bringing together for the first time a selection of reconstructions that make clear the diversity of design and decoration of 12th- and 13th-century cloister arcades throughout England, Wales and Scotland.

FOLLOWING the Norman Conquest a considerable number of new monasteries were created — mostly Benedictine or Cluniac — and often dependencies of large houses in Normandy. Existing Benedictine houses saw the imposition of reforming Norman abbots as, for example, Paul of Caen at St Albans. The new Norman over-lords and their clergy set about rebuilding the fabric of the existing Saxon church to a Norman pattern. In addition to many new foundations in the south, the north of England, a virtual monastic desert in 1066, was soon recolonised by the black monks. Major houses were established at Durham, Selby, Whitby, York, Pontefract and Tynemouth, and these new houses were not slow to establish smaller cells dependent on the mother house. What we know of the early Benedictine cloister arcades is relatively sparse, and the evidence suggests that this is not entirely the fault of the Dissolution. Many English cathedrals were Benedictine and have retained evidence for their cloisters. These show that in virtually every case the early arcades were swept away in the 14th and 15th centuries to be replaced by traceried and vaulted walks. Evidence from non-cathedral Benedictine houses such as Tewkesbury Abbey and Sherborne Abbey clearly shows a similar process at work. Accidents of survival and lack of archaeological investigation have also worked to minimise the evidence of early remains.

In the early 12th century the introduction of new or reformed religious orders spread like a tidal wave throughout Europe. In the literature that of Cîteaux has tended to feature most prominently in the modern popular consciousness. However, in post-Conquest England the Cistercians were pre-empted by the arrival of the canons of the Order of St Augustine, whose foundations spread rapidly and continued

JBAA, vol. 159 (2006), 105–30
© British Archaeological Association 2006
DOI: 10.1179/174767006X147442

to do so after the arrival of the Cistercians.[1] Considering the large number of their houses very little evidence for the form of their early cloister arcades has survived. This paper gives a brief survey of the evidence known to the writer but no doubt other claustral fragments remain to be recognised or have eluded attention. The typical house of canons was modest in scale and generally smaller than that of their Cistercian or Benedictine contemporaries, though some, such as Waltham, Bridlington, Thornton and Guisborough eventually grew large enough to rival even the largest houses of monks. The Benedictine cathedral priories and abbeys were not alone in rebuilding their cloister arcades in the 14th and 15th centuries. As mentioned above a general trend towards greater comfort within all monastic houses in the later middle ages often saw the rebuilding of cloister walks with tracery windows that could be glazed to keep out the weather. Indeed, as we shall see, what we know of two 13th-century arcade designs results from their complete replacement in the 15th century, and the re-use of their materials within the foundations of their replacements. There have been no systematic surveys to quantify the surviving remains of early cloister arcades and this study of necessity focuses on the better and more complete known examples.[2]

The layout of a typical Augustinian house took its form from that first established by Benedictine monks, with the buildings laid out around a square cloister court. The cloister was the hub of any monastic house, and the four covered alleys acted as passageways ensuring communication between the various surrounding buildings. The alley closest to the church (ordinarily the north) formed a place of study and performance of the *lectio divina* or spiritual reading. It was usually fitted out with desks or carrels to facilitate the study process. The generally smaller size of the canons' houses meant that the full range of Benedictine features were often not represented in the overall plan. There could also be variations in the siting of some features. The warming house at Lanercost, for instance, was at the west end of the south range and often the laver was situated at the south end of the west cloister alley, instead of in the south alley. At Hexham and Kirkham the laver was at the south end of the west cloister alley. Similar variations could also occur in Benedictine houses such as Worcester Cathedral Priory where the laver is also in the west cloister alley.

BENEDICTINE CLOISTER ARCADES

IN basic cloister arcade design there is no obvious distinguishing structural feature that could be said to set apart the various orders of monks and canons. Rather it seems that it was the level of decoration, or lack of it, that might distinguish one order from another. Certain cloister designs also had one side of the arches more richly decorated than the other. Indications are that the more richly decorated side tended to face the alleys in Benedictine and Augustinian houses. What we know of early Benedictine cloister arcades in Britain is scant and the most extensive remains, from Henry I's foundation of Reading Abbey, show an arcade supported by a single row of columns — the arches richly decorated with various forms of chevron and beakhead (Fig. 1). It has recently proved possible to reconstruct the form of three differently decorated sections of the arcading.[3] Some of the surviving capitals are also richly carved, but are predominantly of trefoiled scallop design with pellet decoration. It is thought, however, that sculpted capitals may have been set to alternate with the trefoil design in each arcade. Overall it was a rich and impressive piece of architecture that reflected Reading's status as a royal foundation. The survival of other similar capitals,

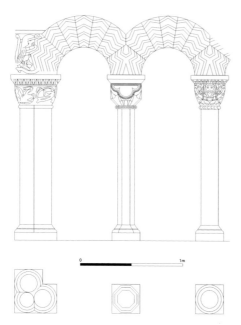

FIG. 1.   Reading Abbey reconstruction drawing of cloister arcade. This shows just one of three known designs for the Reading arcading

Stuart Harrison

some of which have been related stylistically to those at Reading, suggest very similar cloisters existed at other Benedictine houses. Historiated capitals and scallop designs from the Romanesque cloister at Edward the Confessor's Westminster Abbey also indicate a single columnar arcade.[4] Several capitals from Hyde Abbey in Winchester also come from a single columnar arcade and single and double capitals and bases from Winchester Cathedral may have come from the cloister.[5] Similar capitals have also survived at Norwich Cathedral and Lewes Priory. Fragments of paired marble capitals of exquisite design survive from the cloister arcade at Glastonbury Abbey attributed to Henry of Blois.[6] All these examples seem to indicate that the Benedictines may have favoured quite elaborate arcade designs based on the single column type with the paired capitals coming into fashion slightly later, possibly in the 1140s. Surviving French arcades show there could be variations in the single column type with arches grouped in bays between buttresses and a mix of single and paired columns (Fig. 2). Evidence of respond bases at Westminster led W. R. Lethaby to suggest that the Westminster arcade was grouped in bays with larger intermediate supports. The only section of a 12th-century cloister arcade to remain standing in England, a part of the infirmary cloister at Canterbury Cathedral, also employs a mix of single and paired supports, suggesting that something like the type of cloister arcades favoured in 12th-century French monasteries may also have appeared in Britain.

Though the examples cited above hint at considerable variation in the types of supports and arches found in cloisters, by the mid-12th century it is clear that arcades with paired columnar supports were the most popular design, and seem to have largely superseded the single column type, at least for the principal cloister arcades. The arcades of the mid-12th-century great cloister at Canterbury Cathedral seem to have been of this type, and to also have employed decorative designs in the column supports as well as using marbles to create a polychromatic effect. Bases and foliate

FIG. 2.   Cloister arcade with paired shafts
and intermediate four-shaft pier at the
Hôpital Saint-Jean at Angers

Stuart Harrison

FIG. 3.   Restored north alley arcade at
Paisley Abbey

Stuart Harrison

capitals of early Gothic type from St Mary's Abbey at York suggest a cloister arcade
with paired supports, one base of which is covered with graffiti with variants of the
name Richard repeatedly inscribed very carefully.[7] Presumably brother Richard had
become somewhat bored with life in the cloister and took to defacing the fabric
adjoining his carrel. More survives at Iona and Paisley Abbeys in Scotland where sections of much-restored paired-shaft arcades have been re-erected (Fig. 3). The evidence
on which they were re-erected is unrecorded and the reliability of the reconstructions
is questionable.[8] That said they do give the best impression in Britain of what a complete twin-shaft arcade would have looked like. The reconstruction at Paisley consists
of part of the east alley and all of the north. It has simple round-headed moulded
arches with keeled rolls and a band of small nailheads in the soffit hollows and a
mixture of capital types that include waterleaf and crockets. Like some of the capitals
from the cloister at Melrose Abbey, some of the Paisley supports have a round and
octagonal shaft paired together. As restored some of the polygonal shafts also taper
towards the capital from the bases and exhibit hollows worked on the facets. As
restored the arches are set in groups of five or six between solid squared intermediate
support piers, though most of the masonry looks to be new. At Iona there seems to be
more original work re-used in the reconstruction than at Paisley. It has pointed arches
with more complex mouldings and foliate capitals.[9] At Durham Cathedral Priory elements of a single column arcade of early Gothic profile have been identified together
with one springer from a very decorative Romanesque twin-shaft arcade.[10] Fragments
in the farmhouse garden at Marrick Priory, show close affinities with the early Gothic

cloister arcade from Cistercian Jervaulx, a few miles away in the next valley, and show that a relatively modest house of Benedictine nuns could boast a cloister arcade of sophisticated design with elegant moulded arches carried by paired shafts.

At St Dogmael's Priory, a Tironensian house near Cardigan, there are a number of elaborate stiffleaf capitals with circular abaci for a twin-shaft arcade with matching bases. Besides the twin capitals there is a four-shaft cluster, probably from a corner position. There are also plainer twin-shaft moulded capitals. Sections of the arcade show a filleted roll on one angle, with a plain soffit and a chamfer on the other angle (Fig. 4). A section of hoodmould is decorated with leaf designs cut in shallow relief. Some badly damaged base sections suggest that the arcade had intermediate coursed buttresses with four attached shafts somewhat similar to those known from Haverfordwest (see below). The remains include two base sections with tail sections for the buttresses and part of the coursed pier they supported together with a fragmentary capital. The capitals of plain design include one of dumb-bell type that in plan matches with the profile of the buttress base.

A precious survivor is the cloister arcade at West Malling a house of Benedictine nuns (Fig. 5). Recently the subject of a study and publication by Tim Tatton-Brown, this dates to the mid-13th-century with trefoiled arches supported by trefoiled coursed shafts.[11] The spandrels are decorated with *paterae* of varying designs set with stiff leaf decoration. As Tatton-Brown demonstrated in its present form the cloister arcade is a 15th-century reconstruction in which the 13th-century stonework was pulled down and re-erected with new buttressing to support a timber-framed upper floor. The design is very elegant with delicate mouldings and stiffleaf capitals.

From the 13th century there are also much-damaged springers from a twin-shaft arcade at Finchale Priory, a cell of Durham, but the most impressive evidence of a Benedictine cloister arcade of this period comes from Monk Bretton Priory in south Yorkshire (Figs 6 and 7). Discovered when the site was excavated in the 1920s, its full significance was overlooked until the late 1980s. The arcade was of the syncopated form now represented by the sole surviving example at Mont-St-Michel in Normandy, though documentary evidence suggest this design was also used at three other sites in Normandy.[12] It was supported by trefoil shafts with moulded bases and capitals of two different sizes. The arches were lancets moulded with filleted rolls towards the alley side and simply chamfered towards the garth. The two parallel arcades were linked by miniature rib vaults with chamfered ribs. This was a type of arcade that formed a striking and sophisticated alternative to the traditional twin-shaft design. When it was rediscovered and the design reconstructed, Monk Bretton was the only cloister arcade of its type known in the British Isles. Since that time another example has been recognised at Cistercian Tintern, and a similar trefoiled arcade used as a nave screen has been identified at Victorine Keynsham.[13] Other examples of the type perhaps yet remain to be discovered. The geographical and institutional distribution of the syncopated design prove that it was well known as a type, and its use may have been far more common than the archaeological record now indicates.

AUGUSTINIAN CLOISTER ARCADES

THOUGH the evidence of 12th- and 13th-century Benedictine cloister arcades may seem slight, that of the Augustinians is just as poorly represented in the archaeological record. A paired base and scallop capital, now in the south transept and re-erected on modern shafts is all that remains at Bristol Cathedral, though at nearby Keynsham

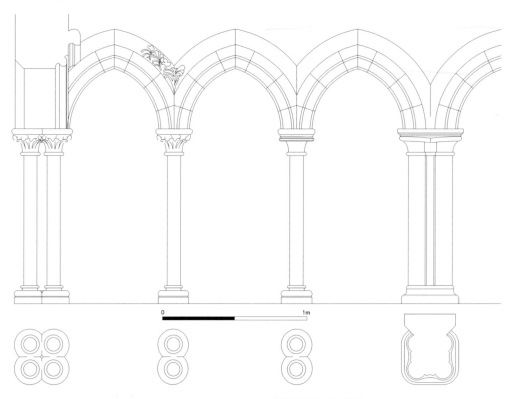

FIG. 4.   St Dogmael's Abbey: reconstruction drawing of the cloister arcade

Stuart Harrison

FIG. 5.   West Malling Abbey cloister arcade

Stuart Harrison

FIG. 6.   Monk Bretton Priory: arches of
cloister arcade assembled together at the
English Heritage Archaeology Store in
Helmsley

Stuart Harrison

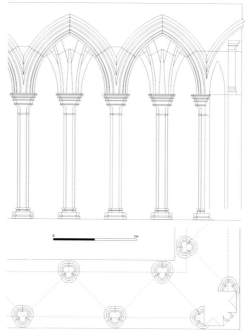

FIG. 7.   Monk Bretton Priory reconstruction
drawing of syncopated cloister arcade

Stuart Harrison

Abbey we are on surer ground. Stonework recently excavated shows a wonderful
selection of elaborately decorated twin scallop capitals of early Gothic date, together
with some sections of paired bases (Fig. 8). One foliate corner support capital indicates a typical arrangement of four shafts. Unfortunately none of the arcade voussoirs
or springers have survived but two spandrel panels have recently been identified.[14]
These show elaborate foliate and shell-like designs with considerable traces of white
limewash and red polychromy. Using these spandrel sections to indicate the scale
of the arches it is possible to give a basic outline of the arcade. Both Keynsham
and Bristol were Victorine houses, one of the side branches of the mainsteam
Augustinians.

At Drax Priory, some moulded capitals, base mouldings and springers for paired
shafts of 13th-century date survive in the garden of Abbey Farm. At Sharlston Hall,
near Nostell Priory, the rebuilding of a wall of the house because of mining settlement
in the 1980s revealed several springers from a relatively plain twin-shaft cloister arcade, presumably from Nostell. Newstead Abbey was converted to a house following
the Dissolution and retains its later cloister court with tracery windows. Displayed in
the east cloister alley are some springers and trefoil bases that most likely originated in
a single column cloister arcade.

The Bridlington Priory Cloister Arcade

THE cloister arcading at Bridlington Priory was unearthed in the 19th century,
probably from within the churchyard as the site of the north cloister alley has clearly

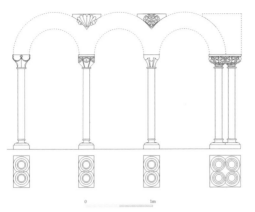

FIG. 8.   Keynsham Abbey: reconstruction drawing of the cloister arcade

Stuart Harrison

been lowered and now sits beneath that of the surrounding churchyard. The arcading was subsequently reassembled from a variety of fragments in 1912 as a memorial to Thomas Harland. A commemorative plaque states it had been discovered in 1877. In a short note in the Yorkshire Archaeological Journal John Bilson had pointed out the absurdity that assembled casts of the arcade were displayed in the Metropolitan Museum, New York, while the real thing was lying in a heap of bits at the priory. This seems to have prompted the reconstruction that we see today (Figs 9 and 10).[15] Bilson presumably had a hand in the reassembly of the arcading and it is notable that it was done with an economic use of new stone. Two separate arcades were re-erected, one of two arches and the other of three. They show that the cloister was a work of some magnificence and Bridlington can claim to have the most elaborate late-12th-century cloister arcading to have survived in England. The two-bay arcade consists of arches decorated with chevron clasping a small angle roll (Fig. 11). The rolls forming the chevrons carry a beading of small pellets along their edges. The triangles of the face chevrons are decorated with flower petals radiating from a circular boss. On the soffits there are similarly decorated diamond chevron panels. The rear face is less sumptuously decorated and lacks the pellets and the angle roll. This clearly indicates there was a directional aspect to the arcade decoration, and it seems likely that the more sumptuously treated side would have faced towards the alley and the plainer towards the garth; though without a corner springer it is impossible to be certain.

The second arcade of three bays carries a different design (Fig. 12). Here there is a large roll on the angle that has a hollow channel or gouging worked along its edge. This is flanked on the extrados with forward-facing chevrons. On the soffit there is a pair of keeled rolls with a single band of chevron between them and a triple band towards the outer edges. Like the first arcade, the three bays have been reassembled with round-headed arches but close inspection shows this to be incorrect. Each arch contains one voussoir that is narrower than the others and which is shaped to act as the apex stone in a pointed arch. The discrepancies in the taper on the joint faces have been made good with mortar. That these pieces originally came from a pointed arch is confirmed by the asymmetrical form of the chevrons on the front face. Closer inspection shows that some voussoirs differ in the detailing of the front chevrons, suggesting slight variations in the decorative scheme. As with the first arcade there is a notable

FIG. 10.   Bridlington Priory: reconstructed arcade of three bays. The arches have been erected back to front so this view shows the slightly plainer rear face. They were also incorrectly re-erected as round arches (see Fig. 12)

Stuart Harrison

FIG. 9.   Bridlington Priory: reconstructed arcade of two bays

Stuart Harrison

difference in the decoration of the front and back, only here what is now the rear of the arcade is the most elaborate with bolder front chevrons. This shows that what now appears to be the front of the arcade is actually the back, and that it was rebuilt in this way to privilege the face that is the least damaged.

Besides the re-erected sections of arcade there are numerous loose capitals, voussoirs and sections of hoodmoulding. Amongst the voussoirs are parts of a third type of arcade (Fig. 13). This has a pair of large rolls on the soffit separated in the centre by chevron that is decorated with bands of nailhead and which has a boss terminal. The front face has a curving roll moulding forming small arches that have a foliate terminal at the base and a trefoil terminal at the apex. The edge of each large front roll has a decorative band of circular pellets flanking a hollow. The rear face is plainer with an angle hollow that is studded with two widely spaced dogtooth ornaments on each voussoir. In the absence of further evidence we cannot tell if the arches were round-headed or pointed, though a round-headed format has been used in the reconstruction. Two sizes of voussoir have been identified with identical decoration. Unfortunately no springer has survived so it is difficult to be sure whether there was any variation in the number of voussoirs in each arch or a mix of sizes.

The two re-erected arcades boast sumptuously decorated hoodmoulds. The most complete examples have deeply undercut vine-trail decoration and the spandrels are embellished with small head stops. Only one survives complete and shows a chubby face with hair in stylised curls. Three others retain only the top of each head with variations in the hair design. Close inspection of the arches shows that there are variations in the hoodmould design. In the three-bay arcade the central arch has a section of hoodmould with a bolder and less undercut design of vine trail. At the right hand end of this arcade and the left hand end of the other the spandrel springers show a third design with undercut acanthus, though this is badly broken and only partially shows the full design. Amongst the loose stones a single fragment of a fourth design is

FIG. 11 (*above left*). Bridlington Priory: reconstruction drawing of chevron-decorated arcade

Stuart Harrison

FIG. 12 (*above*). Bridlington Priory: reconstruction drawing of early Gothic pointed arcade

Stuart Harrison

FIG. 13 (*left*). Bridlington Priory: reconstruction drawing of third arcade

Stuart Harrison

carved with a frieze of undercut leaves that is markedly different from any of the other designs. The survival of this one hoodmould might indicate that there was a fourth lost arcade design.

The arcading was supported on paired bases, shafts and capitals. Only three bases have survived and these all provided for octagonal shafts. Such shafts were used throughout the reconstructed arcades and the three-bay arcade incorporates a couple of sections of original shafting. Malcolm Thurlby, however, pointed out that the surviving capitals, including some used in the reconstruction have circular neckings for round shafts.[16] It seems most likely therefore that the shafts were alternately octagonal and cylindrical. The three surviving bases are slightly different from each other. One has quadrant bosses on the corners with traces of foliate decoration and another spurs on the corners and middle sections. The third type has no spurs or bosses but has a chamfered tiered sub base.

The capitals show the greatest variety of decoration, ranging from plain scallops to intricate linenfold designs with heavy use of pellets. There are several variations on this type and two capitals have small figures carved in the centre of the long side. One of the figures on a linenfold capital has a worn head that in outline is similar to those from the hoodmould stops; suggesting that they were carved by the same hand. Some examples seem to reflect the directional decoration of the arches and have one end that is much plainer. Besides the complex scallop designs there are also vigorously carved Gothic foliate types of capital with considerable use of palmettes. On one example each face is of different design.

Jill Franklin has explored the possible locations of the arcading within the priory buildings, and concluded that it must have originated in the main cloister.[17] Malcolm Thurlby has extensively reviewed the decorative forms and showed links with several buildings in the region. Most notably both Franklin and Thurlby draw comparisons with the architecture of the lost 12th-century choir of York Minster. Since these papers were published more detailed work has been done on the surviving elements of the York choir which reveals an even closer relationship than Franklin and Thurlby were able to demonstrate. They linked the quadrant bosses on the bases and some of the chevron types with those in the York crypt. The type of chevrons on the two-bay arcade occurred in the York choir and the French-inspired mouldings on the three-bay arcade can also be paralleled in the main arcades of the choir. The details suggest that the arcades were begun with round-headed arches, and it seems likely that there was a different design in each alley, each with its own hoodmould. The best represented hoodmould — deeply undercut vine trails with spandrel headstops — seems to have been used on a round-headed arcade because of the length of the voussoirs. It cannot therefore have been used on the three-bay arcade which employed pointed arches. It also seems clear that the lavish scallop and linenfold capitals belong with the round-headed arches. A clear separation in design exists with the three-bay arcade and its Gothic mouldings and pointed arches. It seems most likely that the French-inspired leaf capitals with their palmette designs belong with this arcade. If the hypothetical distribution of elements outlined above is correct, it suggests that as the building of the Bridlington cloister progressed the masons kept pace with work on the York choir, modifying the designs in the process. The initial work at York, in the crypt, was almost wholly late Romanesque in style, but in the choir Romanesque decorative elements were mixed with the latest French-inspired Gothic designs. Seen in this light the Bridlington arcades precisely mirror the developments at York. Trondheim Cathedral is another building whose design has also been closely linked to that of the York choir, and it is notable that the profile of the three-bay arcade at Bridlington shows close affinities with the main arch of the Trondheim chapter house.[18] Thurlby suggested a start date for the cloister arcades while Robert the Scribe was prior (1147–54/9).[19] York is unlikely to have been started before 1154 when Roger Pont l'Eveque became archbishop. The crypt is likely to have been finished by 1166 and the choir was almost certainly complete by 1175. Bridlington is clearly a York derivative and is therefore unlikely to have been started until well after York was underway. This suggests the Bridlington cloister was begun sometime after 1154 and, considering the use of dogtooth in one of the arcades, completion sometime after the York choir. It would not be unreasonable to suggest a period between 1160 and 1180 for its construction.

The Haughmond Abbey Arcade

AT Haughmond Abbey recent excavations revealed parts of a twin-shaft cloister arcade that was supported by early Gothic leaf capitals and carried trefoil arches (Fig. 16).[20] The arches had a plain soffit with small chamfers on the angle, but was surmounted by an internal hoodmould with a roll set in hollows. Above this was an upper stringcourse with dogtooth decoration. Remarkably, several fragments of statuary were also recovered and in one case it proved possible to show that figurative sculpture was carved on a corner springer because segments of the hoodmould survive, attached to the sides of the block. The damaged figure shows the Virgin and Child seated on a throne (Fig. 15). The discovery of the pieces suggested the arcade had been demolished and the resulting fragments were then re-used in the later work. Though only a few fragmentary redressed pieces of the capitals survived the evidence pointes to a rather elegantly designed cloister (Fig. 14). Other fragmentary pieces of sculpture suggest that the statue of the Virgin and Child was not the only statuary employed; possibly the spandrels also had decorative sculpture. In this respect it is an important survival for it demonstrates, like Bridlington, the Augustinian use of sculpture in cloister arcading in the late 12th century.

The Norton Priory Cloister Arcade

THE excavations at Norton Priory showed that the 13th-century cloister arcade, like that at Haughmond, was demolished and replaced by a more substantial design that featured buttressed bays with tracery windows.[21] Little of this later cloister survived the post-Dissolution conversion of the site to a house. In contrast, considerable fragments of the earlier cloister had been re-used in its foundations from which they were recovered by excavation. Several bays of the arcade have been re-erected in the Norton Priory Museum and these, together with numerous other fragments, have been the subjects of a recent reassessment (Fig. 17). The 13th-century arcade featured elegant trefoiled arches supported on groups of three shafts with moulded bases and stiffleaf capitals. The main arches were pointed with rebates into which were set the trefoiled sub arches. The springers of the arcade were decorated with stiff leaf and sculpture as were the spandrels of the trefoils. The re-erected arcade shows trefoiled arches with plain-ended cusps, but the collection of loose stone contains fragmentary cusp ends with foliate terminals showing a variation in the design. The small elongated triangular spandrels of the trefoiled inserts run to a mixture of foliate and figure sculpture. The label stops of the arcade hoodmoulds protrude prominently and include sculpture and stiff leaf motifs. Fragmentary panels show that the main arcade spandrels were decorated with figurative sculpture. The sculptural elements include numerous heads, many with a distinctive widow's-peak hairline (Figs 18 and 19). Two examples show canons with tonsures and cowls. Many of these heads must have been set into the foliage of the capitals as a surviving example shows. The capital foliage is

FIG. 14.   Haughmond Abbey: base and capital fragments from the cloister arcade

Stuart Harrison

FIG. 15.   Haughmond Abbey: statue of Virgin and Child from angle of cloister arcade

Stuart Harrison

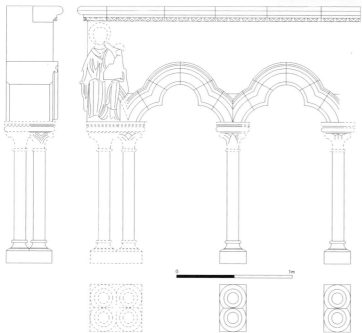

FIG. 16.   Haughmond: Abbey reconstruction drawing of cloister arcade after J. Blair, P. Lankester and J. West

FIG. 17.   Norton Priory: reconstructed arcading displayed in the Norton Priory Museum

Stuart Harrison

FIG. 19.   Norton Priory: carved head hoodmould stop

Stuart Harrison

FIG. 18.   Norton Priory: carved head set in capital

Stuart Harrison

formed of tight balls of stiff leaf that protrude off the main core. Apart from the head sculpture there are examples of fabulous beasts, and what Patrick Greene identified as an otter on one of the label stops. Also found in the foundations of the later cloister arcade was the lower part of a seated effigy, thought by Greene to be that of Christ (Fig. 21). The figure has the part of a rod or staff set between the legs and long folds of fabric spreading down the legs. In the left hand there is a book with a clasp on the cover. An additional piece of the figure has recently been identified forming part of the right side and this seems to show that the right arm was raised, possibly to grasp the staff (Fig. 16). Two other important fragments of the arcade have also recently been identified; a trefoiled base with a squared block at the rear that indicates the arcade was buttressed at regular intervals, and part of the coping of the stylobate built into the later cloister. This has a chamfer on one edge and a roll moulding on the other. The picture that emerges is of a richly decorated piece of architecture covered in sculpture and stiff leaf decoration (Fig. 20). Unfortunately, too few pieces remain to establish if the sculpture was simply decorative or if there was a thematic scheme or cycle set within it.

The Haverfordwest Priory Cloister Arcade

LIKE the arcade from Norton Priory, that at Haverfordwest Priory was also discovered built into the footings of its 15th-century successor.[22] As at Norton this later cloister arcade was almost completely destroyed but enough remained to show it was divided by buttresses into formal bays with traceried windows. The buttresses spanned a drainage channel that formed a water feature in the cloister garth. To support the buttresses the drainage channel was covered by lintels made up of sections of the arches from the earlier 13th-century arcade. These were large stones, moulded on the angles, two of which made up a single pointed arch (Fig. 22). The arches were surmounted by a moulded hood that intersected with a horizontal moulded string-course. The arches were supported on an unusual arrangement of shafts and capitals. As at Norton Priory there were three separate shafts in a cluster, but at Haverfordwest each had its own moulded base. The moulded capitals were similarly treated, there being three separate capitals in each three-shaft group. Remarkably both the bases and capitals had been turned on a lathe and each had a central hole for mounting on the lathe pole. This facilitated the production of finer and more intricate mouldings than could have been achieved using conventional methods for cutting masonry. Above each three-capital group was a single square abacus stone that was decorated with a mixture of foliage and sculpture. In each case these sculptural bands extended along half of each side face and along the whole of the front face; the rest was simply moulded. They include remarkable scenes with fish, leeks, clouds and figures (Figs 23–26). Some figures are so damaged and so constrained by the narrowness of the abacus that it is difficult to understand what they depict. Fortunately a few are better preserved, and one notable example shows a hound pursued by a hare that has seized the hound by the rear paw (Fig. 23). Another features a rabbit-like creature with a lance and pennant. One damaged panel may show a fox dressed in clerical garb preaching.

The arcade stood on a stylobate with a capping that was chamfered at each side (Fig. 28). Other stones show that there were regular buttressed sections with a square coursed pier with a shaft worked on each corner. The capitals were moulded with an integral abacus carved with various sculptural motifs. One example has a pair of goat-like animals with only front legs and wings with tapering bodies ending in curling tails (Fig. 26). Another shows a *sheela-na-gig*, with the subject seen from the rear, bent over so the face peers backwards between the legs (Fig. 27). The broad skirt is thrown upwards to expose the bare buttocks. At the rear of each pier there was a shallow projecting buttress with a sloping capping. The label stops of the hoodmoulds were decorated with sculpture with the head of a bishop amongst the surviving pieces and

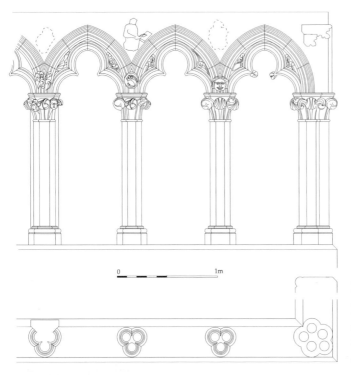

Fig. 20.   Norton Priory: reconstruction drawing of the cloister arcading showing corner arrangement and intermediate buttress

Stuart Harrison

Fig. 21.   Lower half of a statue thought to be a seated figure of Christ found in the cloister at Norton Priory showing additional fragment of right side of statue recently recognised

Stuart Harrison

Fig. 22.   Haverfordwest Priory: assembled
cloister arch
Stuart Harrison

a seated tonsured figure with a book and a key held in the raised right hand; possibly St Peter. Another fragmentary piece shows part of the ear from an animal carving. This highly decorated arcade also made use of contrasting stones to create a polychromatic effect (Fig. 28). The triple shafts, bases, capitals, abaci and arcade arches are of purple Caerbwdy stone, which came from quarries near St Davids. The hoodmoulds and buttressed pier sections and their bases and capitals were made from creamy-brown sandstone. The whole ensemble must have been most impressive, covered, as it was, in sculpture and with contrasting stones. Such architectural polychromy, employing contrasting stones, can be seen in the nearby cathedral and bishop's palace at St Davids and is also known from excavation to have been employed on the crossing arches at Strata Florida Abbey.

Finally, it is worth noting that Haverfordwest was a fairly small Augustinian house; to the extent that much of its architectural detail is of reduced scale. Yet it had a cloister arcade of considerable magnificence. Unfortunately, as at Norton, the sample of surviving sculpture is too small to determine whether there may have been a themed sculptural cycle. The scenes showing various mythical animals, and particularly the hare chasing the hound, may indicate a cycle of allegorical scenes in which the order of the world is turned topsy-turvy. The possible figure of St Peter suggests more seriously religious images, though these seem to have been mixed with more abstract ones.

The Lanercost Priory Cloister Arcade

ONLY a few pieces of arcading can be tentatively identified with the cloister arcade at Lanercost Priory.[23] These include a long rectangular base block with badly damaged upper sections, meaning the precise form of the pier or piers it supported cannot be established. There is also a springer block of unusual design with rolls and filleted roll mouldings on the main decorative side but with simpler quadrant rolls on the plainer side. At the springing is a decorative foliate sprig similar to those on the arches of the nave clerestory. Unfortunately the block is incomplete through re-use and the joint beds are lost. Linked to this springer may be a hoodmould for a pointed arch with a filleted roll on the angle banded at the edge with nailhead. In the spandrel of the hoodmould springer is the headless figure of a woman holding a prayer book. The pieces can be dated stylistically to the second half of the 13th century. If the

FIG. 23. Haverfordwest Priory: detail of abacus showing hare chasing hound

FIG. 24. Haverfordwest Priory: detail of abacus showing leeks and clouds

FIG. 25. Haverfordwest Priory: detail of abacus showing clouds, fish and tonsured head

FIG. 26. Haverfordwest Priory: detail of abacus from a coursed buttress pier showing goat-like creatures with wings, forelegs and tapering bodies

All figures Stuart Harrison

FIG. 27. Haverfordwest Priory: detail of capital from a coursed buttress pier showing *sheela-na-gig* on the abacus

Stuart Harrison

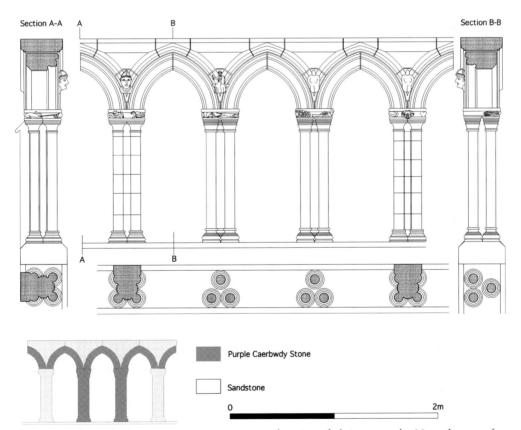

Purple Caerbwdy Stone

Sandstone

FIG. 28. Haverfordwest Priory: reconstruction drawing of cloister arcade. Note the use of different stone to create a polychromatic effect

Stuart Harrison

FIG. 29. Easby Abbey: single arch of cloister arcade assembled together at the English Heritage Archaeology Store in Helmsley
Stuart Harrison

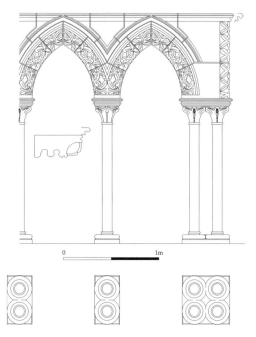

FIG. 30. Easby Abbey: reconstruction drawing of cloister arcade
Stuart Harrison

cloister connection is correct then it suggests a structure of unusual design and some magnificence in terms of sculptural decoration.

PREMONSTRATENSIAN CLOISTER ARCADES

THE branch of canons of the Order of Premontré, known as the Premonstratensians, were to the Augustinian Order what the Cistercians were to the Benedictine. Indeed, they took much of their inspiration from the Cistercians to whom they entrusted the visitation of their houses. They also wore a similar white habit in contrast to the Augustinian black and adopted a more austere lifestyle than regular Augustinian canons, introducing an element of manual labour into the daily routine. The remains of two Premonstratensian cloister arcades survive in the north of England; Easby and Egglestone.

The Easby Abbey Cloister Arcade

NOT a great deal remains from the cloister arcading at Easby Abbey, but what there is enables the reconstruction of the basic design (Fig. 30).[24] The arcade dates to the late 12th or early 13th century, and was supported on the usual twin shafts. A corner springer survives that must have been supported on a cluster of four shafts; a common arrangement in cloister arcading. The arches were decorated with a wide band of foliage, facing towards the alleys (Fig. 29). This was cut in simple relief on the corner springer but deeply undercut over a broad hollow on the voussoirs. Unfortunately, on the surviving pieces most of the foliage has been broken away, leaving just the stubs of the leaves and exposing the broad hollow below. On the right angle of the corner springer there is a vertical band of large dogtooth ornament. There was a moulded hood with unusual dog-leg jointing in the spandrels to lock the stones together and above a horizontal stringcourse. The surviving capitals have turned back palmettes with a small berry cluster between them set below a moulded abacus that includes a roll with fillet. Palmettes also featured in the foliage of the voussoirs. The capitals have lost their lower section so we cannot tell the form of the supporting shafts, round or octagonal. This arcade with its deeply undercut foliage must have been an impressive design.

The Egglestone Abbey Cloister Arcade

THIS was a mid-13th-century cloister arcade with trefoiled moulded arches that deploy three rolls with fillets separated by wide and deep hollows (Fig. 31). The shafts were paired with moulded bases and capitals (Fig. 32), and one four-shaft base shows that it had the typical corner arrangement. A corner springer has an engaged round shaft on the corner angle supported by a small moulded base. The mouldings of the arches emerged from a plain block at the springing. There was a prominent hood-mould that, as at Easby, merges with a horizontal upper stringcourse. The same dog-leg jointing of the spandrel stones that appears at Easby was also used at Egglestone, an arrangement also found on a trefoil-arched cloister arcade at Cistercian Roche Abbey (see the paper on Cistercian cloisters in this volume). Considerable quantities of fragments from the Egglestone arcade survive and exhibit some interesting variations (Fig. 33). These include elements of a doorway through the arcade in which a springer set between a pair of arches was supported by a timber beam. The springer block has mouldings specially worked to accommodate its position and a cut away section for the beam on which it rested. Fragments of two of these springers survive. The timber lintel would have looked unusual but it was a very simple way of creating a doorway through the arcade. The doorway jamb springer has also survived and is cut away to accommodate the end of the timber beam.

An alternative corner arrangement to the four-shaft design has also survived. This shows a corner that was evidently built of solid coursed masonry with paired bases and capitals for a respond on one side. There is also the end respond springer block that the capital supported with a small angle shaft with moulded base on the corner. This is exactly like the four-shaft springer that has survived. The double respond base and capital have seatings for half-round shafts that were clearly of coursed masonry rather than detached design. The return corner is without an arcade springing and must have acted as a filler piece. Sockets cut into double bases suggest some later form of glazing inserted into some of the arches. Egglestone's was an elegant arcade design apparently devoid of sculpture or foliate decoration. This may reflect Cistercian influence on the architecture of the Order, in which respect Egglestone's similarity to the 13th-century infirmary cloister arcade from Fountains Abbey is worth noting.

The above examples form the main cloister arcades that can be reconstructed with some confidence. Other sites run to very much more fragmentary remains, such as the pair of twin scallop capitals from the Gilbertine priory church of Old Malton. Paired bases and capitals of foliate design and late-12th-century date were also recovered in excavations at the site of the Gilbertine priory of St Andrew in York.[25] No doubt with further excavation and investigation more examples will be discovered or recognised.

FIG. 31.   Egglestone Abbey: cloister arcade reassembled in the English Heritage Archaeology Store at Helmsley

Stuart Harrison

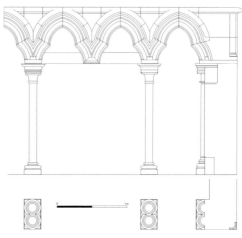

FIG. 33.   Egglestone Abbey: reconstruction drawing of cloister arcade showing alternative corner respond and doorway with timber lintel supporting arches

Stuart Harrison

FIG. 32.   Egglestone Abbey: reconstruction drawing of cloister arcade

Stuart Harrison

126

For instance recent work at Augustinian Felley Priory by Jenny Alexander has identified some fragments that may have formed part of the cloister arcade. What distinguishes the Augustinian and Benedictine arcades from their Cistercian cousins appears to be a lavish use of foliage and sculptural decoration, with the more richly-decorated face set towards the cloister alley. As one might expect Cistercian arcades tend to eschew sculptural elements, relying instead on simple mouldings with relatively plain scallop, leaf, crocket or chalice capitals. The more decorative side faced towards the cloister garth. Even the most elaborate 12th-century Cistercian cloister arcade, Fountains Abbey, had relatively modest waterleaf capitals that were combined with complex mouldings to the trefoiled arches and the use of Nidderdale marble for bases, shafts and capitals to produce a chromatic contrast with the limewashed arches (see the paper in this journal dealing with Cistercian cloister arcades).

On present evidence it seems that the cloisters of the Benedictines and Augustinians in England were timber roofed and it seems that vaulting was avoided before the advent of tracery in the later 13th century. This seems peculiar to the British Isles, for surviving cloisters elsewhere in Europe indicate vaulting was relatively widespread in the 12th century. The archaeological record is also deficient when it comes to the details of cloister layouts, and the whereabouts of features such as doorways, porches and fountain houses. Even at sites that were excavated in the 20th century, there is usually little sign of the arcade walls, and the site is simply marked by modern representational walling. One often wonders on what archaeological basis this representational marking was carried out. At Bridlington we have no record of the layout of the cloister court and at Norton and Haverfordwest the 13th-century arrangements were largely destroyed in the later remodellings. Some houses did feature what must have been architecturally impressive structures, such as Cluniac Much Wenlock Priory where there are remains of a fountain house decorated with figurative panels, though we are lacking any information about the type of cloister arcade to which it was attached.[26] Evidence for another fountain house comes from St Nicholas Priory at Exeter where the paired capitals and bases for its arcades survive but again nothing of the cloister arcade itself.[27] At Durham the cloister fountain house or washing place was described in the Rites of Durham.[28] The circular marble basin of the 15th-century laver still lies in the cloister garth but the fountain house which contained it has been totally destroyed. Excavation of its site showed evidence for the 15th-century structure and traces of an earlier building. These few examples serve to highlight what little we know of the detailed arrangements of British cloister arcades and the few remains of the arcades that have survived show a diversity of decorative forms. The indications are that the earliest arcades had single shafts that were in turn superseded by the twin-shaft design. This seems to have predominated throughout the second half of the 12th century and beyond. In the 13th century the triple-shaft cluster with five shafts at the corners was introduced. This was a new type of design that included the use of inset cusping to the main arches to create a trefoiled effect. The high water mark of the traditional arcade came in the 13th century with the introduction of the syncopated design, an elaborate architectural form of considerable visual complexity. Into this basic mix of architectural designs must be added polychromy, most obviously through the use of contrasting marbles and coloured stones. The use of paint was also of considerable importance but as a perishable medium has left little trace in the archaeological record.

In terms of roofing in Britain we have no survivals from the 12th or 13th centuries and often all that remains are the corbels and sockets for their timbers against the

FIG. 34. Hôpital Saint-Jean at Angers showing roof of cloister walk

Stuart Harrison

surrounding buildings. In its simplest form a cloister roof could be constructed with a series of common rafters for a single sloping roof against the surrounding buildings. Where evidence survives corbels are often trenched to support beams set against the surrounding walls. These beams in turn served to support the cloister roof rafters pegged or trenched into a wallplate resting on top of the arcade. Often a row of angled sockets set below the corbels show where struts to brace the rafters were placed, and these give an indication of the rafter spacing. Where timber cloister roofs have survived in Europe, such as at the hospital of St John at Angers, the carpentry shows more sophisticated treatment where the strut is combined with a curved under rafter to form a segmental arch across the alley (Fig. 34). This arrangement forms a curved collar to brace the roof and makes for a more solid construction that was less likely to push the arcade outwards. The curved segmental arch that was formed by this arrangement of timbers would allow under-boarding or lathe and plastering to form a decorative ceiling. Evidence in the form of sockets for such roofs and ceilings survives in part at Cistercian Rievaulx, and in more complete form at Fountains Abbey. The ceilings of the cloister at Mont-St-Michel are also of this type but in their present form most probably date from the 19th-century restoration by the architect Corroyer. Towards the garth most roofs were probably designed to oversail the arcade in order to throw the rainwater clear. This is the arrangement of the roof at St-Jean in Angers where it is also worth noting that the paired shafts of the arcade are in five bay groups with a larger coursed four-shaft pier between them to stiffen the arcading.

CONCLUSION

THIS brief review of the main evidence for Benedictine and Augustinian cloister arcades of the 12th and 13th centuries shows the relative paucity of the known remains. At many sites, what survives of the cloister amounts to no more than a few battered fragments — often only a few capitals and bases. At very few sites has enough been recovered to reconstruct the form of the arcades with some confidence. Only West Malling and Canterbury Cathedral retain original standing medieval arcades and of these two only that at Canterbury is in its original position. As indicated at the start of this paper numerous arcades built during the 12th and 13th centuries must have been destroyed in later reconstructions. Those that remained at the Dissolution of the monasteries cannot have survived long after. They were simply too fragile to have withstood the ravages of the weather without the protection of a roof. They must also have presented choice targets and easy pickings for those pillaging a monastic site for its stone. In this respect it is worth noting that a stack of cloister capitals was discovered at Rievaulx abbey during the clearance of the site in the 1920s. They were found in the west range, presumably awaiting a sale that never materialised as the new owner tried to maximise his profit from his purchase of the site.

ACKNOWLEDGEMENTS

The research on which this paper is based, as well as that of its Cistercian counterpart, was conducted over many years during which time it has been my good fortune to have been helped by many people. At Reading I was pleased to be invited to work with Ron Baxter. Those who actively participated in helping measure and research some of the material include Paul Barker, Glyn Coppack, Richard Stone and James Goodband. I have also benefited from information and discussion with many people including Malcolm Thurlby, Peter Fergusson, Jenny Alexander, Barbara Lowe, John Weaver, David Sherlock, Tim Tatton Brown, Richard Fawcett, David Robinson, Rick Turner, the late Ann Hamlin, Phillip Lankester, Barbara Harbottle, Andrew Morrison, Richard Morris, David Walsh, Roger Stalley and many others. I must also thank the staff of English Heritage and Cadw for their help on site moving and sorting material.

NOTES

1. D. Robinson, The Geography of Augustinian Settlement, *British Archaeological Reports British series 80*, I and II (1980).
2. Lawrence Keen and Peter Ellis ed., *Sherborne Abbey and School Excavations 1972–76 and 1990* (Dorchester 2005), 67–69 discusses a four-shaft cloister capital and related arches from Sherborne Abbey (now in Sherborne Museum), which may have come from the 12th-century cloister arcade, and also alludes to evidence for cloister capitals or bases at Ivychurch Priory, Abbotsbury, Christchurch Priory, Shaftsbury Abbey, Winchester Cathedral, St Mary de Castro (Leicester), Norwich Cathedral, St Augustine's at Bristol, Wells Cathedral. Prittlewell Priory, Glastonbury Abbey, Battle Abbey, Lewes Priory. To this list can be added several cloister type bases of four-shaft design that can be seen in Kendal parish church (Cumbria).
3. R. Baxter and S. Harrison, 'The Decoration of the Cloister at Reading Abbey', in *Windsor: Medieval Archaeology, Art and Architecture of the Thames Valley*, ed. L. Keen and E. Scarff, *BAA Trans.*, XXV (Leeds 2002), 302–12.
4. W. R. Lethaby, *Westminster Abbey re-examined* (London 1925), 32–37.
5. J. Hardacre, *Winchester Cathedral Triforium Gallery Catalogue* (Winchester 1989), 8–11.

6. G. Zarnecki, R. Gem and C. Brooke, *English Romanesque Art 1066–1200* (London 1984), discusses most of the capitals mentioned above, many of which were exhibited at the Hayward Gallery Romanesque Art Exhibition in 1984.

7. *An Inventory of the Historical Monuments in the City of York*, IV RCHME (London 1975), 22, pls 29d and e. On Canterbury, see the article by Tim Tatton-Brown elsewhere in this volume.

8. Richard Fawcett is of the opinion that much of what we see at Paisley, such as the capitals, was copied from detail surviving elsewhere at the abbey, like the doorway capitals. Personal communication.

9. R. Fawcett, *Scottish Abbeys and Priories* (London 1994), 108. Fawcett also mentions twin-shaft fragments found at Cambuskenneth, Dumfermline, Melrose and Scone. He also briefly discusses later Scottish types at Inchcolm, Oronsay and the reconstructed arcade at Glenluce.

10. S. A. Harrison, 'Observations on the Architecture of the Galilee Chapel', in *Anglo-Norman Durham*, ed. D. Rollason, M. Harvey and M. Prestwich (Woodbridge 1994), 233–34.

11. T. Tatton-Brown, 'The Buildings of West Malling Abbey', *Architectural History*, 44 (2001), 179–94.

12. M. Déceneux, *Mont-St-Michel Stone by Stone* (Rennes 1996), 53–54.

13. S. Harrison, ' A Syncopated Arcade from Keynsham Abbey', in *'Almost the Richest City', Bristol in the Middle Ages*, ed. L. Keen, *BAA Trans.*, XIX (Leeds 1997), 69–70.

14. B. J. Lowe et al., 'Keysham Abbey: Excavations 1961–1985', *Somerset Archaeology and Natural History Society*, 131 (1987), 81–156; B. J. Lowe, S. A. Harrison and M. Thurlby, 'Keynsham Abbey Excavations 1961–1991: Final Report Part I: The Architecture of Keynsham Abbey', *Somerset Archaeology and Natural History Society*, 148 (2005), 92–94.

15. J. Bilson, *Yorkshire Archaeological Journal*, 21 (1911), 174–75; *YAJ*, 22 (1913), 238–39.

16. M. Thurlby, 'Observations on the Twelfth-Century Sculpture from Bridlington Priory', in *Medieval Art and Architecture in The East Riding of Yorkshire*, ed. C. Wilson, *BAA Trans.*, IX (Leeds 1989), 33–43.

17. J. A. Franklin, 'Bridlington Priory: an Augustinian Church and Cloister in the Twelfth Century', in *Medieval Art and Architecture in The East Riding of Yorkshire*, ed. C. Wilson, *BAA Trans.*, IX (Leeds 1989), 44–61. Franklin also mentions the Benedictine cloister capitals from Hyde Abbey and Norwich Cathedral, 46 n.21.

18. C. Wilson, 'The Cistercians as 'missionaries of Gothic' in Northern England', in *Cistercian art and architecture in the British Isles*, ed. C. Norton and D. Park (Cambridge 1986), 86–116.

19. Thurlby, 'Observations on Bridlington', 38–39.

20. J. Blair, P. Lankester and J. West, 'A Transitional Cloister Arcade at Haughmond Abbey', *Medieval Archaeology*, 24 (1980), 210–12.

21. J. P. Greene, *Norton Priory: the archaeology of a medieval religious house* (Cambridge 1989), 111–18. The Norton Priory excavations have yet to be published in detail but at the time of writing the final report is almost complete. The writer has contributed the section dealing with the stonework recovered from the site and the reassessment of the cloister arcade.

22. The extensive excavations at Haverfordwest Priory have yet to be published. The reconstruction drawing of the arcading shown here is based on detailed examination of the loose stonework carried out by the writer during his work for Cadw at the site.

23. H. Summerson and S. Harrison, 'Lanercost Priory, Cumbria', *Cumberland and Westmoreland Antiquarian and Archaeological Society Research Series*, 10 (2000), 118–22.

24. The fragments of the cloister arcades at Easby and Egglestone were presumably found during the Office of Works clearances of the site. They are presently kept in the English Heritage Archaeology Store at Helmsley.

25. R. L. Kemp and C. P. Graves, 'The Church and Gilbertine Priory of St Andrew, Fishergate', in *The Archaeology of York 11: The Medieval Defences and Suburbs*, ed. P. V. Addyman (York 1996), 245–55.

26. J. Pinnell, *Wenlock Priory* (London 1999), 9–10.

27. H. Brakspear, 'Exhibits at Ballots June 22', *Proceedings of the Society of Antiquaries*, 2nd series, 28 (1915–16), 245–50. Nine capitals and three bases were discovered lining a drain at the priory. Brakspear exhibited the capitals at the Society of Antiquaries and calculated the diameter of the circular fountain house to which they belonged as fourteen feet.

28. G. Coppack, *Abbeys and Priories* (London 1990), 86–90.

Cistercian Cloisters in England and Wales Part I: Essay

DAVID M. ROBINSON AND STUART HARRISON

This article has its origins in a paper on Cistercian cloisters presented by David Robinson at the 2004 Rewley House conference on the medieval cloister in England and Wales. Subsequently, it was felt that a JBAA volume dedicated to cloisters would be deficient were it to ignore the very significant work done by Stuart Harrison in enhancing our understanding of white monk cloisters, and that this was the perfect opportunity to bring together the complementary skills of both authors. The paper comes in two parts, an essay and gazetteer.

PERHAPS the most powerful expression of the success achieved by the Cistercian order in medieval Europe was the extraordinary proliferation of its houses.[1] After two centuries of sustained growth, by the beginning of the 14th century there were more than 700 Cistercian abbeys situated in virtually every corner of the Christian west.[2] The total number of foundations in England and Wales eventually stood at about seventy-five (Fig. 1). There were eleven more abbeys in Scotland, and another thirty-five or so in Ireland.[3] Given such large numbers, on the face of it there seems to be considerable potential for comparative architectural study over a very wide area. Indeed, this has been a consistent strand running through Cistercian studies for well over a century. Expectations have been heightened by a recognition of the remarkably strong centralised governance of the order, and by the belief that the fierce drive for self-identity within the movement must have encouraged the adoption of a distinct architectural aesthetic. Time and again, however, scholars have warned of reading too much into the veneer of uniformity which is sometimes thought to characterise Cistercian building.[4] In particular, we must remember that despite the fullness of the order's early narrative and legislative texts, covering widely disparate facets of 'white monk' life, the content is astonishingly vague on the question of architecture.[5] Apart from a single reference to bell towers, there is, as Christopher Holdsworth has pointed out, 'not a word about the size and shape of the buildings in which the monks were to live and pray'.[6]

With this all-important caveat firmly in mind, the purpose of this paper is to look at one rather neglected aspect of Cistercian architecture, namely the cloister garth.[7] We pay particular attention to the surrounding arcades, though other prominent characteristics of the generally four-square open court are also considered. The content focuses very much on the Cistercian cloisters of England and Wales, and to this end is underpinned by the comprehensive gazetteer which follows on from this essay. The paper also presents the opportunity to bring together an important portfolio of English and Welsh arcade reconstructions, a number of them published

JBAA, vol. 159 (2006), 131–207
© British Archaeological Association 2006
DOI: 10.1179/174767006X147460

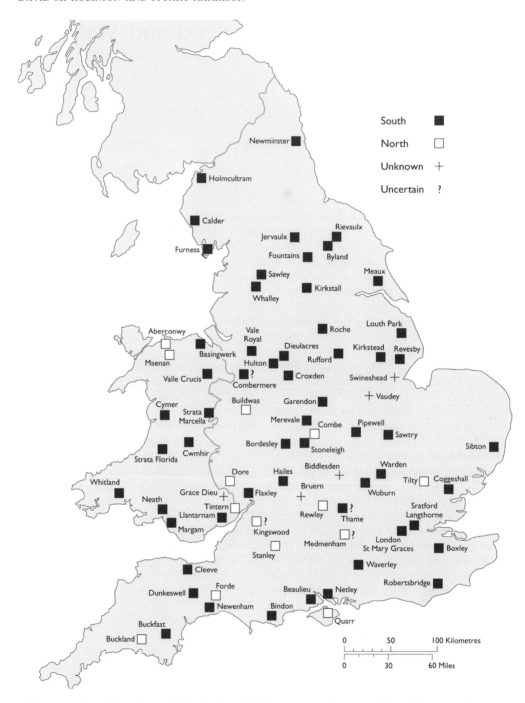

South ■
North □
Unknown +
Uncertain ?

Newminster
Holmcultram
Calder
Rievaulx
Jervaulx
Furness
Fountains
Byland
Meaux
Sawley
Kirkstall
Whalley
Aberconwy
Vale Royal
Roche
Louth Park
Basingwerk
Dieulacres
Kirkstead
Revesby
Maenan
Hulton
Rufford
Valle Crucis
Combermere ?
Croxden
Swineshead +
Cymer
Buildwas
Garendon
+ Vaudey
Strata Marcella
Merevale
Combe
Pipewell
Bordesley
Stoneleigh
Sawtry
Strata Florida
Cwmhir
Biddlesden
Warden
Sibton
Whitland
Dore
Hailes
+
Tilty
Coggeshall
Grace Dieu +
Flaxley
Bruern
Woburn
Neath
Tintern
Rewley
+
Thame ?
Sratford Langthorne
Llantarnam
Kingswood ?
Margam
Medmenham ?
London St Mary Graces
Boxley
Stanley
Waverley
Cleeve
Robertsbridge
Forde
Beaulieu
Netley
Dunkeswell
Newenham
Bindon
Buckfast
Quarr
Buckland

0   50   100 Kilometres
0   30   60 Miles

FIG. 1.   Cistercian abbeys in England and Wales: map to show position of known cloisters
Pete Lawrence for Cadw, Welsh Assembly Government

here for the first time. Our horizons are, however, by no means restricted to these shores. On the contrary, for a fuller appreciation of chronological developments, as well as for an understanding of the significance of individual garth features, it is essential we consider something of the wider European Cistercian context.

The essay is arranged in four principal parts. First, there is an introduction to the basic qualities of the Cistercian cloister, concentrating on its physical attributes while keeping an eye on conceptual interpretations of the space. The second and third sections provide a chronological overview of the development of Cistercian cloister arcading in England and Wales, before and after *c.* 1300. Finally, we consider a number of significant architectural features of the garth, focusing primarily on 'lanes', lavers, collation seats and their associated arcade bays.

QUALITIES OF THE CISTERCIAN CLOISTER

SUCH is the dominance of the cloister (*claustrum*) in medieval monastic planning that it is easy to take its ubiquity for granted. In many ways, the success of its four-square architectural form — especially in northern climes — remains a puzzle. Walter Horn described it as 'one of the great mysteries of medieval architecture'.[8] Nevertheless, the cloister was adopted by virtually every European religious order, almost without question and regardless of any specific ideals. It is rightly seen as the single most inventive and 'enduring achievement' of monastic building.[9]

With one or two significant modifications to the surrounding buildings, the cloister eventually proved fundamental to Cistercian monastic planning. It was a place, as we shall see, in which important liturgical expressions of the community were enacted. Cut off from the outside world both physically and spiritually, the central open court or garth served as a haven of tranquillity at the heart of the abbey complex.[10] On all four sides were passages, usually covered with lean-to roofs, known as cloister walks, galleries, or alleys. Fronted by handsome rhythmic arcades of a generally uniform character, these walks served the practical function of linking church to chapter-house, chapter-house to refectory, and so on. Moreover, they provided an ideal backdrop for processions and other ritual events.

Physical Qualities

THE basic principles underlying the form of the monastic cloister were already well established by the early 9th century, as is witnessed by the celebrated plan of the Carolingian abbey of St Gall.[11] In particular, the St Gall plan shows the cloister to the south of the church, tucked into the angle between nave and transept. In the event, this was the pattern followed by the vast majority of medieval religious houses, and is far and away the most common arrangement among abbeys of the Cistercian order. It was true, for example, of the order's great mother house at Cîteaux (Côte-d'Or), and likewise at St Bernard's abbey of Clairvaux (Aube) (Fig. 2).[12] In so far as one can tell, it also seems to have been the case at the majority of the early foundations in Burgundy and neighbouring Champagne.[13] Nevertheless, it is clear that on occasion particular factors led to the abandonment of the preferred norm. Either through choice, or the lack of it, communities were sometimes prepared to opt for a cloister north of the church.[14] This occurred quite early at Cîteaux's elder daughter at Pontigny (Yonne), for instance, and there is no shortage of other examples spread

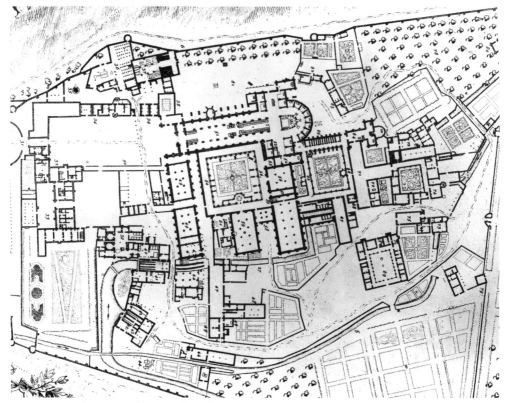

FIG. 2.   Clairvaux Abbey (Aube): detail of a ground plan by Dom Nicolas Milley, 1708
Bibliothèque Nationale de France, Paris

across all areas of France, as at Flaran (Gers), Fontfroide (Aude), Obazine (Corrèze), Silvacane (Bouches-du-Rhône), Le Thoronet (Var), and Vaux-de-Cernay (Seine-et-Oise).[15] Beyond France, well-known examples of northern Cistercian cloisters include Eberbach and Maulbronn in Germany, Moreruela and Poblet in Spain, Alcobaça in Portugal, Melrose in Scotland, and Hore in Ireland.[16] Even so, we are prepared to speculate that fewer than 30 per cent of white monk abbeys followed this pattern.

Among the houses of England and Wales, northern cloisters were certainly in a minority (Fig. 1). No more than thirteen have been recorded so far — compared to fifty-seven southern examples — representing a figure of just under 20 per cent.[17] Interestingly, none of these thirteen was located in the north of England. The majority lay in the west, and perhaps the south-west in particular. The better-known sites with proven northern cloisters include Buildwas, Combe, Dore, Forde, Stanley, and Tintern.[18] By and large, the literature which mentions this fact tends to attribute it to topographical factors, and especially to the practicalities of water supply and drainage.[19]

Turning to the shape and size of the garths themselves, the first point to note is that the Cistercians clearly showed a preference for a symmetrical four-square monastic layout, as depicted for example on surviving early plans of Cîteaux and Clairvaux (Fig. 2).[20] Yet beyond this we have no real way of knowing what instruction founding communities may have been given on setting out their cloisters at an appropriate scale. In any case, it should be remembered that both the shape and size of any particular garth could be modified over time, in line with a major rebuilding programme on the abbey church or monastic buildings.

In attempting to summarise the conclusions which may be drawn from the material in England and Wales, it may not be unreasonable to think of most Cistercian cloister garths as sitting within a median range, few of them varying by more than 20 per cent larger or smaller from a 100 ft square.[21] The outstanding exception at the larger end of the scale was the garth at Byland, which measured a staggering 145 ft (44.2 m) square and covered a total ground area of 21,025 sq. ft (1,953 sq. m). In terms of broad comparison, it is instructive to compare this garth with those at the two wealthiest Benedictine houses in England. In this respect, the cloister at Byland was larger than that of Glastonbury, and was only marginally exceeded by the beautiful 13th-century and later cloister at Westminster Abbey.[22] Another Yorkshire Cistercian house, Rievaulx, had a garth which was comparable in scale to Byland, measuring 140 ft (42.7 m) square. And the cloister at Fountains Abbey, again in the same region, was about 125 ft (38 m) square. In southern England, large cloisters were a feature of the royal foundations at Beaulieu and Hailes, standing at approximately 138 ft (42 m) square and 132 ft (40.2 m) square respectively. Close in scale was the garth at Waverley, which measured about 120 ft (36.6 m) by 124 ft (27.8 m). As regards examples of houses closer to the posited median point, the cloister at Roche in the north was approximately 98 ft (30 m) square, that at Cleeve in the south-west was about 93 ft (28.3 m) square, and that at Bindon in the far south was 90 ft (27.4 m) square. At the smaller end of the scale we might cite the garths at the Welsh houses of Valle Crucis and Cymer, the former measuring around 79 ft (24 m) square, and the latter just 75 ft (23 m) by 72 ft (22 m). Indeed, at a mere 5,400 sq. ft (502 sq. m), the ground area of the garth at Cymer was little more than a quarter of the size of Byland.

When it comes to the specific shape of Cistercian cloisters in England and Wales, there are exceptions to the predominant four-square plan. At Stanley, for instance, the garth was close to trapezoidal. Boxley and Sawley, on the other hand, both had garths which were much longer along the north–south axis than was the case from east–west.[23] By and large, peculiarities of this type were rarely a matter of specific choice by the community in question. In general, they were more likely to have emerged from unforeseen complications in a particular sequence of building campaigns. Then again, the rather unusual arrangements chosen by the community at St Mary Graces in London seem to require further explanation.[24]

Although far from peculiar to the order, the character of an individual Cistercian cloister was very much determined by the nature of its arcades. In England and Wales, for the most part, attempts to visualise cloister walks have to be based on disarticulated architectural fragments, so the importance of the arcade is more apparent when looking at better-surviving examples on the Continent. In particular, it was the arcades which gave a constant rhythm to the layout of the court. In visual terms they tended to conceal the structure of the ranges behind, giving the impression of a unified architectural ensemble, sometimes to buildings of varying date and design.[25] The general point can be made by looking at the surviving 12th-century arcades in the cloisters at Sénanque (Vaucluse) and Fontenay (Côte-d'Or) (Fig. 3), for example, or for that matter in the much less restrained 14th-century work in the garth at Santes Creus in Spain (Fig. 4).[26] At Fontenay, we can be confident that by the time permanent

FIG. 3.   Fontenay Abbey (Côte-d'Or): the cloister garth looking north-east
David Robinson

FIG. 4.   Santes Creus (Catalonia): the cloister garth looking north-east
David Robinson

stone buildings were under construction, cloisters garths with walks and arcades had become essential components within the Cistercian plan.[27] In the general literature, the completion of the church at Fontenay is usually dated to the late 1140s, and the east range is thought to have been constructed *c.* 1150–55. One assumes the cloister followed on from this.[28] The basic framework of the arcades was determined by the buttressed-piers which marked the principal bay divisions. On all sides of the garth, each of the eight bays was then subdivided into paired arches, carried centrally on coupled freestanding colonnettes. It was a formula common in late-12th- and early-13th-century Europe.[29] At Fontenay, as elsewhere, the pier-buttresses were required to support the internal vaults. Here they took the form of pointed barrels, though their precise detail varied from one side of the garth to another. Fontenay also serves to remind us that for many Cistercian communities the original cloister layout, complete with its primary arcades, was deemed perfectly acceptable for the entire Middle Ages.[30]

One other notable physical characteristic of Cistercian cloister arcades, especially in the 12th and 13th centuries, is the comparative rarity of elaborate sculpture.[31] Quirkiness and eccentricity do occur, as with the strange knotted piers used at the angles of the brick arcades at Chiaravalle della Colomba and Chiaravalle Milanese in northern Italy (Fig. 5).[32] Nevertheless, in general terms, early Cistercian arcades are characterised by their sober restraint, and by the almost complete rejection of figure sculpture in particular. On the one hand, considering the austere architectural aesthetic which seems to have defined 12th-century Cistercian buildings in general, this is almost to be expected. But there again we might remember that just as the white

FIG. 5.   Chiaravalle Milanese (Lombardy): pier at the north-west corner of the cloister garth

David Robinson

monks were finding their architectural feet, Romanesque cloister sculpture was flourishing among other monastic orders, not least in Burgundy. In this context, it is impossible to overlook Bernard of Clairvaux's *Apologia* of about 1125, that hard-hitting satire addressed to his Cluniac friend, William of St Thierry.[33] Having condemned the 'immense height' and 'immoderate length' of certain monastic churches, Bernard went on:

What is more, what can justify that ridiculous array of grotesques in the cloister where the brothers do their reading — I mean those extraordinary deformed beauties and beautiful deformities? What place have obscene monkeys, savage lions ... what is the meaning of fighting soldiers or hunters sounding horns? You can see a head with many bodies and a multi-bodied head. Here is a quadruped with a dragon's tail, there an animal's head stuck on a fish. There is a creature beginning as a horse and ending as a goat ... With such a bewildering array of shapes and forms on show, one would sooner read the sculptures than the books ... Ah, Lord! If the folly of it all does not shame us, surely the expense might stick in our throats.[34]

The *Apologia*, and this passage in particular, is much debated. Yet its long-term significance on Cistercian cloister design, or at least the significance of the stance which it might be taken to represent, is hard to underplay. The message was further underlined in one of the order's earliest statutes, which decreed:

Sculptures are never permitted; and the only paintings allowed are on the crosses, which must themselves be only of wood.[35]

Conceptual Qualities

MOVING on from the practical attributes of the cloister walks, there is no doubt that, for all Cistercian communities, the cloister was charged with significant symbolic meaning. Indeed, throughout the order's literature it is not unusual to find the courtyard and its central garden associated with the heavenly paradise, though we must bear in mind that the metaphor of cloister as paradise could be further extended to the entire abbey site, as well as to the monastic life itself.[36] Even so, seen in this broad context, the cloister served not only as a physical entity, but also as an imagined or abstract space, the meaning of which might be enhanced by the symbolism of processions, and by various other liturgical rites carried out within its bounds. Of course, it would be impossible to argue that there was anything exclusively Cistercian in such ideas; they are no less applicable to the Benedictine cloister, or even to the cloisters of the Augustinian canons. Yet at the same time, the importance of white monk cloister liturgy should not underestimated.

Processions were one element of this, even if their frequency was somewhat limited when compared with Benedictine or Cluniac liturgy. In so far as can be judged, by the second half of the 12th century there were just three major annual processions in a Cistercian monastery. One was held on Palm Sunday, the second at Candlemas, and a third took place on Ascension Day.[37] In each of these, the procession began in the church. From the presbytery, the entire abbey community moved out into the cloister, walking around the east, south, and west walks, before returning into the church from the west. The symbolism of the Palm Sunday procession, for example, is very clear, imitating as it did Christ's triumphal entry in Jerusalem.[38]

Aside from these three annual processions, the cloister also featured in the weekly Sunday rite known the *benedictio aquae*, which took place before high mass.[39] As part of this rite, one of the monks aspersed the cloister and the principal monastic

138

buildings with salt and water blessed immediately for the purpose. For Cassidy-Welch, this is another example of the Cistercian attitude towards the 'sacred nature of the claustral landscape'.[40]

THE DEVELOPMENT OF CISTERCIAN CLOISTERS IN THE 12TH AND 13TH CENTURIES

BEFORE turning to the specific evidence for chronological developments in English and Welsh Cistercian cloister design during the 12th and 13th centuries, it is worth mentioning the apparent reluctance among the order's founding fathers to adopt the increasingly standardised claustral monastic plan at all. Despite the practical good sense offered by the Carolingian model, and regardless of its widespread acceptance across late-11th-century Europe,[41] the Cistercians were initially unwilling to accept it without question. Very much in line with their reformist approach to the religious life, and in keeping with their single-minded insistence upon poverty and humility, the founding fathers appear to have experimented with new forms of monastic planning. This is witnessed, in particular, by the earliest layout recorded at St Bernard's Clairvaux, and by the documentary descriptions of the timber buildings raised at various Cistercian sites across Europe.[42] It was a position they may have held for two or three decades, at most, and we have no real way of knowing how temporary such early structures were intended to be. In any case, from the mid-1130s, as the white monks began to build churches and domestic buildings in stone, well-proportioned cloisters definitely became essential components within the basic layout.

The Nature of the Evidence

NOT one Romanesque great cloister of any monastic order remains intact in the whole of England and Wales. In fact, excepting a few bays of the east walk of the infirmary cloister at Canterbury cathedral, one is hard pressed to point to any *in situ* Anglo-Welsh cloister before the traceried arcades and vaulted walks at Westminster Abbey and Salisbury Cathedral, dating from the mid- to late 13th century.[43] It comes as no surprise to learn, therefore, that very little can be said of Cistercian cloisters before *c.* 1160–70. At sites such as Fountains, Rievaulx and Waverley in England, or Margam and Tintern in Wales, although a reasonable amount is known about the disposition of the buildings surrounding the earliest cloister garth, the character of the garth itself and the nature of its arcades and alleys entirely escapes us. Archaeologists and architectural historians have usually tended to fall back on an assumed temporary arrangement, with the not unreasonable suggestion that the initial arcades — if they existed at all — may have been of timber.[44] Our knowledge of stone-built arcades begins to increase for the last three or four decades of the 12th century, and continues on into the mid-13th century. Much of the evidence comes from northern England, though there is also important information from several abbeys in the south and west.

Once again, since nothing survives *in situ*, the details have been derived almost entirely from archaeological investigation. Cumulatively, though, the record is now quite substantial. Indeed, more is known about the design of Romanesque and early Gothic Cistercian cloisters than is the case for any other monastic order in Britain. In part, this can be attributed to the rural settings of white monk abbeys, something which helped prevent their total destruction in the centuries after the suppression. Equally, as a consequence of State guardianship policy on many sites, not least the massive clearance programmes which took place in the early 20th century, we have often inherited large stockpiles of *ex situ* stonework, much of it coming from cloister arcading.[45] The most substantial assemblages are to be found in the north of England, itself a reflection of the greater survival of Cistercian buildings in this region generally. It was a happy coincidence of these two factors — guardianship policy coupled with a large collection of loose stonework — which led to the re-erection of several bays of late 12th-century cloister arcading at Rievaulx Abbey in the 1930s (Fig. 6).[46] Apart from the north of England, there is another comparatively well-preserved group of Cistercian buildings in Wales, six of which are in State care and include significant stonework collections.[47]

These regional imbalances have in turn been reflected in the degree of emphasis which has been given to cloister studies. Scholars have inevitably been drawn to those sites with the best-preserved material evidence. The two present authors have, for instance, worked extensively on Cistercian sites in the north of England and in Wales, and it is a bias which we cannot disguise in the content of the gazetteer entries.[48]

FIG. 6. Rievaulx Abbey: cloister arcade reconstructed at the north-west corner of the garth, late 1160s

Stuart Harrison

Arcades of the Late 12th Century

THE Cistercians made their earliest landfall in Britain in 1128, at Waverley in Surrey. By 1152, the year in which the order's General Chapter tried to call a halt on further foundations, there were already close to fifty houses in existence in England and Wales.[49] Meanwhile, the English Benedictines had definitely begun building elaborate stone cloister arcades, as witnessed by the richly sculptured capitals of the 1120s or 1130s from Reading and Hyde abbeys, along with the marginally later programme known from the Glastonbury of Bishop Henry of Blois.[50] The extensive collection of architectural fragments from Reading reveals an arcade of decorative round-headed arches supported on single colonnettes, a pattern which was probably repeated at Hyde. At Glastonbury on the other hand, the capitals indicate that the arcades were arranged with supports of both single and paired colonnettes, probably in an alternating pattern. Then, as the century progressed, it seems an exclusively paired arrangement became the most popular choice.[51] In the event, when we are first able to pick up on evidence for Cistercian arcades, they are almost always of paired design.

Specifically from the north of England, we now have a wide range of information on late-12th-century arcades from the great cloisters at Byland, Calder, Fountains, Jervaulx, Kirkstall, Newminster, Rievaulx, Roche, and perhaps Sawley.[52] Typically, but not exclusively, these arcades featured the by-then close to ubiquitous rows of paired columns, all featuring moulded bases and moderately decorative capitals. The columns in turn supported a sequence of round-headed or pointed arches, with mouldings to the soffits and at least one side. In broad terms, the more decorative façade was almost always placed on the garth side, with the plainer work facing inwards towards the alleys.[53]

Today, the clearest expression of the form can be seen in the re-erected sections of arcading at the north-west corner of the cloister garth at Rievaulx (Fig. 6).[54] In this case the arcade arches were supported on alternating pairs of circular and octagonal colonnettes, with a four-shaft grouping at the corner. There is a common base pattern, but the capitals feature a variety of scalloped and waterleaf designs. The arch mouldings are fairly bold and are surmounted externally by a chamfered hood-mould. The composition is completed with a moulded eaves cornice, which must have taken the wall-plate carrying the timbers of the lean-to roof.[55] Enough evidence survives on site to demonstrate there were segmental-arched ceilings beneath the lean-to roofs over each alley (Fig. 7). In terms of dating, the blend of late Romanesque and early Gothic forms found in the capital sculpture would fit with a date close to the end of Ailred of Rievaulx's abbacy, that is the late 1160s.

Thereafter, the suggested sequence of main northern cloister arcades begins with Kirkstall (Fig. 49). The arches here were again round headed, though with full-blown Gothic detailing to the capitals, indicating a date of *c.* 1170–75.[56] Byland possibly overlapped with the Kirkstall scheme. Here, the arcades were presumably in place in time for the arrival of the community from its temporary home at nearby Stocking in 1177.[57] Their general character is revealed in the reconstruction at the site museum (Fig. 8), but variations are known in both the form of the shafts and the capitals (Figs 22–24). After Byland, it is no great surprise to find that the main cloister arcading built at its daughter house of Jervaulx was closely related (Figs 44–47). All of the arcade arches were again round headed, and a date in the late 1170s or early 1180s seems most probable.[58]

FIG. 7.   Rievaulx Abbey: reconstruction drawing showing the east cloister alley as it may have appeared in the late 12th century. Note the segmental-arched ceiling

English Heritage

FIG. 8.   Byland Abbey: cloister bases and capitals of the mid- to late 1170s, reconstructed with modern shafts at the site museum

Stuart Harrison

FIG. 9. Roche Abbey: pointed cloister arcade of *c.* 1180–90 reconstructed for the exhibition entitled 'Abbeys: Yorkshire's Monastic Heritage', held in the Yorkshire Museum in York, 1988

Stuart Harrison

Towards the end of the 12th century, round-headed arches began to be replaced by pointed or trefoiled forms, mouldings became more complex, and dog-tooth decoration made an appearance. At Newminster, for example, arcades with slender shafts, moulded bases, leaf capitals, and pointed arches with a prominent hood-mould were built *c.* 1180–85 (Fig. 50).[59] And, at much the same time, the community at Roche also began work on arcades with two-centred arch heads, here supported on waterleaf capitals (Fig. 9). Remarkably, however, at some point along one of the alleys, the design of the arcade was changed. Instead of the simple pointed arches, the masons now employed a far more elaborate trefoiled design, featuring complex roll mouldings and enriched with a band of dog-tooth decoration (Figs 51–52). The bulk appears to have been painted white, but with some of the architectural detailing picked out in red.[60] The change of design presumably reflects a slightly prolonged constructional sequence. Yet there is no sign of any concern on the part of the masons or the abbey community, and it is certainly a pattern encountered elsewhere.

The most elaborate of these late-12th-century northern arcades, and probably the last in the sequence, was that built at Fountains (Figs 28–30). All of the arches were of the trefoiled form found in the second phase at Roche, but here they featured even more complex mouldings. Painted in brilliant white, the arches must have stood in stark contrast to the twined colonnettes, waterleaf capitals and moulded bases, all of which were executed in grey Nidderdale marble. In much of the established literature on Fountains, these handsome great cloister garth arcades have usually been attributed to Abbot Robert of Pipewell (1170–80), who, according to the foundation history of the house, 'erected sumptuous buildings' (*edificia construxit sumptuosa*).[61] But fresh research on the relative chronologies of major Cistercian buildings in the north of England points to a different conclusion, and it now seems more likely the main Fountains arcades were built in the time of one of Pipewell's successors, either William (1180–90) or Ralph Haget (1190–1203).[62]

FIG. 10. Rievaulx Abbey: reconstructed infirmary cloister arcade, late 1160s
Stuart Harrison

Before leaving the north of England, a smaller sub-set of late-12th-century Cistercian arcade forms should be noted. These have generally been found away from the great cloister, with the principal characteristic of the group being the fact that the arches were carried on single rather than paired colonnettes. The earliest examples would appear to be the arcading from the infirmary cloister garth at Rievaulx and the arcading representing the lay brothers' cloister garth at Fountains (Figs 10, 31), both of which date from the mid- to late 1160s. A marginally later form has also been identified at Jervaulx, which probably also came from a lay brothers' cloister (Fig. 48).[63] A section of the Rievaulx infirmary arcades has been re-erected on the site (Fig. 10).[64] Like those from the great cloister, the arches were again round-headed, but here they were much plainer in style. The single shafts featured simple chalice capitals, and were arranged in an alternating pattern of octagonal and circular forms. In essence, the composition was a modest, or scaled-down version of the principal arcades.

Nothing like the same amount of evidence for late-12th-century Cistercian cloister arcades has so far been uncovered in the south of England or in Wales. Even at Bordesley Abbey, a site which has seen extensive excavation over a very long period, the quantity of evidence revealed from the initial cloister arcading is small.[65] Nevertheless, enough material has been uncovered to show that the early Bordesley arcades were not unlike those in the north, at least in terms of their general character. A twin scalloped capital is evidence of the usual paired colonnette arrangement, and a moulded base indicates there were four-shaft groupings at the corners. The work may have been completed in the 1160s.[66]

Fragments of a late-12th-century arcade of a somewhat different design were excavated by Harold Brakspear at Waverley Abbey around 1900. The evidence came from the east and south alleys, and was dated by Brakspear to *c.* 1180. Interestingly, the arches were carried on an alternate arrangement of coupled circular columns and single octagonal ones, all with Purbeck marble bases.[67] Aside from this distinct variation, however, one other example must serve to demonstrate the widespread occurrence of early twin-colonnette forms throughout the country. Investigations at Whitland Abbey in south-west Wales in the early 1920s, led to the discovery of coupled capitals and bases from early cloister arcades, perhaps dating to the late 12th century.[68]

Arcades of the 13th Century

TWIN-COLUMNED cloister arcades were to remain popular with the Cistercians in England and Wales well into the 13th century, despite further stylistic advances made in line with early Gothic taste. At Furness in the north-west, for instance, twin-shafted arcades were raised in the first quarter of the century. These were almost certainly of trefoil-headed design, with moulded bases and capitals to the shafts (Figs 37–38).[69] Extensive use was made of a fine grey marble, all cut and polished to a very high standard of finish. Based on the tentative reconstruction offered here (Fig. 42), these arcades may be regarded as updated versions of those in the great cloister at Fountains.[70]

In the south and west of England, other early-13th-century twin-shafted cloister arcades are known for example from Beaulieu, Bindon, Buildwas and Stanley.[71] At Buildwas, the only specific remains on site today are the narrow stylobates surrounding the garth, but *ex situ* fragments reveal the character of the early-13th-century detail.[72] In their early-20th-century excavations at Beaulieu, Hope and Brakspear found evidence of open arches and coupled columns featuring moulded capitals and bases, all standing on low stylobates.[73] Similar arrangements were again identified by Brakspear at Stanley.[74] There is no close date for the work at either of these last two sites, yet it is unlikely the cloister arcading was finished much before 1250.

Very much in contrast with these by now increasingly conservative twin-colonnette forms were the arcades begun by the communities at Dore and Tintern abbeys in the second and third quarters of the 13th century. Apart from anything else, the details as reconstructed on paper demonstrate that the Cistercians in the south-west were by this date happy to give their cloister masons a great deal of free rein, allowing them to experiment with increasingly inventive forms for the arcades (Figs 11, 27, 55).

The monks at Dore were engaged in programmes to enlarge both their church and cloister buildings in the initial decades of 13th century, with most of the work completed before *c.* 1250.[75] In other words, during the time of Abbot Stephen of Worcester (*c.* 1236–57), the community must have been ready to undertake work on new cloister walks and arcades. In fact, recent investigations of *ex situ* stonework at the site have located just enough material to posit a reconstruction of cloister arcading of precisely this date bracket (Fig. 27).[76] An unusual but elegant design is revealed, featuring tall cinquefoil arches with filleted roll mouldings. On the garth side of the arches there was a prominent rebate, intended to accommodate a second band of

FIG. 11.   Tintern Abbey: reconstruction drawing to show the syncopated arcading in the
north-east corner of the cloister in the late 13th century

Cadw, Welsh Assembly Government

moulded voussoirs. But the particular interest of this Dore arcading is the fact it was
supported on groups of detached triple shafts, further increased to five individual
colonnettes at the corner angles. In so far as the evidence allows, all of the shafts had
moulded bases and stiff-leaf capitals. To date, this is the only definite example of
Cistercian cloister arcading in England and Wales known to have featured triple-shaft
supports, though it may be compared to the evidence from several Augustinian sites.[77]

The new cloister arcades introduced at Tintern, probably in the mid- to late 13th
century, proved to be more inventive still (Figs 11, 55). Over much of the previous
three to four decades, the community had been busy extending and rebuilding its three
main ranges of claustral buildings. So extensive was the programme on the east and
north ranges, in particular, it had presumably been necessary for the builders to sweep
away any existing 12th-century cloister arrangements.[78] Whether the monks had been
prepared to forego the use of the cloister walks for an extended period is unclear, but
in any case the arcades on all four sides of the garth were eventually laid out afresh. In
essence the design of the new scheme was based upon two separate rows of elegant
trefoil-headed arches, the details having been recovered entirely from *ex situ* stonework fragments. Of particular interest, the arches were set out in a somewhat unusual
syncopated pattern, in which both the inner and outer rows were independently
carried upon free-standing colonnettes, all of them probably featuring plain moulded

146

capitals and bases.[79] Although the height of the colonnettes can only be estimated, it was their staggered spacing which created the syncopated rhythm to the composition at large.

Taken as a whole, one has to accept that Tintern's 13th-century cloister layout incorporated a degree of eccentricity. It is clear, for example, that the form of the arch heads must have varied around the four sides of the garth, and very probably on the internal and external faces. Indeed, no fewer than five alternate moulding profiles have been identified, some featuring a semicircular enclosing arch others not (Fig. 55). It is also clear that the builders used at least two different stone types. Yet at the same time, the generally accomplished form of the arcades indicates that the community had chosen to engage a mason capable of producing precisely such a novel design. The confident use of micro-vaulting linking the two rows of arches, for instance, may well reflect the fact he had already worked on a similar cloister arcade elsewhere. In common with earlier examples, the Tintern vault ribs projected diagonally from the rear spandrel of each springer in the inner and outer arcades, forming a series of small pointed arches of zigzag plan. One further detail is testimony to the sophistication of the Tintern design — the clever use of pointed arches in half-bay widths along at least one side of the garth so as to align inner and outer arcade bays, and allow an opening to connect walk and garth.[80]

Taking into account the comprehensive reworking of the Tintern claustral ranges in the early 13th century, the balance of probability suggests this novel cloister scheme could not have been started much before *c.* 1245–50. Contrary to such a proposal, one should cite the somewhat earlier 13th-century date (*c.* 1225–50) preferred by Jackie Hall for cloister arcades of a similar character at Croxden (Fig. 26).[81] Admittedly these were not of complex syncopated form, instead featuring a standard arrangement of trefoil-headed arches supported on paired columns with moulded capitals and bases. Even so, the detailing is comparable in broad terms with that at the Welsh house. There again, among the earliest moulding profiles in the Tintern assemblage, one can pick out quite definite similarities with those of the Salisbury Cathedral workshop of the 1260s.[82] Moreover, other elements in the Tintern design find close parallels in works of the last years of the 13th century, and even later.

In sum, it may be suggested that Tintern's syncopated cloister arcades were begun *c.* 1245–50, with, in all probability, all four sides of the garth included in the original scheme. This would mean that the southern arcade and its walk must initially have been built against the north wall of the Romanesque abbey church.[83] Key differences which have been identified in the moulding profiles of the cloister arcades doubtless reflect the complex later constructional history of the garth. From *c.* 1269, for instance, the community began work on a brand new abbey church.[84] As completed, this led to a deepening of the north–south cloister axis, presumably making it necessary to reposition the southern arcade and to insert linking sections into the east and west sides, perhaps *c.* 1300.

Before progressing with further developments in England and Wales, we must recognise that despite the degree of novelty introduced to the arcades at Dore and Tintern, by the standards of some contemporary white monk cloisters on the Continent their basic design was beginning to look old-fashioned. In particular, they were still covered with timber lean-to roofs, whereas the open arcades would have meant the actual cloister walks were left exposed to the winter elements. Meanwhile, in parts of France and elsewhere, the Cistercians had been willing to take part in new experiments in cloister arcading and vaulting. At Heiligenkreuz in Austria, for instance, the elegant rib-vaulted cloister walks had apparently been at least partially glazed at the

FIG. 12. Heiligenkreuz Abbey (Austria): cloister alley, *c.* 1220–50

John Goodall

FIG. 13. Noirlac Abbey (Cher): north walk of cloister from garth

John McNeill

time of their original construction, *c.* 1220–50 (Fig. 12).[85] Later in the century, with bar tracery to the fore, yet further possibilities for arcade design were opened up. At the French abbey of Noirlac (Cher), for example, although the disposition of the late-12th-century buildings remained unchanged, around 1270 the community decided to update the entire cloister court, a programme which extended well into the 14th century (Fig. 13). Vaulted throughout, the phasing of the work is reflected in the various tracery patterns around the garth, some of which shows evidence of glazing.[86] At much the same time, the monks at Maulbronn in Germany were busy constructing vaulted walks on three sides of their cloister garth. Each bay featured quadripartite ribs, with French-inspired tracery to the arcades.[87]

In England and Wales there is precious little yet discovered of late-13th-century Cistercian cloisters to compare with these impressive Continental examples. Netley and Hailes are two sites which, given their dates and royal connections, present themselves as possibilities, but too little evidence has survived on which to base an informed judgement.[88] It is, therefore, of especial interest to note the record of possible traceried arcades at Strata Marcella. The suggestion was made by the excavators of 1890, based on the recovery of fragments of a Geometrical tracery showing no sign of glazing, with the cloister seen as the most likely source.[89]

THE DEVELOPMENT OF CISTERCIAN CLOISTERS IN THE LATER MIDDLE AGES

BY far the most significant change in the design of monastic and cathedral cloisters in England and Wales during the late 13th and 14th centuries was the introduction of vaulting, accompanied by traceried arcades towards the garth. As noted above, two of the earliest schemes of this type appear to have been the east walk at Westminster Abbey (begun 1253) and the cathedral garth at Salisbury (perhaps completed by 1266).

The pace began to increase towards the end of the 13th century, with Lincoln (from 1295) and Norwich (from 1297), and continued unabated through the 14th century with the ongoing works at Westminster, and with fresh schemes at the likes of Gloucester, Worcester, and Canterbury (from 1397).[90] But for all this, the English and Welsh Cistercians appear to have remained no more than bit players, possibly until well into the 15th century.

From documentary evidence it is known that a new cloister was consecrated at Pipewell in 1312, though sadly no information is available on its form.[91] Again, written sources reveal that in 1373 the community at Boxley Abbey commissioned the mason Stephen Lomeherst to built new cloister alleys on all four sides of the garth. The surviving contract provides precise details of the proposed arcade walls, which were to support columns of two sizes with tracery above. There is, though, no mention of a vault, and it seems each alley was to sit merely beneath a timber roof (*subtus meremium*).[92]

Archaeological evidence from Stanley Abbey appears to confirm this preferred English pattern. Here, the arcades were almost certainly rebuilt afresh in the 14th century. They were carried on walls 2 ft (0.6 m) thick, but no positive sign of glazing has been recovered and the absence of buttresses again argues against vaulting.[93] The evidence from two sites in the north-east of Wales is even more telling. Although the cloister arcades at Basingwerk and Valle Crucis were rebuilt in the mid- to late 14th century, not only were the alleys to remain unvaulted, the arcades were to remain completely open and without tracery.

The *ex situ* fragments which allow for a reconstruction of the Basingwerk arcading was recovered during clearance of the site in the early 1920s.[94] The pieces introduce a new and not unstylish twist on the paired colonnette arrangement of the 12th century (Fig. 21). Instead of the freestanding columns employed in earlier arcades, the Basingwerk masons appear to have carved twin shafts from the same block of masonry, linking them together with a thinner plate or web of stone. In outline at least, the form of the shafts and their bases was octagonal, whereas the mouldings to the capitals ran through in combined unbroken fashion. The arches were of pointed form with cusped soffits, each bay separated by sunken triangular spandrels. The arrangements at Valle Crucis, in what must have been near-contemporary cloister arcades, were very similar, although the bay spacings were rather narrower than at Basingwerk (Fig. 56).[95]

Although this new style arcading in the two Welsh abbeys retained the slim elegance of the earlier coupled-shaft arrangement, it had the advantage of greater strength. Generally known as a dumb-bell pier form, it was particularly characteristic of Irish Cistercian cloisters in the later Middle Ages.[96] Interestingly, fragments of dumb-bell piers are also known from Furness and Tintern. The Tintern material, which is extensive, is unlikely to represent replacement arcades for the main cloister, though it could well have come from a late-medieval reworking of the infirmary garth.[97]

The distinct lack of evidence for traceried and vaulted 14th-century cloister alleys at Cistercian abbeys in England and Wales is in marked contrast to what is known from a number of sites on the Continent. At Maulbronn, for instance, the work begun on the cloister walks and their arcades in the 13th century culminated with the northern alley and its associated fountain house laver, perhaps as late as *c.* 1314–69 (Fig. 14).[98] Foremost among such 14th-century white monk cloister work, however, is that at the Catalan monastery of Santes Creus. Here, from 1313, the 12th-century arcades were to be entirely swept away, and replaced by a far more ornate scheme of traceried Gothic

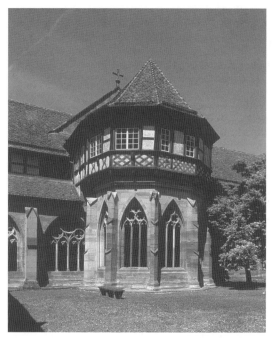

FIG. 14. Maulbronn Abbey (Germany): cloister garth look north-east, and showing fountain house laver

Malcolm Thurlby

FIG. 15. Bordesley Abbey: reconstruction of the north-east corner of the cloister alleys *c*. 1400, based on excavated fragments

David A. Walsh: Copyright, Bordesley Abbey Project. Reproduced with permission

design (Fig. 4). The work began with the north gallery, under the direction of Bertran Riquer, who was also responsible for the tomb canopy of King James II of Aragon (1291–1327) in the abbey church. But, from 1331 until *c*. 1341, the work fell under the control of the English master mason, Raynard Fonoyll. He produced the flamboyant (curvilinear) tracery and highly elaborate elements within the overall scheme. The capitals, for example, are rich in historiated detail, including the Creation and Fall of Adam and Eve on the south-west corner pier, scenes of grotesques and hybrids, and what appear to be two self-portraits of Fonoyll himself.[99] Such a scheme was of course the very antithesis of that sober restraint urged by St Bernard of Clairvaux in his *Apologia* of *c*. 1125.[100] But by now the Cistercians had come a very long way.

To date, the only hard architectural evidence which is available on English or Welsh Cistercian traceried arcading before the mid-15th century comes from Bordesley. The form of the arcades has been reconstructed by David Walsh, based on fragments excavated at the north-east corner of the garth (Fig. 15). He dates the scheme to *c*. 1400.[101] Externally, the bay divisions were marked by prominent buttresses set at regular intervals, and internally by engaged respond shafts set on polygonal bases. In each bay, above a lower tier of wall panelling, there was a three-light window with Perpendicular tracery to the head. Although by this time one might expect the internal

Fig. 16. Hailes Abbey: view of the cloister from the south-west, with standing fragmentary bays of 15th-century arcades in foreground
David Robinson

shafts to have carried up to stone vaults, nothing resembling rib fragments or webbing was located during the excavation, and a timber roof is again more likely.[102]

Even on into the 15th century, timber roofs were still not unusual in rebuilt Cistercian cloisters across England and Wales. At the comparatively wealthy Yorkshire abbey of Byland, for example, all four cloister walks were reconstructed with glazed tracery windows, perhaps around 1450. The bays were defined by substantial buttresses and the windows featured four lights with major and minor mullions, but there is no indication of stone vaulting.[103] Similarly, at the rather smaller Welsh house of Strata Florida, buttressed arcades were introduced to the north and east sides of the garth around the middle of the 15th century (Fig. 54).[104] In each of the regularly spaced standard bays there was a five-light window. It is possible that only the heads of the lights were glazed, from the point where horizontal glazing bars were set. Once again, despite the buttressing, there is no indication of vaults over the alleys.

It was probably in the third quarter of the 15th century that two Cistercian communities in the south-west finally broke with the trend for wooden cloister roofs, those at Hailes and Tintern. The dating of the new work at Hailes is uncertain, though it has been suggested it was begun under Abbot William Whitchurch around 1460.[105] All four walks were to receive new glazed arcades, with ten bays to each walk. Three shattered bays survive on the south-west side, with ample evidence to show they contained four-light windows with Perpendicular traceried heads (Figs 16, 43). More significantly, the alleys were vaulted in stone. Each bay was covered with a stellar design incorporating major and minor ribs, and with a large heraldic boss eventually set in the crown.[106] In places the ribs were set awkwardly into the earlier surrounding buildings, here supported on angel corbels. The heraldry on the bosses suggests the construction programme may have been continued (or perhaps modified) in the 16th century.

At Tintern meanwhile, in 1411–12 the monks had only been concerned to repair the roofs of their existing cloister walks. Then, at much the same time as the work began at Hailes, a complete rebuilding was begun, probably under Abbot Thomas Colston (*c.* 1460–86).[107] The prompt may have come from William Herbert, earl of Pembroke (d. 1469), who had been the abbey's lay steward and patron since the 1450s. In his will, Herbert made provision for his funerary monument in the abbey church, offering any surplus in the endowment 'to build new cloisters'. As is evident from the thickened wall foundations around the edges of the garth, a degree of progress was definitely made. Moreover, in south-east corner of the court, there are traces of the intended design against the north transept wall, including evidence of construction on at least four lavish stone-vaulted bays. It is unfortunate that the full extent of progress before the suppression remains uncertain.

Two final cloister schemes, again in the south-west, must be mentioned in closing. The first of these, at Cleeve, may again have been started in the late 15th century, though it was certainly continued under the last abbot, William Dovell.[108] The evidence survives on the west side of the garth, where it seems a two-storeyed treatment was envisaged. The seven-bay arcade, of at least two phases, was certainly glazed, but the alley remained unvaulted. Just before the suppression, in 1534, a legacy was left to Cleeve by the vicar of Stogumber for 'the newe bewylding of the clawsta', suggesting Dovell intended to progress the work to other sides of the garth.

The second of these late south-western cloister schemes was implemented at Forde during the time of the last abbot, Thomas Chard (1506–39).[109] Chard was not only an ambitious reformer, he was aware of the importance played by architecture in projecting an appropriate image. Apart from his grand new domestic apartments, he set out to completely remodel the cloister walks. From what was achieved on the north side, it was undoubtedly one of the most ambitious Cistercian cloister designs ever attempted in England. There was a large four-light glazed window in each of the six bays, the tracery pattern being repeated on the inner wall of the alley. The windows were surmounted by a decorative parapet featuring a frieze of quatrefoils enclosing shields of arms, initials, and devices. Inside, the vault responds and their springers indicate plans for fan vaulting, though this does not seem to have been completed before the suppression.

By way of conclusion, it must be said there appears to be nothing distinctly Cistercian in any of the late-medieval white monk cloister schemes identified in the south-west. The communities involved, and especially their architecturally ambitious abbots, were clearly unworried by a feeling that in replacing their outmoded arcades they might lose any spiritual or conceptual link with earlier generations of monks. Not unlike the greater Benedictine houses of the same region, their primary concern may have been comfort, stimulated by a new emphasis in what Julian Luxford calls 'internal patronage'.[110]

FEATURES OF THE WALKS AND THE GARTH

IN the Cistercian cloister, as in any other, the four walks or alleys served the practical function of linking the various surrounding buildings. In a very real sense, though, these spaces also represented 'the home of the monk'.[111] After all, when not at the work of God in the abbey church, the cloister was where he spent much of his day. In the north alley, that is the alley next to the church, carrels or desks were provided for reading and writing, at least during the later Middle Ages.[112] An inventory made at Rievaulx soon after its suppression in 1538, for instance, records 'the deskes ther called carolls' among the contents of the cloister.[113] And, in a similar suppression inventory made at Pipewell, the clerk noted that in the cloister 'the munkes seatys are sould for xxiiijs. iiijd.'.[114] It was presumably at their carrels, or on earlier stone benching, that the monks undertook the meditative or spiritual reading (*lectio divina*) encouraged in the Rule of St Benedict.[115] For one 12th-century Cistercian, this was to be taken very seriously: Abbot Richard (d. 1149) of Melrose wrote that a 'cloister without literature is a tomb for living men'.[116] The north alley, meanwhile, was also the scene of the collation, something which is examined in more detail below.

At the northern end of the east cloister alley was the book cupboard or book room (*armarium*), conveniently situated close to where the volumes were studied.[117] Nearby, it seems a writing tablet (*tabula*) was displayed, on which the roster for the monks with weekly duties was kept. Recesses to house such tablets are known from Fountains and Rievaulx.[118] The main feature of the south cloister alley was the laver, the place where the monks washed before going into the refectory for meals. The laver was also used in the important weekly rite known as the *mandatum*, again considered in more detail below. Finally, as a reminder of its wider purposes, the cloister walks were the place where the monks had their tonsures shaved at set points in the year, and it was one of the locations in which they were allowed to sit and rest after periodic blood-letting.[119]

Although archaeology has so far told us very little, it seems likely that for much of the 12th and early 13th centuries the cloister alleys at most English and Welsh Cistercian abbeys were at best paved with stone slabs.[120] A statute passed by the order's General Chapter in 1194 presupposes burial in cloister alleys was not unusual. However, raised grave slabs were presumably seen as a potential danger, leading to the prescription in this statute that henceforth they were to be reduced to a level flush with the cloister flooring.[121] Across Britain as a whole, tile pavements were probably introduced to cloister walks sparingly over the course of the later 13th century,[122] though they were undoubtedly to become more common in the later Middle Ages. When Stanley in Wiltshire was excavated in 1905, for example, the 14th-century paving in the west cloister walk 'was found in a very perfect state' for over 40 ft (12.2 m).[123] Today, more commonly, it is just occasional fragments which are encountered, as is the case at Buildwas, or in the west alley at Byland.[124] In Wales, definite evidence of tile pavements in cloister alleys is recorded from Basingwerk and Neath.[125]

As to the central open garth itself, there has been no reported modern excavation on any English or Welsh site which would allow for confident insights into its probable layout. Yet from what has been recovered elsewhere, the presumption is that garden beds, filled with flowers, herbs, and perhaps fruit trees, were divided by a series of paths leading out from the cloister alleys.[126]

The Lay Brothers' Lane

ONE very distinctive, not to say unique, characteristic of Cistercian cloisters is the occasional presence of a so-called 'lane' on the west side of the garth, described by Marcel Aubert as the 'ruelle des convers'.[127] Where it occurred, this rectangular open space separated the back of the west cloister walk from the lay brothers' accommodation in the west range. Both for Aubert, and for Anselme Dimier, the lane was sufficiently commonplace for it to be included in their versions of a 'standard' Cistercian plan.[128] Indeed, as one very clear mark of its significance, a lane definitely featured in the mature mid-12th-century claustral layouts at both Cîteaux and Clairvaux (Fig. 2).[129]

Such lanes were often relatively narrow spaces, appearing (in plan at least) as no more than passages. Clairvaux is the best French example of the form, though it also appeared at 12th-century Aiguebelle (Drôme) and Fontfroide, and again at the

13th-century royal abbey of Royaumont (Val-d'Oise).[130] Much the same pattern featured at Casamari and Fossanova in Italy, Alcobaça in Portugal, and at Mellifont in Ireland.[131] English and Welsh examples of the type are known from Beaulieu, Buildwas, Byland, Neath, Rufford and Sawley.[132] In marked contrast to this pattern, the width of the lane at Cîteaux was such that it could almost be described as a court-yard. The same could be said of the arrangements at Clairmont (Mayenne) in France, Villers in Belgium, Eberbach in Germany,[133] and Kirkstall, Stanley, and perhaps Whitland in England and Wales.[134]

The exact purpose of the lane, together with the reasons for its occurrence at some sites and absence at others, has been much debated. At the end of the 19th century, there was a rather vague suggestion that it was intended merely to cut off the sound of the 'noisy trades' carried out by the lay brothers within the west range itself. But as Hope pointed out, 'this will not do'.[135] A more plausible proposal was put forward as early as the 1880s by Micklethwaite, who wondered whether the lane may in fact have served as the lay brothers' cloister.[136] This particular view has continued to find its supporters,[137] who further point out that when a lane is absent from a site, there is sometimes a separate cloister court or yard for the *conversi*, as identified against the outer face of the west ranges at Fountains and Jervaulx.[138] More recently, Fergusson has sought to explain the differences by reference to the changing nature of the relationship between monks and lay brothers in the second half of the 12th century. The absence of lanes and enclosing walls at Fountains and Rievaulx may, he says, reflect 'the more egalitarian values associated with the earlier period'. But as tensions between the two groups grew later in the century, there was an ever increasing need for more formal segregation.[139]

Fountain House and Wall-Mounted Lavers

ONE of the more prominent features known from Cistercian cloister garths on the Continent is some form of centrally planned fountain pavilion, a small but distinctive building usually found projecting from the alley adjacent to the refectory.[140] In essence, this was the place where the monks washed themselves before going into the refectory for meals.[141] The structure might be square, circular, or polygonal, within which the laver basin itself was fed with a constant flow of running water. Such pavilions appear on early plans of Cîteaux and Clairvaux (Fig. 2),[142] and other good French examples are known from Fontenay, Le Thoronet (reconstructed), and Valmagne (Hérault).[143] Elsewhere there are fine survivals at Alcobaça in Portugal, Santes Creus and Poblet in Spain (Fig. 17), Bebenhausen and Maulbronn (Fig. 14) in Germany, and Heiligenkreuz, Neuberg and Zwettl in Austria.[144]

It has been suggested that such free-standing lavers are to be expected at a number of early Cistercian foundations in Britain, with plausible claims having been made for Buildwas, Byland, Fountains and Kirkstall.[145] And indeed, the foundations of one such 12th-century structure are to be seen in the cloister garth at Melrose in Scotland.[146] It seems, however, they were less favoured after the third quarter of the 12th century, their decline seeming to coincide with the rebuilding of south claustral ranges generally, and with the emergence of the preferred Cistercian refectory orientation, that is on a north–south axis at right angles to the cloister.[147] From this point on, British white monk lavers were more commonly placed in recesses positioned within the façade of the northern refectory wall.[148] Nonetheless, the move was not universal, as is witnessed by the remains of the very handsome, and once vaulted, octagonal

FIG. 18.   Rievaulx Abbey: wall-mounted laver
to the left of the refectory doorway
English Heritage

FIG. 17.   Poblet Abbey (Catalonia):
fountain pavilion laver, *c.* 1200
David Robinson

fountain pavilion surviving in the cloister garth at Melifont in Ireland, dating to *c.* 1200–10.[149]

The earliest example of a British wall-mounted laver is almost certainly that which survives in the south alley at Fountains. Now thought to date from *c.* 1185, it was a paired arrangement in which the laver basins or troughs were set in recesses on either side of the refectory doorway.[150] Something very similar was introduced at Rievaulx shortly afterwards, and was again associated with the rebuilding of the monks' refectory (Fig. 18).[151] Later examples, which run through to the late 13th century, include Beaulieu, Cleeve, Forde, Hailes, Neath, Netley, and Tintern (Fig. 11).[152]

Aside from their use by the monks for washing their hands before entering the refectory for meals, we can be confident that both wall-mounted and pavilion lavers were designed so that they could accommodate the liturgy associated with the *mandatum*.[153] This important weekly rite had originally been prescribed in the Rule of St Benedict, and involved a symbolic washing of the brethren's feet.[154] This action — indicative of humility and exemplary charity — was clearly done in imitation of Christ washing the feet of the Apostles before the Last Supper. Such was the significance of the *mandatum* to the early Cistercians that St Bernard suggested it should be made the eighth sacrament.[155] The basic rite was performed every Saturday, when the washing was enacted by those monks appointed to serve as the kitchen helpers for the week.[156] On Maundy Thursday, as part of an expanded programme for the *mandatum* liturgy, the abbot himself washed the feet of twelve members of the community: four monks,

FIG. 19. Byland Abbey: base of entrance doorway to the late-13th-century collation porch in the north cloister alley. The paired respond bases show where it was inserted into the original twin-shaft arcade

Stuart Harrison

FIG. 20. Strata Florida Abbey: collation bay projecting from the north cloister arcade wall, mid-15th century

Cadw, Welsh Assembly Government

four novices, and four lay brothers.[157] To help facilitate both these ceremonies, lavers set into the refectory façade sometimes featured benching above the washing trough, allowing the monks to sit with their feet close to the water. Traces of such benches have been identified at Fountains and Rievaulx, and also at Vaux-de-Cernay (Yvelines) in France.[158]

Collation Seats and Arcade Bays

THE last aspect of the Cistercian cloister garth to be considered is the general custom within the order of holding the brief evening ceremony known as collation (*collatio*, lit. conference) in the alley adjacent to the church.[159] The origins of the ceremony go back to the Rule of St Benedict, which decreed that after Vespers the community should sit together to listen to a reading before going into the church for Compline.[160] The ceremony took its name from the *Collationes* of St John Cassian (d. 435), one of the books recommended for reading.[161] Essentially, we might look for three structural indications connected with the collation. The first is a stone bench, running along the wall of the church, on which the monks sat during the reading.[162] Secondly, given that the abbot would usually have presided at the centre, there may be signs that his seat or throne was distinguished by a prominent architectural frame. Finally, opposite the abbot's seat, there was sometimes a projecting bay in the cloister arcading. This was the location of the lectern, and the place where the reader took up his position.

By far the most elaborate surviving abbot's seat, together with associated benching, is to be found at the French abbey of Cadouin in the Dordogne. The handsome composition, which includes figure sculpture, dates from the second half of the 15th century. To the left of the seat, the kneeling figure of an abbot with his monks is usually identified as the likely builder, Peter de Gaing (1455–75).[163] Nothing so grand is found in England and Wales, though there is a shallow recess with a trefoiled head representing the abbot's seat in the north alley at Cleeve,[164] and at Tintern (though robbed of its dressed stone) there is a similar recess with a pointed head, in this case also accompanied by stone benching.[165] Further examples of abbot's seats or thrones are known from Melrose in Scotland,[166] and from Graiguenamanagh and Grey in Ireland.[167]

The strongest evidence for the importance of a distinct bay in which the collation lectern could stand comes from a documentary source. In 1373, the monks at Boxley contracted the mason Stephen Lomherst to build new cloister arcades on all sides of their garth, erecting one per year. In the third year, Lomherst was to work on the alley next to the church, where he was also to build a pulpit for the collation (*pulpitum collationis*).[168] Architectural evidence for such bays in England comes, for instance, from Byland. There, in the north cloister alley, there are clear indications of a 13th-century collation bay having been inserted into the 12th-century cloister arcading (Fig. 19).[169] And, a geophysical survey suggests a similar bay may have existed at Fountains.[170] There is, finally, further evidence from two sites in Wales. At Strata Florida Abbey, in addition to slight traces of stone benching at the east end of the nave wall, there is a shallow canted bay projecting out from the middle of the north cloister alley, undoubtedly representing the position of the collation lectern (Fig. 20).[171] Then again at Whitland, the possibility of a collation bay in the same cloister alley has been revealed through geophysical survey.[172]

Of course, in Wales, as in the rest of the Cistercian world, such is the rarity of architectural evidence for the abbot's seat or throne that we might assume such permanence was not always considered necessary, and that wood may have sufficed in many instances. Collation bays, on the other hand, are more likely to have left archaeological evidence, and the chance of further discoveries seems high.[173]

NOTES

1. For introductions to the Cistercians, their ideals, and their place in western monasticism, see L. J. Lekai, *The Cistercians: Ideals and Reality* (Kent, Ohio 1977); M. Pacaut, *Les moines blancs: Histoire de l'ordre de Cîteaux* (Paris 1993); B. M. Bolton, 'The Cistercians', in *The Dictionary of Art*, ed. J. Turner, 34 vols

(London 1996), VII, 346–53; J. Burton, 'The Cistercian adventure', in *The Cistercian Abbeys of Britain: Far From the Concourse of Men*, ed. D. Robinson (London 1998); reprinted in paperback (London 2002), 7–33; D. H. Williams, *The Cistercians in the Early Middle Ages* (Leominster 1998); C. H. Lawrence, *Medieval Monasticism: Forms of Religious Life in Western Europe in the Middle Ages*, 3rd edn (Harlow 2001), 172–98. A controversial account of the order's origins is given in C. H. Berman, *The Cistercian Evolution: The Invention of a Religious Order in Twelfth-Century Europe* (Philadelphia 2000).

2. On the growth of the order and the distribution of its houses, see F. Van der Meer, *Atlas de l'ordre cistercien* (Paris and Brussels 1965); R. A. Donkin, *The Cistercians: Studies in the Geography of Medieval England and Wales* (Toronto 1978), 21–31; R. Locatelli, 'L'expansion de l'ordre cistercien', in *Bernard de Clairvaux: Histoire, mentalités, spiritualité*, Sources chrétiennes, 380 (Paris 1992), 103–40; Williams, *Cistercians in the Early Middle Ages*, 1–30.

3. Precise calculations are often difficult; one has to remember the many temporary sites and aborted foundations. For the Cistercians in England and Wales, see D. Knowles and R. N. Hadcock, *Medieval Religious Houses: England and Wales*, 2nd edn (London 1971), 112–28; D. Knowles, *The Monastic Order in England*, 2nd edn (Cambridge 1963), 208–66; J. Burton, 'The foundation of the British Cistercian houses', in *Cistercian Art and Architecture in the British Isles*, ed. C. Norton and D. Park (Cambridge 1986), 24–39; J. Burton, *Monastic and Religious Orders in Britain, 1000–1300* (Cambridge 1994), 63–77; Robinson, *Cistercian Abbeys of Britain*, 64–205 (which includes Scotland). For the Irish houses, see A. Gwynn and R. N. Hadcock, *Medieval Religious Houses: Ireland* (London 1970), 114–44; R. Stalley, *The Cistercian Monasteries of Ireland* (London and New Haven 1987).

4. For early, but still pertinent views, see M. Aubert, 'Existe-t-il une architecture cistercienne?', *Cahiers de civilisation médiévale*, 1 (1958), 153–58. The most recent overview is T. Kinder, *L'Europe Cistercienne* (La Pierre-qui Vire 1997); trans. edn, *Cistercian Europe: Architecture of Contemplation*, Cistercian Studies Series, 191 (Kalamazoo 2002). See also J.-B. Auberger, *L'unanimité cistercienne primitive: mythe ou réalité?*, Cîteaux: Commentaria cistercienses, studia et documenta, 3 (Achel 1986); Berman, *Cistercian Evolution*, 23–39.

5. The most important edition of the order's early legislative framework (with a commentary and notes) is now *Narrative and Legislative Texts from Early Cîteaux*, ed. C. Waddell, Cîteaux: Commentaria cistercienses, studia et documenta, 9 (Brecht 1999). Throughout the remainder of the paper, we alternate between references to the Cistercians and the 'white monks'. The white monk label emerged very early in the order's history, as witnessed in Walter Daniel's late-12th-century *Life of Ailred of Rievaulx*: 'These remarkable men … were known as the white monks after the colour of their habit, for they were clothed angel-like in undyed sheep's wool … Thus garbed … [they] shine as they walk with the very whiteness of snow.' For this, see P. Matarasso ed., *The Cistercian World: Monastic Writings of the Twelfth Century* (London 1993), 153; and on the Cistercian habit generally, see J. France, *The Cistercians in Medieval Art* (Stroud 1998), 72–82.

6. C. Holdsworth, 'The chronology and character of early Cistercian legislation on art and architecture', in Norton and Park ed., *Cistercian Art and Architecture*, 40–55, at 55; see also the important views made on this very same point in P. Fergusson, *Architecture of Solitude: Cistercian Abbeys in Twelfth-Century England* (Princeton 1984), 10–16.

7. There is a brief introduction in Kinder, *L'Europe cistercienne*, 129–38; and the Irish evidence is well covered in Stalley, *Cistercian Monasteries of Ireland*, 153–62; see also the interesting summary of various points in T. Coomans, *L'abbaye de Villers-en-Brabant: Construction, configuration et signification d'une abbaye cistercienne gothique*, Cîteaux: Commentaria cistercienses, studia et documenta, 11 (Brussels and Brecht 2000), 298–303. As sources for illustrations of many of the cloisters (and their features) mentioned in this paper, see Van der Meer, *Atlas*; A. Dimier, *L'art cistercien: hors de France* (La Pierre-qui-Vire 1971); A. Dimier, *L'art cistercien: France*, 3rd edn (La Pierre-qui-Vire 1982); Kinder, *L'Europe cistercienne*, 113–28, 145–60; J.-F. Leroux-Dhuys, *Cistercian Abbeys: History and Architecture* (Paris and Cologne 1998), passim.

8. W. Horn, 'On the origins of the medieval cloister', *Gesta*, 12 (1973), 13.

9. R. Stalley, *Early Medieval Architecture* (Oxford 1999), 182–84; Stalley, *Cistercian Monasteries of Ireland*, 51; C. Brooke, *The Age of the Cloister: The Story of Monastic Life in the Middle Ages* (Stroud 2003), 6–8.

10. This point is made in W. Braunfels, *Monasteries of Western Europe: The Architecture of the Orders* (London 1972), 41; Stalley, *Early Medieval Architecture*, 182. In the early Cistercian statues there was a clear statement that the proper dwelling-place for a monk, according to the Rule of St Benedict, 'ought to be the cloister': *Narrative and Legislative Texts*, 410 (Capitula XVI), 459 (Instituta VI).

11. On the origins of the cloister, see Horn, 'Origins of cloister', 13–52; and the essay by John McNeill in this volume. The principal work on the St Gall plan remains W. Horn and E. Born, *The Plan of St Gall: A Study of the Architecture and Economy of, and Life in a Paradigmatic Carolingian Monastery*, 3 vols (Berkeley 1979), I, 241–45. See also Braunfels, *Monasteries of Western Europe*, 31–46; K. J. Conant,

Carolingian and Romanesque Architecture, 800 to 1200, 4th edn (1978), new impression (New Haven and London 1993), 55–59; Stalley, *Early Medieval Architecture*, 184–88.

12. For Cîteaux, see M. Plouvier and A. Saint-Denis ed., *Pour une histoire monumentale de l'abbaye de Cîteaux, 1098–1998*, Cîteaux: Commentaria cistercienses, studia et documenta, 8 (Brecht and Dijon 1998), 123–64; for Clairvaux, J.-F. Leroux ed., *Histoire de Clairvaux: Actes du colloque de Bar-sur-Aube/Clairvaux 22 et 23 juin 1990*, Association renaissance de l'abbaye de Clairvaux (Bar-sur-Aube 1991), passim. The architecture of both sites is reviewed in its regional context in A. K. M. Kennedy [Gajewski], 'Gothic architecture in northern Burgundy in the 12th and early 13th centuries' (unpublished Ph.D. thesis, Courtauld Institute of Art, London 1996). Summaries of recent views (published and unpublished) will be found in D. M. Robinson, *The Cistercians in Wales: Architecture and Archaeology 1130–1540* (London 2006), passim.

13. Of course, one has to bear in mind just how little is known of Cistercian building before the middle years of the twelfth century. For Cistercian cloisters in France in general, see M. Aubert, *L'architecture cistercienne en France*, 2nd edn, 2 vols (Paris 1947), I, 107–34; II, 1–33.

14. We have found no significant investigation of this aspect of the subject in the scholarly literature. Before any broad conclusions can be drawn, more explanations may be required on a case by case basis. For views on the high incidence of northern cloisters in nunneries, for example, see R. Gilchrist, *Gender and Material Culture: The Archaeology of Religious Women* (London 1994), 92–149.

15. Most of these sites feature in Dimier, *L'art cistercien*, passim. Lists of fifty southern and thirty-four northern French cloisters are given in Aubert, *L'architecture cistercienne*, 112, n. 1. For a useful guide to all the Cistercian abbeys of France, giving map locations and access details, see B. Peugniez, *Routier cistercien: Abbayes et sites, France, Belgique, Luxembourg, Suisse* (Moisenay 2002).

16. For most of these, see Dimier, *L'art cistercien: hors de France*, passim; for Maulbronn, U. Knapp, *Das Kloster Maulbronn: Geschichte und Baugeschichte* (Stuttgart 1997), 34–35; for Melrose, Robinson, *Cistercian Abbeys of Britain*, 144–48; for Hore (and the layout of Irish Cistercian cloisters generally), Stalley, *Cistercian Monasteries of Ireland*, 53–56, 58. For a very full corpus of Cistercian plans, not always indicating the position of the cloister, see A. Dimier, *Recueil de plans d'eglises cisterciennes*, 2 vols and supplement (Paris 1949–67).

17. For the details, see the gazetteer at the end of this paper. Ground plans showing the position and scale of the cloister at almost all Cistercian sites in England and Wales (as well as Scotland) will be found in Robinson, *Cistercian Abbeys of Britain*, 64–205.

18. Bibliographical sources for these sites and their cloisters are given in the gazetteer.

19. As is suggested for northern Cistercian cloisters in France: Aubert *L'architecture cistercienne*, I, 112–16. For England and Wales, see, for example, R. Stone, 'The monastic precinct', in *A Definitive History of Dore Abbey*, ed. R. Shoesmith and R. Richardson (Woonton 1997), 125–38; D. M. Robinson, *Tintern Abbey*, 4th edn (Cardiff 2002); D. M. Robinson, *Buildwas Abbey* (London 2002).

20. Aubert, *L'architecture cistercienne*, 11, 109; Plouvier and Saint-Denis, *L'abbaye de Cîteaux*, 138, 145–46.

21. Roger Stalley wonders if the 100 ft (30.5 m) square cloister was 'something of a European norm', understood as such by the Cistercians as by other monastic orders: Stalley, *Cistercian Monasteries of Ireland*, 54. In part, this is based on a commentary on the Rule of St Benedict written *c.* 845–50 by Hildemar of Corbie. Hildemar declared that 'it was generally held that the cloister should be a hundred feet square and no less because that would make it too small': quoted in Horn and Born, *Plan of St Gall*, I, 184; see also Braunfels, *Monasteries of Western Europe*, 41, 237–38. For comments on the variation in size across Europe, see Coomans, *L'abbaye de Villers-en-Brabant*, 229, 551 (note 113).

22. The Westminster cloister was begun in 1253 and completed in the second half of the 14th century. It measured about 140 ft (42.7 m) north–south by 151 ft (46 m) east–west, enclosing a ground area of 21,140 sq. ft (1,964 sq. m): RCHME, *An Inventory of Historical Monuments in London, I, Westminster Abbey* (London 1924), 76–77; C. Wilson, P. Tudor-Craig, J. Physick and R. Gem, *Westminster Abbey* (London 1986), 80–85; J. Harvey, *Cathedrals of England and Wales*, 3rd edn (London 1974), 251. Bury St Edmunds was another wealthy English Benedictine house with a large cloister garth, something in the region of 155 ft (47.2 m) square.

23. For a discussion of the Sawley (and Boxley) arrangements, see G. Coppack, C. Hayfield and R. Williams, 'Sawley Abbey: the architecture and archaeology of a smaller Cistercian abbey', *JBAA*, 155 (2002), 22–114, at 70–71, 80–81, 109–10.

24. The 1980s excavations at St Mary Graces, the last Cistercian foundation in England, are not yet published in full. In interim reports, the cloister is shown detached from the abbey church, and separated from it by an open yard; see I. Grainger and D. Hawkins, 'Excavations at the Royal Mint site 1986–1988', *The London Archaeologist*, 5 (1984–88), 429–36; Robinson, *Cistercian Abbeys of Britain*, 136–37. However, it appears this is to be modified in a forthcoming monograph by Ian Grainger and Christopher Phillpotts. A new interpretation is given to the features initially thought to represent the main cloister. This is more likely

to represent a garth and walks attached to the chapel of the Holy Trinity (*c.* 1350–53), effectively representing the community's initial buildings. Within a decade, a new church was begun to the north-east, and a cloister started on the south side. Even so, the alignment of the posited east alley with something that looks very like a 'walking place' in a mendicant church remains most intriguing. Furthermore, the first cloister was retained within the layout of the mature abbey. We are grateful to Barney Sloane for bringing us up to date on developments in the forthcoming excavation report.

25. Braunfels, *Monasteries of Western Europe*, 97–98; Stalley, *Early Medieval Architecture*, 182.

26. Illustrations of Sénanque and Fontenay appear in Dimier, *L'art cistercien*, 70, 89–92, 107, 138; Santes Creus appears in Dimier, *L'art cistercien: hors de France*, 251, 266–67, and in Leroux-Dhuys, *Cistercian Abbeys*, 325–27. The Fontenay cloister is discussed in Aubert, *L'architecture cistercienne*, II, 6–9; J.-B. Auberger, *Mystère de Fontenay: La spiritualité de saint Bernard en majesté* (La Pierre-qui-Vire 2001), 87–95. For Sénanque, see Aubert, *L'architecture cistercienne*, II, 6–7; M. Thibout, 'L'abbaye de Sénanque', *Congrès Archéologique* (Comtat-Venaissin), 121 (1963), 365–76; C. Brou ed., *Notre-Dame de Sénanque Abbey* (Rennes 2003), 46–51. For Santes Creus, J.-F. Cabestany, *Real Monasterio de Santes Creus* (Barcelona 1997), 55–63; B. Rosenman, 'The tomb canopies and the cloister at Santes Creus', in *Studies in Cistercian Art and Architecture: Volume Two*, ed. M. P. Lillich, Cistercian Studies Series, 69 (Kalamazoo 1984), 229–40.

27. As pointed out in the subsequent section of this paper, it seems the Cistercians of the late 11th and early 12th centuries initially rejected the standard monastic plan.

28. For a note of caution on these traditional dates, see Robinson, *Cistercians in Wales*, 63–65, 77, plus notes, and Stuart Harrison's forthcoming article on the dating of Fontenay in the revue *Cîteaux* (2007).

29. Stalley, *Early Medieval Architecture*, 182–83.

30. In general terms, the lack of a later replacement was not necessarily related to insufficient wealth or patronage: the decision to keep the original seems to have been a matter of deliberate choice.

31. One important and quite remarkable exception is to be found in the cloister of the Cistercian nuns at Las Huelgas in Spain. Here, the miniature church façade carved on the face of one capital is taken to represent an intimate representation of the entry to the heavenly paradise. It is illustrated in S. Tobin, *The Cistercians: Monks and Monasteries of Europe* (London 1995), 19. The subject has been explored by Dr Rose Walker.

32. Both are illustrated in Leroux-Dhuys, *Cistercian Abbeys*, 166–67, 170–71; see also A. M. Caccin, *L'Abbazia di Chiaravalle Milanese* (Milan 1979), 47–49.

33. For the fullest analysis (with a transcript), see C. Rudolf, *The 'Things of Greater Importance': Bernard of Clairvaux's Apologia and the Medieval Attitude Towards Art* (Philadelphia 1990).

34. There are transcripts of this passage in, for example, Rudolf, *Things of Greater Importance*, 283; Braunfels, *Monasteries of Western Europe*, 242; Matarasso, *Cistercian World*, 57. Of course, as Rudolf argues (at 125–57), Bernard may not have been criticising capital sculpture *per se*, but uses it as a vehicle to question artistic distractions from monastic contemplation in general.

35. *Narrative and Legislative Texts*, 413 (*Capitula XXVI*), 464 (*Instituta XX*).

36. For a recent consideration of the theme see, in particular, M. Cassidy-Welch, *Monastic Spaces and their Meanings: Thirteenth-Century English Cistercian Monasteries* (Turnhout 2001), 47–71, passim. On the different usages of the words *claustra* and *claustrum* during the Middle Ages, P. Meyvaert, 'The medieval monastic claustrum', *Gesta*, 12 (1973), 53–54; Brooke, *The Age of the Cloister*, 7.

37. For the liturgy associated with these, see *Les 'Ecclesiastica Officia' cisterciens du XIIème siècle*, ed. D. Choisselet and P. Vernet, Documentation cistercienne, 22 (Reiningue 1989), chap. 17 (Palm Sunday), chap. 29 (Ascension Day), chap. 47 (Candlemas). For more on the theme of processions, see Cassidy-Welch, *Monastic Spaces*, 58–61.

38. Cassidy-Welch, *Monastic Spaces*, 59–60.

39. *Ecclesiastica Officia*, chapter 55.

40. Cassidy-Welch, *Monastic Spaces*, 61.

41. The St Gall plan of *c.* 820–30 was of course the clearest demonstration of the model, for which see Horn and Born, *Plan of St Gall*; also the paper by John McNeill in this volume. As one of the primary examples of the way this had become formalised by the mid-11th century, we might consider the arrangements at Burgundian Cluny (i.e. Cluny II): Conant, *Carolingian and Romanesque Architecture*, 146–48; Braunfels, *Monasteries of Western Europe*, 54–58.

42. On the earliest Cistercian buildings, with reference to their lack of central cloister planning, see J. O. Schaefer, 'The earliest churches of the Cistercian order', in *Studies in Cistercian Art and Architecture: Volume One*, ed. M. P. Lillich, Cistercian Studies Series, 66 (Kalamazoo 1982), 1–12; P. Fergusson, 'The first architecture of the Cistercians in England and the work of Abbot Adam of Meaux', *JBAA*, 136 (1983), 74–86; G. Coppack, '"According to the form of the order": the earliest Cistercian buildings in England and their context', in *Perspectives for an Architecture of Solitude: Essays on Cistercians, Art and Architecture in Honour of Peter Fergusson*, ed. T. N. Kinder (Turnhout 2004), 35–45.

43. In other essays in this volume Tim Tatton-Brown discusses the infirmary cloister at Christchurch Priory, Canterbury, while John McNeill and Stuart Harrison mention the '*in situ*' arcade in the south cloister walk at the abbey of Benedictine nuns at West Malling in Kent, perhaps dating to the 1220s. They remind us, however, that Tim Tatton-Brown has shown this arcade was dismantled and reassembled before the suppression. The east walk at Westminster was begun by Henry of Reyns in 1253: see note 22, above; Wilson et al., *Westminster Abbey*, 80–81. For Salisbury, see T. Tatton-Brown, 'The cloisters of Salisbury Cathedral', *Friends of Salisbury Cathedral 65th Annual Report* (1995), 6-10 (though the dates here have always been controversial).

44. See, for example, L. Butler, 'The Cistercians in England and Wales: a survey of recent archaeological work 1960–1980', in Lillich ed., *Studies in Cistercian Art and Architecture: One*, 88–101, at 93.

45. For introductions to the impact of State guardianship, see Fergusson, *Architecture of Solitude*, xxii–xxiv, 163–64; Robinson, *Cistercians in Wales*, 11–15.

46. P. Fergusson and S. Harrison, *Rievaulx Abbey: Community, Architecture, Memory* (New Haven and London 1999), 36, 211.

47. Robinson, *Cistercians in Wales*, 11–12.

48. There is undoubtedly more evidence of English and Welsh Cistercian cloister arcading waiting to be uncovered. The authors welcome information from readers who may be able to correct or add to the entries in the gazetteer.

49. On the statute which sought to control further foundations, see *Narrative and Legislative Texts*, 492–93 (*Instituta XXVI*). The numbers included some eleven houses incorporated into the order from the congregation of Savigny in the merger of 1147, for which see Knowles, *Monastic Order*, 250–51.

50. The assemblages from all three sites are illustrated and described in G. Zarnecki, J. Holt and T. Holland ed., *English Romanesque Art 1066–1200* (London 1984), 167–73, 184–85. The Reading arcades are covered further in R. Baxter and S. Harrison, 'The decoration of the cloister at Reading Abbey', in *Windsor: Medieval Archaeology, Art and Architecture of the Thames Valley*, ed. L. Keen and E. Scarff, BAA Trans., xxv (Leeds 2002), 302–12. Henry of Blois was abbot of Glastonbury between 1126 and 1171.

51. See the paper by Stuart Harrison on Benedictine and Augustinian cloisters in this volume.

52. Details of all will be found in the gazetteer. The use of 'great' here is intended to distinguish the principal cloister from that of the infirmary or other areas.

53. A note of caution must be sounded here. Without the presence of a corner springer, it is sometimes impossible to be sure of the orientation of the arcading. Also, for the most part, the archaeological evidence of these 12th-century arcades is too scant to determine if they were buttressed at intervals.

54. Fergusson and Harrison, *Rievaulx Abbey*, 87, 137; P. Fergusson, G. Coppack and S. Harrison, *Rievaulx Abbey* (London 2006), 17, 19, 27.

55. As pointed out in the gazetteer entry, the *ex situ* cloister material suggests certain variations on the basic form described here.

56. The Kirkstall arcades were first considered in W. H. St John Hope and J. Bilson, *Architectural Description of Kirkstall Abbey*, Thoresby Society Publications, 16 (Leeds 1907), 27–28, fig 21.

57. Fergusson, *Architecture of Solitude*, 69–72.

58. The Jervaulx arcades were first considered in W. H. St John Hope and H. Brakspear, 'Jervaulx Abbey', *Yorkshire Archaeological Journal*, 21 (1911), 315–16.

59. B. Harbottle and P. Salway, 'Excavations at Newminster Abbey, Northumberland, 1961–63', *Archaeologia Aeliana*, 4th series, 42 (1964), 146, 148.

60. G. Coppack, *Abbeys: Yorkshire's Monastic Heritage* (London 1988), 8–9; P. Fergusson, *Roche Abbey* (London 1990), 14–15; G. Coppack, *Abbeys & Priories* (Stroud 2006), 93–94.

61. For previous considerations of these arcades, see W. H. St John Hope, 'Fountains Abbey', *Yorkshire Archaeological Journal*, 15 (1900), 339–41; Coppack, *Abbeys*, 29; G. Coppack and R. Gilyard-Beer, *Fountains Abbey* (London 1993), 30; G. Coppack, *Fountains Abbey: The Cistercians in Northern England* (Stroud 2003), 68.

62. The fresh research, as yet unpublished, is by Stuart Harrison.

63. Details of all three are given in the gazetteer. The Jervaulx arcade was considered in Hope and Brakspear, 'Jervaulx Abbey', 343.

64. Fergusson and Harrison, *Rievaulx Abbey*, 110, 116–17; Fergusson, Coppack and Harrison, *Rievaulx Abbey*, 27.

65. This can presumably be attributed, in no small measure, to the fact the 12th-century arcades were replaced around 1400. For a summary of the excavations, which began in 1969, see G. Astill, S. Hirst and S. M. Wright, 'The Bordesley Abbey project reviewed', *Archaeol. J.*, 161 (2004), 106–58.

66. On the recovery of material, see D. A. Walsh, 'A rebuilt cloister at Bordesley Abbey', *JBAA*, 132 (1979), 43. For the capital and base, P. Rahtz and S. Hirst, *Bordesley Abbey, Redditch, Hereford–Worcestershire: First Report on Excavations 1969–1973*, BAR, British Series, 23 (Oxford 1976), 142, 146; S. M. Hirst, D. A. Walsh and S. M. Wright, *Bordesley Abbey II: Second Report on Excavations at Bordesley*

Abbey, Redditch, Hereford–Worcestershire, BAR, British Series, 111 (Oxford 1983), 264–65. The proposed date is given in Astill, Hirst and Wright, 'Bordesley Abbey', 150.

67. H. Brakspear, *Waverley Abbey*, Surrey Archaeological Society (Guildford 1905), 35–37.

68. A. W. Clapham, 'Three monastic houses of south Wales', *Archaeologia Cambrensis*, 76 (1921), 208. In passing, it is also worth noting that the coupled form was common at Cistercian sites in Ireland during the late 12th and early 13th centuries, for which see Stalley, *Cistercian Monasteries of Ireland*, 153–54.

69. The Furness arcades were considered in W. H. St John Hope, 'The abbey of St Mary in Furness, Lancashire', *Transactions of the Cumberland and Westmorland Antiquarian and Archaeological Society*, 16 (1900), 257–58.

70. As at Fountains, the Furness builders used marble to create polychromatic effects. Interestingly, something like these two northern English arcades was reported at Graiguenamanagh in Ireland in 1892, including paired shafts in blue limestone, paired capitals, and round arches with trefoiling: Stalley, *Cistercian Monasteries of Ireland*, 154.

71. For Bindon, see RCHME, *An Inventory of Historical Monuments in the County of Dorset*, 5 vols (London 1952–75), II, ii, *South-East*, 404.

72. Robinson, *Buildwas Abbey*, 11, 14.

73. W. H. St John Hope and H. Brakspear, 'The Cistercian abbey of Beaulieu, in the county of Southampton', *Archaeol. J.*, 63 (1906), 152.

74. H. Brakspear, 'The Cistercian abbey of Stanley, Wiltshire', *Archaeologia*, 60 (1906–07), 506.

75. Robinson, *Cistercians in Wales*, 118–21, 190–91, 207, 246.

76. S. Harrison, 'The loose architectural detail', in Shoesmith and Richardson ed., *Dore Abbey*, 75–76; Robinson, *Cistercians in Wales*, 172–73.

77. There are also suggestions for Hulton and Dieulacres, for which see the gazetteer entries. Mid-13th-century cloister arcades carried on triple shaft groups are known from the Augustinian priories of Norton in Cheshire and Haverfordwest in Pembrokeshire, though both were adorned with figure sculpture. For Norton, see J. P. Greene, *Norton Priory: The Archaeology of a Medieval Religious House* (Cambridge 1989), 111–18. See also Stuart Harrison's essay on Benedictine and Augustinian cloisters in this volume.

78. For the rebuilding programmes, see Robinson, *Tintern Abbey*, 29–31. For the new cloister, S. Harrison, 'The thirteenth-century cloister arcade at Tintern Abbey', in *Cardiff: Architecture and Archaeology in the Medieval Diocese of Llandaff*, ed. J. R. Kenyon and D. M. Williams, BAA Trans., XXIX (Leeds 2006), 86–101; Robinson, *Cistercians in Wales*, 172–75.

79. To date, only one moulded corner capital for a triple-shaft group has been identified, though more possibilities for both capitals and bases appear in early photographs.

80. Very few examples of syncopated cloister arcades have so far been identified, although it is reasonably certain that the form originated before the 1220s. The only extant instance of the design occurs not in Britain, but at the Benedictine abbey of Mont-Saint-Michel (Manche) in Normandy, apparently completed by 1228. For this, and other examples of the basic form, see L. Grant, *Architecture and Society in Normandy, 1120–1270* (New Haven and London 2005), 165–67; Harrison, 'cloister arcade at Tintern Abbey', 99–101; Robinson, *Cistercians in Wales*, 174.

81. Dr Hall has identified three possible design forms in the cloister arcade fragments she has recovered at Croxden: J. Hall, 'Croxden Abbey: buildings and community', 2 vols (unpublished Ph.D. thesis, University of York, 2003), I 54–56, 176–81; II, figs A11–A17.

82. A point made by Dr Richard Morris on the basis of an initial consideration of the fragments (pers. comm. 1989–90). The best parallels are with the Salisbury chapter-house detailing. For recent views on the date of this work, see S. Brown, *Sumptuous and Richly Adorn'd: The Decoration of Salisbury Cathedral* (London 1999), 28–31.

83. The Tintern cloister garth was positioned to the north of the church (Fig. 1).

84. For which, see Robinson, *Cistercians in Wales*, 124–37.

85. J. Hayward, 'Glazed cloisters and their development in the houses of the Cistercian order', *Gesta* (1973), 93–109, at 97.

86. Aubert, *L'architecture cistercienne*, II, 15–16, 18–20; Hayward, 'Glazed Cloisters', 96–97; Dimier, *L'art cistercien*, 259. Hayward, in 'Glazed Cloisters', 97, also mentions that the arcades at Loccum in Germany were glazed in the late 13th century.

87. The south walk at Maulbronn was begun *c.* 1214–20. The work on the north, east and west arcades dates from after 1270: Knapp, *Maulbronn*, 79–82, 96–114, passim.

88. As discussed in the subsequent section of this paper, the 13th-century arcades at Hailes were replaced in the late 15th century. See also the gazetteer entries for further details.

89. M. C. Jones and S. W. Williams, 'Excavations on the site of Strata Marcella Abbey — Report on excavations at Strata Marcella Abbey, near Welshpool', *Montgomeryshire Collections*, 25 (1891), 173 and pl. 8. Given the nature of their sketch drawings, one must accept this as no more than a very tentative suggestion.

90. See, in general, G. Webb, *Architecture in Britain: The Middle Ages* (London 1956), 155–57; Harvey, *Cathedrals*, 145, 251. For Norwich, see F. Woodman, 'The Gothic Campaigns', in *Norwich Cathedral: Church, City and Diocese, 1096–1996*, ed. I. Atherton, E. Fernie, C. Harper-Bill and H. Smith (London 1996), 165–78; for Westminster, Wilson et al., *Westminster Abbey*, 80–85.

91. H. Brakspear, 'Pipewell Abbey, Northamptonshire', *Associated Architectural Societies' Reports and Papers*, 30 (1909–10), 301, 307.

92. L. F. Salzman, *Building in England Down to 1540* (Oxford 1952), 448–50; P. J. Tester, 'Excavations at Boxley Abbey', *Archaeologia Cantiana*, 88 (1973), 135, 153–56. J. Harvey, *English Medieval Architects: A Biographical Dictionary Down to 1550*, 2nd edn (Gloucester 1984), 185–86. As noted in the gazetteer, the scheme may not have been completed to plan in all alleys.

93. Brakspear, 'Cistercian abbey of Stanley', 506.

94. Robinson, *Cistercians in Wales*, 14, 175–77, 229.

95. The material was first identified in the 1890s, but no capitals seem to have been recorded. See H. Hughes, 'Valle Crucis Abbey', *Archaeologia Cambrensis*, 5th series, 11 (1894), 171–72, 274–75; 12 (1895), 6–7; Robinson, *Cistercians in Wales*, 175–76, 290–93.

96. The earliest known Irish example seems to be that constructed at Jerpoint Abbey *c.* 1390–1400. The re-erected arcade has arches placed in groups of three set between solid rectangular piers. At Inch, St Mary's Dublin and Holycross, earlier arcades were replaced with open cusped arches. At Bective the cusped arches were not continuous but set in groups of three within an enclosing arch. These and other late-medieval Irish arcades are discussed in Stalley, *Cistercian Monasteries of Ireland*, 154–61.

97. Robinson, *Tintern Abbey*, 60–62. There was also a late-medieval covered arcade linking a doorway in the north aisle of the presbytery with the infirmary court and abbot's lodging. One only has to look at the evidence from Fountains (see gazetteer) to appreciate the potential for arcading in such arrangements.

98. Knapp, *Maulbronn*, 46–47, 118–21. Knapp's dates may be too late for other commentators. See, for instance, H. Grüger, 'Cistercian fountain houses in central Europe', in *Studies in Cistercian Art and Architecture: Volume Two*, ed. M. P. Lillich, Cistercian Studies Series, 69 (Kalamazoo 1984), 201–22, at 207, where the fountain house is dated to *c.* 1250. Cistercian fountain house lavers are considered in the next section of this paper.

99. Rosenman, 'Santes Creus', 231-32, 236-37; Cabestany, *Santes Creus*, 54–61; N. de Dalmases and A. Pitarch, *Història de l'Art Catalá, Vol III: L'Art Gòtic* (Barcelona 1984), 114–19; Harvey, *Medieval Architects*, 109–10. There are good illustrations of some of the sculpture in Leroux-Dhuys, *Cistercian Abbeys*, 119.

100. Rudolf, *Things of Greater Importance*, 283.

101. Walsh, 'Bordesley Abbey', 43–49.

102. Walsh was more cautious when writing in 1979, saying 'It cannot be determined at this time what kind of roofing the cloister walks possessed': ibid., 47–48.

103. S. Harrison, *Byland Abbey* (London 1990), 12. Byland was unusual among the abbeys of Yorkshire in this regard. The wealthy houses at Fountains, Jervaulx and Rievaulx, for instance, all seem to have been perfectly content to retain their 12th-century arcades through to the suppression.

104. C. A. R. Radford, *Strata Florida Abbey* (London 1949); Robinson, *Cistercians in Wales*, 177–78, 272; D. M Robinson, *Strata Florida Abbey — Talley Abbey*, 3rd edn (Cardiff 2007), 51–52.

105. As in J. G. Coad, *Hailes Abbey*, 2nd edn (London 1993), 7–8, 21. See also, W. Bazeley, 'The abbey of St Mary, Hayles', *Transactions of the Bristol and Gloucestershire Archaeological Society*, 22 (1899), 259–60, 265–66.

106. The vault form is clear from the half-bay reconstruction in the grounds of the site museum. The bosses are displayed in the museum itself.

107. Robinson, *Tintern Abbey*, 17, 36–37, 48–49; Robinson, *Cistercians in Wales*, 177, 281–85.

108. R. Gilyard-Beer, *Cleeve Abbey*, 2nd edn (London 1990), 11–13, 46–47.

109. For the latest views on Chard's building campaigns, see A. Emery, *Greater Medieval Houses of England and Wales 1300–1500*, 3 vols (Cambridge 1996–2006), III, *Southern England*, 560–65. The dates of Chard's abbacy are taken from here and correct the more frequently given 1521–39. See also, RCHME, *An Inventory of the Historical Monuments in Dorset*, 5 vols (London 1952–75), I, *West*, 242; L. Monckton, 'Late Gothic architecture in south west England', 2 vols (unpublished Ph.D. thesis, University of Warwick, 1999), I, 304–14.

110. We make this connection only in the very broadest terms: J. M. Luxford, *The Art and Architecture of English Benedictine Monasteries, 1300–1540* (Woodbridge 2005), 51–113. As one clear demonstration of the similarities between this late Cistercian work and that of, say, the Benedictines in the south-west, one only has to compare the striking resemblances found between Chard's scheme at Forde and the near-contemporary cloister work at Muchelney: Monckton, 'Late Gothic' I, 307; J. Goodall and F. Kelly, *Muchelney Abbey* (London 2004), 10–11, 15–16. Aside from these closing remarks on late Cistercian cloisters

in England and Wales, we should not entirely overlook those late medieval examples built on the Continent. Three examples will suffice: Villers in Belgium, Cadouin (Dordogne) in France, and Bebenhausen in Germany. At Villers, the south and west galleries were reconstructed as part of a programme of late-15th-century works: Coomans, *L'abbaye de Villiers-en-Brabant*, 294–95. At Cadouin elaborate new vaulted galleries were erected on the north, east and south sides of the cloister in two main phases between about 1455 and 1504: J. Gardelles, 'L'abbaye de Cadouin', *Congrès Archéologique*, 137 (1979), 146–78. The work at Bebenhausen includes net vaults and dates from 1471–96: M. Köhler, *Die Bau- und Kunstgeschichte des ehemaligen Zisterzienserklosters Bebenhausen: Der Klausurbereich*, Veröffentlichungen der Kommission für geschichtliche Landeskunde in Baden-Württemberg, Reihe B/124 (Stuttgart 1995). Of course, in addition to this late-medieval work, if abbeys survived the Middle Ages (as notably in France and Italy), cloisters sometimes received further attention in later centuries.

111. Williams, *Cistercians in the Early Middle Ages*, 240.

112. In the case of those houses with northern cloisters, the relevant alley was on the south side of the garth.

113. Fergusson and Harrison, *Rievaulx Abbey*, 229.

114. Brakspear, 'Pipewell Abbey', 301.

115. For Cistercian reading and intellectual pursuits, see Lekai, *The Cistercians*, 227–47; Williams, *Cistercians in the Early Middle Ages*, 97–108.

116. *Claustra sine literatura, Est vivi hominis sepultura*: quoted in Williams, *Cistercians in the Early Middle Ages*, 100.

117. Kinder, *L'Europe cistercienne*, 241–44.

118. Coppack and Gilyard-Beer, *Fountains Abbey*, 30; Fergusson, Coppack and Harrison, *Rievaulx Abbey*, 17. For weekly duties, see *Ecclesiastica Officia*, chapters 104–08.

119. *Ecclesiastica Officia*, chapters 85, 90.19–20.

120. From the comprehensive excavations at Bordesley, it is known that the floor of the presbytery in the abbey church itself was paved with no more than plain stone slabs up to about 1200: Hirst, Walsh and Wright, *Bordesely Abbey*, 28, 35–38. In excavations (1970) in the south-west corner of the cloister at Valle Crucis, Butler found no surviving trace of a floor or paving: L. A. S. Butler, 'Valle Crucis Abbey: an excavation in 1970', *Archaeologia Cambrensis*, 125 (1976), 86.

121. *Twelfth-Century Statutes from the Cistercian General Chapter*, ed. C. Waddell, Cîteaux: Commentaria cistercienses, studia et documenta, 12 (Brecht 2002), 285. Burial within Cistercian cloister galleries is potentially a whole separate strand of investigation. Santes Creus is one well-known site where a series of grand sarcophagi rest in niches set into the wall of the nave in the north gallery: Cabestany, *Santes Creus*, passim. See, also, Coomans, *L'abbaye de Villiers-en-Brabant*, 288–91, 301. The theme of burial at white monk abbeys is explored in a special edition of the journal *Cîteaux*, 56 (2005); J. Hall and C. Kratzke, ed., *Sepulturae Cistercienses: Burial, Memorial and Patronage in Medieval Cistercian Monasteries*.

122. Generally, see C. Norton 'Early Cistercian tile pavements', in Norton and Park ed., *Cistercian Art and Architecture*, 228–55; J. M. Lewis, *The Medieval Tiles of Wales* (Cardiff 1999), 1–13.

123. Brakspear, 'Stanley Abbey', 506.

124. For Buildwas, Robinson, *Buildwas Abbey*, 14; for Byland, J. Stopford, *Medieval Floor Tiles of Northern England: Pattern and Purpose — Production Between the 13th and 16th Centuries* (Oxford 2005), 236–42, passim, 280, 283. Stopford's survey of northern English tiles is instructive in showing just how little survives from cloister alleys at any site.

125. Lewis, *Medieval Tiles of Wales*, 227, 241, 245.

126. For general comments on gardens, see Fergusson and Harrison, *Rievaulx Abbey*, 65–66, and their reconstructions at 88–89, 134–35. At Jervaulx Abbey, in extremely dry weather, differential dieback in the grass of the cloister garth indicates the presence of paths. These radiate from a central circular feature in a cross-shaped plan to the mid-point of each alley.

127. Aubert, *L'architecture cistercienne*, I, 53; II, 122–23. This is taken up in Kinder, *L'Europe cistercienne*, 311, 329; see also Braunfels, *Monasteries of Western Europe*, 77–79.

128. Aubert, *L'architecture cistercienne*, II, facing 1; Dimier, *L'art cistercien*, 39–41.

129. Aubert, *L'architecture cistercienne*, I, 11, 109; II, 122.

130. Plans in ibid., I, 110, 115, 121.

131. Dimier, *L'art cistercien: hors de France*, 197, 209, 298; R. Stalley, 'Mellifont Abbey: a study of its architectural history', *Proceedings of the Royal Irish Academy, Section C*, 80 (1980), 263–354, at 301, 313.

132. Plans of all of these will be found in Robinson, *Cistercian Abbeys of Britain*, 64–205, passim. Further sources are listed in the gazetteer.

133. For Clairmont, see Aubert, *L'architecture cistercienne*, I, 178–79; for Villiers, Coomans, *L'abbaye de Villiers-en-Brabant*, 292–93, 413, 427–28, 545–48; for Eberbach, Dimier, *L'art cistercien: hors de France*, 104, 124.

134. Robinson, *Cistercian Abbeys of Britain*, 64–205, passim; Robinson, *Cistercians in Wales*, 295.

135. Hope, 'Fountains Abbey', 381–82; Hope and Bilson, *Kirkstall Abbey*, 58.

136. J. T. Micklethwaite, 'Of the Cistercian plan', *Yorkshire Archaeological Journal*, 7 (1882), 239–58.

137. Williams, *Cistercians in the Early Middle Ages*, 249.

138. Details are given in the gazetteer.

139. Fergusson and Harrison, *Rievaulx Abbey*, 56–58.

140. See, in general, Braunfels, *Monasteries of Western Europe*, 101, 103; M. P. Lillich, 'Cleanliness with godliness: a discussion of medieval monastic plumbing', in *Mélanges à la mémoire du père Anselme Dimier*, ed. B. Chauvin, 3 vols in 6 (Arbois 1982–87), III, 5, 123–49; Grüger, 'Cistercian fountain houses in central Europe', 201–22; Kinder, *L'Europe cistercienne*, 135–38; Williams, *Cistercians in the Early Middle Ages*, 246–47; J. Bond, 'Monastic water management in Britain: a review', in *Monastic Archaeology: Papers on the Study of Medieval Monasteries*, ed. G Keevill, M. Aston and T. Hall (Oxford 2001), 88–136, at 115–16.

141. *Ecclesiastica Officia*, chapters 76.4–8, 108.15–16.

142. Aubert, *L'architecture cistercienne*, II, 26; Braunfels, *Monasteries of Western Europe*, 80; Plouvier and Saint-Denis, *l'abbaye de Cîteaux*, 138, 145–46. In P. Didron, ed., *Annales Archaéologiques*, 3 (Paris 1845), 231, describes the laver at Clairvaux as 'Une grande fontaine don't le bassin est d'une pière d'une pièce, ayant de longueur plus de qualtre toises, et tout à l'entour gecte yaue par divers conduitz'.

143. Aubert, *L'architecture cistercienne*, II, 25–31. The Fontenay pavilion has been lost, though an indication of its form is provided in a reconstruction by Viollet le Duc, reproduced by Aubert. The simple late-12th-century structure at Le Thoronet was restored in 1924.

144. Many of these are illustrated in Van der Meer, *Atlas*, passim; Leroux-Dhuys *Cistercian Abbeys*, passim; see also Dimier, *L'art cistercien: hors de France*, passim; Grüger, 'Cistercian fountain houses', passim. The approximate dates are: Alcobaça (13th century), Santes Creus (late 12th century), Poblet (late 12th century), Bebenhausen (*c.* 1400), Maulbronn (*c.* 1250, or early 14th century), Heiligenkreuz (late 13th century), Neuberg (*c.* 1300), Zwettl (early 13th century).

145. See, for example, Coppack, *Fountains Abbey*, 65; Coppack, *Abbeys & Priories*, 154–56 (for Kirkstall and Byland); Robinson, *Buildwas Abbey*, 11, 21; see also gazetteer entries. For further context on freestanding lavatoria in England, W. H. Godfrey, 'English cloister lavatories as independent structures', *Archaeol. J.*, 106, supplement for 1949 (1952), 91–97.

146. R. Fawcett and R. Oram, *Melrose Abbey* (Stroud 2004), 175–76.

147. On the general point, see P. Fergusson, 'The twelfth-century refectories at Rievaulx and Byland abbeys', in Norton and Park ed., *Cistercian Art and Architecture*, 160–80; Robinson, *Cistercians in Wales*, 156–57, 201–09.

148. That is in the wall face contained within the south cloister alley (or the north alley in the case of northern garths). Lillich, in 'Cleanliness with godliness', 140–41, goes so far as to suggest this recessed form of laver may have been invented by the Cistercians to cope with the cold winters encountered in northern Britain.

149. Stalley, 'Mellifont Abbey', 310–12, 348–50; Stalley, *Cistercian Monasteries of Ireland*, 170–72. Professor Stalley argues the Mellifont pavilion was an addition to the original cloister arcading and suggests it was of English inspiration, owing less to Cistercian preference for this form on the Continent.

150. Hope, 'Fountains Abbey', 360–61; Coppack, *Fountains Abbey*, 64–65. The date of *c.* 1185 is based on new research of Stuart Harrison. Glyn Coppack prefers the 1170s.

151. The refectory dates from the time of Abbot Sylvanus (1167–88): Fergusson and Harrison, *Rievaulx Abbey*, 142–47.

152. Bond, 'Monastic water management', 117–18. The key features are all described in the gazetteer entries, where further sources are also given. More work needs to be done at Continental sites to determine the frequency (or otherwise) of lavers which were not housed in pavilions. At Notre-Dame-de-l'Épau (Sarthe) and Vaux-de-Cernay, for example, there appear to have been early-13th-century wall-mounted lavers: Aubert, *L'architecture cistercienne*, II, 25, 28; J.-Y. Bernier, *L' Épau, une abbaye cistercienne* (Paris 1988); A. C. Rochet, 'The refectory wing of the Cistercian abbey of Vaux-de-Cernay', in *Studies in Cistercian Art and Architecture: Volume Five*, Cistercian Studies Series, 167 (Kalamazoo 1998), 187–210, at 196, 199. On the other hand, in the 15th century, the community at Villers replaced its earlier laver (of uncertain form) with a three-bay rectangular structure, forming only a shallow projection into the garth. It is described by Coomans as 'exceptional': Coomans, *L'abbaye de Villiers-en-Brabant*, 272–76, 300. Yet something similar seems to have been built at Wettingen in Switzerland in the 13th century: Grüger, 'Cistercian fountain houses', 209.

153. For accounts of the rite and its importance, see Fergusson, 'twelfth-century refectories', 178–80; Fergusson and Harrison, *Rievaulx Abbey*, 149; Lekai, *The Cistercians*, 374; Cassidy-Welch, *Monastic Spaces*, 61–62.

154. *The Rule of St Benedict*, ed. J. McCann (London 1976), chapter 35. On its importance to early post-Conquest Benedictine communities in England, see *The Monastic Constitutions of Lanfranc*, ed. D. Knowles and C. N. L. Brooke (Oxford 2002), 4–5, 52–58.

155. Lillich, 'Cleanliness with godliness', 147.

156. *Ecclesiastica Officia*, chapter 108.32–43.

157. *Ecclesiastica Officia*, chapter 21.23–42. On Maunday Thursday, another version of the rite, known as the *mandatum pauperum*, took place in one of the cloister walks. A further version was employed for visiting guests: *Ecclesiastica Officia*, chapters 21.7–19, 107.

158. Hope, 'Fountains Abbey', 361; Fergusson and Harrison, *Rievaulx Abbey*, 149; Rochet, 'Vaux-de-Cernay', 196, 199.

159. For general context, see R. Gilyard-Beer, 'Boxley Abbey and the *pulpitum collationis*', in *Collectanea Historica: Essays in Memory of Stuart Rigold*, ed. A. Detsicas (Maidstone 1981), 123–31; Kinder, *L'Europe cistercienne*, 133–34; Williams, *Cistercians in the Early Middle Ages*, 240–41.

160. *Rule of St Benedict*, chapter 42. The English Benedictines do not appear to have had a fixed place for the collation. In the 11th century, Archbishop Lanfranc's constitutions decreed it was to take place in the chapter-house: *Monastic Constitutions of Lanfranc*, 218–19; Gilyard-Beer, 'Boxley', 123.

161. For the Cistercian practice, see *Ecclesiastica Officia*, chapter 81.

162. It is unlikely, however, that benching alone will provide conclusive proof of a collation alley: Gilyard-Beer 'Boxley', 129.

163. Aubert, *L'architecture cistercienne*, II, 20–26; Gardelles, 'L'abbaye de Cadouin', 146–78; France, *Cistercians in Medieval Art*, 95.

164. Gilyard-Beer, 'Boxley', 125, 130; Gilyard-Beer, *Cleeve Abbey*, 11.

165. Robinson, *Tintern Abbey*, 49. Gilyard-Beer's view, in 'Boxley', 130, that the rectangular depression in the cloister opposite the position of the abbot's seat represents a projecting reader's bay is unconvincing. An undated photograph in the site archive held by Cadw shows that a trial trench was dug here at some point. From what can be seen, there are no strong indications of walls or foundations.

166. Fawcett and Oram, *Melrose Abbey*, 178; Gilyard-Beer, 'Boxley', 125, 130.

167. A. Hamlin, 'Collation seats in Irish Cistercian houses: Grey Abbey, County Down and Graiguenamanagh, County Kilkenny', *Med. Archaeol.*, 27 (1983), 156–57; Stalley, *Cistercian Monasteries of Ireland*, 160–62.

168. Salzman, *Building in England*, 448–50; Tester, 'Boxley Abbey', 153–56. Harvey, *Medieval Architects*, 185–86; Gilyard-Beer, 'Boxley', 129, 131. Ironically, as noted in the gazetteer, the work may not have been completed to plan.

169. Harrison, *Byland Abbey*, 12; Gilyard-Beer, 'Boxley', 128, 130.

170. Coppack, *Fountains Abbey*, 68, where it is suggested the bay contained the abbot's seat.

171. Robinson, *Strata Florida Abbey — Talley Abbey*; Gilyard-Beer, 'Boxley', 127, 130.

172. N. Ludlow, 'Whitland Abbey, Carmarthenshire: a Cistercian site re-examined, 1994–99', *Archaeologia Cambrensis*, 151 (2002), 64, 73.

173. The two phases of projecting porch at Jerpoint in Ireland have been known about for some time: Gilyard-Beer, 'Boxley', 127, 130; Stalley, *Cistercian Monasteries of Ireland*, 161–62. But another has only recently been excavated, at Tintern Minor in County Wexford.

Part II: Gazetteer

STUART HARRISON AND DAVID M. ROBINSON

Following the abbey name, modern local authority location, and dates of foundation and suppression, most of the entries in this gazetteer are divided into three main sections. The *Summary* begins by noting the position of the cloister (Fig. 1), followed by an indication of what is known about the overall form of the garth. If available, an approximate date for any arcades is given, and notable features of the garth and its alleys are mentioned. Where there is more extensive information, particularly in the cases where cloister arcades have been reconstructed on paper, a longer entry is given in the section marked *Details*. The *Bibliography* is not exhaustive for any site. It provides the key references to remarks on cloisters, their arcades, and other features of the garth. Comparative ground plans of almost all known English and Welsh cloister garths, drawn to a common scale, are given in D. M. Robinson ed., *The Cistercian Abbeys of Britain: Far from the Concourse of Men* (London 1998); reprinted in paperback (London 2002).

ABERCONWY (Conwy), 1186–1283

Summary: north; form of the garth unknown; no information on arcades, though presumably 13th century.

Bibliography: D. M. Robinson, *The Cistercians in Wales: Architecture and Archaeology 1130–1540* (London 2006), 34, 169, 225.

BASINGWERK (Flintshire), 1131/32–1536/37

Summary: south; full form of garth known from clearance excavations; late-14th-century arcades; lane?

Details: The form of the cloister garth at Basingwerk was uncovered during Office of Works clearance excavations after 1923. Measuring approximately 92 ft (28 m) north–south and a modest 78 ft (23.7 m) east–west, it was arranged at a significant angle to the nave of the abbey church. The west range may well have been separated from the garth by a substantial lay brothers' lane, the arrangements not unlike those of its mother house at Buildwas.

Nothing is known of the assumed late-12th- or 13th-century arcades at Basingwerk. However, the early clearance works also uncovered *ex situ* fragments (mainly capitals and bases) of a 14th-century arcade. In this, pointed arches with cusped soffits, each bay separated by sunk triangular spandrels, were supported on paired octagonal shafts. The shafts were probably linked with a thin web of masonry in dumb-bell fashion (Fig. 21). The fragments, identified in photographs and drawings, have not yet been located in storage. The details are very similar to what is known of a contemporary cloister arcade at nearby Valle Crucis Abbey.

Bibliography: Robinson, *Cistercians in Wales*, 34, 175–76, 227–28; D. M. Robinson, *Basingwerk Abbey*, 2nd edn (Cardiff 2006), 8.

BEAULIEU (Hampshire), 1203/04–1538

Summary: south; full form of cloister known; 13th-century arcades; lane, and laver in south alley.

Detail: The cloister at Beaulieu measured 138 ft (42 m) east–west by 137 ft (41.7 m) north–south.
On the west side of the garth there was an open lay brothers' lane, 16 ft 6 in. (5 m) wide.

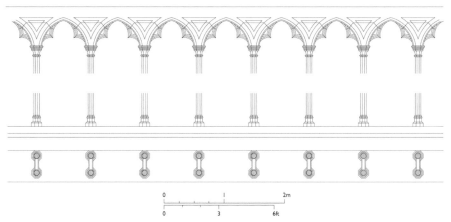

FIG. 21. Basingwerk Abbey: reconstruction of 14th-century dumb-bell cloister arcading

Pete Lawrence, for Cadw, Welsh Assembly Government

During a programme of excavations in 1900–06, Hope and Brakspear identified a number of fragments of 13th-century cloister arcading, consisting of coupled columns with moulded capitals and bases, 'all in Purbeck Marble'. The width of the walls supporting the arcades towards the garth (the stylobates) was 1 ft 7 in. (0.48 m). The work may have been completed in time for a ceremony of dedication in June 1246.

There was a mid- to later-13th-century laver to the east of the refectory doorway in the south alley of the garth. It appears to have been especially fine, with three moulded arches supported on freestanding columns. The laver basins themselves stood in a vaulted recess behind the open frontage.

In the north alley, set into the south wall of the nave, was a row of seven large pointed recesses, the bases of which were about 2 ft 9 in. (0.84 m) above the floor of the cloister. Hope and Brakspear were inclined to look for a structural explanation. Similar recesses featured in the same location at Beaulieu's daughter house at Hailes.

Bibliography: W. H. St John Hope and H. Brakspear, 'The Cistercian abbey of Beaulieu, in the county of Southampton', *Archaeol. J.*, 63 (1906), 129–86, at 151–53, 158–59, 163; Robinson, *Cistercian Abbeys of Britain*, 68–69.

BIDDLESDEN (Buckinghamshire), 1147–1538

Summary: position not known with certainty; several features of the garth could still be seen in 1712, but these were gone by 1735.

Bibliography: B. Willis, *The History and Antiquities of the Town, Hundred, and Deanry of Buckingham* (London 1755), 150–64; Peter Fergusson, *Architecture of Solitude: Cistercian Abbeys in Twelfth-Century England* (Princeton 1984), 111–12; Robinson, *Cistercian Abbeys of Britain*, 70.

BINDON (Dorset), 1171/72–1539

Summary: south; full form of garth known; no information on arcades.

Detail: The full cloister garth at Bindon was 90 ft (27.4 m) square, but none of the inner arcade walls remain *in situ*. Among loose fragments at the site, the RCHME note there are 'several bases of coupled shafts and a square base from the angle of the cloister arcade'.

Bibliography: RCHME, *An Inventory of Historical Monuments in the County of Dorset*, 5 vols (London 1952–75), II, ii, *South-East*, 404–06; Fergusson, *Architecture of Solitude*, 112–13; Robinson, *Cistercian Abbeys of Britain*, 70–71.

BORDESLEY (Worcestershire), 1138–1538

Summary: south; approximate form of cloister known; arcades of the mid-12th century and *c*. 1400.

Detail: Somewhat limited excavations were carried out at Bordesley by James Woodward in 1864. His plan of the site (since modified by Rahtz and Hirst) shows a cloister garth of around 105 ft (32 m) square. However, David Walsh has suggested the east–west measurement was likely to have been larger. In a long programme of excavations since 1969 (directed variously by Philip Rahtz, Sue Hirst, Sue Wright and Grenville Astill), several areas of the garth have been examined with considerable care. The work on the north-east corner has been published, and more reports are set to follow.

Walsh's report on the north-east angle is concerned with the discovery of fragments of a traceried arcade of about 1400. But by way of introduction he also refers to the unearthing of many fragments of *ex situ* stonework 'whose form and scale would be appropriate to a cloister arcade of the second half of the 12th century'. The material was found scattered in archaeological levels representing later periods. Two of the better pieces have been published (in other reports on the Bordesley work): a double-scalloped capital and a quadruple base in oolitic limestone. In a recent summary paper by Astill, Hirst and Wright, it is suggested that 'the Romanesque cloister arcade was completed in the 1160s'.

As to the traceried arcades of *c*. 1400, enough evidence has been uncovered to support a very reasonable reconstruction (Fig. 15) of the turning at the north-east corner. The bays were determined externally by buttresses and internally by engaged shafts set on polygonal bases. The internal measurement of each bay was 6 ft (1.85 m). Within each bay was a three-light window with Perpendicular tracery to the head. There is evidence that at least parts of the cloister were glazed, although the alleys do not appear to have been vaulted.

Bibliography: J. M. Woodward, *The History of Bordesley Abbey* (London and Oxford 1866); P. Rahtz and S. Hirst, *Bordesley Abbey, Redditch, Hereford–Worcestershire: First Report on Excavations 1969–1973*, BAR, British Series, 23 (Oxford 1976), 142, 146; S. M. Hirst, D. A. Walsh and S. M. Wright, *Bordesley Abbey II: Second Report on Excavations at Bordesley Abbey, Redditch, Hereford–Worcestershire*, BAR, British Series, 111 (Oxford 1983), 264–65; D. A. Walsh 'A rebuilt cloister at Bordesley Abbey', *JBAA*, 132 (1979), 42–49; G. Astill, S. Hirst and S. M. Wright, 'The Bordesley Abbey project reviewed', *Archaeol. J.*, 161 (2004), 106–58; Fergusson, *Architecture of Solitude*, 113–14; Robinson, *Cistercian Abbeys of Britain*, 72–73.

BOXLEY (Kent), 1143/46–1538

Summary: south; form of cloister known from excavation; late-12th- and late-14th-century arcades?; collation bay.

Detail: The Boxley cloister garth was of unusual rectangular form, measuring approximately 82 ft (25 m) east–west, but 125 ft (38 m) on the longer north–south axis. In 1373, the abbot and convent contracted Stephen Lomherst to rebuild their (late-12th-century?) cloister. The full contract has been published by Salzman. According to its terms, Lomherst was to build one alley each year, on walls 2 ft 6 in. (0.76 m) high and 1 ft 6 in. (0.46 m) thick. The form of 'larger' and 'smaller' columns was also specified, and above these was to be tracery. In the alley adjoining the church (where he was also to build a new processional doorway and four new windows in the nave), Lomherst was to construct a *pulpitum collationis*, presumably a projecting collation bay. It is not certain how far the work progressed. In his excavations (1971–72), Tester found evidence that both the width and the surviving footings of the north and west alleys differ from those of the south and east. He suggested that the north and west alleys were reconstructed by Lomherst, but that the older south and east alleys were retained.

Bibliography: L. F. Salzman, *Building in England Down to 1540* (Oxford 1952), 448–50; P. J. Tester, 'Excavations at Boxley Abbey', *Archaeologia Cantiana*, 88 (1973), 129–58, at 135, 153–56; R. Gilyard-Beer, 'Boxley Abbey and the *Pulpitum Collationis*', in *Collectanea Historica: Essays in Memory of Stuart Rigold*, ed. A. Detsicas (Maidstone 1981), 123–31; Fergusson, *Architecture of Solitude*, 114–15; Robinson, *Cistercian Abbeys of Britain*, 73–74.

BRUERN (Oxfordshire), 1147–1536
Summary: position not known with certainty; no information on garth or arcades.
Bibliography: Fergusson, *Architecture of Solitude*, 115; Robinson, *Cistercian Abbeys of Britain*, 74.

BUCKFAST (Devon), 1136–1539
Summary: south; form of garth known only from excavations in the 1880s; no information on arcades.
Bibliography: Fergusson, *Architecture of Solitude*, 115–16; Robinson, *Cistercian Abbeys of Britain*, 75–76.

BUCKLAND (Devon), 1278–1539
Summary: north; form of garth unknown; no information on arcades.
Bibliography: Robinson, *Cistercian Abbeys of Britain*, 76–78.

BUILDWAS (Shropshire), 1135–1536
Summary: north; full form of garth known; 13th-century arcades; lane.
Detail: The form of the northern cloister garth at Buildwas is known from clearance excavations, undertaken from 1925, by the Office of Works and its successors. It measures some 82 ft (25 m) north–south by 91 ft (27.7 m) east–west. There was a lay brothers' lane on the west side, and there is some evidence to indicate a freestanding laver in the north-west corner of the garth.

Both on the site, and at English Heritage's museum store at Atcham, there are a number of *ex situ* fragments representing a paired-shaft arcade. The most prominent items are several twin capitals with stiff-leaf decoration, suggesting an early-13th-century date for construction.
Bibliography: Fergusson, *Architecture of Solitude*, 116–17; Robinson, *Cistercian Abbeys of Britain*, 78–80; D. M. Robinson, *Buildwas Abbey* (London 2002), 11, 14.

BYLAND (North Yorkshire), 1134/77–1539
Summary: south; full form of garth known; late-12th- and 15th-century arcades; collation porch; laver; lane.
Detail: At 145 ft (44.2 m) square, the vast cloister garth at Byland is the largest Cistercian example known from the British Isles. On the west side was a most unusual lay brothers' lane. Although not especially wide, it would have been roofed, and it was equipped with a remarkable row of thirty-five niche seats along one side.

During clearance excavations by the Office of Works in 1924, a considerable number of *ex situ* fragments from Byland's late-12th-century cloister arcades were uncovered. In particular, twin capitals and bases had survived on the site, reused as rubble in the walls of the late-medieval replacement arcades. The stones were collected and the better-preserved examples were eventually re-erected on modern shafts on the veranda of the site museum (Figs 8, 22–23). Less complete examples remain in the English Heritage reserve collection.

The bases are unusual in that they have a chamfered stepping to the sides of the sub-base. Of yet greater interest, there are examples intended for both round and octagonal shafts, indicating an alternating rhythm to the arcades. As it happens, all those on display at the site are for twin round shafts. The surviving capitals are mainly of waterleaf design (Fig. 22), though there is a solitary scallop example (Fig. 23). Some capitals have leaves that are of an

FIG. 22. Byland Abbey: twin-waterleaf capital from cloister arcading, 1170s
Stuart Harrison

FIG. 23. Byland Abbey: twin-scalloped capital and springer from cloister arcading, 1170s
Stuart Harrison

unusual shape with an emphatically horizontal underside to the main leaves. Some of the circular waterleaf tips are worked with spirals. Other differences in the designs are mainly in the form of the motifs placed centrally between the main leaves. Two fragmentary springers of the arcade arches also survive (Fig. 23), giving the profile of the soffit, but unfortunately not that of the side of the arches. Comparison with the similar arcades from Jervaulx Abbey (see below) suggests that the Byland work would also have featured a hood-mould. The overall design is clearly of early Gothic inspiration, though with a few old-fashioned elements such as the scallop capitals lingering on. In sum, the arcades were presumably one of the last works to be completed on the monastic buildings. They are likely to have been in place before 1177, the year in which the monks arrived at Byland from their temporary (1147–77) home at Stocking.

In the late 13th century, a collation porch was introduced to the centre of the north alley, projecting into the garth. This meant the removal of two bays of the late-12th-century arcade and the provision of responds where the arcades met the new porch. As the porch was retained when the cloister was rebuilt (see below) the bases of these responds survive. Their height shows that the original stylobate supporting all four arcades was just over 2 ft (0.64 m) high. In addition, the spacing of the responds almost certainly equates to a bay width of the original arcade. Taken together, all these elements allow for a reconstruction (Fig. 24). Although the form of the hood-mould has not been recovered, it was probably similar to those at Jervaulx and Newminster (see below). The collation porch was square in plan, with elegant tracery windows of Geometric design, parts of which survive in the site stone collection. The entrance sill stone shows that the doorway was subdivided in two by a mullion, rising to tracery. The porch was also vaulted, as shown by a surviving corner springer.

In the 15th century, all four cloister walks were reconstructed with glazed tracery windows. The bays were defined by buttresses with a moulded plinth. Some of the window sills survive at the east end of the north alley. They show that the windows had moulded jambs and sills and were divided into four main lights with major and minor mullions. The site has produced only a few fragments of tracery and it has not proved possible to fully recover the tracery design of the windows, though indications are that they were of Perpendicular style.

A further discovery made during the Office of Works clearance of the cloister in the 1920s was that of fragments of a marble laver. They indicate a facia decorated with a frieze of leaves. Presumably smashed so as to recover the lead from its pipes at the time of the

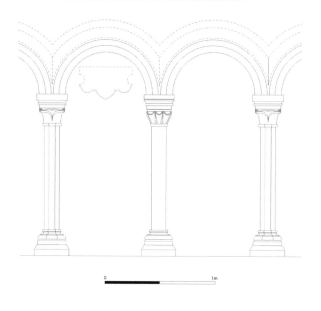

FIG. 24.   Byland Abbey:
reconstruction drawing of cloister
arcading, 1170s
Stuart Harrison

suppression, the laver pieces reveal evidence of regularly spaced holes where these pipes sat. Taps were probably fitted to the pipes, and they must have been set over a basin or trough. The lack of any seating at either side of the refectory doorway suggests the laver must have been positioned elsewhere, perhaps in the cloister arcading, or within a fountain pavilion in the garth, though no positive trace can be identified today.

Bibliography: S. Harrison, *Byland Abbey* (London 1990), 12; G. Coppack, *Abbeys & Priories* (Stroud 2006), 154–55; Fergusson, *Architecture of Solitude*, 69–83, 117–18; Robinson, *Cistercian Abbeys of Britain*, 81–83.

CALDER (Cumbria), 1142–1536

Summary: south; conjectural outline of garth known; late-12th-century arcades.

Detail: Clearance and general excavation of Calder were carried out by A. G. Loftie in 1880–81. His summary plan provides an outline of the cloister garth, though clear information on the west side is lacking.

A few fragments of the cloister arcade survive on the site. They show evidence of a pointed arcade of late-12th or early-13th-century date (Fig. 25). The springers have a plain block at the base from which the arch mouldings begin to emerge. Three different arch profiles survive, of which type 'A' seems to have been the most prevalent. One springer has type 'B' on one side and type 'C' on the other. Type 'C' has a central filleted roll and might indicate a later insertion or alteration to the design, perhaps for a doorway. There was presumably a hood-mould but this has yet to be identified. The capitals show variants of leaf and waterleaf

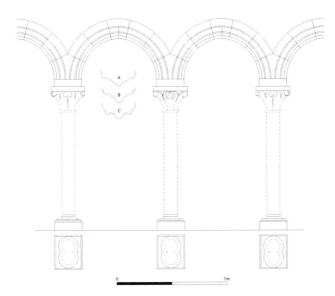

FIG. 25. Calder Abbey: reconstruction drawing of cloister arcading, late 12th or early 13th century

Stuart Harrison

designs, but no complete example survives. The bases are moulded but have lost their upper profile.

The Calder arcade is much reduced in scale from the examples recorded at other northern Cistercian houses, probably reflecting the wealth and aspirations of the community in general. This reduced architectural prominence is reflected in the form of the bases and capitals. Instead of the usual paired colonnettes, they had a single shaft dressed to look like a pair. The arches were also narrower in width from what one finds at several of the Yorkshire abbeys.

Bibliography: A. G. Loftie, *Calder Abbey, its Ruins and History* (London 1892); Fergusson, *Architecture of Solitude*, 118; Robinson, *Cistercian Abbeys of Britain*, 84–85.

CLEEVE (North Somerset), 1186/98–1536

Summary: south; full form of garth known; late-medieval arcade; collation seat; laver.

Detail: The cloister garth at Cleeve is very well preserved, measuring approximately 93 ft (28.3 m) square. Today there is no trace of the assumed 13th-century arcade walls above ground. However, during excavations of the monks' latrine area (1980–85), fragments of twin marble capitals, bases, and a hood-mould springer from a cloister arcade, of *c.* 1220–50 were recovered. It is possible this material comes from the main cloister arcade; equally, though, it may derive from an infirmary arcade, the roofline of which can be seen adjacent to the latrine, running against the outer wall of the monks' dormitory.

Much of the west cloister alley remains intact. On this side, at least, the arcade was rebuilt in the late 15th or early 16th century, with some of the work definitely carried out by Cleeve's last abbot, William Dovell. It was a seven-bay, Perpendicular-style arcade, buttressed towards the garth. From the surviving fabric (the four northernmost bays are the best preserved), it is clear that each bay featured a four-light glazed window with a tracery head. On the basis of a considerable legacy left to Cleeve by the vicar of Stogumber in 1534, for 'the newe bewylding of the clawsta', it may be argued that Dovell intended to progress the work to the other three sides of the cloister.

Mid-way along the north cloister alley, against the south wall of the church, a shallow trefoil-headed recess would have provided an architectural frame for the abbot's seat during

FIG. 26.   Croxden Abbey:
reconstruction of cloister
arcading, 13th century
Jackie Hall

the collation reading. In the south alley, the remains of a broad, wall-recessed laver survived
the rebuilding of the refectory in the late 15th century.

Bibliography: R. Gilyard-Beer, *Cleeve Abbey*, 2nd edn (London 1990), 11–13, 23, 25, 46; C. J.
Guy, 'The excavation of the reredorter at Cleeve Abbey, Somerset', *Somerset Archaeology
and Natural History*, 142 (1999), 1–40, at 35–39; S. Harrison, *Cleeve Abbey* (London 2000),
3–4, 11, 29; Fergusson, *Architecture of Solitude*, 119–20; Robinson, *Cistercian Abbeys of
Britain*, 85–88.

COGGESHALL (Essex), 1140–1538

Summary: south; form of garth partially recovered; possible late-12th- and 15th-century arcades.

Details: A scalloped capital and waterholding base attributed to the cloister suggest an arcade of
the 1160s or 1170s. There are also reports of 15th-century arcading having been found.

Bibliography: RCHME, *An Inventory of the Historical Monuments in Essex*, 4 vols (London
1916–23), III, 165–67; J. S. Gardner, 'Coggeshall Abbey and its early brickwork', *JBAA*, 108
(1955), 19–32, at pl. 6, no. 2; Fergusson, *Architecture of Solitude*, 120–21; Robinson,
Cistercian Abbeys of Britain, 88–89.

COMBE (Warwickshire), 1150–1539

Summary: north; almost full form of the garth known; 15th-century arcades.

Details: The form of the original (late-12th-century?) arcades is unrecorded. They were replaced,
at least in part, in the late 15th century. Sections of these later arcades were incorporated into
the post-suppression house on the site, itself modified several times. In the courtyard of what
is now a hotel, there are three surviving bays on the north side and seven on the west side.
They feature cusped four-light windows, each with tracery beneath a four-centred head.

Bibliography: VCH, *Warwick*, VI (Oxford 1951), 72–73; Fergusson, *Architecture of Solitude*,
121–223; Robinson, *Cistercian Abbeys of Britain*, 89–90.

COMBERMERE (Cheshire), 1133–1538

Summary: south?; form of garth unknown; no information on arcades.

Bibliography: Fergusson, *Architecture of Solitude*, 122; Robinson, *Cistercian Abbeys of Britain*,
90.

CROXDEN (Staffordshire), 1176–1538

Summary: south; form of garth known; 13th-century arcades; traces of another cloister alley to the east of the east range.

Detail: The cloister garth at Croxden was recorded in plan in the early 20th century by Lynam, though its form was presumably clarified further during clearance by the Office of Works after 1936, especially in the 1950s. It measures approximately 110 ft (33.5 m) east–west by around 120 ft (36.6 m) north–south. Documentary sources, not least the abbey's own chronicle (begun in the late 13th century), provide a number of references to cloister building works. The chronicle records that, in the early 14th century, Abbot Richard of Shepshed (*c.* 1329–37) retiled all four roofs of the alleys, employing some 25,550 tiles. Repairs to the cloister were again carried out in 1374, and from the late 15th century there is a reference to Abbot John de Checkley-Walton (*c.* 1467–1507) making a cloister. The meaning is obscure, but a full rebuilding scheme may have been contemplated, even if not fully carried out.

Jackie Hall has recently reconstructed the form of the 13th-century cloister arcades at Croxden, highlighting three design variations, which she suggests were built either late in the abbacy of Thomas of Woodstock (1178–1229), or early in the abbacy of Walter of London (1242–68). The basic design, thought to have come from the principal garth, continued the tradition of coupled columns with moulded capitals and bases, here supporting trefoiled arches with hood-moulds, which, although not syncopated, bear comparison with the marginally later Tintern forms (Fig. 26).

To the east of the east range, excavations in the 1970s revealed evidence of covered walks, including what looks like two sides of the infirmary cloister. *Ex situ* stonework fragments recovered, notably capitals and bases, certainly belonged to cloister arcades.

Bibliography: C. Lynam, *The Abbey of St Mary, Croxden, Staffordshire* (London 1911); P. Ellis, 'Croxden Abbey, Staffordshire: a report on excavations 1956–7 and 1975–7', *Staffordshire Archaeological and Historical Society Transactions*, 36 (1994–95), 29–51, at 36–38, 46–48; J. Hall, 'Croxden Abbey: buildings and community', 2 vols (unpublished Ph.D. thesis, University of York, 2003), I, 54–56; II, figs A11–A17; Fergusson, *Architecture of Solitude*, 122–23; Robinson, *Cistercian Abbeys of Britain*, 91–92.

CWMHIR (Powys), 1176–1537

Summary: south; form of garth known only in conjectural outline, based on excavations of the 1890s; nothing known of arcades.

Bibliography: Robinson, *Cistercian Abbeys of Britain*, 94–96; Robinson, *Cistercians in Wales*, 34, 230–35.

CYMER (Gwynedd), 1198/99–1537

Summary: south; form of garth known from clearance excavations, measuring some 72 ft (22 m) north–south by 75 ft (23 m) east–west; nothing known of arcades.

Bibliography: D. M. Robinson, *Cymer Abbey* (Cardiff 1995); Robinson, *Cistercian Abbeys of Britain*, 97–98; Robinson, *Cistercians in Wales*, 34, 235–39.

DIEULACRES (Staffordshire), 1214–1538

Summary: south; form of garth unknown; possible 13th-century arcade.

Detail: A triple-shaft base survives reused in farm buildings at the site, and may have come from the cloister arcades. A similar base is known from nearby Hulton Abbey. An inventory taken at the time of the suppression refers to the '*glasse, ieronn*, [and] *the monks settes*' in the cloister.

Bibliography: M. E. C. Walcott, 'Inventories and valuations of religious houses at the time of the Dissolution', *Archaeologia*, 43 (1871), 201–49, at 214–17. W. D. Klemperer, 'Dieulacres Abbey', *West Midlands Archaeology*, 38 (1995), 66–72; W. D. Klemperer, R. K. Morris, J. Price and R. Barnett, *Survey of Dieulacres Abbey*, Stoke-on-Trent City Museum Archaeological Unit Report, 46 (Stoke-on-Trent 1995); Robinson, *Cistercian Abbeys of Britain*, 100.

DORE (Herefordshire), 1147–1536

Summary: north; outline of garth known only in conjectural form; 13th-century arcades; lane?

Detail: The largely buried remains of the cloister garth at Dore were first explored by Roland Paul at the turn of the 19th century. His conjectural plan of 1904 (one of at least six published versions by Paul) has been refined in studies by both the present authors. Admittedly the evidence is rather complex, but, in so far as it can be taken at this stage, a starting point may be to suggest that by the mid-13th century the garth measured approximately 108 ft (33 m) square. On the west side (according to Paul's records) there may have been a lay brothers' lane, measuring some 25 ft (7.6 m) wide. Alternatively, this could be a misinterpretation of only partially excavated walls. Indeed, it is just possible that the space seen by Paul as a lane may have been the position of the 12th-century west range, replaced in the 13th century by a larger building sited further out from the cloister. If this was the case, there is also a chance that the width of the earlier range was incorporated into a modified cloister. The result would have been a markedly rectangular garth, measuring more than 130 ft (39.6 m) across the east–west axis.

The fragments now believed to have come from Dore's 13th-century cloister arcades were probably excavated by Paul, though he never reported their discovery in print. Until recently the pieces lay unrecognised in a collection of other *ex situ* stonework in the ambulatory of the abbey church. As reconstructed on paper, they are shown to represent an elegant arcade featuring comparatively tall cinquefoil arches (Fig. 27). On the rear (in this case to the garth side) there was a rebate to accommodate a separate band of moulded voussoirs. The arches, which featured filleted roll mouldings, were supported on triple-shaft groups with moulded bases and stiff-leaf capitals. At each of the corner junctions (it can be assumed), the arches were carried on a cluster of five shafts, represented in the stone collection by one badly damaged capital. Interestingly, some of the fragments of the inner band mouldings retain traces of red paint.

In general terms, there are distinct similarities between the reconstructed form of the Dore arcade and that known from the Augustinian priory at Norton in Cheshire. There, too, the arches featured separate trefoiled sub-arches set in a rebate (see the paper on Benedictine and Augustinian cloister arcades in this volume). In addition, the five-shaft corner arrangement was common to both sites. The Norton arcade has been dated to the mid-13th century (after a fire of 1236). At Dore, it may be posited that construction of the arcade followed on from earlier 13th-century claustral works, probably in the time of Abbot Stephen of Worcester (*c.* 1236–57). The extent to which the similarities in the constructional elements between the two schemes were more than coincidental awaits further contextual investigation.

The possibility of another cloister arcade at Dore, dating from the 14th or 15th century, is suggested by a single badly damaged capital of dumb-bell design.

Bibliography: R. W. Paul, 'The church and monastery of Abbey Dore, Herefordshire', *Transactions of the Bristol and Gloucestershire Archaeological Society*, 27 (1904), 117–26; S. Harrison, 'The loose architectural detail' and 'The cloister ranges and a fresh look at the chapter house', in *A Definitive History of Dore Abbey*, ed. R. Shoesmith and R. Richardson (Woonton 1997), 63–76, 113–24, at 75–76, 117–20; Fergusson, *Architecture of Solitude*, 94–100, 111; Robinson, *Cistercian Abbeys of Britain*, 101–04; Robinson, *Cistercians in Wales*, 34, 172–73, 243–46.

DUNKESWELL (Devon), 1201–1539

Summary: south; garth known in conjectural form; no information on arcades.

Bibliography: Robinson, *Cistercian Abbeys of Britain*, 107.

FLAXLEY (Gloucestershire), 1151–1536

Summary: south; form of garth unknown beyond speculative outline; nothing known of arcades.

Bibliography: Fergusson, *Architecture of Solitude*, 124–25; Robinson, *Cistercian Abbeys of Britain*, 108–09.

Garth Side   Alley Side

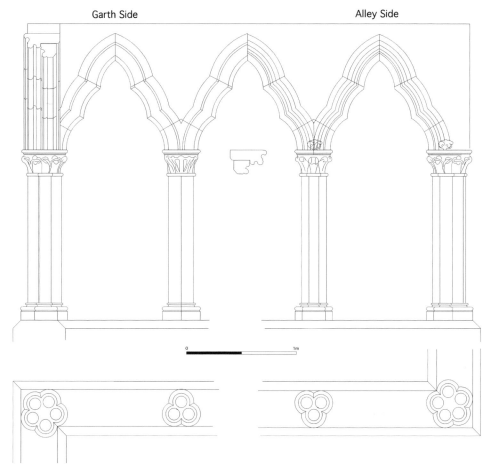

FIG. 27.   Dore Abbey: reconstruction of cloister arcading, *c.* 1236–57

Stuart Harrison

FORDE (Devon), 1136–1539

Summary: north; garth known only in conjectural form; 16th-century arcade; laver in north alley.

Detail: Brakspear produced a conjectural outline of the full cloister garth at Forde to accompany his 1913 account of the abbey. The dimension from east–west, the limits of which survive, was about 82 ft (25 m). Brakspear proposed similar limits along the north–south axis, and he may well be correct. In the 13th century, a laver was recessed into the outer wall of the northern alley, just to the east of the doorway into the north–south refectory. And, although once blocked by 16th-century works, three bays of its wall arcading are today exposed to view.

Nothing is known of the original (late-12th- or early-13th-century?) arcades, but they might have survived into the 16th century. Then, as part of a very extensive programme of alterations and additions to the house, Forde's last abbot, the ambitious reformer Thomas Chard (1506–39), began to completely remodel the cloister walks. He made greatest progress on the north side, but the scheme was probably interrupted by the suppression. The six-bay north alley, with a modified corner bay at either end, was retained as part of the post-suppression house.

The alley was buttressed towards the garth. Within each bay was a large four-light window organised around a Y-tracery pattern with through reticulation. The transomed lights featured ogee heads and cinquefoil cusping. Quatrefoil panels occupy the spandrels above two-centred heads. In turn, the windows were surmounted by a decorative parapet featuring a frieze of quatrefoils enclosing shields of arms, initials, and devices. Inside the alley, the pattern of the windows was largely repeated as blind tracery against the north wall. Between the bays there are vault responds supporting fan vault springers, although the vault itself does not appear to have been completed before the suppression. All in all, Chard's work at Forde represents one of the most ambitious Cistercian cloister schemes known from Britain.

Bibliography: H. Brakspear, 'Forde Abbey', *Archaeol. J.*, 70 (1913), 498–99; RCHME, *An Inventory of the Historical Monuments in Dorset*, 5 vols (London 1952–75), I, *West*, 242; L. Monckton, 'Late Gothic architecture in south-west England', 2 vols (unpublished Ph.D. thesis, University of Warwick, 1999), I, 304–14; A. Emery, *Greater Medieval Houses of England and Wales 1300–1500*, 3 vols (Cambridge 1996–2006), III, *Southern England*, 560–65; Fergusson, *Architecture of Solitude*, 125; Robinson, *Cistercian Abbeys of Britain*, 109–10.

FOUNTAINS (North Yorkshire), 1132–1539

Summary: south: full form of garth known; late-12th-century arcades; collation bay in north alley; paired lavers in south alley; details of the infirmary cloister arcades (*c.* 1220–47), and of the lay brothers' cloister and its arcades, are also known.

Detail: Fountains was of course the largest and most important Cistercian monastery in the British Isles. The overall form of the great cloister garth at the centre of the complex had effectively been established by the mid-12th century, though in detail it was to see further modification through the second half of the century. To the west, there appears to have been a lay brothers' cloister situated outside the west range. And, to the east, cloister walks were certainly a feature linking the main claustral complex with the infirmary hall and its associated structures.

By great good fortune, Fountains retains more evidence of cloister arcading from these areas than is the case at any other white monk abbey in the country. In terms of dating, the fragments span the late 12th to the mid-13th centuries. The pieces were all discovered in excavations by John Richard Walbran in the mid-19th century. Early photographs show that a large quantity of moulded stone, including the bulk of the main cloister fragments, was collected and stacked in the east guest house. However, Walbran left much of the loose stone from the infirmary cloister arcading lying on the walls which had originally supported it. In a subsequent rearranging of the site, this material was placed in a large dump adjoining the great infirmary hall. In the 1980s, all the loose stone from the site was removed to an English Heritage storage area where it still remains.

The great cloister garth was approximately 125 ft (38 m) square. In the established literature, the arcades are usually attributed to Abbot Robert Pipewell (1170–80), who — it says in the abbey's foundation history — 'erected sumptuous buildings' (*edificia construxit sumptuosa*). However, fresh research (by Stuart Harrison) looking at the whole relative chronology of Cistercian buildings in the north of England leads to a different conclusion. The findings (as yet unpublished) indicate Pipewell's sumptuous buildings are more likely to have been the chapter-house and guest houses. The construction of the cloister arcades is better placed in the period 1180–95, that is in the time of Abbot William (1180–90), or of his successor, Ralph Haget (1190–1203). The scheme, in any case, represented the culmination of works to rebuild the east, west and south cloister ranges. And, comparing the details with the cloister arcading recorded at Kirkstall, Byland, Jervaulx, Newminster, and Roche, it seems clear the Fountains work must have followed most of them in sequence. The exception may have been Roche, where the phasing perhaps overlapped with that at Fountains.

Fig. 28. Fountains Abbey: assembled arch from main cloister arcading, late 12th century

Stuart Harrison

The arches of the Fountains arcades were of trefoiled form, and featured highly complex mouldings (Fig. 28). They were supported on twin bases, shafts, and capitals all made from Nidderdale marble. The capitals were of waterleaf design and the bases had griffes or corner spurs. Considerable traces of white limewash remain on the surviving springers and vous-soirs. The white painted arches must have stood in stark contrast to the grey polished Nidderdale marble supports. The corner arrangements reveal a variant of what might be considered the usual four-shaft grouping (Fig. 29). At Fountains there were three shafts of standard round section, but with a small trefoiled shaft on the corner angle. The three shafts supported the corner capital whereas the trefoiled shaft rose higher and supported a separate foliate capital at wall-plate level. In turn, this capital is likely to have carried a timber wall rib. The rib itself projected diagonally across the angle of the alley towards the far corner of the garth. Wall scars on the buttresses flanking the refectory doorway show that there was a ceiling of segmental curvature over the alleys and thus the timber rib would have marked the intersection of the ceilings in the corners. Sockets in the cloister corners show where the ribs were supported. To accommodate the cloister ceiling a string-course was inserted into the walls of the surrounding buildings, which in turn gives a clue as to the height of the arcades.

Other springers show that in each corner of the arcades there were moulded diagonal arches that spanned across the angle within the garth (Fig. 31). These small diagonal arches were intersected at their apex by a much thinner half-arch or rib springing out from the main corner springer. The purpose of the diagonal arch was to carry the wall-plate around the corner of the cloister. This introduced a triangular section at the junction of the alley roofs so that the tiles could be run around the corner without the need for a valley between each alley. It was a simple yet practical solution to this problem and its use here raises the question of how the corner junctions may have been treated at other sites.

An indication of an important variation in the main Fountains arcade design comes from a springer which shows that a second arcade intersected with the first at right angles. This suggests the presence of a porch, or possibly a collation bay in the north alley. However, geophysical survey of the garth has shown what appears to be a similar projection from the south alley, in front of the refectory doorway.

The main Fountains arcade was of early Gothic form, but is more elaborate and shows considerable advances on the examples known from Kirkstall, Byland, and Jervaulx. The arch profile, in particular, was far richer and made up of delicate rolls and angle fillets. Adding to its impact were the polychromatic effects of limewash and marble. All in all, it must have been a highly impressive structure, rightly seen as the most elaborate 12th-century Cistercian cloister arcade yet known from Britain.

In the south alley of this main cloister garth, to either side of the refectory doorway, there are handsome arcaded recesses. It is thought these could represent the earliest Cistercian wall-mounted laver in Britain; they are almost certainly the earliest surviving instance of the

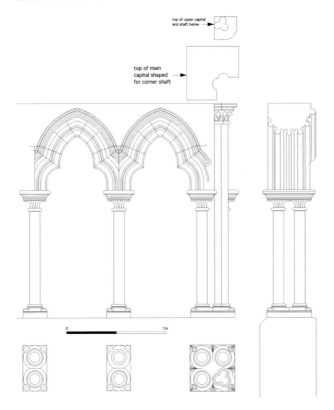

top of upper capital
and shaft below →

top of main
capital shaped →
for corner shaft

FIG. 29.   Fountains Abbey: reconstruction drawing of the main cloister arcades showing the corner arrangement from the alley side, late 12th century
Stuart Harrison

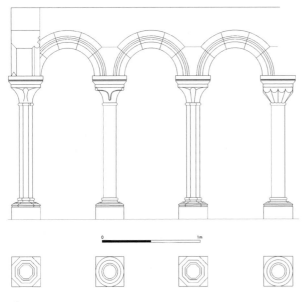

FIG. 30.   Fountains Abbey: reconstruction drawing of the single column arcading that formed part of a secondary cloister court on the outer side of the west range, late 1160s
Stuart Harrison

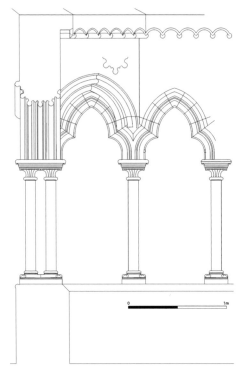

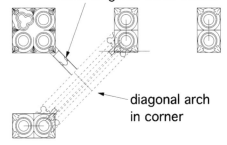

small diagonal rib in corner

diagonal arch
in corner

FIG. 31. Fountains Abbey: reconstruction
drawing of the main cloister arcades showing the
diagonal arch spanning the corner angle within
the garth, late 12th century

Stuart Harrison

form. The arcade arches, in both round and pointed forms, were carried on marble bases,
shafts, and capitals set on a broad stone bench. In front of the arcades were the continuous
metal troughs or basins where the monks washed before going into meals. The troughs were
fitted with lead pipes and bronze taps.

Fragments of a second arcade uncovered by Walbran indicate a much earlier, rather
plainer, and less-advanced design to that of the main garth (Fig. 30). The arches were round
headed and carried just a simple roll moulding. They were supported on a single row of
columns featuring moulded bases and capitals in both scallop and simple leaf forms. The
columns alternated in a round and octagonal pattern, not unlike the infirmary cloister arcade
at Rievaulx, or a further arcade known from Jervaulx.

As to its location, the best fit appears to be with the outer side of the west range. Here,
against the outer face of the west wall, there are corbel supports and marks for a pentice roof

running from the church southwards to the position of the lay brothers' day stairs. Evidence of roof supports can also be seen returning westwards against the south-west corner of the nave. In addition, geophysical survey of the area has revealed the outline of a rectangular court with an inner line almost certainly marking the position of arcade walls. In other words, this seems to have been a western cloister for use by the lay brothers, and it is the most likely location for the single column arcade. When it was first built, in the third quarter of the 12th century, it stood against the first west range. When the surviving, larger, west range was constructed, the cloister must have been reduced in size, the east arcade being moved and re-erected.

During the abbacy of John of Kent (1220–47), the Fountains community began work on a new infirmary complex. Looted for its stone in the late 16th century, and almost completely buried, the infirmary was rediscovered during Walbran's excavations in the mid-19th century. However, mistakenly, Walbran thought he had found the abbot's house. Not until the end of the 19th century were the structures firmly identified as the infirmary complex and its associated cloister alleys by William St John Hope.

The 13th-century infirmary cloister arcade at Fountains did not conform to the traditional rectangular court plan. This was because it fulfilled a dual purpose, serving not just as a place for the infirm monks to relax, but also as a covered passageway from the infirmary hall to the abbey church. To begin with this passage was of L-shaped plan, extending westwards from the infirmary hall doorway and then turning northwards through 90 degrees to connect with the Chapel of Nine Altars at the east end of the abbey church, also built by Abbot John of Kent. As the cloister was a freestanding passageway there was no rear wall. Instead there were two sets of parallel arcades in each section of the alleys, with the passage formed between them. The passage on the east–west axis had elegant trefoiled arches supported on paired shafts (Fig. 32). Because of the freestanding nature of the design, the arches were arranged in groups, and then at regular intervals there were blind arches with external buttresses. As the blind arches followed the same spacing and design as the open arches, the rhythm of the arcades went uninterrupted. The shorter alley on the north–south axis was of a different design, in which trefoiled arches were supported on larger single shafts (Fig. 33). The outline of its sloping roof can be seen against the south wall of the Nine Altars Chapel, giving an indication of the overall height of the structure.

The bases and capitals in both arcades were moulded, though in the east–west alley they varied in height. In fact, the alley itself sloped up towards the east, presenting the architect with a problem in the design of the arcading. The base walls were set out to follow the slope of the ground, and therefore the arcades also had to be arranged to follow this slope. To cope with the sloping inclination of the base wall, the bases of the paired shafts were set into shallow rebates cut into the top of the wall. Above, the capitals had to be stepped up in height from west to east, following the inclination of the base wall. To further cope with these arrangements, the arch keystones of the arcade were asymmetrical in design, accommodating the slope, the changing height of the capitals, and of the arches (Fig. 32).

In places there were wide doorways through the alleys. These had moulded respond bases, set at the end of each base wall and standing on their own tiered sub bases. To accommodate the roof-plate the doorway arches must have been segmental in form. All that remains today are parts of the stylobates and some of the bases of the arcades and buttresses. Fortunately, when Walbran excavated the cloister he discovered numerous sections of collapsed arcading and these survive in the English Heritage stone store. Measurement and detailed study of these has enabled most of the design details to be recovered.

Shortly after its completion, the east–west infirmary alley was extended westwards to connect with the east range. The design followed the pattern of the earlier twin-shaft arcade, but with simpler mouldings to the arch heads. One section complete with base, shaft, capital, and springer survives *in situ* and gives a good guide to the height of the arcades (Fig. 34). It is part of a blind arch section and retains a buttress standing to full height on the exterior, though this is largely immured in later masonry. Enough is visible to show a steeply sloping top capping to the buttress, adding yet another of the design details. The arcades here have

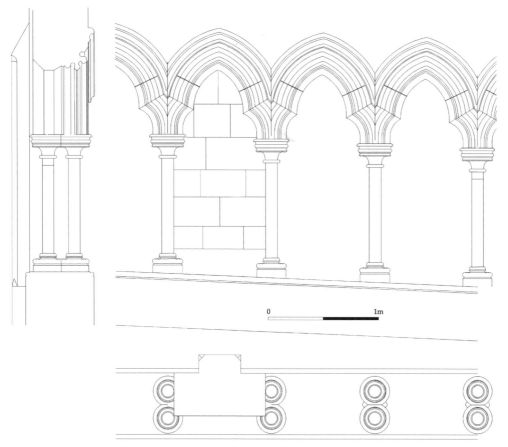

0   1m

FIG. 32.   Fountains Abbey: reconstruction drawing of the twin-shaft arcade forming the eastern
cloister passageway, built by Abbot John of Kent (1220–47)

Stuart Harrison

mouldings with rolls and filleted rolls set between hollows, and they were surmounted by a
prominent hood-mould (Fig. 35). The paired bases have developed beyond the waterholding
type, with three superposed rolls over a circular sub base. The details suggest a date late in
the abbacy of John of Kent, probably around 1240–47.

In the late 15th century, an upper storey was added to the infirmary cloister arcading,
probably (as with the infirmary cloister at Rievaulx) to form a long gallery. This included
partial rebuilding of the western section of the cloister. Some arches were blocked up with the
addition of buttresses and large stone bases for first-floor fireplaces and chimney-stacks, all
of which must have disfigured the original elegant design.

It is worth mentioning one other arcade which has been recorded at Fountains. Although
strictly not a cloister work, its similarity to such late 12th-century forms is striking. The
relevant fragments were again excavated by Walbran in the mid-19th century and they belong
to the galilee porch at the west front of the abbey church. Such was the depth of debris
against the west front of the church, the presence of the porch came as an unexpected
discovery. Contemporary photographs show the arches of the arcading laid out in front of

183

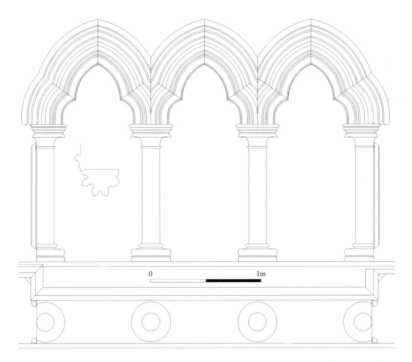

0   1m

FIG. 33.   Fountains Abbey: reconstruction drawing of the single-shaft arcade forming the
northern cloister passageway, built by Abbot John of Kent (1220–47)

Stuart Harrison

the galilee shortly after their discovery, and its seems that nearly all of the original eighteen
arches had survived. Three arches were subsequently rebuilt at the north end of the porch
(Fig. 36). They have twin shafts with moulded bases and scallop capitals supporting round-
headed arches. As with the lay brothers' cloister, the arches have a simple roll moulding and
angle fillet or arris on the angle. The rest of the arcade was cleared away to the east guest
house and is now in the English Heritage stone store on the site. It includes respond springers
from the end of the arcade and some bases and twin capitals which show that, besides scallop
designs, simple leaf capitals were also employed.

It seems clear from the mouldings that this twin-shaft galilee arcade and the single-shaft
lay brothers' arcades were near-contemporary constructions, probably going up in the
mid- to late-1160s. The closest parallel to both is the work seen in the main arcades at
Rievaulx Abbey. All three show a similar mix of late Romanesque and early Gothic detailing.

Bibliography: W. H. St John Hope, 'Fountains Abbey', *Yorkshire Archaeological Journal*, 15
(1900), 269–402; at 332–35, 339–41; G. Coppack, *Abbeys: Yorkshire's Monastic Heritage*
(London 1988), 29; G. Coppack and R. Gilyard-Beer, *Fountains Abbey* (London 1993),
30–31, 48, 52–53; G. Coppack, *Fountains Abbey: The Cistercians in Northern England*
(Stroud 2003), 68, 79–80; Fergusson, *Architecture of Solitude*, 38–48, 126; Robinson,
Cistercian Abbeys of Britain, 111–15.

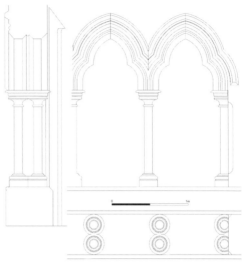

Fig. 34 (*above left*). Fountains Abbey: surviving base, shaft, capital, and springer of the western cloister passageway (1220–47). Immured in the later masonry behind it is a complete external buttress

Fig. 35 (*above*). Fountains Abbey: reconstruction drawing of the twin-shaft western cloister passageway, built by Abbot John of Kent, *c.* 1240s

Stuart Harrison

Fig. 36 (*left*). Fountains Abbey: the galilee porch arcading re-erected in the 19th century from fallen fragments

Stuart Harrison

185

FIG. 37 (*above left*). Furness Abbey: highly polished marble base from the early-13th-century cloister arcading
Stuart Harrison

FIG. 38 (*above*). Furness Abbey: highly polished marble capital from the early-13th-century cloister arcading
Stuart Harrison

FIG. 39 (*left*). Furness Abbey: moulded twin-capital from cloister arcading, with foliage decoration
Stuart Harrison

FURNESS (Cumbria), 1124/27–1537

Summary: south; form of garth known; early-13th-century arcades.

Detail: The 12th-century cloister garth at Furness was approximately 103 ft (31.2 m) square. In the early 13th century, however, when the southern claustral range was rebuilt (including the refectory), the opportunity was taken to extend the garth in that direction. Thereafter, the north–south axis across the court measured around 135 ft (41 m).

Nothing is known of the original 12th-century arcades at Furness, although Hope confidently stated they were 'no doubt of wood'. In any case, these were replaced in the early 13th century by brand new arcades, in which extensive use was made of a fine grey marble. On the site itself, a single trefoiled base survives at the north-east corner of the garth. But there is also a sizeable group of *ex situ* fragments (mainly capitals and bases), some on display in the site museum, and others kept in the English Heritage reserve collection. Some of the bases have foliate decoration set between the intersections of the circular sub-bases (Fig. 37). One base is unfinished and only roughed out to shape. Matching these examples of marble bases, there is a well-preserved capital of moulded design (Fig. 38). In all cases, the pieces are cut and polished to a very high standard of finish. Then, in addition to the marble examples, the Furness stone collection also includes paired cloister capitals executed in the local sandstone. These have moulded sections with leaf decoration set between them (Fig. 39).

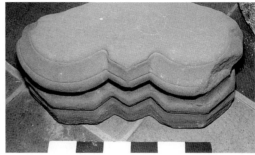

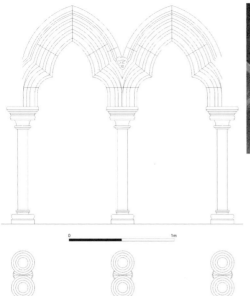

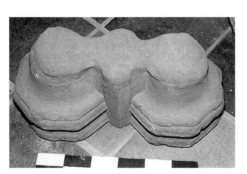

FIG. 40 (*above left*).   Furness Abbey:
reconstruction drawing of the early 13th-century
cloister arcading
Stuart Harrison

FIG. 41 (*above*).   Furness Abbey: dumb-bell base
Stuart Harrison

FIG. 42 (*left*).   Furness Abbey: dumb-bell capital
Stuart Harrison

Another surviving element of the early-13th-century arcades is a single fragmentary corner springer. Its form indicates a trefoil-headed design. It has a foliate boss in the spandrel, but unfortunately the many complex rolls and hollows in its profile are very badly damaged. Some idea of its appearance can be gained from the trefoiled blind arcading in the chapter-house vestibule, which also features marble bases and capitals. The cloister springer seems to have been stilted, and a further clue to the overall form comes from one worn spandrel hood-mould for trefoiled arches decorated with a head stop. Taken together, the fragments allow for a tentative reconstruction of the completed 13th-century arcades (Fig. 40). In effect, the design may be regarded as an updated version of the late-12th-century great cloister arcades at Fountains.

Other fragments from the site include shafts of dumb-bell form with moulded bases and capitals (Figs 41–42). These probably represent a secondary cloister, elsewhere in the abbey complex, probably dating from the 14th or 15th centuries.

Bibliography: W. H. St John Hope, 'The abbey of St Mary in Furness, Lancashire', *Transactions of the Cumberland and Westmorland Antiquarian and Archaeological Society*, 16 (1900), 221–302, at 257–58; Fergusson, *Architecture of Solitude*, 126–27; Robinson, *Cistercian Abbeys of Britain*, 116–19.

GARENDON (Leicestershire), 1133–1536

Summary: south; form of garth only partially recovered; nothing known of arcades.

Bibliography: Fergusson, *Architecture of Solitude*, 127; Robinson, *Cistercian Abbeys of Britain*, 119–20.

GRACE DIEU (Monmouthshire), 1226–1536

Summary: unknown; no information on garth or arcades.

Bibliography: Robinson, *Cistercian Abbeys of Britain*, 121–22; Robinson, *Cistercians in Wales*, 247–48.

HAILES (Gloucestershire), 1246–1539

Summary: south; full form of garth known; late-medieval arcades; laver.

Detail: The vast size of the cloister garth at Hailes is one indication of the ambition which lay behind this comparatively late Cistercian royal foundation. At approximately 132 ft (40.2 m) square, it was among of the largest built by the white monks in southern England.

According to the Hailes chronicler, the initial construction programme at the abbey proceeded at close to breakneck speed. By 1251, in addition to the church and all the principal monastic buildings, 'a large and spacious cloister walk' was apparently ready for dedication. It would not be surprising if this prestigious house featured cloister arcades of early tracery design. Sadly, however, too little evidence of the 13th-century work has survived to indicate its precise form. One *ex situ* fragment, a moulded coupled-column base in blue lias, could be from the cloister, but this is not certain (pers. comm. Richard Lea).

In any case, it was probably Abbot William Whitchurch who began rebuilding the cloister with glazed and vaulted walks, around 1460. It appears to have been a comprehensive programme, leading to significant modifications to several of the doorways and other features around the edge of the garth. Three fragmentary bays of the inner arcade survive at the southern end of the west alley, the middle one retaining some of its tracery (Fig. 16). When the evidence is coupled with *ex situ* fragments, a reconstruction is possible (Fig. 43). Of even greater interest, when this same area was excavated by Bazeley at the turn of the 19th century, six superb heraldic bosses were recovered in addition to large quantities of vaulting and some tracery. On the basis of the heraldry (which requires more detailed study), there is a suggestion that erection of the cloister vaults (at least) may well have extended into the early 16th century.

Around the inner walls of the garth, the vault ribs were carried on angel corbels, three of which survive near the north-east corner, one with a fragment of the vault ribs. An indication of the appearance of the alleys is gained from the *ex situ* vault rib fragments reassembled in a half bay as part of the site museum displays.

In the south alley, eastwards of the refectory doorway, there is a wide recessed laver under a plain segmental arch. The arch soffit is decorated with foil-headed panels. Dating from the 15th century, it must have replaced an earlier laver.

In the north alley, set into the eastern end of the nave south wall, were five large arched recesses with shaft responds and moulded capitals. The arrangement was not unlike that at Beaulieu, though here the recesses have sometimes been interpreted as book cupboards.

Bibliography: W. Bazeley, 'The abbey of St Mary, Hayles', *Transactions of the Bristol and Gloucestershire Archaeological Society*, 22 (1899), 257–71, at 259–60, 265–66; W. St C. Baddeley, *A Cotteswold Shrine: Being a Contribution to the History of Hailes, County Gloucester, Manor, Parish and Abbey* (London 1908); J. G. Coad, *Hailes Abbey*, 2nd edn (London 1993), 7–8, 13, 21; Robinson, *Cistercian Abbeys of Britain*, 122–25.

HOLMCULTRAM (Cumbria), 1150–1538

Summary: south; form of garth not recorded; nothing known of arcades.

Bibliography: S. Harrison, 'The architecture of Holm Cultram Abbey', in *Carlisle and Cumbria: Roman and Medieval Architecture, Art and Archaeology*, ed. M. McCarthy and D. Weston,

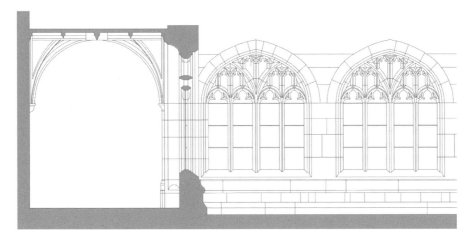

0 ————————————————— 5 metres

0 ————————————————— 15 feet

FIG. 43.   Hailes Abbey: reconstruction drawing showing the south-west corner of the cloister, as remodelled in the late 15th century

Richard Lea, for English Heritage

BAA Trans., XXVII (Leeds 2004), 239–56; Fergusson, *Architecture of Solitude*, 127–29; Robinson, *Cistercian Abbeys of Britain*, 125–26.

HULTON (Staffordshire), 1218/20–1538

Summary: south; full form of garth known from excavation; possible 13th-century arcades.

Detail: The cloister garth at Hulton appears to have been about 95 ft (30 m) square. A single trefoil base and fragments of shafts found during excavations may well represent 13th-century cloister arcading. A similar triple-shaft group arrangement is known from Dore, and is suspected at Dieulacres.

Bibliography: W. D. Klemperer and N. Boothroyd, *Excavations at Hulton Abbey, Staffordshire, 1987–1994*, Society for Medieval Archaeology Monograph, 21 (Leeds 2004), 84, 193; Robinson, *Cistercian Abbeys of Britain*, 127.

JERVAULX (North Yorkshire), 1145/56–1537

Summary: south; form of garth known; late-12th-century arcades; evidence of lay brothers' cloister; laver.

Detail: The main or great cloister garth at Jervaulx was not quite square, measuring 115 ft (35 m) east–west, 108 ft (33 m) down the length of the eastern side, and just over 110 ft (33.5 m) down the west side. The outline of a further cloister has been traced on the outer side of the west claustral range, presumably intended for use by the lay brothers. The known *ex situ* fragments of the cloister arcading were discovered when the site was cleared in the early 19th century. The pieces were subsequently analysed and drawn by Hope and Brakspear, but they did not show the complete range of material or the full detail of the designs.

On the site today there are several twin bases of both octagonal and round shaft form standing on a low wall in the north alley. These are clearly not *in situ* and have been reset. Lying around the cloister are numerous springers and voussoirs, including three of the four

189

corner springers, one of which (from the north-east corner) has a vertical angle moulding decorated with a foliate trail (Fig. 44). The springers from the north-west and south-west corners of the garth remain near to their original positions. Other springers have migrated from the cloister to the infirmary area.

The arcade arches were all round-headed, but two types of arcade profile have been identified. From the corner springers it seems that the south, east, and north alleys were all of one profile (Figs 45–46). This featured a central keel flanked by large rolls and with a small pointed arris set between them. The pattern is very similar to that employed in the late-12th-century Byland cloister arcade. The springers had a plain base block, a feature used extensively in the choir arches of York Minster, built by Archbishop Roger de Pont l'Eveque (1154–81). In contrast, the alley on the west side of the garth had a different arch profile. Again there was a central keel and flanking rolls, but here with a small hollow set between them. Also, the west arcade featured what may be described as decorative crockets set at the springing of the arches.

The three surviving corner springers show that the arches carried a hood-mould, though only on the side of the arcade which faced out to the garth (Fig. 47). Two versions of hood-moulding survive, one with a small keeled roll, the other with a small gouged roll. Few sections of the capitals have survived, but what there are show early Gothic foliate designs. The twin bases meanwhile have the same chamfered stepping on the sub-base as those at Byland, perhaps a stylistic link between the cloister arcades at Jervaulx and those at its mother house. In turn, it may be suggested the Jervaulx arcades were erected in the late 1170s or early 1180s, following on from Byland. Both works were in any case early Gothic compositions.

The remains of the second arcade at Jervaulx lie on the west wall of the west range and comprise sections of bases, springers, and voussoirs (Fig. 48). It was a single column arcade, with alternating round and octagonal shafts. One capital for a round shaft has leaf

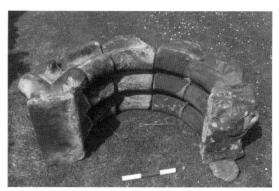

FIG. 44 (*left*). Jervaulx Abbey: corner springer of cloister arcades, late 1170s or early 1180s. It is one of three that have survived at the site
Stuart Harrison

FIG. 45 (*above*). Jervaulx Abbey: assembled cloister arcade arch, late 1170s or early 1180s
Stuart Harrison

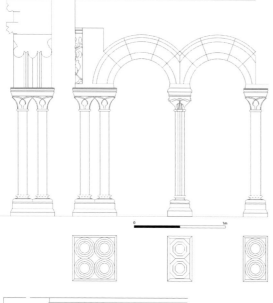

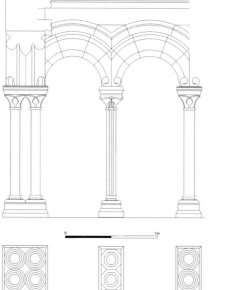

FIG. 46 (*left*).   Jervaulx Abbey: reconstruction drawing of cloister arcading, showing the alley side appearance with corner springer and section through arcade
Stuart Harrison

FIG. 47 (*below left*).   Jervaulx Abbey: garth side view of arcading from west alley, showing decoration at springing level and different profile of arches
Stuart Harrison

FIG. 48 (*below*).   Jervaulx Abbey: reconstruction drawing of the single shaft arcade that stood against the west wall of the west range
Stuart Harrison

decoration of early Gothic style. The arches were relatively plain with a roll on one side and a chamfer on the other. The location of the pieces suggests that the arcade must have served as the lay brothers' cloister, situated on the outer side of the west range. Perhaps, as at Fountains, it formed part of a rectangular court. In general appearance, it must have looked very similar to the infirmary cloister arcade at Rievaulx.

During recent consolidation works at the site, the sill of a wall laver recess, set east of the refectory doorway, was uncovered. Apart from an indication of the laver's extent, the

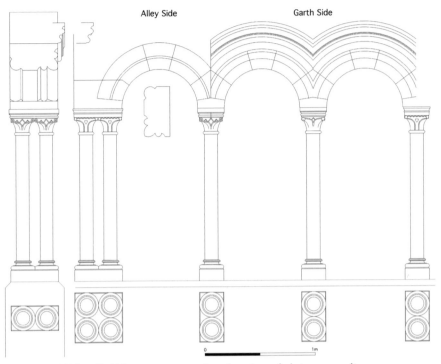

Alley Side   Garth Side

FIG. 49.   Kirkstall Abbey: reconstruction drawing of cloister arcading, *c.* 1170–75

Stuart Harrison

discoveries include architectural fragments in the walling above. These indicate clustered foliate corbels of 12th-century design, and these may have formed part of the arcading set above the laver sill.

Bibliography: W. H. St John Hope and H. Brakspear, 'Jervaulx Abbey', *Yorkshire Archaeological Journal*, 21 (1911), 303–44, at 315–16, 343; Fergusson, *Architecture of Solitude*, 84–85, 129; Robinson, *Cistercian Abbeys of Britain*, 128–29.

KINGSWOOD (Gloucestershire), 1139–1538

Summary: north?; form of garth unrecorded; nothing known of arcades.

Bibliography: E. S. Lindley, 'Kingswood Abbey, its lands and mills' *Transactions of the Bristol and Gloucestershire Archaeological Society*, 73 (1954), 115–91, at pl. xx; Fergusson, *Architecture of Solitude*, 129–30; Robinson, *Cistercian Abbeys of Britain*, 130.

KIRKSTALL (Leeds), 1147/52–1539

Summary: south; form of garth known; late-12th-century arcades; laver; lane.

Detail: The late-12th-century cloister garth at Kirkstall was about 115 ft (35m) square. On the west side was a lay brothers' lane, about 26 ft (8m) wide. The known fragments of the arcade were presumably discovered during the early programme of excavation and fabric consolidation in the 1890s. They were first mentioned (and illustrated) by John Bilson, at which time they were stored in the transept chapels. The pieces are now in secure storage at the site.

The remains include several springers and voussoirs with keeled mouldings (Fig. 49). At the base of each springer is a plain section of block from which the mouldings emerge. Such plain springing blocks were a notable feature of the 12th-century choir of York Minster, built by Archbishop Roger de Pont l'Eveque (1154–81). Fragments of the hood-mould also survive.

Nearly all these pieces show signs of recutting for later reuse, and indeed voussoirs from the cloister can be seen reused in the upper parts of the refectory west2 wall. As to the capitals, although unfortunately none are complete, several sections with waterleaf and volute designs do survive. No two are identical. A surviving corner springer shows how the arcade corners were treated, and also provides evidence that the hood-mould must have been set on the garth side.

Notably, the Kirkstall arcades were built from limestone, in contrast to the rest of the buildings on the site which are of millstone grit. Presumably this was because a finer finish could be cut in the limestone. Stylistically, the arcades appear to have been the last element of the claustral ranges to have been completed. They reflect the very latest French-inspired early Gothic detailing, notably in the capitals and moulding designs. This is in contrast to earlier construction programmes at the site. The majority were still firmly rooted in Anglo-Norman Romanesque, with only minimal early Gothic detailing. In sum, Kirkstall may have been the first Cistercian house in England to introduce full-blown Gothic to its main cloister arcades — it is certainly the earliest example so far identified. Construction is likely to have been carried out marginally earlier than that at Byland, perhaps *c.* 1170–75.

In the later Middle Ages, probably in the 15th century, it seems the main cloister was enlarged. The wall dividing the lay brothers' lane was demolished and the lane area incorporated into the garth. Presumably the original arcading was largely destroyed at this time and replaced with tracery designs. However, no positive proof of this later arcading has yet been discovered.

In the 12th-century cloister arrangements at Kirkstall there does not appear to have been a wall-mounted laver, and it is thought a fountain house may have existed towards the south-east corner of the garth. In the 13th century, however, a wall laver was constructed to the east of the refectory doorway. It featured a trefoil-headed arcade of eight arches, supported on moulded and foliate corbels. The detached, eastern end, of the laver basin has survived and is now on display in the visitor centre. It represents a squared stone trough with supports for seats set along the back, and with holes for pipes in the end. Although very worn, part of one of the projecting trefoil-shaped seats remains *in situ* at the east end of the laver.

Bibliography: W. H. St John Hope and J. Bilson, *Architectural Description of Kirkstall Abbey*, Thoresby Society Publications, 16 (Leeds 1907), 27–28, fig 21; Fergusson, *Architecture of Solitude*, 48–51, 130; Robinson, *Cistercian Abbeys of Britain*, 132–34.

KIRKSTEAD (Lincolnshire), 1139/87–1537
Summary: south; form of garth unrecorded in detail; nothing known of arcades.
Bibliography: Fergusson, *Architecture of Solitude*, 130–31; Robinson, *Cistercian Abbeys of Britain*, 134–35.

LLANTARNAM (Torfaen), 1179–1536
Summary: south; form of garth unrecorded; nothing known of arcades.
Bibliography: Robinson, *Cistercian Abbeys of Britain*, 135–36; Robinson, *Cistercians in Wales*, 169, 249–50.

LONDON, 1350–1538/39
Summary: south; partial form of garth recorded from excavation; 14th-century arcades.
Detail: The overall plan of St Mary Graces in London, the last Cistercian foundation in England, was not of conventional form. In interim reports,the cloister is shown to be of rectangular plan, detached from the abbey church, and separated from it by an open yard. However, the interpretation is to be modified in a forthcoming monograph by Ian Grainger and Christopher Phillpotts. This particular cloister may have become secondary, with a slightly more conventional arrangement subsequently built to the north-east (see note 24). Fragments of late-14th-century Perpendicular-style tracery recovered from the excavations provides an indication of arcade forms, though it may prove difficult to determine from which of the two cloisters.

Bibliography: I. Grainger and D. Hawkins, 'Excavations at the Royal Mint site 1986–1988', *The London Archaeologist*, 5 (1984–88), 429–36, at 432–34; Robinson, *Cistercian Abbeys of Britain*, 136–37.

LOUTH PARK (Lincolnshire), 1137/39–1536

Summary: south; form of garth known only in conjectural outline, based on excavations of the 1870s; nothing known of arcades; laver?

Detail: There is documentary evidence to suggest the cloister and lay brothers' cloister were completed by Abbot Richard de Dunham (1227–46). There is a vague suggestion of a free-standing pavilion laver in the garth.

Bibliography: E. Venables, 'Louth Park Abbey', *Associated Architectural Societies' Reports and Papers*, 12 (1873–74), 41–55; Fergusson, *Architecture of Solitude*, 131–33; Robinson, *Cistercian Abbeys of Britain*, 137.

MAENAN (Conwy), 1284–1537

Summary: north; form of garth unrecorded; nothing definite known of arcades.

Bibliography: Robinson, *Cistercian Abbeys of Britain*, 64–65; Robinson, *Cistercians in Wales*, 34, 250–53.

MARGAM (Neath Port Talbot), 1147–1536

Summary: south; form of garth not fully recorded; nothing known of arcades.

Detail: Margam must have had stone-built cloister arcades by the late 12th or very early 13th century, but nothing is known of their form. There are indications, based around the east processional doorway, that parts (at least) of the garth were remodelled in the 14th century, in which case the arcades too may well have been replaced at this time.

Bibliography: Robinson, *Cistercian Abbeys of Britain*, 138–41; Robinson, *Cistercian in Wales*, 34, 175, 256, 258.

MEAUX (East Yorkshire), 1150–1539

Summary: south; form of garth unrecorded; 13th-century arcades.

Detail: According to the 14th-century Meaux chronicle, the monks' cloister was begun in stone by Abbot Alexander (1197–1210). The work was finished in the time of Abbot Hugh (1210–20). In excavations by G. K. Beaulah a 13th-century twin capital for round shafts was found reused in the base wall of the east cloister alley. The capital was of simple moulded design (pers. comm. Kenneth Beaulah). The reuse of this capital in the walls of a later cloister arcade is paralleled at Byland Abbey.

Bibliography: Fergusson, *Architecture of Solitude*, 133–36; Robinson, *Cistercian Abbeys of Britain*, 141–42.

MEDMENHAM (Buckinghamshire), 1201/04–1536

Summary: north?; form of garth unknown; nothing known of arcades.

Bibliography: Robinson, *Cistercian Abbeys of Britain*, 143–44.

MEREVALE (Warwickshire), 1148–1538

Summary: south; full form of garth unrecorded; no details of arcades.

Bibliography: VCH, *Warwickshire*, IV (London 1947), 142–44; Fergusson, *Architecture of Solitude*, 136; Robinson, *Cistercian Abbeys of Britain*, 148.

NEATH (Neath Port Talbot), 1130–1539

Summary: south; full form of garth exposed; nothing known of arcades; lane; traces of laver recesses in south alley.

Detail: The full form of the cloister garth at Neath, including the position of the arcade walls, was recovered during clearance excavations in 1924–34, and in subsequent investigation by the Ministry of Works. The garth measures some 97 ft (29.6 m) east–west by 119 ft (36.3 m) north–south. There was a comparatively narrow lay brothers' lane on the west side. Recessed lavers flanked the doorway into the north–south refectory in the south alley, in an arrangement not unlike that at Tintern. There is currently no information on the form of the cloister arcades, though some clue may be found in a large but overgrown collection of *ex situ* stonework on the eastern margins of the site.

Bibliography: Robinson, *Cistercian Abbeys of Britain*, 149–51; Robinson, *Cistercians in Wales*, 34, 206, 263–65; D. M. Robinson, *Neath Abbey*, 5th edn (Cardiff 2006).

NETLEY (Hampshire), 1239–1536

Summary: south; full form of garth known, no information on arcades; laver.

Detail: The cloister garth at Netley was approximately 115 ft (35 m) square. The arcades were presumably built in the mid- to later 13th century. In the south alley, to the east of the refectory doorway was a wall-recessed laver. It was divided by shafts into four bays.

Bibliography: J. Hare, 'Netley Abbey: monastery, mansion, ruin', *Proceedings of the Hampshire Field Club and Archaeological Society*, 49 (1993), 207–27; Robinson, *Cistercian Abbeys of Britain*, 151–53.

NEWENHAM (Devon), 1247–1539

Summary: south; partial form of garth known only from antiquarian observation; nothing known of arcades.

Bibliography: Robinson, *Cistercian Abbeys of Britain*, 155.

NEWMINSTER (Northumbria), 1138–1537

Summary: south; form of garth known; late-12th-century arcades.

Detail: The cloister garth at Newminster was approximately 128 ft (39 m) square. The arcade walls are known from excavation, and appear to have been buttressed towards the garth.

Several bays of arcading were re-erected *c.* 1913–14 by the then owner, Mr George Fenwick, his work viewed and photographed by members of the Society of Antiquaries of Newcastle-upon-Tyne in 1914. However, the reconstructed material does not lie on the line of any original alley wall, somewhat confusing the layout of the site.

The work is early Gothic in form (Fig. 50), with the slender twin shafts supporting leaf capitals. Some of the capitals have had new lower sections grafted on to make good ancient damage. The arches are pointed. Details of the mouldings show triple rolls separated by small angle fillets or arrises. The central roll was keeled. There is a prominent hood-mould featuring a roll moulding. Apart from the pointed arches, the details of these Newminster arcades are very similar to those at Byland and Jervaulx. A date of *c.* 1180–85 may be suggested.

When the re-erected arcades were photographed by F. H. Crossley around 1935, one section was supported by raking iron stays (Fig. 50). This has since partly collapsed. Today, due to the much overgrown nature of the site, the arcades are very difficult to see, though parts have clearly started to fall.

Bibliography: Anon., 'Newminster Abbey', *Proceedings of the Society of Antiquaries of Newcastle-upon-Tyne*, 3rd series, 6 (1915), 209–11, pl. facing 209; F. H. Crossley, *The English Abbey*, (London 1935), pl. 87; B. Harbottle and P. Salway, 'Excavations at Newminster Abbey, Northumberland, 1961–63', *Archaeologia Aeliana*, 4th series, 42 (1964), 95–171, at 146, 148; Fergusson, *Architecture of Solitude*, 136–38; Robinson, *Cistercian Abbeys of Britain*, 156–57.

OXFORD (see Rewley)

PIPEWELL (Northamptonshire), 1143–1538

Summary: south; conjectural outline of garth plotted; nothing known of arcades.

Detail: Following the dedication of a rebuilt church at Pipewell in 1311 (an extended eastern arm?), a new chapter-house and cloister were consecrated in 1312. Brakspear gives the dimensions of the cloister as *c.* 103 ft (31.3 m) square.

FIG. 50. Newminster Abbey: cloister arcading re-erected on the site in about 1913–14, late 1170s or early 1180s

F. H. Crossley

Bibliography: H. Brakspear, 'Pipewell Abbey, Northamptonshire', *Associated Architectural Societies' Reports and Papers*, 30 (1909–10), 299–313, at 301, 307; Fergusson, *Architecture of Solitude*, 138; Robinson, *Cistercian Abbeys of Britain*, 157.

QUARR (Hampshire), 1132–1536
Summary: north; approximate outline of garth known from 'very summary' excavations of 1891; no information on arcades.
Bibliography: Fergusson, *Architecture of Solitude*, 138–39; Robinson, *Cistercian Abbeys of Britain*, 158.

REVESBY (Lincolnshire), 1143–1538
Summary: south; form of garth not fully recovered; no information on arcades.
Bibliography: T. Baker, 'Recent excavations on the site of Revesby Abbey', *Associated Architectural Societies' Reports and Papers*, 10 (1869), 22–25; Fergusson, *Architecture of Solitude*, 139–40; Robinson, *Cistercian Abbeys of Britain*, 159.

REWLEY (Oxfordshire), 1281–1536
Summary: north; form of garth unclear; no detail of arcades.
Bibliography: D. Wilkinson, 'Rewley Abbey', *Oxford Archaeological Unit Annual Report 1993–94*, 19–21; Robinson, *Cistercian Abbeys of Britain*, 160; J. Munby, A. Simmonds, R. Taylor and D. Wilkinson, *From Studium to Station: Rewley Abbey and Rewley Road Station, Oxford* (Oxford 2007).

RIEVAULX (North Yorkshire), 1132–1538
Summary: south, form of garth known; late-12th-century arcades; paired lavers in south alley; form of infirmary cloister and its arcades also known.
Detail: The form of the great cloister at Rievaulx was firmly established during the time of Abbot Ailred (1147–67). At about 140 ft (42.7 m) square, it was close to the largest garth ever built by the Cistercians in Britain, and today it stands as perhaps the best-known example.

Numerous fragments of the late-12th-century cloister arcades were uncovered when the site was excavated in the 1920s, including capitals, bases, and sections of the eaves cornice.

These were cleared away and stored in a dump to the east of the church. Meanwhile, good evidence had survived for the form of the stylobate on which the arcades had stood. In the 1930s, the Minister of Works suggested that there was enough material to allow for a reconstruction of several bays on the site. Initially, two arches were re-erected in 1934, and this proving successful additional arches were soon added.

It is evident from the reconstructed bays (Fig. 6) that the arches were round headed and featured roll mouldings on the angle. They were supported on the usual 12th-century arrangement of twin shafts, here with moulded bases and decorative capitals. In more detail, we find two variations of arch form. Both of them had a chamfered hood-mould, though in one case there were three voussoirs with plain soffits and, in the other, five voussoirs with chevron hollows on the soffits. Nevertheless, all of these details were firmly rooted in the Romanesque style. The capitals, on the other hand, featured a broad mix of Romanesque scallop and early Gothic leaf capitals. This implies a transitional phase, perhaps dating from the late 1160s. The work finds its closest parallel in lay brothers' cloister arcades and the galilee porch arcade at Fountains Abbey.

Among the other *ex situ* fragments of stonework from Rievaulx, there is evidence for additional minor variations in the form of the main cloister arcades, including the occurrence of pointed arches in some section or sections. The shafts clearly alternated between round and octagonal forms, and the variants in capitals and base mouldings indicate a partial rebuilding. One explanation for such rebuilding is the known redevelopment of the south claustral range, including a new refectory, late in the time of Abbot Sylvanus (1167–88). This is bound to have required modifications to the south cloister alley. These changes aside, various details of sockets and string-courses on the walls of the south range show that, just as at Fountains, there was a segmental-arched ceiling over the Rievaulx alleys. Capitals set into the northern corners of the garth indicate the probable presence of a diagonal timber rib marking the junction of the ceilings at the corners. Again, similar evidence also survives at Fountains.

In the south alley, to either side of the refectory doorway, there are the remains of wide recesses filled with arcading and featuring trefoil-headed arches (Fig. 18). Each recess contained a trough-like laver, the place where the monks washed before meals. There were semi-circular seats set along the base of the arcading behind the laver troughs. In the Rievaulx suppression inventory, the lavers were described as being of 'lead overcast with pewter'.

Following the successful re-erection of the north-west corner of the main cloister arcade in 1934, a similar exercise was undertaken in Rievaulx's infirmary cloister (Fig. 10). Here, the form of the garth was again established during Ailred's abbacy. It measured about 78 ft (23.8 m) north–south by some 75 ft (22.9 m) east–west. The arcades again featured alternating round and octagonal shafts, but in this case it was a single column form. The arches were much plainer, having only simple chamfers, though the capitals do show considerable variety. In the re-erected sections, the corner capital is a cluster of three scallop capitals, whereas simple chalice capitals sit on the individual piers. Part of the abacus has a simple form of chevron decoration. Other related loose capitals carry vigorous waterleaf designs with distinctive double loops at the base of the foliage, also a hallmark of the capitals at nearby Byland Abbey.

This Rievaulx infirmary cloister was largely destroyed in the late 15th century, when the infirmary at large was converted to serve as the abbot's lodging. The northern arcade and part of the eastern arcade were retained in some form, providing a passage leading from the main cloister towards the abbot's new block of accommodation. The work survived as a result of being encased within later walling which supported a long gallery on the first floor.

Bibliography: P. Fergusson and S. Harrison, *Rievaulx Abbey: Community, Architecture, Memory* (London 1999), 87, 110, 116–17, 137, 142; P. Fergusson, G. Coppack and S. Harrison, *Rievaulx Abbey* (London 2006), 17, 19, 27; Robinson, *Cistercian Abbeys of Britain*, 160–64.

ROBERTSBRIDGE (East Sussex), 1176/1250–1538

Summary: south; form of garth unrecorded; possible early Gothic arcades.

Detail: Fergusson refers to architectural fragments in the former vicarage garden at Salehurst, including a base with angle spurs, 'almost certainly from the cloister'.

Bibliography: L. F. Salzman, 'Excavations at Robertsbridge Abbey', *Sussex Notes and Queries*, 5 (1934–35), 206–08; Fergusson, *Architecture of Solitude*, 140–41; Robinson, *Cistercian Abbeys of Britain*, 164–65.

ROCHE (Rotherham), 1147–1538

Summary: south; form of garth known; late 12th-century arcades; laver.

Detail: Excavations were undertaken at Roche in the 1880s, though the cloister garth was only really explored and cleared after 1921, as part of an Office of Works programme directed by Charles Peers. As determined at the time of its initial construction in the late 12th century, the garth measured approximately 98 ft (30 m) square.

Presumably, the many sections of late-12th-century cloister arcading that survive from Roche were uncovered during of the Office of Works clearances. Among the individual fragments are bases, capitals, springers, voussoirs and spandrel stones. Some are now stored on site, others are kept in the English Heritage reserve collection.

Some years ago, a number of the twin bases, along with the corresponding capitals of waterleaf design, were recovered from the collection of loose stonework on the site. For a period, they were set up in the site exhibition room. Modern shafts were employed, and a concrete lintel was painted to look like the arcading. But the display was eventually dismantled. In 1988, not only were the capitals and bases brought back together, they were united with the other surviving parts of the arcades which had hitherto remained scattered throughout the collection. They were to be assembled in an exhibition entitled 'Abbeys: Yorkshire's Monastic Heritage', held in the Yorkshire Museum in York. In all, enough stonework was brought together to allow for the erection of four arches in a corner situation (Fig. 9). The assembly required the provision of a new corner springer. Following the exhibition, the arcade was again dismantled and has since remained in English Heritage storage. At one stage provisional plans were made to re-erect it on south-east corner of the site, and exploratory excavations were undertaken to establish the position of the cloister arcade wall. Interestingly, this led to the discovery that the central cloister garth was sunk below the level of the surrounding alleys (pers. comm. Glyn Coppack). Small fragments of a cloister base were also recovered in this excavation.

The Roche arcading was clearly a very fine architectural composition. The arches themselves were of pointed design with elegant keeled mouldings and conge decoration at the springings. There was a hood-mould outside the arches, and the spandrels were decorated with small quatrefoils and other ornaments. One notable aspect of the design was the provision of holes through some of the spandrels for iron tie bars to hold the arcade in place. Presumably the bars spanned the cloister alleys and were secured to the surrounding buildings.

Part-way along one alley there was a distinct change in the design of the arcade (Figs 51–52). One surviving springer has the standard pointed design to one side, but the beginnings of a much more elaborate trefoiled design on the other (Fig. 51). Not only did this trefoiled arcading have far more elaborate mouldings, it was also decorated with a band of small dog-tooth. Although few other fragments of this type seem to have survived, sufficient spandrel panels and hood-mould keystones survive to show there were at least ten such arches. The spandrel panels were decorated with small abstract leaf designs and employed a dog-leg jointing system to lock the stones together. This type of jointing was also used later at the Premonstratensian houses of Easby and Egglestone (see the paper on Benedictine and Augustinian cloister arcades in this volume).

It may seem odd that the Roche cloister should undergo such a radical change of design in mid-arcade. The initial design was clearly much indebted to the still potent influence of French early Gothic in the north of England during the 1170s and 1180s. However, the

Fig. 51. Roche Abbey: cloister arcade springer showing change from pointed to trefoiled arches, *c.* 1180–90
Stuart Harrison

Fig. 52. Roche Abbey: reconstruction drawing of cloister arcading showing a corner arrangement and the change from pointed to trefoiled arches, *c.* 1180–90
Stuart Harrison

detailing suggests a slightly later date than the cloister arcades at its mother house of Newminster. Then again, the trefoil-headed work at Roche looks very similar to the main cloister arcade at Fountains Abbey (perhaps built c. 1185–95), in whose family Roche sat as a granddaughter house. Perhaps this new and influential work was the significant factor behind Roche's decision to change the design.

In the south alley of the garth, although badly robbed out, the position of laver arcades can be discerned to either side of the refectory doorway. The western example retains evidence for one moulded base at the west end. Wall robbing has exposed the points where channels for pipework and drainage were positioned.

Bibliography: Coppack, *Yorkshire's Monastic Heritage*, 8–9; P. Fergusson, *Roche Abbey* (London 1990), 14–15; Coppack, *Abbeys & Priories*, 93–94; Fergusson, *Architecture of Solitude*, 62–66, 141–42; Robinson, *Cistercian Abbeys of Britain*, 165–67.

RUFFORD (Nottinghamshire), 1146–1536

Summary: south; outline of garth recorded; no information on arcades.

Bibliography: C. McGee and J. Perkins, 'A study of the Cistercian Abbey at Rufford, Nottinghamshire', *Southwell and Nottinghamshire: Medieval Art, Architecture, and Industry*, ed. J. S. Alexander, *BAA Trans.*, XXI (Leeds 1998), 83–92, at 88; Fergusson, *Architecture of Solitude*, 142–43; Robinson, *Cistercian Abbeys of Britain*, 167–68.

SAWLEY (Lancashire), 1147–1536

Summary: south; full form of garth known from excavation; late-12th- or early-13th-century arcades; lane.

Detail: The cloister garth at Sawley was notably elongated along the north–south axis, measuring 128 ft (39 m), as opposed to 88 ft (27 m) east–west. The only comparable English example is Boxley. Even more unusual at Sawley was the absence of a west cloister alley, though there does seem to have been a lay brothers' lane.

Amongst the *ex situ* stone collection from the site are three springers and one voussoir from a cloister arcade of the late 12th or early 13th century. The pieces were presumably found during the 19th-century clearance of the site. They are relatively plain, but feature triple rolls between sinuous hollows on one angle and a chamfer on the other (Fig. 53). The arcade arches were probably made up from three voussoirs, giving a round-headed form, as shown in the reconstruction drawing. Although no capitals or bases appear to have survived, they were almost certainly of the twin shaft type.

Bibliography: G. Coppack, C. Hayfield and R. Williams, 'Sawley Abbey: the architecture and archaeology of a smaller Cistercian abbey', *JBAA*, 155 (2002), 22–114, at 70–71, 80–81, 109–10; Fergusson, *Architecture of Solitude*, 143–44; Robinson, *Cistercian Abbeys of Britain*, 170–71.

SAWTRY (Cambridgeshire), 1147–1536

Summary: south; outline of garth recorded in the early 20th century, measuring c. 110 ft (33.5 m) east–west by c. 105 ft (32 m) north–south; no information on arcades.

Bibliography: S. I. Ladds, 'Sawtry Abbey, Huntingdonshire', *Transactions of the Cambridgeshire and Huntingdonshire Archaeological Society*, 3 (1914), 295–322, 339–74, at 303; Fergusson, *Architecture of Solitude*, 144, 146; Robinson, *Cistercian Abbeys of Britain*, 172.

SIBTON (Suffolk), 1150–1536

Summary: south; garth recorded in conjectural outline; no information on arcades; traces of laver; lane?.

Detail: The fragmentary and overgrown remains at Sibton have not been studied or recorded in detail. A ground plan of 1892 by T. E. Key was published by Hope with his own commentary. On this evidence, the cloister garth was about 98 ft (30 m) square, with a broad west lane of around 32 ft (9.8 m) wide. On the south side, in the façade of an east–west refectory, there are traces of a recessed two-bay laver with moulded arches.

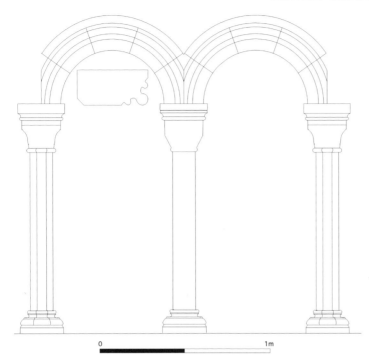

0   1m

Fig. 53. Sawley Abbey: reconstruction drawing of the arches from the main cloister arcades

Stuart Harrison

Bibliography: W. H. St J. Hope, 'Sibton Abbey', *Proceedings of the Suffolk Institute of Archaeology and Natural History*, 8 (1894), 54–60; Fergusson, *Architecture of Solitude*, 146; Robinson, *Cistercian Abbeys of Britain*, 172–73.

STANLEY (Wiltshire), 1151/54–1536

Summary: north; form of garth known from excavations; 13th- and 14th-century arcades; lane.

Detail: Harold Brakspear excavated Stanley in 1905. He discovered a northern cloister garth which was not quite square, measuring 105 ft (32 m) east–west by 100 ft (30.4 m) north–south. There was apparently a lay brothers' lane or court on the west side, approximately 27 ft (8.2 m) wide.

    Brakspear also uncovered evidence for the 13th-century cloister arcades in the form of moulded bases and capitals for coupled shafts. The pieces, made from a blue lias marble, were found chiefly reused in the church, as core work in the 14th-century pulpitum. Brakspear reasoned that the cloister arcades were themselves rebuilt in the 14th century, and were set on walls 2 ft (0.6 m) thick. He found a few fragments of moulding to support this view. The walls were unbuttressed, indicating that the roofs remained of timber construction.

Bibliography: H. Brakspear, 'The Cistercian abbey of Stanley, Wiltshire', *Archaeologia*, 60 (1906–07), 493–516, at 506, 512; Fergusson, *Architecture of Solitude*, 147–48; Robinson, *Cistercian Abbeys of Britain*, 173–75.

STONELEIGH (Warwickshire), 1141/54–1536

Summary: south; form of garth not fully recorded; no firm detail of arcades.

Bibliography: R. K. Morris, 'From monastery to country house: an architectural history of Stoneleigh Abbey, 1156–c. 1660', in *Stoneleigh Abbey: The House, Its Owners, Its Lands*, ed. R. Bearman (Stoneleigh 2004), 15–61, at 37–38, 58; Fergusson, *Architecture of Solitude*, 138–39; Robinson, *Cistercian Abbeys of Britain*, 148–49.

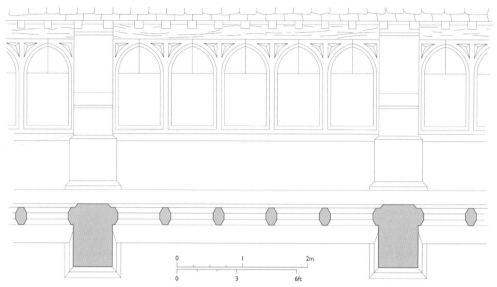

FIG. 54.   Strata Florida Abbey: reconstruction drawing showing one bay of the
mid-15th-century cloister arcades

Pete Lawrence (after Stuart Harrison), for Cadw, Welsh Assembly Government

STRATA FLORIDA (Ceredigion), 1164–1539

Summary: south; form of garth partially known; early-13th- and 15th-century arcades; collation
bay.

Detail: Knowledge on the cloister garth at Strata Florida derives from excavations in the 1880s by
Stephen Williams, and from clearance operations by the Office of Works in the years after
1931. On the northern side, the garth was approximately 98 ft (29. 8 m) wide from east–west.
The north–south dimension has yet to be recovered (the southern end lies beyond the
guardianship boundary currently managed by Cadw).

In the accounts of his late-19th-century excavations, Williams reports finding evidence of
twinned capitals and bases from a cloister arcade. His brief description is accompanied by an
illustration of one such a capital. A narrow band of dog-tooth decoration framed within
the mouldings suggests an early 13th century date. What appears to be the same capital has
recently been relocated (by Stuart Harrison), although it is unfortunately incomplete. It is not
impossible that this particular piece was originally a twin capital, but its style suggests it is
more likely to have been part of the chapter-house doorway.

At some point towards the end of the Middle Ages, probably in the mid-15th century,
some (at least) of the Strata Florida cloister arcades were rebuilt, with the principal evidence
surviving for the north and east sides. The northern alley, for example, was arranged in five
bays by regularly placed buttresses. There were five lights to the standard bays, with iron
glazing bars set horizontally near the springing of the pointed heads (Fig. 54). The heads may
have been glazed. A broadly similar design to this late Welsh cloister arcade may be seen,
reconstructed, at Glenluce Abbey in Scotland. There several bays have been re-erected in the
eastern alley outside the chapter-house.

In the northern alley at Strata Florida, the middle bay of the rebuilt cloister was canted
outwards. This undoubtedly represents the position of the lectern for the collation reading.

Bibliography: S. W. Williams, *The Cistercian Abbey of Strata Florida: Its History and an Account
of the Recent Excavations Made on the Site* (London 1889), 206 and pl. facing 206 no. 2;
S. W. Williams, 'On further excavations at Strata Florida Abbey', *Archaeologia Cambrensis*,

5th series, 6 (1889), 24–58, at 34 and pl. facing 32, no. 2; C. A. R. Radford, *Strata Florida Abbey* (London 1949); Robinson, *Cistercian Abbeys of Britain*, 176–79; Robinson, *Cistercians in Wales*, 35, 171, 177–79, 193, 270–72; D. M Robinson, *Strata Florida Abbey — Talley Abbey*, 3rd edn (Cardiff 2007).

STRATA MARCELLA (Powys), 1170–1536
Summary: south; form of garth recorded in conjectural outline, based on excavations of the 1890s; 13th-century arcades?
Detail: The conjectural outline of the garth at Strata Marcella measures about 75 ft (28.9 m) square. Among the *ex situ* stonework excavated at the site in 1890 were fragments of Geometrical tracery, with no sign of grooves for glazing. The excavators suggested it may have formed part of the cloister arcade.
Bibliography: M. C. Jones and S. W. Williams, 'Excavations on the site of Strata Marcella Abbey — Report on excavations at Strata Marcella Abbey, near Welshpool', *Montgomeryshire Collections*, 25 (1891), 149–96, at 173 and pl. 8; Robinson, *Cistercian Abbeys of Britain*, 179–80; Robinson, *Cistercians in Wales*, 35, 275–76.

STRATFORD LANGTHORNE (Essex), 1135–1538
Summary: south; form of garth not fully recovered; no information on arcades.
Bibliography: B. Barber, S. Chew, T. Dyson and B. White, *The Cistercian Abbey of St Mary Stratford Langthorne, Essex: Archaeological Excavations for the London Underground Limited Jubilee Line Extension Project*, MoLAS Monograph, 18 (London 2004), 32, 75; Fergusson, *Architecture of Solitude*, 149–50; Robinson, *Cistercian Abbeys of Britain*, 180–81.

SWINESHEAD (Lincolnshire), 1135–1536
Summary: position unclear; nothing known of form of garth or arcades.
Bibliography: Fergusson, *Architecture of Solitude*, 150; Robinson, *Cistercian Abbeys of Britain*, 184.

THAME (Oxfordshire), 1137–1539
Summary: south?; nothing known on form of garth or arcades.
Bibliography: Fergusson, *Architecture of Solitude*, 150–51; Robinson, *Cistercian Abbeys of Britain*, 184–85.

TILTY (Essex), 1153–1536
Summary: north; form of garth known in outline, based on limited excavations and aerial photography; no information on arcades.
Bibliography: F. W. Galpin, 'The abbey church and claustral buildings of Tilty', *Transactions of the Essex Archaeological Society*, new series, 18 (1926), 89–95; Fergusson, *Architecture of Solitude*, 151; Robinson, *Cistercian Abbeys of Britain*, 185–86.

TINTERN (Monmouthshire), 1131–1536
Summary: north; form of garth known; evidence of 13th- and 15th-century arcades;
paired lavers in north alley, collation seat in south alley; form of infirmary garth also known.
Detail: The cloister garth at Tintern was situated to the north of the abbey church and was first laid out in the 12th century, measuring a rather modest 76 ft (23.2 m) north–south. The arrangements on the west side of the garth at this time are uncertain, and nothing can be said of the original arcades. Following an extended programme of rebuilding on the claustral ranges in the first decades of the 13th century, all four cloister alleys were to be given new arcading. From *c.* 1269–1301, however, the scheme was complicated by the removal of the 12th-century Romanesque church on the south side of the garth and its replacement by a new abbey church. This resulted in an expansion of the garth southwards, presumably necessitating (at the very least) extensions to the new arcades on the east and west sides.

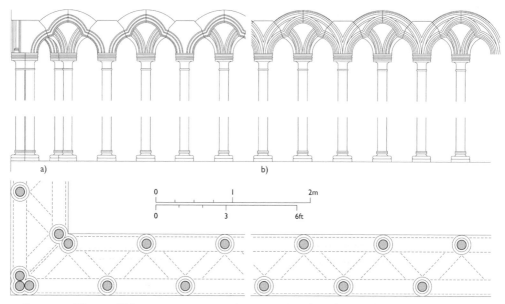

FIG. 55.   Tintern Abbey: reconstruction drawing of mid- to late-13th-century syncopated
cloister arcading, showing two forms of design

Pete Lawrence (after Stuart Harrison), for Cadw, Welsh Assembly Government

From the early 14th century, the full garth measured about 100 ft (30.5 m) north–south by
110 ft (33.5 m) east–west.

Considerable quantities of the 13th-century Tintern cloister arcades have survived at the
site. The many *ex situ* fragments were presumably identified or uncovered in the various
State clearances programmes extending back to 1901. From the 1920s, the pieces were
displayed with all other *ex situ* fragments on a terrace at the northern end of the site. There
many of them remain, their present condition a significant cause for concern.

As reconstructed on paper, the design of this Tintern arcading could be said to form the
high-water mark of Cistercian cloister designs before the advent of tracery overwhelmed
earlier concepts. In essence, the Tintern design was based on two parallel rows of elegant
trefoil-headed arches linked by miniature rib vaults. Novelty and complexity were introduced
by the fact these arches were independently carried on free-standing colonnettes set out in a
staggered or syncopated pattern (Figs 11, 55). Within the full portfolio of trefoiled arch forms
recovered, there are for example considerable variations in the arch mouldings, and also in
terms of whether there was an enclosing arch or just a plain trefoil head. Only one capital of
moulded design has so far been identified, and this is possibly cut from a pale grey marble to
contrast with the stone arches.

Close scrutiny of the limited documentary evidence and known structural sequences at the
site suggest that work on arcade could not have been started before *c.* 1245–50, and a date
extending into the 1260s would not be unreasonable. Following the marginally later rebuilding of the abbey church, and the extension of the cloister garth southwards, the arcades must
have seen further work towards the end of 13th century. Potential elements of the additional
arcading have been identified, and again show a variety of trefoiled designs and moulding
profiles, though generally retaining the earlier syncopated form. Some of this later arcading

was distinguished with gables outlining the arches, perhaps forming doorways through to the garth.

By the beginning of the 15th century (1411–12), the Tintern community was seeking funds to repair the existing cloister roofs. In due course, it was probably Abbot Thomas Colston (*c.* 1460–86) who chose to embark on a complete rebuilding programme, no doubt prompted by an endowment offered to the community in the will of William Herbert, earl of Pembroke (d. 1469), 'to build new cloisters'. A degree of progress was quite definitely made before the suppression, with the traces of four lavish stone-vaulted bays surviving in the south-east corner of the garth.

In the north alley of the Tintern cloister, to either side of the refectory doorway, there was a large arched recess with a richly moulded head. As with the central doorway, the jambs of these arches comprised multiple clusters of attached and detached shafts. Each recess contained a trough-like laver, where the monks washed before meals. The paired arrangement is not unlike the earlier examples found at Fountains and Rievaulx.

In the south alley, against the wall of the nave of the second abbey church, there is a shallow recess with a pointed head. It almost certainly represents the position where the abbot sat during the collation reading.

To the north-east of the great cloister, the full form of Tintern's infirmary cloister garth is also known. It was about 84 ft (25.6 m) east–west by 71 ft (21.6 m) north–south and was again surrounded by arcades. The form of these arcades is unclear, though it is tempting to suggest they were based on a form of dumb-bell pier with linked polygonal colonnettes, numerous fragments of which survive at the site.

Bibliography: S. Harrison, 'The thirteenth-century cloister arcade at Tintern Abbey', in *Cardiff: Architecture and Archaeology in the Medieval Diocese of Llandaff*, ed. J. R. Kenyon and D. M. Williams, *BAA Trans.*, XXIX (Leeds 2006), 86–101; D. M. Robinson, *Tintern Abbey*, 4th edn (Cardiff 2002), 31, 36–37, 48–49, 62; Robinson, *Cistercians in Wales*, 35, 172–75, 177, 281–85.

VALE ROYAL (Cheshire), 1274–1538

Summary: south; form of garth not fully recovered; no information on arcades.

Bibliography: Robinson, *Cistercian Abbeys of Britain*, 192–93.

VALLE CRUCIS (Denbighshire), 1200/01–1536/37

Summary: south; full form of garth known; 14th-century arcades.

Detail: Butler suggests that the original intention at Valle Crucis had been to provide a cloister 79 ft (24 m) square. In the event, the north–south axis was eventually up to 5ft (1.5 m) longer on the west side. The arrangements in the garth, including the position of the arcade walls, became fully clear after an excavation in 1970.

There is no record of any cloister arcading built prior to the 14th century. However, following the reconstruction of the east range around 1325–50, new arcades were introduced to at least that side of the garth, if not all four sides. Fragments of the arcade, in which pointed arches with cusped soffits were supported on paired dumb-bell type shafts were discovered by Hughes in the late 19th century (Fig. 56). Butler (pers. comm.) says fragments of this type were put in store in the early 1960s. The reconstructed form of this Valle Crucis arcade shows it to have been very similar to that known from Basingwerk.

In the south-east corner of the garth, there are the remains of a walled rectangular basin. It is possible it marks the site of the monks' laver, otherwise not represented in the admittedly low surviving walls of the south range.

Bibliography: H. Hughes, 'Valle Crucis Abbey', *Archaeologia Cambrensis*, 5th series, 11 (1894), 169–85, 257–75, at 171–72, 274–75; and 12 (1895), 5–17, at 6–7; C. A. R. Radford, *Valle Crucis Abbey*, 12th impression (London 1976), 22–23; L. A. S. Butler, 'Valle Crucis Abbey: an excavation in 1970', *Archaeologia Cambrensis*, 125 (1976), 80–126, at 86, 93; Robinson, *Cistercian Abbeys of Britain*, 194–97; Robinson, *Cistercians in Wales*, 35, 175–76, 290–93.

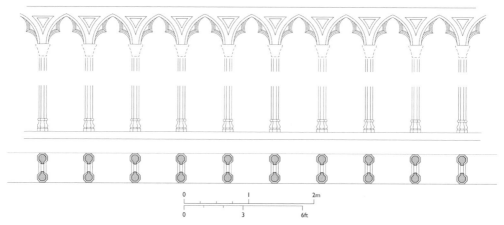

FIG. 56.   Valle Crucis Abbey: reconstruction drawing of 14th-century cloister arcading

Pete Lawrence, for Cadw, Welsh Assembly Government

VAUDEY (Lincolnshire), 1147–1536

Summary: not known with certainty; form of garth unrecorded; no information on arcades.

Bibliography: Fergusson, *Architecture of Solitude*, 149–50; Robinson, *Cistercian Abbeys of Britain*, 197–98.

WARDEN (Bedfordshire), 1136–1537

Summary: south; form of garth partially recovered; no information on arcades.

Bibliography: G. T. Rudd and B. B. West, 'Excavations at Warden Abbey in 1960 and 1961', *Bedfordshire Archaeological Journal*, 2 (1964), 58–72; Fergusson, *Architecture of Solitude*, 152; Robinson, *Cistercian Abbeys of Britain*, 198–99.

WAVERLEY (Surrey), 1128–1536

Summary: south; full form of garth known from excavations; late 12th-century arcades.

Detail: Harold Brakspear suggested that the earliest cloister at Waverley was about 96 ft (29.3 m) square. The east and south alleys (if not all), were probably rebuilt around 1180. Brakspear reported finding parts of the rebuilt arcading. It featured alternating coupled circular columns and single octagonal ones, with bases made from Purbeck marble. Two bases of either form were found towards the south-east corner. The nature of the arcade itself was not clear, though Brakspear felt the alternate pattern of the bases suggested 'it was probably somewhat different from the usual series of trefoiled arches'.

  Following the completion of a new abbey church in the mid- to later 13th century, the cloister was extended northwards. In addition, part of the west range was removed to allow for an extension of the garth in that direction. As completed, the size of the garth was 120 ft (36.6 m) north–south by 124 ft (37.8 m) east–west. Brakspear found one base of a coupled column of the enlarged arcading, but felt it was impossible to say if it matched the alternating arrangement of the earlier work. In the 15th century, the cloister floors were raised some 3 ft (0.91 m) and the open arcades were partially blocked with solid walls.

Bibliography: H. Brakspear, *Waverley Abbey*, Surrey Archaeological Society, (Guildford 1905), 35–37, pl. 14; Fergusson, *Architecture of Solitude*, 153–54; Robinson, *Cistercian Abbeys of Britain*, 199–201.

WHALLEY (Lancashire), 1296–1537

Summary: south; form of garth recorded; no information on arcades; laver in south alley.

Bibliography: Robinson, *Cistercian Abbeys of Britain*, 202–03.

WHITLAND (Carmarthenshire), 1140–1539

Summary: south; conjectural outline of garth recorded; possible late-12th- and 15th/16th-century arcades; lane.

Detail: A conjectural outline of the cloister garth at Whitland has recently been put forward on the basis of standing structures and geophysical survey, with a suggestion that it was approximately 98 ft (30 m) square. The evidence is inconclusive, but there appears to have been a broad lay brothers' lane on the west side, up to 42 ft (13 m) wide. Geophysical anomalies may also indicate the presence of a collation bay in the north alley.

Clapham reported seeing coupled capitals and bases from the (late-12th-century?) cloister arcade in the grounds of Whitland Abbey House, though none has been found in more recent summary investigations of *ex situ* stonework. Ludlow suggests the cloister arcades may well have been replaced in the late 15th or early 16th century, based on the amount of Perpendicular-style tracery recovered from the recent excavations.

Bibliography: A. W. Clapham, 'Three monastic houses of south Wales', *Archaeologia Cambrensis*, 76 (1921), 205–14, at 208; N. D. Ludlow, 'Whitland Abbey, Carmarthenshire: a Cistercian site re-examined, 1994–99', *Archaeologia Cambrensis*, 151 (2002), 41–108, at 69, 73, 76; Robinson, *Cistercian Abbeys of Britain*, 204–05; Robinson, *Cistercians in Wales*, 35, 171, 177, 294–96.

WOBURN (Bedfordshire), 1145–1538

Summary: south; form of garth not fully recorded; no information on arcades.

Detail: Two early-18th-century plans of the post-suppression house by John Sanderson (d. 1774), now in the Woburn Abbey archive, allow for a partial recovery of the garth and the disposition of the principal monastic ranges around it (copies of plans supplied in pers. comm. from Diane Duggan).

Bibliography: Fergusson, *Architecture of Solitude*, 154–55; Robinson, *Cistercian Abbeys of Britain*, 205.

Architecture and Meaning in Cistercian Eastern Ranges

JACKIE HALL

The uniformity of Cistercian claustral ranges allows for a level of analysis beyond the functional attribution of different spaces. Even in the absence of sculptural iconographic schemes, it is possible to detect meaning in surviving remains. In this paper, the entrances from the east cloister alley into the various rooms of the east range are shown to be carefully nuanced and to display a range of meanings. While the importance of the chapter-house is stressed by the architectural enrichment of its façade, the relative status of the book room and the parlour appears to have changed over time.

CISTERCIAN cloisters are famously uniform, and so the identification of the rooms of the east range need not detain us long.[1] Aside from living tradition and the buildings themselves, much of our information on the location and function of the claustral buildings comes from the *Ecclesiastica Officia*, one of the early documents that make up the so-called *consuetudines* of the Cistercians. It was used from the late 19th century — a formative time in the interpretation of monastic buildings — to identify the different parts of the cloister.[2] The *Ecclesiastica Officia* describes in detail liturgical practice, everyday activities and the duties of monastic officials; references to buildings are therefore largely incidental, dealing with matters such as who should be where and when. The route of the Sunday procession is arranged so as to asperge by turn the chapter-house, parlour, dormitory and latrine, followed by the warming room, refectory, kitchen, and cellar, thus confirming the order of those spaces.[3] The *Ecclesiastica Officia* also locates two parlours, 'next to the kitchen and in the cellar' and 'next to the chapter-house' and hints at the location of a bookroom between the chapter-house and the church, since lights must be placed in front of the *armarium* to light the way from the chapter-house to the choir.[4] Because of this, for the last century and more, the narrow space adjacent to the church has been interpreted at most Cistercian abbeys as a bookroom to the west, which opened onto the cloister, and a vestry or sacristy to the east, which opened into the transept.[5]

In a conventionally aligned cloister, with the church on the north side, the chapter-house can be found south of the bookroom and the parlour south of that (as identified by the *Ecclesiastica Officia*). South of the parlour, entrances may lead to the day stairs, to an eastward-leading passage or slype and to the dayroom or dormitory undercroft (often entered by a door from a passage).[6]

THE CHAPTER-HOUSE FAÇADE

THE chapter-house façade almost invariably dominates the east range, with an ornate central doorway flanked each side by an unglazed window or an arch dropping to the

JBAA, vol. 159 (2006), 208–21
© British Archaeological Association 2006
DOI: 10.1179/174767006X132998

floor. This interpenetration of cloister alley and chapter-house has been interpreted as deriving from a desire to enable lay-brothers to follow proceedings as well as monks.[7] At Cistercian abbeys, lay-brothers held their own chapter in a separate room every Sunday, except on those occasions (some sixteen times a year) when they listened to the abbot's sermon during the chapter of the choir monks.[8] At the height of Cistercian prosperity, it may well have been the case that joint numbers of monks and lay-brothers were too great to fit into the chapter-house proper. At Rievaulx, for instance, in 1142 there were 300 community members in total (although many of the lay brothers would have lived on granges outside the abbey) and numbers grew under the abbacy of St Aelred (1147–67).[9] In England and Wales, it is possible that this usage is responsible for the development of vestibules in the first bay adjacent to the cloister, usually contemporary with an enlargement of the chapter-house east of the range, as for instance at Fountains and Furness.[10] Although in other orders, as for instance at Benedictine Chester or Augustinian Bristol, the opportunity was taken to increase the grandeur of the chapter-house by raising its vault well above the height of the east range upper floor, this does not seem to have been common in Cistercian houses. Apart from the exceptional Rievaulx Abbey, there is little evidence to suggest that Cistercian chapter-houses did have high ceilings, even where vestibules exist. At Furness, the upper windows of the dormitory are still visible; elsewhere the projecting bays alone are not extensive enough to have housed the whole community in the prosperous times in which they were built.

At Croxden Abbey (Staffordshire), instead of making a vestibule within the width of the east range, the cloister alley itself was converted into an antechamber, at the same time as the main room was extended two bays eastwards, and the interior remodelled. The connection between the alley and the chapter-house was created by the insertion of a vault over the alley using the same rib moulding as the interior. The importance of the alley space may have been further stressed by the addition of a substantial porch built within the garth.[11]

Although the openness of the chapter-house to the cloister alley could have been used to advantage when the numbers of lay-brothers and monks combined was high, Professor Stein-Kecks has recently argued convincingly that this could not have been the original reason that their façades developed in that way, since privacy was important to many chapter-house proceedings. While she suggests the reason may have been pragmatic (to create more light) or symbolic (at Cluny, to dignify the entrance to the holy space of the infirmary chapel, which was attached to the rear of the chapter-house),[12] even from an early date the façade itself had become a *topos* of chapter-house architecture. So much so that the façade remained identifiable even when, as in some English examples, it no longer connected the cloister alley with the chapter-house. Where there is a vestibule, as for example at Fountains (Fig. 1) or Benedictine Chester, the façade fronting the cloister still declares the space behind to be a chapter-house — there is no differential architecture for vestibule façades and chapter-house façades. At Furness (Fig. 2), and perhaps also at Fountains, the arches flanking the chapter-house door lead not into the chapter-house vestibule but into book cupboards.[13] None the less, these arches are treated in the same way as the central doorway, which does lead into the chapter-house (via the vestibule). The appearance of cloister-chapter-house interpenetrability is often a sham, but is maintained, perhaps, in order to affirm the chapter-house as the central element of the east claustral range, and to emphasise the importance of that element.

FIG. 1.   Fountains Abbey: east range from cloister, chapter-house and parlour entrances
Jackie Hall

FIG. 2.   Furness Abbey: east range from south
Jason Wood

BOOKROOMS, PARLOURS, PASSAGES AND UNDERCROFTS

UNLIKE the chapter-house façade, the façades of the smaller spaces to the south, and of the bookroom to the north, are not instantly recognisable. In order to understand them collectively, individual examples must first be understood in relation to their own east range.

The starting point for this particular investigation was Croxden Abbey, and it is still a good place to begin, because at Croxden each doorway in the east range is different from the others (Figs 3–5). The northern end of the east range — the lower part of the south transept wall and the north jamb of the bookroom door — may predate the arrival there of the monks in 1179, while the remainder belongs to the time of the first abbot, Thomas Woodstock (1178–1229).[14] It was built in a single, though perhaps lengthy, building campaign. There are signs of pauses at regular intervals — south of the bookroom, south of the chapter-house and south of the parlour. In most cases, these pauses are probably no more than seasonal building breaks, the possible exception being the break between the bookroom and the chapter-house, the latter completed in a rather different style, sometime in the first quarter of the 13th century. After this, the range appears to have been built fairly swiftly. This continuous building sequence led not to a stylistic homogeneity but to a series of very individual spaces, with a series of equally individual entrances.

Viewed from the cloister the openings of the east range can be characterised as moderately and conventionally decorated (the bookroom); ornately decorated (the chapter-house façade); moderately and eccentrically decorated (the parlour) and rather plain (the slype). The bookroom entrance arch has three moulded orders, all carved on the square and each sporting a sharply pointed keel as the principal moulding. Only the middle order is supported on simple foliate capitals (slightly different north and south, indicating the building break). The openings of the chapter-house façade each had four ornately moulded external orders plus a hoodmould (the inner orders now missing), and two internal orders, all supported by moulded bases, shafts and stiff-leaf capitals (Fig. 4). Between each major *en-delit* shaft was a minor coursed shaft with its own capital and base.

Externally, the parlour entrance is quite different from that of the chapter-house. The capitals are very simply moulded, although those below the hoodmould sport tendrils, which sweep outwards. The three orders of the arch bear no relation to each other or to those of the chapter-house (Fig. 5). The inner order is elaborately moulded with beaks and a roll-and-three-fillets; the middle order is chamfered, and the outer order is the oddest of all, with a series of cusps carved over a small keeled roll, like some sort of degraded gothic beakhead (the internal outer order is only chamfered). This order is quite without parallel at Croxden although similar features can occasionally be seen elsewhere. The slype has a hoodmould and chamfered arches of two orders, supported on simple capitals like those of the parlour door.

At first sight, the degree of decoration is a direct reflection of the importance of the room behind. However, excepting chapter-houses, it is not obvious that the status of the rooms, as advertised architecturally, is uniform in Cistercian east ranges. To make sense of the individual decoration of the doorways at Croxden, therefore, it is worth looking at a sample of other Cistercian houses to establish whether there might, in fact, be method in Croxden's madness.

Comparative analysis is limited by the small numbers of Cistercian ranges that survive in a sufficiently complete state, and discussion here is further limited to

FIG. 3.   Croxden Abbey: book room door and north window of chapter-house,
viewed from cloister

English Heritage

FIG. 4.   Croxden Abbey: chapter-house façade, viewed from cloister

Jackie Hall

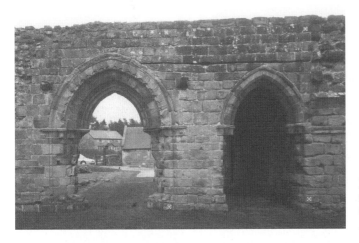

FIG. 5. Croxden Abbey: entrances to parlour and slype, viewed from cloister
English Heritage

English and Welsh examples; it is possible to reach some conclusions. Looking at the earliest examples first, the east ranges of Fountains, Kirkstall and Buildwas all date to *c.* 1150–80, with Fountains probably the first (Figs 1, 6 and 7).[15] Although there are manifest differences in architectural richness between these abbeys, there is remarkable consistency in the relative treatment of the elements of the façade. It goes without saying that the arches of the chapter-house façade are the most sumptuous, but at Fountains the parlour door is equally grand while the Kirkstall and Buildwas parlour openings are only slightly less rich. The bookroom entrances make a stark contrast — in each case a single arch without moulding, chamfer or capital (although Kirkstall's has a hoodmould). At Fountains and Kirkstall the slype/dorter undercroft doorways are plainer than their respective parlour doors (Buildwas does not have a slype separate from the parlour). A little later (*c.* 1180–90), the east range of Combe Abbey in Warwickshire is slightly different, with the doorways to both north and south as rich as the arches to the chapter-house and chevron was used on the outer orders of most of the arches.[16]

More examples survive from the 13th century than from the 12th, including Furness, Tintern, Beaulieu, Netley and Hailes, as well as Croxden (Figs 2 and 8–11).[17] At Furness, every doorway in the façade is rather ornate. The chapter-house arches, or rather the chapter-house vestibule doorway and flanking book cupboards, have five moulded orders (the lost inner orders probably dividing each arch into two), while the parlour and slype doorways each have four rather different orders. Although badly eroded, the parlour arch appears to have a raised section in the middle of each outer-order voussoir, a little like billet, but running across all the mouldings (Fig. 8).

Tintern is closer to the earlier examples, with a parlour door like that of the chapter-house and a plain slype entrance (the arches are lost, but the lower parts of the jambs remain). The bookroom entrance, however, belongs to the early 14th century and was particularly ornate (Fig. 9). Beaulieu also has an ornate bookroom entrance added in the 14th century — a double doorway of which only the Purbeck marble bases survive — while the book niche on the south transept wall is vaulted with moulded ribs and Purbeck bases, shafts and capitals. South of the rich chapter-house entrance the parlour/slype has a segmental chamfered arch (no capitals or shafts) and

213

Fig. 6.   Fountains Abbey: east range from cloister, south transept and entrance to book room
Jackie Hall

Fig. 7.   Kirkstall Abbey: east range from cloister
Jackie Hall

FIG. 8.   Furness Abbey: parlour doorway, detail

Jackie Hall

FIG. 9.   Tintern Abbey: bookroom entrance, from cloister

Jackie Hall

the entrance to the dormitory undercroft is almost equally plain, with simple chamfered jambs. Netley's east range (Fig. 10) was probably complete by around 1260 and, unsurprisingly, it shares some features with that of Beaulieu, its mother-house. Like Beaulieu, the capitals, shafts and bases are of Purbeck marble throughout the east range. The chapter-house façade is of three orders with complex arch mouldings; the bookroom has one moulded order and one chamfered order with, according to Brakspear, a trefoil oculus over the doorway.[18] The doorway to the parlour/slype by contrast is very plain, with no capitals and shafts and a single chamfered order, and there is a similar doorway to the dormitory undercroft. Also a daughter of Beaulieu, Hailes' conventual buildings were complete by 1251. Once more, the bookroom/ sacristy entrance (the partition is lost) was moderately complex with double trefoil doorways and a quatrefoil oculus. The details of the chapter-house entrance are mostly lost but appear to have been similar, perhaps with more orders and tracery in the windows. The entrances to the parlour/slype and to the dormitory undercroft are both much lower and both round-headed; the parlour doorway is multi-foiled below and the mouldings of the undercroft doorway are noticeably less complex.

Later still in the 13th century, the east range of Calder Abbey is distinguished by a completely plain parlour/slype and a bookroom which occupies part of the chapter-house.[19] There is no separate space between the church and the chapter-house. This must partly be due to the smallness of the cloister at Calder, and to the enduring poverty of the house. Valle Crucis, in north Wales, also has a small cloister and has a similarly compressed east range, which was largely rebuilt in the mid-14th century (Fig. 11). The (very plain) opening south of the chapter-house doorway leads to the day stairs, while that to the north leads to a shallow book cupboard fronted on the cloister side by a flamboyant tracery screen. The chapter-house door itself is quite severe, with two orders of continuous mouldings, and the entrance to the broad passage south of the daystairs matches it. North of the chapter-house, the entrance to the sacristy/bookroom dates to the first phase of building at Valle Crucis (following its foundation in 1201). Unusually, these two houses have abandoned the convention of an enriched chapter-house entrance — was this deliberate or a function of poverty or remoteness?

The east range of Whalley Abbey in Lancashire belongs to the later 14th century.[20] In the south transept and west wall of the sacristy (which is not accessible from the cloister) are three large deep book cupboards, completely unmoulded. The chapter-house vestibule has simple traceried windows and a doorway of three continuous moulded orders with fleurons, all of which are embellished with crocketed hoodmoulds. The parlour door is the same as that of the chapter-house, minus the fleurons and crockets, while the slype entrance is smaller and simpler still, with two orders, the inner supported by a capital.

DISCUSSION

THE comparative evidence confirms what we already know — that the chapter-house is marked out as the most important element in any given east walk, and almost always has a façade of three arches. The entrances to either side do not follow such a clear pattern. The entrances to (separate) slypes and to dormitory undercrofts appear to be universally of less architectural pretension than the other doorways of the east range other than the early bookrooms. These early bookrooms, along with the niches at 14th-century Whalley, contrast with their respective parlours and are plain to a

FIG. 10.   Netley Abbey: east range from cloister
Jackie Hall

FIG. 11.   Valle Crucis Abbey: east range from cloister
David Robinson

fault — treated as nothing more than oversized cupboards. Most of the later examples, starting with Combe and including Croxden, appear to be moderately decorated and occasionally, as at Valle Crucis and Tintern, are treated with as much elaboration as the chapter-house — in these latter instances the flourish added in the 14th century. In this company, the use of the chapter-house façade to house books at some abbeys does not seem so strange. The *lectio divina* always played an important role in Cistercian life, as is evident from the *Ecclesiastica Officia*, and the apparent rise in the architectural status of the bookroom is intriguing. Does it imply an overt emphasis on the role of learning by the later convents?[21] Is it a reflection of regional identity (the early plain ones being mostly in the north)? Or is it a desire on the part of the architect or convent to provide a more fitting neighbour to the chapter-house and to raise the architectural level of the whole cloister?

On the far side of the chapter-house, the parlour was a place for permissible conversation during the hours of reading and of work, but the *Ecclesiastica Officia* makes it clear that access was not free but had to be granted by the prior. He arranged his own work in the parlour, and this may have been where he distributed the necessary tools for the monks' work.[22] One wonders if the presence of the prior alone was enough to guarantee the architectural signposting of the parlour as a special place, since the activities within seem far from special. Yet at Fountains, Kirkstall, Buildwas, Combe, and a little later, Tintern, the parlour entrance is framed in exactly the same way as the chapter-house. In addition to the external architectural embellishment of the parlour, there is evidence that it was also enriched internally. This is shown at Croxden by the delicate responds of the vault (like those of the chapter-house, although the capitals are moulded rather than carved) and the unique rib designs. At Saint-Jean-des-Vignes, Soissons (Augustinian), Bonde and Maines have suggested that a small space in the south range with architectural embellishment 'comparable to liturgically-charged spaces' and including a decorated tiled floor, may have functioned as a high status parlour. They consider that it may have acted in this way before the building of a separate abbot's lodging, as a place where the abbot might converse both with monks and élite secular visitors.[23] Aside from occasional records of business transactions in parlours,[24] an architectural link with the secular world might perhaps be suggested at Furness, where the parlour door shares its distinctive raised motif (which, like the cusped motif of Croxden's parlour, has its origins in English Romanesque) and its moulding details with the north transept north door. One explanation for the unusual transept door is that it was the entrance to a lay chapel within the north transept, prior to the building of the gatehouse chapel.[25]

Elsewhere, as for instance at Augustinian Worksop Priory (Fig. 12), and at Calder Abbey such distinctive decorative designs can be seen in the west doors of the conventual church, while at Kirkstall it is the north door of the abbey church (which faces the gatehouse) that is so distinguished (Fig. 13).[26] These are all doorways through which high status secular guests may have passed. Thus it is just possible that Croxden's eccentric parlour entry may be an architectural indication that lay folk might enter here (as porches were on guest halls).[27] The relatively few abbeys where such contrasts — in either parlour or church entrances — can be pinpointed, however, suggests caution, especially at Worksop, where the entrances belong to a late Romanesque tradition (albeit with early gothic bases, shafts and capitals).[28] It is not at all clear that such a device would have been comprehensible to everybody, and at best it seems only to have been used in a particular region (the northern half of England) and for a limited time (the early 13th century).

FIG. 13.   Kirkstall Abbey church: showing north
door into nave aisle

Jackie Hall

FIG. 12.   Worksop Priory: west front,
north door

Jackie Hall

Elsewhere, Beaulieu, Netley, Calder and to a lesser extent Hailes, all gathered round the middle third of the 13th century, have markedly plain parlour entrances, by comparison with their respective chapter-houses and in each case the parlour probably also acted as the slype. The lack of architectural distinction in these examples suggests a lowering of status of this space, and we should entertain the possibility that some of the activities associated with earlier parlours had moved — perhaps to the warming room or to the day room. Conversations with high ranking visitors, meanwhile, may have now taken place in the abbot's lodgings, which were beginning to be built around this time.[29]

Although at first sight immutable, the Cistercian east range can be seen as a place that subtly mediated changing functions and changing attitudes. The unchanging character of the chapter-house at the centre of the façade, by contrast, emphasises the importance of order and discipline at the heart of monastic life throughout the Middle Ages.

ACKNOWLEDGEMENTS

This paper started as part of my doctoral thesis at the Centre for Medieval Studies, University of York. I am therefore grateful for all the useful comments made at that time by my supervisors, Christopher Norton and Jane Grenville, and for the financial support from English Heritage, which enabled me to start it, and the Ochs Scholarship from the British Archaeological

Association, which enabled me to finish it. I am especially grateful for John McNeill's review of the text in its later stages, and to Jason Wood and David Robinson for permission to use their photographs.

NOTES

1. The uniformity of the Cistercian cloister is often remarked upon, leading to the notion that a blind monk of the order might find his way round any of its abbeys. However, as Christopher Brooke noted, 'relatively few monks travelled and relatively few were blind'; 'Reflections on the Monastic Cloister', in *Romanesque and Gothic: Essays for George Zarnecki*, ed. N. Stratford (Woodbridge 1987), 21.

2. It was first made widely available in this country in 1878 when a version was published by Philippe Guignard in *Les Monuments Primitifs de la Règle Cistercienne* (Dijon 1878). J. T. Micklethwaite may have been the first to make use of it when he published 'Of the Cistercian plan', *Yorkshire Archaeological Journal*, 7 (1882), 239–58. Following him, both Hope and Brakspear used the early Cistercian documents made available by Guignard in interpreting the physical evidence that they revealed in the course of numerous excavations. MS Dijon 114, dating from around 1185, was used as the basis for both the 1878 edition and for the central text of the modern edition *Les Ecclesiastica officia: Cisterciens du XIIeme siècle*, ed. D. Choisselet and P. Vernet (Reiningue 1989), which is the one quoted in this article.

3. *Ecclesiastica Officia*, ch. 55.

4. *Ecclesiastica Officia*, ch. 117.23, 113.13 and 74.

5. See for instance W. H. St John Hope, 'The abbey of St Mary in Furness, Lancashire', *Transactions of the Cumberland and Westmorland Antiquarian and Archaeological Society*, 16 (1900), 260. It has recently been suggested that the space was originally all sacristy, only later partitioned (T. Kinder, *L'Europe Cistercienne* (La Pierre-qui-Vire 1998), 241–43), but in fact all references to the vestry in the *Ecclesiastica Officia* are in relation to church services, in which the vestry is entered from the church (chs 13.3, 23.21–23, 53.11 and 55.16). There was never any need for a sacristy to be entered from the cloister. Structurally, of course, partitions are later and many no longer survive.

6. Only early cloisters have stairs in the east range; from around the 1160s refectories were realigned and cloisters begun after this used some of the space created in the south range for the day stairs. See P. Fergusson, 'The 12th Century Refectories at Rievaulx and Byland Abbeys', in *Cistercian Art and Architecture in the British Isles*, ed. E. C. Norton and D. Park (Cambridge 1986), 170.

7. H. Stein-Kecks, provides a useful summary of this view, although it is one she argues against. See H. Stein-Kecks, '"Claustrum" and "capitulum": Some Remarks on the Façade and Interior of the Chapter House', in *Der Mittelalterliche Kreuzgang*, ed. P. K. Klein (Regensburg 2004), 159–60.

8. C. Waddell ed., *Cistercian Lay Brothers. Twelfth Century Usages with Related Texts* (Brecht 2000), 183–84.

9. P. Fergusson and S. Harrison, *Rievaulx Abbey* (London 1999), 47 and 64.

10. For Fountains, see G. Coppack and R. Gilyard-Beer, *Fountains Abbey* (London 1993), 32; and G. Coppack, *Fountains Abbey*, 2nd edn (Stroud 2003), 57–58; for Furness, Hope, 'Furness Abbey', 258–67.

11. J. Hall, 'Croxden Abbey: Buildings and Community' (unpublished Ph.D. thesis, University of York, 2003), 67–68. Only the foundations survive of the porch, and without excavation it is impossible to say whether they are medieval or post-dissolution — they appear to contain re-used worked stone.

12. Stein-Kecks, '"Claustrum" and "capitulum"', 164, 167.

13. This possibility at Fountains is suggested in Coppack and Gilyard-Beer, *Fountains Abbey*, 32, and Coppack, *Fountains Abbey*, 58.

14. For the full building history of the east range, see Hall, 'Croxden Abbey', 65–77.

15. For Fountains, see W. H. St John Hope, 'Fountains Abbey', *Yorkshire Archaeological Journal*, 15 (1900), 343–48; and Coppack and Gilyard-Beer, *Fountains Abbey*, 10–11. For Kirkstall, W. H. St. John Hope and J. Bilson, *The Architecture of Kirkstall Abbey Church, with some general remarks on the Architecture of the Cistercians* (Publications of the Thoresby Society 16, 1907), 3–4, 27–30; P. Fergusson, *Architecture of Solitude: Cistercian Abbeys in 12th Century England* (Princeton 1984), 48–51; and D. Robinson ed., *The Cistercian Abbeys of Britain* (London 1998), 132. Most recent architectural research has been directed at the church, while the excavations of the 1950s and 1960s barely touched the east range; S. Moorhouse and S. Wrathmell, *Kirkstall Abbey: The 1950–64 Excavations: a Reassessment* (Wakefield 1987), 8 and 12. For Buildwas, see Fergusson, *Architecture of Solitude*, 116–17; G. Coppack, *The White Monks: the Cistercians in Britain 1128–1540* (Stroud 1998), 51–53; and D. Robinson, *Buildwas Abbey* (London 2002).

16. Fergusson, *Architecture of Solitude*, 121–22; *The Victoria History of the County of Warwick*, 2 (London 1902), 72–73; Robinson ed., *Cistercian Abbeys*, 89–90.

17. For the architecture of the east range of Furness, see particularly Hope, 'Furness Abbey', 258–67; S. Harrison and J. Wood, *Furness Abbey* (London 1998); and Robinson ed., *Cistercian Abbeys*, 117. For Tintern, see D. Robinson, *Tintern Abbey*, 4th edn (Cardiff 2002), 30 and 50–52; for Beaulieu, see particularly W. H. St John Hope and H. Brakspear, 'The Cistercian Abbey of Beaulieu in the County of Southampton', *Archaeol. J.*, 63 (1906), 131–39 and 153–56; and V. Jansen, 'Architectural Remains of King John's Abbey, Beaulieu (Hampshire)', in *Studies in Cistercian Art and Architecture 2*, ed. M. P. Lillich (Kalamazoo 1984), 82. For Netley, see VCH *County of Hampshire*, 3 (London 1908); C. A. F. Meekings, 'The Early Years of Netley Abbey', *Journal of Ecclesiastical History*, 30 (1979), 1–37; and Robinson ed., *Cistercian Abbeys*, 151–53. For Hailes, see D. Winkless, *Hailes Abbey, Gloucestershire* (Stocksfield 1990), 7–19; Robinson ed., *Cistercian Abbeys*, 122–25.

18. VCH *Hampshire*, 474. This feature is now lost.

19. For description and comments on the architecture of Calder, see M. C. Fair, 'Calder Abbey', *Transactions of the Cumberland and Westmorland Antiquarian and Archaeological Society*, 53 (1954), 80–97; Fergusson, *Architecture of Solitude*, 118; and Robinson ed., *Cistercian Abbeys*, 84–85.

20. Little has been written about the architecture of Whalley Abbey, but see N. Pevsner, *North Lancashire* (B/E, London 1969), 259–60; O. Ashmore, *A Guide to Whalley Abbey*, 5th edn (Blackburn 1996); and Robinson ed., *Cistercian Abbeys*, 202–04.

21. A university education and the ownership of books were increasingly seen as important from the mid-13th century onwards; L. J. Lekai, *The Cistercians: Ideals and Reality* (Kent, Ohio 1977), 77–90. Bell suggests that the numbers of books rose greatly in the 14th century, even if cistercian reading habits remained somewhat old-fashioned; D. Bell, 'Monastic Libraries: 1400–1557', in *The Cambridge History of the Book in Britain*, ed. L. Hellinga and J. B. Trapp (Cambridge 1999), 229–54.

22. *Ecclesiastical Officia*, chs 72 and 75.

23. S. Bonde and C. Maines, 'Elite Spaces in Monastries of the Reform Movement and an Abbot's Parlour at Augustinian Saint-Jean-des-Vignes, Soissons (France)', in *Religion and Belief in Medieval Europe. Papers of the Medieval Europe Brugge 1997 Conference 4*, ed. G. d. Boe and F. Verhaeghe (Zellik 1997), 43–53.

24. D. H. Williams, *The Cistercians in the Early Middle Ages* (Leominster 1998), 243.

25. J. C. Dickinson, 'Furness Abbey, an Archaeological Reconsideration', *Transactions of the Cumberland and Westmorland Antiquarian and Archaeological Society*, 67 (1967), 61–62; Fergusson, *Architecture of Solitude*, 60–61; Hope, 'Furness Abbey', 242.

26. For Calder Abbey, see Fergusson, *Architecture of Solitude*, 118 and pl. 58.

27. For guesthalls, see R. Rowell, 'The Archaeology of Late Medieval Monastic Hospitality' (unpublished Ph.D. thesis, University of York, 2000), 208.

28. The possible origins of the Worksop façade are discussed at length by J. P. McAleer, 'Southwell, Worksop and Stylistic Tendencies in English Twelfth-Century Facade Design', in *Medieval Architecture and its Intellectual Context: Studies in Honour of Peter Kidson*, ed. E. Fernie and P. Crossley (London 1990), 61–72. He rules out Cistercian influence. The possible meanings of the decorative scheme of the west doors are not discussed, unsurprisingly since they are not unusual within a late Romanesque context. It may be that, in relation to Croxden, Worksop represents only an example of the types of model available to the Croxden master who designed the parlour door.

29. There is only definite evidence of a contemporary abbots' lodging at Netley, but this does not rule out their existence elsewhere.

Lincoln Cathedral Cloister

JENNIFER S. ALEXANDER

Lincoln cathedral's cloister dates from the late 13th century, with one range rebuilt in 1674 by Wren. It serves to provide access to the chapter-house which was already standing by the time of its construction. The current appearance of the cloister can, in part, be attributed to a 19th-century restoration by Pearson, who incorporated parts of the earlier corridor, which the cloister builder had demolished, in the later work. The evidence for this earlier structure is assessed and the role of the cloister, and its antecedents, is examined.

AS a secular cathedral, Lincoln has no suite of buildings for which the covered walks of a cloister are an essential means of access, but Lincoln follows Salisbury, Exeter and Wells in having one[1] (Fig. 1). The present structure at Lincoln serves as a passageway to the chapter-house and gives access to offices and the library, although at the time it was built the latter was housed elsewhere.[2] Other secular cathedrals, or major churches, like York, Lichfield and Southwell, link their chapter-houses to the churches by short corridors and these also act as vestibules.

Lincoln's medieval cloister is single-storeyed with an open traceried arcade and wooden vault with carved bosses.[3] It dates from the end of the 13th century with one range partially rebuilt in the 17th century as a two-storeyed wing and named after its designer as the Wren library. It lies on the north side of the cathedral occupying most of the space between the east and west transepts, and it is connected to the cathedral by a short passage (Fig. 2). As at Salisbury, the south walk is positioned away from the wall of the cathedral choir, leaving a space that was used by workmen until the recent past.

The hill-top site of the cathedral, with its steep fall-off to the south, means that a northern cloister was inevitable, but its layout was affected by two additional factors: the medieval deanery lay close by to the north west, and the polygonal chapter-house had already been built to the north east in the early 13th century.[4] The archaeological evidence is that a pentice originally provided the link between the chapter-house and the north-east transept, although the relationship between the pentice and the chapter-house, in terms of their use, is not clear, and it is this that was replaced by the current cloister.

THE CLOISTER ARCADES

THE three medieval walks of the cloister have the same form of tracery to the arcade; an oculus of unencircled pointed and rounded trefoils above pairs of trefoil headed lights, under a pointed quatrefoil (Fig. 3). The oculus repeats the tracery form of the east window oculus of Ripon cathedral, dated to between 1286–96,[5] but without the intrusion of the lower section of the window into the oculus, and with the cusps

JBAA, vol. 159 (2006), 222–48
© British Archaeological Association 2006
DOI: 10.1179/174767006X133005

FIG. 1.   Lincoln's cloister and north-west transept from the north-east

Jennifer Alexander

unpierced. The screen tracery has shafts and capitals with naturalistic foliage to the main mullions, although some of the foliage tends towards the bulbous seaweed-type of the post-naturalistic period. The clustered shafts of the mullions descend through the blocked lower section of the arcade onto polygonal bases and on the outer face, the buttresses between the bays end in diagonally set finials. The rear walls of the north, west and south walks are completely plain. On the east side the rear wall now has an arcade of pointed arches supported on clusters of shafts that flank the portal to the chapter-house.

THE CLOISTER VAULT

THE vault is wooden with carved wooden bosses. Wooden vaults are not uncommon, as Hearn and Thurlby have shown, but wooden cloister vaults are less familiar, and Lincoln's cloister vault is the only one included in their study.[6] The vault is a hybrid form, a sort of quasi-sexpartite vault where the intermediate ribs are curved down from the ridge rib, resembling a barrel vault with ribs. The ribs rise from stone springers that die into the wall, and the intermediate ribs are socketed into the wall. There was no wall rib. This arrangement leaves a section of blank walling between the angled vault web and the arched head of the tracery on the arcade side. The two

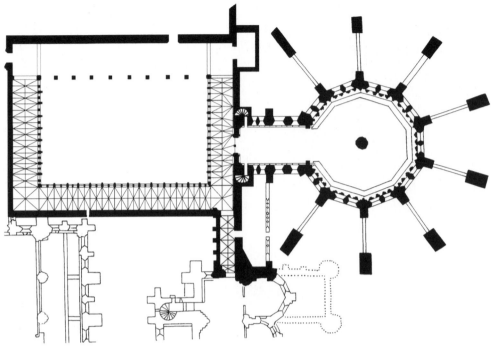

FIG. 2.   Plan of the cloister
Jennifer Alexander

southern corner bays are configured differently (Fig. 4). The double span is arranged as a regular sexpartite bay with a horizontal intermediate rib. Again no wall rib was used.[7]

The cloister bosses

VERY few of the cloister bosses depict religious subjects, and the rest comprise the largest group of grotesques and genre scenes in the whole cathedral. This is perhaps a reflection of the more secular form of the cloister at Lincoln. The subjects of the bosses include an incomplete set of the labours of the months, foliage, several religious images, and real and mythical animals (Fig. 5). The bosses have been studied recently and comparisons made to the marginal drawings of the medieval manuscripts of the slightly later East Anglian school.[8] The foliage bosses are carved with naturalistic foliage, with the exception of one boss that still has stiff-leaf, although with small fruit forms. The species of the plants have been identified as oak, vine, and maple with a rose in bloom also occurring.[9] None of the bosses has the later, less naturalistic, more bulbous foliage. There is no trace of any colouring left on the ribs or the bosses to indicate that this vault was highly coloured, although Brighton records that traces of a pale ground remain on some of the bosses and he suggests that the vault was originally highly coloured.[10]

Fig. 3.   Cloister west walk from the south

Jennifer Alexander

Fig. 4.   South-west corner of the cloister

Jennifer Alexander

The cloister layout

THE rectangular layout of the cloister resulted in the east and west walks originally having ten bays and the north and south fourteen (Fig. 2). The Wren library range is wider than the medieval north walk it replaced and one bay had to be removed from both the east and west ranges to accommodate it; the vault springer for the lost bay remains in the east walk (Fig. 6). The rear wall of the north walk was retained in the

FIG. 5.   East walk, roof boss depicting a hare,
over the entrance to the chapter-house

Jennifer Alexander

FIG. 6.   North walk east end, from the south

Jennifer Alexander

17th century and bears the marks of the removed medieval vault. The overall layout of
the medieval walks is fairly precise, the north and south walks are both 117 ft 9
in (35.9 m) in length, the west walk is 91 ft (27.73 m), and the east walk 90 ft 9 in
(27.68 m). Visually, and practically, the ten by fourteen bay rectangle of the cloister
arcade is the equivalent of a square and the diagonal of its side, which is an elegant
solution to the design problems imposed by the restrictions of the site. Each arcade
bay measures almost exactly 6 ft 6 in (2.00 m) long which strongly suggests that all
the tracery for the arcade screens was made at the same time. A certain amount of
adjustment was necessary in their construction, but this does not exceed 1 ¼ in
(30 mm) along the length of the arcades on the three sides. This accuracy was not
achieved in the relative placing of the arcades and rear walls, however, each walk
varies in width along its length, with the west walk the most accurately laid out,
having a difference of only 1 ½ in (40 mm) between the width of its north and south
ends. The east walk is the least regular; the difference there is 5 ½ in (135 mm).
The vault springers, which emerge from the rear wall, are also precisely spaced, with
the exception of the east rear wall where the vault has been remodelled.[11]

The date of the cloister

THE cloister is dated by two documents; the first is a letter of 1296 to the dean from Bishop Sutton, requesting permission to build a wall abutting the dean's stable to erect the north side of the cloister, and the second is John de Schalby's note of Bishop Sutton's personal involvement in the cloister's construction. In the register of Bishop Sutton the text of the letter from Sutton to Dean Willoughby dated 23 July 1296 is quoted:

Ad decorem ecclesiae nostrae confratres vestri quoddam claustrum in area ante capitulum eiusdem ecclesiae nobis ad hoc dantibus occasionem, decenter metantes, murum eiusdem ex parte australi iam laudabiliter erexerunt in altum. Sane situs loci, et dispositio fundamenti huismodi fabricae, necessario exigunt, ut praetendunt, quod alter paries correspondens super murum stabuli vestri ex parte boreali, super solum ecclesiae constructum, ut dicitur, sine vestro dispendio construatur, domo ipsa sicut prius salva manente; et super hoc ut consensum praestetis sicut intelleximus, capitulum specialiter vobis scribit.

Considering the embellishment of our church your brethren, having taken with our permission the measurements of the cloister located in front of the chapter-house, have decided to build an elevation on the southern wall, and deserve praise for doing so. They maintain that the other façade, corresponding to it, on the northern side above the wall of your stable and resting on the foundation of our church, can be built without your incurring any expense and without your building being in any way altered or threatened.[12]

John de Schalby, who was Bishop Sutton's registrar, added that Sutton gave fifty marks towards the cloister's construction, which indicates that work was underway before the bishop's death in 1299.[13] The implication of the letter is that deanery buildings had encroached upon land belonging to the cathedral and that the northern boundary between the cathedral's land and that of the deanery had not been clearly established. The wording of the proposal to build the cloister north wall on this land offers a compromise that would enable both buildings to occupy the site. It also suggests that the dean was not one of the parties pressing for the construction of the cloister.

Any resolution of the situation seems not to have been permanent, however. A later dean, John Macworth (1412–51), reclaimed some of this disputed land and was charged in 1437 with demolishing part of the cloister and building his stable over part of its wall. This involved constructing the stable against the outside wall of the north range, and resulted in damage to the cloister roof from its gutter and dampness from it; stone had apparently also been removed from the cloister wall for use in the stable.[14] In 1441 the dean was forced to choose between removing the stable or paying a yearly rent for it.[15] The stables, or a replacement, were still immediately behind the north cloister wall in 1649 and they are shown on the 19th-century plan of the deanery. The extent of Dean Macworth's dilapidations is hard to assess; the rear wall of the north range still retains the scars from the wooden vault of the 13th-century range and it is only in the end bays that there is any evidence of alterations to the vault. There are clumsy channels cut into the rear wall at the east and west ends of the north wall that show where an angled web has been inserted below the level of the arched vault, and these may have been part of the repairs made during Macworth's period (Fig. 6).

Resolution of the disputed site of the north cloister came after the Restoration when Dean Michael Honywood, who was appointed in 1660, set about restoring both the liturgical life of the cathedral and the fabric of its building. The cathedral had been attacked during the Civil War, and the library, which was over the end of the east and north ranges, was burned; this conflagration followed an earlier fire in 1609.[16] Honywood included the sum of £300 for 'the needfull reparations of the cloyster' in 1662.[17] Twelve years later Dean Honywood entered into a contract for the construction of the new library over a new north range of the cloister for the sum of £780, and the earlier sum may well have been required for the first stage in the planned rebuilding rather than for general restoration work. There would have been costs for the clearance of the site ready for work to begin, the range is described as 'now ruined' in the contract; the fee for Sir Christopher Wren as architect, and for Mr Tompson, the model-maker.[18] The contract is very specific about the re-use of materials; the builders are only to have the stone which is not carved or moulded and they are to re-use this material exclusively in the building. Some of the moulded work turned up in the buttresses that had been added to the west walk when these were removed in 1883;[19] this was probably 17th-century work. The roof was clearly almost totally removed by 1674 since the contract refers to the builders having the lead that was left, although it only amounted to about a yard in breadth. The contract specifies that the rear wall was to remain; it refers to removing the coping from it and the thickening of its upper stages where it is deemed to be too thin for the building work proposed. The old library over the north end of the east range was retained and demolished in 1789, when a doorway was made in the north-east corner of the cloister and a new staircase constructed.[20] A small part of this structure survives in a restored form.

THE DEANERY

THE origins of the dispute over the boundary with the deanery can be traced back to the late 12th and early 13th centuries when land was provided for the dean's residence. The deanery lay to the north of the cathedral on Eastgate, sharing a site with the buildings of the Works Chantry, which extended from the road out of Minster Yard as far as the Close Wall gate; this lay slightly to the west of the Roman Eastgate. Both the Works Chantry and the deanery were demolished in the 19th century, but the line of their frontages can be assessed from the surviving Atton Place that preserves the alignment of the Works Chantry gatehouse in its east wall, and a much-altered wall on Eastgate contains material from both buildings.[21]

First mention of the deanery is in the period of Dean Richard Fitzneal (1184–89), when a house in the 'atrium' of the cathedral was rebuilt to provide the dean's residence; previously there had been no specific house for him. Dean Richard made over the property to his successors in perpetuity, and further land grants extended the site eastwards. One parcel of land, between the gate of Eastgate and the dean's house, was the subject of a complex leasing arrangement and the later endorsements on the final concord refer to it being partly within the dean's dwelling, but also partly within the cathedral cloister. This may be the same land cited in a charter of Dean William de Thornaco from c. 1230, that was a grant both to extend the landholding of the deanery and also to increase the size of the cemetery.[22] A further boundary to the north was also breached in the 13th century when it was reported that the dean's kitchen and brewhouse had been built either five, or six, feet across the king's highway of Eastgate, with their outer stone wall abutting the king's wall.[23]

Antiquarian drawings and plans show the layout and appearance of the deanery and the Works Chantry, and these are supplemented by a survey taken in 1649. The deanery was a series of linked buildings arranged around a courtyard, with a gateway

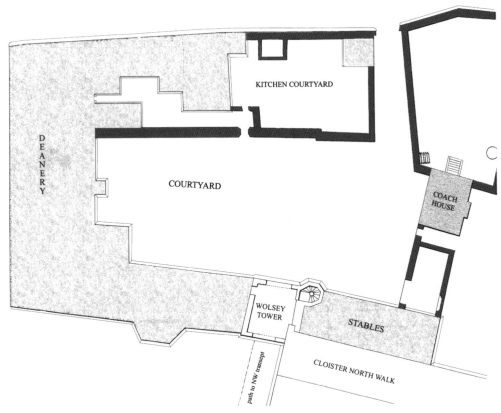

KITCHEN COURTYARD

DEANERY

COURTYARD

COACH HOUSE

WOLSEY TOWER

STABLES

path to NW transept

CLOISTER NORTH WALK

FIG. 7.   Plan of the deanery, after Betham
Jennifer Alexander

to Eastgate and a gatehouse tower on the opposite range that abutted the cloister's north range and faced the cathedral. The layout of the buildings was irregular. The south range, shown on the plan made between 1827 and 1847 by Edward Betham, surveyor to the dean and chapter, lay approximately at right angles to the other ranges, but its angle changed slightly at the gatehouse tower so that the tower met the corner of the cloister, and another block then lay immediately behind the north cloister (Fig. 7).

The tower had been built by Dean Robert Flemyng (1451–83), together with the building identified as the stable behind the cloister north range, but more probably a replacement with a different function.[24] None of the other buildings could be precisely dated. The fragments of a three-light window preserved in the Eastgate wall seem to date from *c.* 1230, with a dog-tooth moulding and nook shafts on moulded bases, and this probably dates this part of the wall. Jones also suggests that the eastern range of the deanery had been built against a late-15th-century wall.[25]

FIG. 8. North-west transept portal and exterior corner of the cloister

Jennifer Alexander

THE FUNCTION OF THE CLOISTER

THE relative positions of the cloister and the deanery indicate that a decision had been made to keep the two structures completely separate. Flemyng's tower, and doubtless its predecessor, was positioned opposite the north-west transept so that the pathway between the tower and the door in the centre of the transept façade formed a ceremonial path for the dean, flanked by the outside wall of the cloister. The south-west corner of the cloister was carefully laid out just to the east of the portal on the western transept (Fig. 8), but not connected to it, so that the dean did not walk directly through the cloister to reach his residence from the cathedral. There was no access into the cloister from the deanery until the period of Wren's north range when the doorway in the north-west corner was cut through and a second door constructed between the upper chamber of the gateway tower and the new library. This would have been entirely appropriate since Dean Honywood was paying for the building and had donated his own books to the library, but was deemed much less so in the 13th century.[26]

The effect of not opening the cloister from the transept, however, was to deprive the cloister of a possible liturgical function. At Salisbury, by contrast, there is a doorway in that position that allows the south walk of the cloister to form part of a processional route with a return doorway into the west end of the nave, and this has been described as the main purpose of the cloister.[27] There are additional minor doors to the exterior in the east and west walks. Wells has a cloister doorway in the transept with a return doorway in the western bay of the nave that will have enabled its use for processions. The transept door also aligned with a second portal at the south end of the range, that allowed direct access from the bishop's palace, with a further processional door in the south-east corner and other minor doors. Exeter's cloister doors are at the east and west ends of the nave aisles, on the monastic model, and would therefore have usable for processions. The cloister is no longer standing and it is not possible to determine what other entrances it may have had. Lincoln's arrangement of entry to the cloister by a single door that in turn leads into the short vestibule makes it much less suitable for processions, and it may never have been used in this way.

An alternative function for the Lincoln cloister may have been to provide the route to a burial ground for the more senior members of the cathedral chapter in the garth, although there is no evidence of any means of access to it now. Any doorway into the garth must have been sited in the north range, and of sufficiently small scale not to have affected the layout of the vault since there is no indication of any special arrangement of the vault webs on the rear wall. There is enough space within the width of a single bay of the cloister arcade to fit a pair of doors and the height is also adequate for this. A further, but distinctly utilitarian, purpose for the cloister was to provide access to the masons' yard, the 'Nettles Yard', sited behind the south range, but this must always have been a secondary function.

Bishop Oliver Sutton's involvement in the construction of the cloister is significant. Sutton had been dean of Lincoln before becoming bishop, and had overseen much of the building of the Angel Choir in which he was to be buried in 1299, his tomb appropriately positioned between the two shrines for St Hugh on the north side of the choir. Preparatory to building the cloister, Sutton negotiated for a new site for the cathedral's main burial ground. He arranged for the canons to take over the graveyard of the redundant church of St Bartholomew, beyond the west gate of the castle, to use as their cemetery in 1295, and two years later assigned the whole site to the canons.[28] The position of the original cemetery for the cathedral has not been firmly established, but the documentary references, cited above, strongly suggest that it lay on the site that the cloister now occupies. Sutton also enclosed the area around the cathedral by building walls with gates to the north and west, and gave the site for the Vicars' Court on the south side of the cathedral.[29] The construction of the cloister, that closed off the north side of the cathedral between the deanery and the city wall, can be seen as part of the same separation of the cathedral from the city and creation of an area of seclusion for the cathedral canons.

THE SEQUENCE OF CONSTRUCTION OF THE CLOISTER

THE sequence of construction of the cloister can be determined by an examination of the documentary and archaeological evidence. The letter of 1296 suggests that the south walk had already been laid out and awaited the construction of its screen wall towards the garth. The request for agreement to construct the north wall means that the west wall had also, at least, been laid out, but no work had started on replacing the east walk, which was retained from an earlier period. The archaeological evidence supports this reading. The east range is not centred on the chapter-house portal,

FIG. 9. Exterior of the rear wall of the south walk

Jennifer Alexander

which it surely would have been had this range been constructed first. Evidence for its being from an earlier phase is discussed below. The south walk's rear wall was probably the first part to be built since it differs from the other two medieval walks in its form (Fig. 9). Visible both on the outside and inner face of the upper level of the wall are the remains of tall rectangular openings that are now blocked, linked by a chamfered string-course. These have a deep splay to the interior and must have been intended as windows to light an upper level of the cloister, above the vault. This would suggest that the original plan was for a two-storeyed range on the model of Norwich or Coventry Whitefriars. These features are not found on the west and north exterior walls, which implies that the plan was abandoned before their outer walls had been built, or even during the construction of the south wall, since the height of the lintels of the windows suggests that the wall was meant to have risen higher.

The uniformity of the surviving walks suggests a rapid sequence of construction and the evidence of the tracery and the c. foliage sculpture support a date of *c.* 1290–1300 for the main building. This means that the cloister was started during the end of work on the Angel Choir. Further evidence for this can be found by comparing the moulding profiles of the cloister and the altar furnishings of the Angel Choir, including the shrine of Little St Hugh, which belong to the last period of the Angel Choir work. The similarities are marked and the mouldings belong to the group of roll and hollow base types found in the last decades of the 13th century, frequently encountered in the East Midlands region.[30]

THE CLOISTER PASSAGEWAY

THE main cloister is connected to the cathedral by a vaulted passageway of a similar period (Fig. 10). The passage arcade has the same tracery as the main cloister, but it is glazed, and left uncarved on the side towards the works yard. All the mullions have shafts and capitals, not just the major mullions as in the main cloister. Naturalistic foliage is used, oak, hawthorn, maple and vine are predominant, with ivy used for two capitals, and there are also two examples of bubbly seaweed foliage (Fig. 11). A stone quadripartite rib vault with a ridge rib springs from capital level, different in form to the quasi-sexpartite vault of the main cloister. The bosses also have natural-istic foliage and reproduce the form of the Angel Choir aisle bosses, even having some of the same subjects. The rear wall is plain and the vault springs from corbels, one of which has oak leaves and acorns.

It would seem that the passageway was built shortly after the main cloister. The doorway between the two is centred on the passage, whereas the earlier door from the north-east transept is off-set (Fig. 12).

RESTORATION HISTORY

THE present appearance of the cloister can be attributed to John Loughborough Pearson's restoration from the last quarter of the 19th century. Repair work had been underway in the earlier 19th century and work is also documented from the third quarter of the 18th century. Most of this involved repairs to boards in the vault, or to relaying paving, but more substantial work had been undertaken in 1787 when the lead on the roofs was replaced by Westmoreland slate, with the possible exception of part of the east range.[31] The windows in the passageway were restored by J. C. Buckler in 1867, and he was urged by the sub-dean to glaze the three medieval walks of the cloister.[32] Pearson's first report, dated 23 June 1875, revealed the cloisters to be in a dangerous state with the walls no longer vertical. The foundations were inad-equate and required underpinning, the walls were bulging outwards and the buttresses added to correct this were also on poor foundations. The roof needed additional strengthening to prevent it pushing the walls out further. The arcades would require rebuilding and it was proposed that the slate roof should be replaced by a lead one.[33]

The west walk's arcade was found to be the most seriously out of true, and Pearson began work in 1881 to dismantle it and rebuild it on new foundations. Advice was sought from the Diocesan Architectural Association who proposed that the later buttresses, and the walling between the mullions, should be allowed to remain, although, since the infill walling was not bonded in, it clearly was not part of the original build.[34] Pearson chose to ignore the advice on the larger buttresses and they have all been removed. Espin's drawing, published in 1813, shows the larger buttresses alternating with the more slender ones (Fig. 13): Pearson reduced them all to the same size and was able to confirm the medieval appearance of these by reference to the examples that are partially buried in Wren's responds.

The west walk occupied the works department until 1885 when the carpenters com-pleted the repairs to the vault. Restoration had already started on the south walk. It too was taken down and rebuilt, although Pearson did state that it could be repaired without this.[35] The masons spent eighteen months on the stonework, but the carpentry work was delayed by the men being required for other work in the cathedral, and the vault was not finished until after July 1889.[36] The work on the east walk progressed with the dismantling of the vault in 1889, and the restoration was virtually complete by 1890 when the lead was cast for its roof.[37] The whole cloister restoration was finished by 1898 when the Clerk of Works reported to the dean and chapter on Pearson's work.[38]

No restoration of the north walk was undertaken, but Pearson did include a proposal for the Wren library in his initial report in 1875. Included in a list of 'other works not vital to the structure yet of vast importance as respects its appearance' was the removal of 'the north side of the cloister arcade ... and erection of a wing to restore the cloisters to their original form'. This subtly worded paragraph passed

FIG. 11.   Passageway capital
Jennifer Alexander

FIG. 10.   Passageway from north-east
transept looking north
Jennifer Alexander

FIG. 12.   Passageway looking south
Jennifer Alexander

FIG. 13.   Drawing of the chapter-house and cloister
Drawn by Espin, 1813

without the dean and chapter noticing that Pearson intended to remove the Wren library and, although he did not receive immediate support for the proposal, it did not provoke an adverse reaction at the time. It was only in 1892 when the plans were published that the wrath of the SPAB descended on Pearson and the scheme was abandoned.[39]

PEARSON'S RESTORATION OF THE EAST RANGE

PEARSON'S restoration of the south and west walks of the cloister was sensitive and for the most part unobtrusive, and he seems to have fulfilled his claim that only the minimum of new stonework was used. The renewed stonework can be identified easily by the mason's mark on it since the medieval stonework has no marks, and by the graffito of one of Pearson's masons, 'R. Hague, 1891', on the upper walling of the east range.[40] It is a testament to his work that few people are aware that he actually took down and rebuilt the medieval ranges. His work on the east walk was more radical however; there he brought back an arcade that had flanked the chapter-house

235

in the period before the cloister was built, and combined it with the supports for the wooden vault. This arcade had formed part of the earlier access to the chapter-house, referred to in Bishop Sutton's letter as 'the cloister in front of the chapter-house', that is, the pentice that linked the chapter-house to the north-east transept. Considerable traces of this remain above the east range vault and its appearance can be reconstructed. It was clearly very different in scale and design to the cloister, and in its relationship to the chapter-house.

The wall arcade dated from the same period as the chapter-house, and the evidence for it was uncovered during Pearson's restoration of the cloister. In a letter of 11 January 1890, discovered by Christopher Brighton, Pearson wrote to the sub-dean about the re-exposure of the 'beautiful arcading which existed on this east side of the cloister on each side of the doorway now only brought to light', which he hoped to be able to restore.[41] Permission was granted and Pearson designed the continuous arcade of sharply pointed arches on grey polished limestone shafts, rather than the freestone shafts of the example, still visible where his masons exposed it, in the corner behind the cloister door. The bench that the arcade stands on was also re-established and the chapter-house portal modified (Fig. 14). The portal had consisted of a large central arch, divided into two by a pair of decorated arches supported on a cluster of slender shafts; this in turn was flanked by two pointed arches with dogtooth between the shafts that were set back from the portal. Espin's drawing (Fig. 15) shows the flanking arches with their three fluted shafts instead of the four now present, and the vault ribs sprung from the portal capitals.[42] Pearson recreated an outer order for the flanking arches, together with a new shaft and capital to support each side (Fig. 16). He also changed the role of the outer shaft of the portal from the springing point of the vault ribs to the support for the new outer order for the portal, reasoning that this had been the original arrangement. He then created a new springing point for the vault. The early 19th-century text describes these shafts and their capitals being 'in a very mutilated state' but tidied up by Espin in the drawing, and the ones there now are doubtless all Pearson's.[43]

The arcade, with the exception of the surround to the chapter-house door, must have been removed when the late 13th-century cloister vault was built since it occupied the area needed for the vault springing. In rebuilding it, Pearson had to carry out a substantial remodelling of the vault, pushing up all the vault springers from their existing site above the portal capitals to the arcade spandrels, and shortening the ribs on the east side (Fig. 17). The most northerly bay is the least affected and this retains its original springing. Pearson also gave the vault a wall rib, which he arranged over the wall arcade in groups of three arches to regularise what is now a markedly asymmetric vault (Fig. 18). His solution to the problem of the spacing was to regard the east and west sides of the vault as separate entities that met at intervals, and he abandoned the concept of discrete bays for the east side (Fig. 19).

Pearson's reworking changed the geometry of the vault considerably and several of the bosses had to be altered to accommodate a different number of ribs, while others had ribs brought in at changed angles. This is most apparent on the sixth boss, of the man killing the pig, where two redundant rib spurs can be seen (Fig. 20), or on number fifteen where an extra rib has been added and the angel's wing removed. The bosses were photographed when the vault was dismantled and this enables comparisons to be made with the current state of the bosses. It is clear that certain bosses were intended to fit an asymmetric arrangement of ribs from the start, such as the one showing a hare from over the chapter-house portal that has three ribs on one side but

FIG. 14. Chapter-house portal and arcade
Jennifer Alexander

FIG. 15. Drawing of the chapter-house portal
Drawn by Espin, 1813

FIG. 16.   Chapter-house portal south side,
showing new arch moulding and capital
Jennifer Alexander

FIG. 17.   East walk vault from the south
Jennifer Alexander

FIG. 18.   East walk wall-rib
Jennifer Alexander

only one on the other (Fig. 5). This demonstrates how the original builder accommodated the layout of the portal in the late 13th century. The portal was the equivalent
of two and a half bays of vaulting, and so an alternative form of sex-partite vault was
used for the eastern side in this area while the western side retained the regular form.
It provided a logical solution to the problem by using two extra diagonal ribs that
sprang from the outer order of the portal and met the ridge rib in the centre of the
transverse rib. Two halves of the diagonal ribs in these bays were omitted to make
room for them.[44] The rest of the east side of the vault repeated the regular layout of
the west side and bay divisions were standardised.

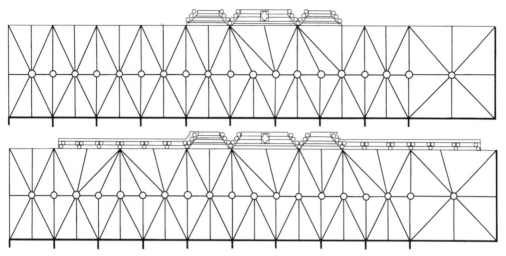

FIG. 19.   Schematic plan of the east walk vault, a. before Pearson, b. after Pearson
Jennifer Alexander

FIG. 20.   East walk vault roof boss, of the man killing the pig, with redundant rib spurs

Jennifer Alexander

FIG. 21.   East walk, space above the vault from the south

Jennifer Alexander

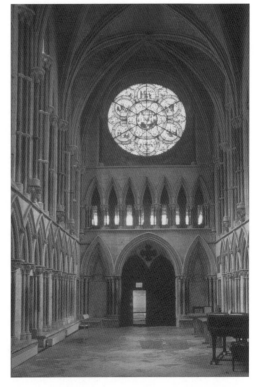

FIG. 22.   Chapter-house interior from the east, taken in July 2003

Jennifer Alexander

THE EVIDENCE FOR AN EARLIER CLOISTER

The 13th-century pentice

EVIDENCE survives in the roof space of the east walk that the earlier pentice had a simple lean-to roof and no vault. The corbels for a wall plate surviving below the apex of the current vault leave insufficient space for a vault above the wall arcade. In the same space there is a row of ten rectangular openings, also below the level of the current roof, that align with the gallery across the west end of the chapter-house (Fig. 21). On the interior the jambs of these openings are clearly visible, and, when the lead was temporarily removed from the east cloister walk in 2003, it allowed the windows to be illuminated to great effect (Fig. 22). The openings are square-headed and delineated at the base by a chamfered string-course. Any evidence of possible arched-heads has been masked by the heavy timber of the later roof's wall-plate, but the irregular alignment between these openings and the internal arcade makes this less likely, and there is no suggestion on the interior of their having been remodelled.

The presence of these openings means that the west front of the chapter-house presented a slightly more elaborate façade in the mid-13th century than it does now. Comparison with the contemporary north-west transept façade reveals that it was by far the less elaborate of the two (compare Figs 23 and 1), having chamfered rather than richly moulded arches and no additional shafting, and with its round window isolated in a blank wall. The same cannot be said of the interiors of both façades, however, where the extent and form of the enrichment is very similar, and the two structures share elements such as circular windows above glazed galleries (compare Figs 22 and 24). Of the two interiors, the design of the chapter-house is actually the more successful in combining the elevation of the wall with the fit of the vault, and this reveals a different priority behind the two designs.

Unlike the transept end wall, the chapter-house west wall does not continue the elevations of the lateral walls, since the wall passage does not continue across there, and this has allowed the designer to create a different proportion scheme for the west wall. By lowering the height of the portal zone, and keeping the middle zone in proportion, the round window with its semi-circular enclosing arch fits comfortably under the vault. It avoids the awkward fit of the high vault from which the transept suffers, and which is only partly solved by forcing the ridge rib to climb steeply to clear it. The priority for the designer of the transept façade has been to create a spectacular exterior with its levels the same as those of the transept north and south sides, whereas the chapter-house designer has allowed the exterior to be secondary to the interior. He has also created a building more elaborate on the interior than the exterior. The date of this part of the chapter-house has been established, the timbers in the roof were felled in 1216, which means that the façade must have been going up at the same time as that of the transept.[45] The chapter-house roof itself has not been dated, although the start of the building works of the masonry structure can be placed in the first Gothic building campaign. The chapter-house has a narrow course of Alwalton marble at the base of the walls, presumably intended to act as a type of damp course, and this material has been closely identified with the work of the first early Gothic builder, in the period up to *c*. 1200.[46]

The earlier pentice as vestibule

THE role of the pentice in relation to the chapter-house must now be examined. The rectangular bays that open into the polygonal space of Lincoln's chapter-house are usually referred to as its vestibule, but this raises a number of questions. In no other non-monastic English chapter-house is there a vestibule that is as open to its chapter-house as this one is. Instead Southwell, Lichfield and York share the same arrangement of a polygonal chapter-house, which could be closed off with doors, and a separate vestibule that leads to it (Fig. 25). The vestibule forms a corridor between the church and the chapter-house and can, in turn, be closed off from both buildings. The spaces are narrow, although upper storeys can be included in the plan. Benches, or more elaborate seating in the case of Lichfield, are provided and the areas can be regarded as separate meeting spaces, distinct from the chapter-house. This is further achieved by siting the vestibule at a right angle to the chapter-house portal. Lincoln's 'vestibule' cannot have been used in the same way and would not have provided a second meeting chamber that was private to the main chapter-house. Instead the pentice outside may have provided this facility and it is probably better to consider that as its primary function. It was separated from both the transept and the chapter-house by doors, to create a distinct, and private, space and had a bench for seating, and as such is comparable to the examples at the other secular buildings.

There is no evidence that the pentice ended just beyond the chapter-house portal with a return wall. Pearson restored the wall arcade beyond the portal, as far as the

FIG. 23.   Chapter-house from the cloister
Jennifer Alexander

FIG. 24.   North-west transept interior
from the south
Jennifer Alexander

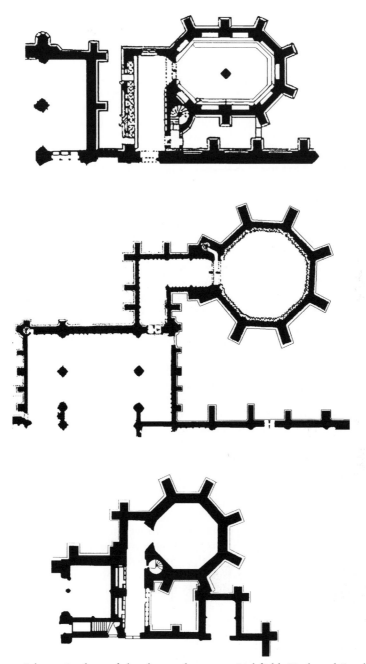

FIG. 25.   Schematic plans of the chapter-houses at Lichfield, York and Southwell

Jennifer Alexander

arch into the 17th-century range, but a narrow band of stone that represents the bench on the rear wall can still be seen in bay ten, which suggests that it originally extended further still. The rear face of the wall to the north of the chapter-house is clearly of three different periods. The lower section of the wall is part of the chapter-house build and has the continuation of its plinth and string-courses across it. It stops abruptly after about 3 m (10 ft), that is before the end of Pearson's arcade, and is butt-jointed to a later wall of greater thickness. Both of these sections are capped by an upper section that may have been that added by John Hayward in the late 18th century when the old library was taken down. Hayward submitted an estimate that included 'building up ashlar work in the line of the old library and continuing the battlements wall from thence to the corner of the Chapter house in the same manner as the battlements at the south end of the same building'. [47]

The rear wall alignment is the course of the Roman wall which was probably chosen as a fixed point early on in the layout of the cathedral since it also underlies the eastern crossing. The Roman wall continues northwards to join the Roman Eastgate that had been given to the bishop as his residence by Henry I. The new Bishop's palace on the south side of the cathedral was under construction from the early 13th century, [48] that is, at the same time as the construction of the chapter-house itself, but the building on the Eastgate site continued in use as a domestic structure until the 15th century and it is not apparent at what stage in the construction of the new palace that the bishop gave up the Eastgate as his residence. The pentice may therefore have had a second function as an entrance to the cathedral from the bishop's palace. One piece of evidence suggests this.

The portal on the north-east transept is on the outer face of the wall, so that the entrance appears to be from the pentice, not into it. The portal appears to be of early-13th-century date, although it has been heavily restored, but it clearly belongs to a period before the construction of the passageway to the cloister since it is not aligned with the passage or its vault (Fig. 12). The later reworking of this area perpetuates this arrangement in the layout of its bosses, which are meant to be read from north to south. However, the pentice may not have been envisaged by the transept builder. The opening is secondary to the transept wall (Fig. 26); it interrupts the double wall arcade and cuts through its bench, the string-course above has had to be re-worked to provide enough space for the shallow head of the arch, and the portal is squeezed up against the buttress on the outside. Additionally, the window above the doorway has been blocked for most of its height, to disguise the pentice roof, and advantage has been taken of this to create a strong-room above the pentice with a complex access arrangement. It is possible that the chapter-house was built first and its covered access afterwards. There is a blocked partially built doorway in the chapel adjacent for which there is no apparent purpose in the medieval building. It is conceivable that it may have been intended to provide the entrance to a pentice which would have been sited a little further to the east.

POSSIBLE EARLY-GOTHIC CLOISTER

THERE is one piece of documentary evidence that reveals that the chapter had considered building a cloister in the period before the chapter-house was built. A document of the 1180s, probably from 1184–87, refers to a parcel of land being assigned to a canon named Samson with the proviso that the grant would be rescinded if the chapter required the land to build a cloister. [49] The date of the document is

FIG. 26.   North-east transept north
wall with doorway into cloister
passage

Jennifer Alexander

imprecise, which is unfortunate. Although it probably refers to the first half of the
decade and relates to the Romanesque building that was brought down in 1185, were
it to date from after 1186 then the cloister was being considered for the new building
for Bishop Hugh, 1185–1200, planned soon after his appointment, in which case it
would have been the work of the mason who built the early Gothic choir. The possibility of a cloister conceived by the master of the complex spatial intricacies, and
structural bravado, of the choir, is a very intriguing one.

NOTES

1. The date of Salisbury's cloister has not been firmly established, although the dendro dates point to
a 1260s completion of both the cloister and chapter-house. The debate is summarised in Sarah Brown,
Sumptuous and Richly Adorn'd: The Decoration of Salisbury Cathedral (London 1999), 28. At Exeter the
earlier work is no longer standing, but documentary evidence points to it having a cloister by the later 13th
century; see N. Pevsner and P. Metcalf, *The Cathedrals of England Southern England* (London 1985), 123.
The chapter-house at Wells is on the opposite side of the cathedral to the cloister and is accessed by a

passageway that continues on to the hall of the Vicars' Choral. Warwick Rodwell's excavations have provided a considerable amount of new evidence for the cloister at Wells. There is documentary evidence for a mid-11th-century cloister, although its site remains uncertain, but a cloister was added to the north of the late Saxon cathedral in the later Romanesque period. This was demolished when the Gothic cathedral was built and lies partly under its south transept. The new building was intended to have a cloister on its south side from the start of work in the 1180s, and a grand portal was built in the transept western aisle. This was in turn replaced by the current structure, between c. 1420–1508, with upper storeys to the east and west ranges. Warwick Rodwell, *Wells Cathedral Excavations and Structural Studies, 1978–93* (London 2001), 99–101, 143, 245.

2. The cathedral is known to have had a library since at least the middle of the 12th century, although it is not known where the books were kept, and it is possible that there was no need for a single repository for the books; see M. T. Clanchy, *From Memory to the Written Record*, 2nd edn (Oxford 1993), 157. After 1255 they were housed in the upper part of the south-west chapel of the north-east transept (now the treasury) where ten recesses in the walls mark the sites of the book cupboards. A new library was built over the east walk of the cloister in 1420–22 that extended from the chapter-house to the north-east corner of the cloister, of which substantial, although reworked, sections survive. This was damaged by fire in 1609, and later in the Civil War, and rebuilt by Charles Hodgson Fowler in 1909–14; it was also affected by the construction of the Wren library. See below.

3. The cloister has not been the subject of a detailed study to date. There have been three studies of the roof bosses of the cloister, but the architecture has not been examined outside the general literature on the cathedral; see E. Venables, 'The bosses of the eastern walk of the cloisters of Lincoln Cathedral', *Associated Societies Reports and Papers*, 20 (1899), 179–83; C. J. P. Cave, 'The Roof Bosses of Lincoln Cathedral', *Archaeologia*, 85 (1935), 25–36; and C. R. Brighton, *Lincoln Cathedral Cloister Bosses* (Lincoln 1985).

4. An additional feature that may have caused problems for the cloister-builder was the structure associated with a Roman pavement that was discovered in the south-east corner of the garth. It was rediscovered in the 1790s when a large amount of soil was removed from the garth, and appears on early-19th-century plans of the cloister with a shed over it; see for example Espin's plan published in 1814. The shed was described as 'an eyesore' in 1867 and removed soon after, when the pavement was lifted. The work is itemised in the reports of the clerks of the works to the dean and chapter, Lincolnshire Archives Office, D&C A/4/13.

5. Jean Bony, *The English Decorated Style* (Oxford 1979), 73, n. 20.

6. M. F. Hearn and Malcolm Thurlby, 'Previously Undetected Wooden Ribbed Vaults in Medieval Britain', *JBAA*, 150 (1997), 48–58.

7. The northern corners had the same arrangement but both seem to have been altered at a later date and larger versions of the angled vaults built beneath them. The scarring for this remains but it has been crudely cut and looks like a reworking, perhaps in connection with later repairs, see below.

8. Brighton, *Cloister Bosses*, 49.

9. Brighton, *Cloister Bosses*, 10–29.

10. Brighton, *Cloister Bosses*, 6.

11. This was carried out in the 19th century, see below.

12. 'The Rolls and Register of Bishop Oliver Sutton, vol. 5 1280–1296', in R. M. T. Hill ed., *Lincoln Record Society*, 60 (1965), 170–71.

13. '... claustrum ecclesiae fieri procuravit et de suo L marcas contulit ad constructionem eiusdem.' *The Book of John Schalby concerning the Bishops of Lincoln and their Acts*, cited in E. Venables, 'The Architectural History of Lincoln Cathedral', *Archaeol J.*, 40 (1883), 159–90, 377–418, at p. 406.

14. 'Item dicit quod decanus, inconsulto capitulo, edificauit stabulum suum infra mansum suum decanalem super murum claustri borialem, per cuius stillicidia dampnificatur tectum claustri, et eciam plures lapides politos de ipsos muro ad hoc opus et pro illo tempore prostrauit per quod timetur de maiori dampnacione in futurum quam modo suspicatur', and 'Item decanus lapides scuerarij, scilicet claustri, conuertit in stabulum equorum, quod a multis doctoribus sacrilegium reputator', *Detecta in Visitacione* W. Alnewyke, Lincoln'. *Episcopi 1437*, printed in C. Wordsworth ed., *Statutes of Lincoln Cathedral*, part ii (Cambridge 1897), 374, 390. '... Decanus magnam partem muri claustri Ecclesie ibidem demoliri, et stabulam unam super residuam partem muri eiusdem construi fecit, Capitulo inconsulto, et absque eius voluntate, sciencia vel assensu.' *Laudum W: Alnewike Episcopi Lincoln (Aᵒ 1439)*, no. 33, Wordsworth, *Statutes*, 193. As Wordsworth points out in his introduction, Bishop Alnwick had a considerable task in dealing with the charges levelled against Dean Macworth by the canons, and the matter of the stables was only one of many alleged misdeeds. Wordsworth is surely incorrect in stating that the bishop did not pursue the matter of the stables, see below.

15. Bishop Alnwick's Visitation Book, 1441, 24 April 1441, Wordsworth, *Statutes*, 450.

16. Margaret Bowker, 'Historical survey, 1450–1750', in *A History of Lincoln Minster*, ed. Dorothy Owen (Cambridge 1994), 191.

17. Naomi Linnell, 'Michael Honywood and Lincoln Cathedral Library', in *Close Encounters: English Cathedrals and Society Since 1540. Studies in Local and Regional History no. 3*, ed. D. Marcombe and C. S. Knighton, University of Nottingham Dept of Adult Education (Nottingham 1991), 82. Dean Honywood's notes are LAO D vii/3/C/7.

18. LAO D&C CIII/31/1/1. The contract was with William Evison, builder, signed on 2 June 1674, the work to be completed by the feast of St Martin Bishop (presumably St Martin of Tours, 11 November)

19. Venables, 'Architectural History', 407.

20. LAO Chapter Acts A.3.15, 338–9, A.14.13, estimates from William Lumby and John Hayward for the work. I am grateful to Dr Nicholas Bennett for this reference.

21. Stanley Jones, Kathleen Major and Joan Varley, *The Survey of Ancient Houses in Lincoln 3: Houses in Eastgate, Priorygate, and James Street* (Lincoln 1990), 8.

22. Stanley Jones suggests that the cemetery referred to is the cloister garth, although at this stage the cloister had not been built. Jones, *Survey of Ancient Houses*, 20. The document is LAO, Dij 81/2 no. 31, published in 'Final Concords of the County of Lincoln vol. 2 1197–1208', in C. W. Foster ed., *LRS*, 17 (1920), 332–33.

23. The complex situation is detailed in the 'Registrum Antiquissimum of the Cathedral of Lincoln x', in K. Major ed., *LRS*, 67 (1973), 256–57.

24. Jones, *Survey of Ancient Houses*, 30. The building shown in the drawings by E. J. Willson and his son, T. J. Willson, had two doorways that appear to be of domestic size, too small to admit horses, and this building does not correspond to the 1649 description of '2 bayes of rough stone buildings covered with Tile used for two small stables and 1 small room, and over the same are 2 rooms used for haylofts'. E. Venables, 'A Survey of the Houses in the Minster Close of Lincoln, taken by order of Parliament in 1649 and 1651, with explanatory notes and additions', *AASRP*, 19 (1887–88), 73.

25. Jones, *Survey of Ancient Houses*, 24.

26. The medieval door in the north range has been cut through an existing wall and was probably installed during the construction of the new deanery in 1847 to provide access directly into the cloister. It continues to serve this purpose for the choristers of the cathedral school who now occupy the building.

27. Thomas Cocke and Peter Kidson, *Salisbury Cathedral Perspectives on the Architectural History* (London 1993), 10.

28. J. F. W. Hill, *Medieval Lincoln* (Cambridge 1948), 146.

29. The completion of the close wall was effected by his successors, with the remains of the Roman city wall included and strengthened, so that the entire site and its inhabitants could be safeguarded, see Dorothy Owen, 'Historical survey, 1091–1450', in Owen, *Lincoln Minster*, 152–53.

30. R. K. Morris, 'The Development of Later Gothic Mouldings in England, *c*.1250–1400 part 2', *Journal of the Society of Architectural Historians*, 22 (1979), 26.

31. LAO D&C A/4/13. The instructions for the removal of the old library over the north end of the east range specifically stated that the roof was to be remade as a lead roof in this region. This is dated two years after the slate roof was ordered for the rest of the cloister. The slate roof required repair in 1833–35, D&C C IV 55, Gen. Receipts.

32. LAO D&C A/4/13, the proposal was not adopted. The passageway arcade wall is still noticeably out of true.

33. LAO D&C The Ark 22/13.

34. LAO D&C The Ark 22/17, Clerk of Works six-monthly report 13 January 1883.

35. LAO D&C The Ark 22/17, Clerk of Works six-monthly report 12 January 1885.

36. LAO D&C The Ark 22/17, Clerk of Works six-monthly reports 11 July 1887, 23 January 1888, and letter from J. J. Smith to Dean and Chapter, July 1889.

37. LAO D&C The Ark 22/29, Bills and Wages 1884–1900, wages bill for June–December 1890.

38. LAO D&C The Ark 22/20.

39. LAO D&C The Ark 22/13; A. Quiney, *John Loughborough Pearson* (London 1979), 194.

40. Robert Hague, stonemason, is listed in the surviving wages accounts between 1858–89. By 1876 he was one of the highest paid members of the team. LAO D&C CIV 55, Audit Vouchers.

41. Brighton, *Cloister Bosses*, 61, n. 26, citing (as then) uncatalogued letters in the Clerk of Works office.

42. This drawing from 1813 is confirmed by Arthur Foster's measured drawing of 1886/7.

43. J. and H. S Storer, *The History and Antiquities of the Cathedral Church of Lincoln* (London, nd, *c*. 1813), page titled 'q'.

44. Plans published in 1813 and 1851 show a different arrangement of the east vault, with ribs missing and others extended over several bays. This must reflect the vault in an unrestored state. The published plans of the cathedral all show the pre-Pearson arrangement of the vault.

45. The transept façade is dated by a description of its window in the Metrical Life of St Hugh, written in the 1220s; see Charles Garton ed., *The Metrical Life of St Hugh* (Lincoln 1986), 4.

46. Jennifer S. Alexander, 'Building stone from East Midlands Quarries: Sources, Transportation and Usage', *Medieval Archaeology*, 39 (1995), 107–35.

47. LAO D&C A/4/13. It is undated but must be from shortly after 1789.

48. H. Chapman, G. Coppack and P. Drewett, *Excavations at the Bishops Palace, Lincoln 1968–72*, Society for Lincolnshire History and Archaeology Occasional Publications, 1 (1975), 6.

49. 'Registrum Antiquissimum of the Cathedral of Lincoln IX', in K. Major ed., *LRS*, 62 (1968), no. 2603, 196–97. The land was between Canon Samson's property and the gate of the Bedern, which Dorothy Owen places on the south side of the cathedral; see Owen, 'Historical survey', 124. There is, however, insufficient room for a cloister alongside the Romanesque, or later, nave on the south, whereas the space on the north side is more than adequate.

Experimental Architecture? Vaulting and West Country Cloisters in the Late Middle Ages

LINDA MONCKTON

Complex and spatially adventurous vaults have come to be seen as a critical element in the development of Decorated architecture. By the second quarter of the 14th century it is the West Country that had become the most significant region within England for experiments in vaulting designs. This paper examines the history of late medieval vaulting from the perspective of a series of West Country cloisters, many of them demolished or little studied, in order to assess the role of the cloister in the evolution and development of lierne vaulting in late medieval England. It is shown that the meditative, liturgical and processional uses of cloisters made them an obvious showcase for the most extravagant architectural effects. A number of particular vault designs were employed, two of which — the fan and the lierne — became the preferred options for prestige projects in the early 15th century. Fan and lierne vaults were not in competition for recognition or status and both were fundamental to the creation of the Perpendicular cloister.

THE West Country has long been acknowledged as an area of seminal importance for the development of late medieval architecture in England, and is celebrated in particular for its stone vaulting. This paper sets out to examine the development of vaulted cloisters in this region and assess their contribution to the wider architectural history of the 14th and 15th centuries. As always with the study of medieval buildings, the gaps in knowledge are many and the abandonment of many rural monasteries following their Dissolution has led to significant losses. In places, the monastic church was lost, but the claustral ranges survived through conversion into farm buildings. However, the cloister walks themselves served no obvious purpose that warranted their upkeep. Notable exceptions to this do exist, most famously, Lacock Abbey, where the cloister was incorporated into the house constructed by William Sharrington. Such examples, however, are rare. Conversely, churches originally associated with regular communities that did survive often lost their claustral buildings. Whilst the exceptions are well known (Gloucester, Norwich, Durham, Canterbury, etc.), the number of churches that lost their cloister is very much greater. Whilst most of this destruction can be dated to the mid-16th century, some cloisters fortunate to escape 16th-century demolition faced new threats of fire and civil war in the 17th century. The cathedral cloisters of St Paul's, Exeter and Peterborough were lost in these ways.

   Despite these losses, it is still clear that the 14th century saw a considerable amount of claustral construction or, more usually, reconstruction. Standards were set high by

JBAA, vol. 159 (2006), 249–83
© British Archaeological Association 2006
DOI: 10.1179/174767006X133014

the new 13th-century cloisters of Westminster Abbey and Salisbury Cathedral. Subsequently, through the 14th and into the early 15th century, Romanesque cloisters were regularly demolished and replaced. At present, too many cloisters remain unexcavated or poorly understood for it to be possible to write a comprehensive architectural history of the late medieval cloister. However, more information has become available on sites either excavated or assessed over the past thirty years, and a preliminary attempt to take an overview of the development of the 14th-century cloister seems appropriate.

As the processional link between the great church and the conventual ranges, cloisters invite a grand architectural design. Yet in scale they were not so large as to encounter the structural problems inherent in vaulting the main body of the church itself. Cloister walks are, in fact, ideal spaces for developing new ideas in vaulting, even more so than the, arguably comparable, architectural space of the church aisle. In a region acknowledged for its interest in vaulting, it is perhaps hardly surprising to discover that West Country cloisters may have made a crucial contribution to this reputation.

THE CURRENT PERSPECTIVE

IN terms of known structures one might represent the architectural history of the Gothic cloister as one punctuated by a series of milestone buildings. The great cloister at Salisbury, constructed *c.* 1260,[1] seems to have set a new standard in cloister building (Fig. 1). Its ambitious, Rayonnant-inspired design, closely emulating that of the most prestigious royal works in the country, at Westminster Abbey — its uniform character and rapid construction, are all factors that might have contributed towards its success. As a secular foundation, without monastic ranges, it stood as an isolated processional route. Its completed state contrasted to the smaller scale of the earlier cloister at Exeter, also a secular cathedral, which had been constructed in the first two decades of the 13th century to connect the church with the entrance to the contemporaneous chapter-house. Both the large bays of the east walk of Westminster and the whole of the cloister at Salisbury were vaulted with stone quadripartite vaults. Architecturally, therefore, cloisters were already being treated in a manner comparable to their adjacent churches.

Perhaps the next milestone building should be that of the cloister of St Paul's Cathedral, with its famous garth and chapter-house, known to have been begun in 1332 and constructed to designs by William Ramsey.[2] Cited by all concerned with the origins of the perpendicular style, the St Paul's cloister has a number of distinguishing features. It was small, two-storeyed, and a polygonal chapter-house occupied almost the whole of the garth. The well-known Hollar engraving provides the best record of the overall appearance of the cloister, indicating that the upper storey had tracery lights with blind tracery spandrels, although it does not record the appearance of the tracery of the lower level, which had been lost by the mid-17th century (Fig. 2).[3] Most published sources suggest that this lower storey was lit by three-light windows, with hexagons above and blind tracery spandrels.[4] Details of the interior of the lower storey are known through drawings of the responds and other moulded details as recorded by Penrose during excavations on the site (published by him in the 1880s, and again by Harvey in the 1970s) (Fig. 3).[5] Collectively, this provides most of the evidence on which an assessment of the overall character of St Paul's and its stylistic followers is

FIG. 1.   Salisbury Cathedral: cloister, north walk
John McNeill

based. Its closest followers are buildings in the south-east, most notably Westminster Abbey (from 1344) and Canterbury Cathedral (cloister and nave *c.* 1390).[6]

The possible appearance of the vaults in either of the two walks at St Paul's, however, is not discussed in the published literature. That the lower storey was vaulted in stone is implicit in the responds and related buttresses. Furthermore a large number of vault rib fragments from the cloister survive in the historic stone collection at St Paul's Cathedral. Amongst these, three fragments of intersecting ribs with the same profile, containing foliate bosses, make it clear that the vault was a simple tierceron, with a large boss at the central point and smaller ones at the subsidiary intersections. Furthermore, Richard Lea has tentatively suggested that tiercerons were also used in the vaulted chamber of the adjacent chapter-house.[7] Secondary support for this might be adduced from the south cloister walk at Westminster Abbey, whose detailing is derived from St Paul's, which is itself covered by a tierceron vault. Although Ramsey's work at St Paul's was highly influential, both in its general impact on the development of Perpendicular and its particular impact on certain later 14th-century buildings in the south-east,[8] Ramsey's straightforward approach to vaulting was not favoured in the west of England, where the next milestone building is located.

The Benedictine abbey of Gloucester, as it was, houses what is surely England's most famous set of cloister walks — elaborately panelled with tracery on all surfaces and covered by what is traditionally considered to be the first structural fan-vault (Fig. 4). That the cloister was commenced during the abbacy of Thomas Horton

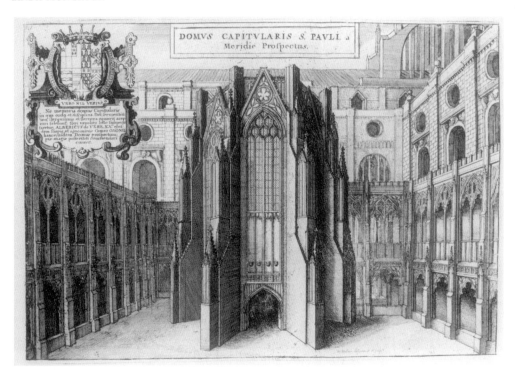

DOMVS CAPITVLARIS S. PAVLI.
Meridie Prospectus.

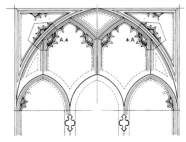

FIG. 2. Old St Paul's Cathedral, London: engraving of cloister and chapter-house by Wenceslaus Hollar

Courtesy of Dr John Scholfield/Molas

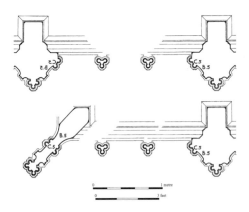

FIG. 3. Old St Paul's Cathedral, London: lower cloister walk, mouldings showing responds and mullions, after J. H. Harvey

Richard Lea

FIG. 4.   Gloucester Cathedral: cloister, east walk to south
John McNeill

(1351–77) is stated in the 15th-century monastic *Historia*, which specifies that Horton's work extended from the north nave aisle to the door of the chapter-house.[9] Leedy suggests that the building evidence indicates the north rather than the south part of the east walk was completed first, the rest of the cloister following in a single campaign and that the fan vault was not part of the original design but an addition.[10] Leland attributes the cloister to Abbot Walter Frowcester (1381 to 1412),[11] during which period it does seem that most of the work was done, and it is to this period that Leedy attributes the cloister vault.[12] It is far more likely, however, that the fan vault does indeed date to the earlier phase. The logical sequence for cloister construction, as with Exeter and Westminster, is to complete first the route between the church and the chapter-house. Indeed, the Gloucester chronicle is explicit on this point. Moreover, Christopher Wilson has already put forward convincing reasons why Leedy's assessment of the technical differences in construction at the north end of the east walk have nothing to do with the building sequence.[13] There is no evidence on site that leads one to assume the fan vault is not part of the original design or construction. The sequence accepted here is that the first phase of the cloister, probably under construction during the 1360s, was followed by the north transept (1368–72) under a new master mason, who then went on to complete the cloister for Abbot Frowcester from 1381.[14] The design of the cloister clearly changes in the second phase, with a simpler wall panelling design first encountered in the east bay of the south walk, and a revised tracery design for the fan vaulting in the subsequent bay. Other details, including sub-bases and bases also show modifications at this point.

FIG. 5. Worcester Cathedral: cloister, south walk, looking west

R. K. Morris

Those cloisters that survive and are dateable to the years after the start of the Gloucester cloister seem to reject the fan-vaulted model in favour of a particular type of lierne vault. Cloisters at Worcester Cathedral, Lacock Abbey and Wells Cathedral, for example, all share a common vault design, albeit one whose detailing is varied, combining a tierceron vault with liernes to form an octagon around the central boss. The east walk of Worcester cloister is likely to be broadly contemporary with the modernisation of the chapter-house, which took place between 1386–87 and 1392.[15] Certainly by the 1390s references to work on the cloister walks is found in documents, and this work continues until the 1430s. Large sculptural bosses dominate the vault at Worcester, with the presence of the lierne ribs providing additional intersections for the presence of more bosses than would be available with a tiercceron vault (see Figs 5 and 12 iv). It fits into a tradition of historiated cloisters where the design of the

FIG. 6.   Lacock: Cloister, north walk to east
John McNeill

FIG. 7.   Wells Cathedral: cloister, east walk
Linda Monckton

vault itself is secondary. In contrast, at Lacock Abbey and Wells Cathedral the success of the cloister walks is a more purely architectural effect. The cloister at Lacock is undated, although Brakspear places it in the early 15th century, and a stylistic assessment of its mouldings suggests a date for the reconstruction of most of the cloister of *c*. 1400–20 (Figs 6 and 12 v).[16] This is supported by a *terminus ante quem* provided by the north walk lavatorium, which shows the painted image of Agnes Frary, abbess from 1429 to 1445.[17] Almost contemporary with this is Wells, where work is known to have started on the replacement of the 12th-century cloister before 1424, when Bishop Bubwith bequeathed money in his will for the completion of the east walk with a library above (Figs 7 and 12 vi).[18] A pause in work occurred after the eighth bay was reached,[19] and the southern half of the walk was not completed until 1457–58 when references to its paving can be found.[20] Work to the west walk followed in the 1460s under Bishop Beckington, probably being completed after his death in 1465,[21] and the south walk was finally reconstructed between *c*. 1489 and 1509.[22]

Whilst the character of the Worcester vault is, essentially, determined by its historiated bosses, there is a close visual relationship between the designs at Lacock and Wells. The type of vault design found there became popular from the late 14th century, and can be found, with slight modifications, for example, in the nave aisles of

Winchester Cathedral (1390s), the chantry chapel of Richard Beauchamp, Earl of Worcester in Tewkesbury Abbey (1421/22), the gatehouse of All Souls College, Oxford (1440s), the Fitzjames Gateway in Merton College (1497), and the presbytery aisles of Winchester Cathedral in the early 16th century.[23] Gloucester, by contrast at this date, stands apparently isolated. Fan vaulting is most commonly associated with late-15th- and early-16th-century buildings, many of which owe a debt to Gloucester's technology rather than having a specific affinity. Several questions are raised by this. First is there any evidence that the Gloucester cloister design was directly emulated, or was it seen as too distinctive to be precisely copied? Secondly, how were designs for lierne vaults generated, and is the presence of several lierne vaults of the same or closely similar designs a sign of the stagnation of architectural ideas in the region? The remainder of this paper will deal with these issues in turn.

GLOUCESTER AND THE FAN VAULTING TRADITION

THE construction of the Gloucester south transept in 1331 to 1336 was a precocious attempt to extend the principles of architectural articulation across all surfaces, an interest which was to become the hallmark of Perpendicular architecture. However, the transept, and its immediate successors, the presbytery and choir, were tempered by the need to apply the new style to an existing Romanesque elevation. By contrast, the cloister was relatively free from such constraints, for although it replicated the plan, and re-used the rear walls of its 12th-century predecessor, the walks could effectively be built anew. By the 1360s, when work began on the east cloister walk, the idea of applying a grid of tracery over all surfaces was already well established at Gloucester. However, although Gloucester developed a notable, and remarkably creative, internal architectural dynamic, it is not wholly impervious to outside influence, and the lining of the interior walls of the cloister with fully developed blind tracery designs is strongly reminiscent of work at the Aerary porch, Windsor (constructed, just before Gloucester, in 1353–54, although probably designed by 1349) (Fig. 8).[24] This building was comparatively small, with two square bays, in which an 'overarching architectural logic' is applied to the walls and the vault which, as a result become 'visually integrated'.[25] Whilst the principles of the tracery grid and surface decoration of the Aerary porch may be traced back to the works of Michael of Canterbury, and the design, and protracted construction, of St Stephen's, Westminster,[26] the parallel between the Aerary porch and Gloucester has a bearing on more than the general spread of Perpendicular architecture. First, the vault of the Aerary has already been acknowledged as a precursor to fan vault designs, not least because of its use of jointed ashlar masonry.[27] Secondly, the scale of the work at the Aerary porch is similar to that in a small cloister, and the two bays provide not just an entrance to the adjacent (unvaulted) cloister which was being constructed contemporaneously, but provided access to the door leading to the treasury above. It may, therefore, have seemed an appropriate model for the application of blind tracery to the interior walls of a cloister. The design of the Gloucester cloister is dated to not long after the Windsor porch was completed, being between 1351 and 1377, and most likely the early 1360s. Certain details at Gloucester may even demonstrate an awareness of the St Paul's cloister as discussed above. At St Paul's a band of quatrefoils divides the upper and lower exterior elevations of the cloister, and link directly to the mullioned blind panels beneath the upper storey windows (see Fig. 2). The work at the cloister in

FIG. 8.   St George's
Windsor: Aerary Porch

John Goodall

Gloucester therefore shows a continued awareness of south-eastern models.[28] Its fully developed fan vault, however, was not, it seems, a direct copy of any existing model.

So to return to a question posed above — once established, was the Gloucester cloister design influential? Any attempt at an answer, at present, is clouded by a lack of information about a number of crucial buildings within a 25-mile radius of Gloucester. As Leedy has stated 'it is impossible to determine the architectural contributions of the now destroyed West Country abbeys of Winchcombe, Evesham and Circencester'.[29] Unfortunately this essentially remains true, although a brief comment on Evesham may be warranted.

FIG. 9. Evesham Abbey:
fragment from Abbey Manor
David Kendrick

The only surviving fragment of the Evesham cloister complex that survives *in situ* is the decorated arch that led from the east cloister walk into the chapter-house vestibule, both the arch and the new decagonal chapter-house being constructed during the abbacy of John de Brokehampton (1284 to 1316), probably between 1284 and 1295.[30] He also constructed the east walk of the cloister and a 'large fine dormitory', in other words a complete new east range.[31] The implication is that the north, south and west walks remained in their Romanesque state, having been begun in the late 11th century and continued in the second and third quarters of the 12th century.[32] Documentary evidence suggests that at least the north walk of the Romanesque cloister was then replaced in the following century, being rebuilt by Abbot Ombersby *c.* 1375.[33] The Evesham chronicle only refers to the north walk at this time, and there is no other evidence as to whether the other walks were rebuilt also. When the abbey site at Evesham was excavated between 1811 and 1834 by its then owner Edward Rudge, many architectural fragments were moved to Abbey Manor.[34] A large number of stones still survive in the garden of this house, many arranged (in nothing like their original disposition) as garden features or furniture. Further large fragments were buried close by. During preliminary investigations of the site a number of interesting fragments were discovered.[35] In particular, a series of pieces survive from a section of panelled wall organised according to a hierarchy of mullions. In one of these can be seen blind panelled tracery, with a row of quatrefoils and an adjacent row of trefoil-headed lights (Fig. 9).[36] Close parallels to this exist at Gloucester, where rows of quatrefoils set within panelled and mullioned walls were first used in the south transept, maturing in the presbytery before going on to become a hallmark of the cloister design. Another possible link with Gloucester is manifest in a fragmentary respond from Evesham, discovered in the same location at Abbey Manor, cut with three rolls each flanked by canted fillets.[37] The use of rolls flanked by canted fillets was introduced to the Gloucester presbytery design in 1337, and used in subsequent works within the cathedral as well as in buildings showing direct links with Gloucester (the choir of Great Malvern, for example). All of these fragments appear to belong to a

FIG. 10. Tewkesbury Abbey: north-east angle of former cloister

John McNeill

screen wall, shown by the presence of simpler mullions indicating panelling on the reverse face of some.[38]

Although it is tempting to associate these fragments with a cloister walk at Evesham, known to be under construction in the 1370s, the fact they are mostly double-sided makes it more likely that they belong to a chapel screen or tomb. Moreover, the details evident at Evesham ultimately derive from the earlier works at Gloucester dating from the 1330s. At Gloucester, these features were adopted in the more or less continuous building campaigns which followed on from the south transept, and drew heavily on its most innovative features, resulting, as Wilson has cogently argued, in Gloucester becoming 'by the 1350s ... [the] centre of Perpendicular architecture'.[39] Whatever the provenance of the Evesham fragments, they offer a tantalising glimpse of what was architecturally possible, and confirm that relations with Gloucester could be close. The presence of a fragment of fan-vault springer within the same garden raises further questions about the nature of this relationship. Even if, as seems likely, these fragments did not belong to a lost panelled, and possibly fan-vaulted, north cloister walk, in the matter of some undetermined micro-architectural composition, Evesham was among the earliest of Gloucester's imitators.

The question of whether or not Gloucester was too distinctive to be precisely copied is easier to answer. Of those buildings generally regarded as being influenced by Gloucester, the best known are probably the small-scale work of the north-west porch at Exeter Cathedral and the cloister at Tewkesbury Abbey.[40] In isolation these might not suggest that the Gloucester cloister had much beyond a limited and local influence. The former was constructed by Robert Lesyngham, master mason at Exeter between 1376 and 1394, but notably from Gloucester.[41] And the cloister at Tewkesbury Abbey, long acknowledged as a direct response to Gloucester, is a mere 10 miles up the river Severn, and is a monastery whose architecture has a long history of sharing in developments at Gloucester. What survives of the cloister at Tewkesbury is fragmentary, though it is still clear that it never achieved the coherence of Gloucester (Fig. 10). It is known that by the early 16th century work was still not complete,[42] and the *in situ* remains suggest that the north walk was not vaulted in stone. Richard Morris has suggested that the east walk was vaulted with a stone fan vault and argues that this walk at least, can be dated, in part by the presence of a new processional door into the church, to the second quarter of the 15th century.[43] But rather than an isolated copy of a nearby and closely related neighbour, the Tewkesbury cloister appears to be only one of a possible series of related cloister designs all closely copying Gloucester as a direct model.

Recent archaeological excavation at the cathedral-priory site at Coventry has revealed a large number of stones relating to a late medieval cloister. These are currently being studied and assessed by Richard Morris, who has suggested the cloister must have employed panelled internal walls, and that their design indicates an awareness of Gloucester.[44] Just to confuse the picture, there is currently no evidence that these walks were actually vaulted, and it may be that the Gloucester model, as at Tewkesbury, was adapted to the circumstances or wealth of the moment. However, the Coventry work is currently dated by Morris to *c.* 1400, which serves to reinforce the immediate impact of the aesthetic of the Gloucester design in the West Country and in the Midlands.[45] Rather than an isolated work of genius, the Gloucester cloister was granted the most sincere form of flattery, that of imitation.

Leedy, in assessing the influence of Gloucester, is interested in a form — the fan vault — rather than its location. After noting the north-west porch at Exeter and Hugh Herland's timber vault at Winchester College, he identifies a hiatus, stating that no fan vaults were built between 1412 (the latest date for fan-vault designs at Gloucester and Tewkesbury) and the late 1430s (the date at which Leedy attributes the design of the large-scale fan vault in the Sherborne Abbey chancel).[46] In searching for a rationale behind this pause, Leedy cites rising costs in the building industry in the first thirty years of the 15th century. Recent research does flatly contradict this view, however, suggesting that fan vaults continued to be designed through the 1420s. Most notably the Sherborne chancel vault is now generally acknowledged to have been designed in its present form before the fire of 1437, and probably as early as *c.* 1425;[47] while the Beauchamp Chapel at Tewkesbury, with its pendant fan vaulted 'vestibule', has most recently been redated to 1421/22, rather than the 1430s as previously.[48]

In summary, the Gloucester cloister model was influential in the West Country in the late 14th and early 15th century. Despite the clear significance of the design, and the ease with which its details could be closely copied, however, it did not have the field to itself, and, as was suggested towards the beginning of this paper, between *c.* 1380 and 1420 the Gloucester tradition was paralleled by a lierne vault design.

The next part of this paper will assess the origins and development of this parallel tradition, with a view to asking whether the appearance of similar sets of designs presupposes a stagnation of architectural ideas.

LIERNE VAULTS AND THEIR DEVELOPMENT AS A VIABLE ALTERNATIVE

THOMAS OF WITNEY's design for the pulpitum at Exeter Cathedral (1317–26) is probably the earliest net vault in England.[49] Its design is notable for the way in which a simple cross-vault is combined with diagonals stretching across two net vault bays and a triple ridge rib (Fig. 11 vii), and lies behind a sequence of large scale complex lierne vaults at Tewkesbury and Gloucester.[50] In the western bay of the pulpitum Witney introduced kite or lozenge shapes (Fig. 11 ix), probably imported directly from

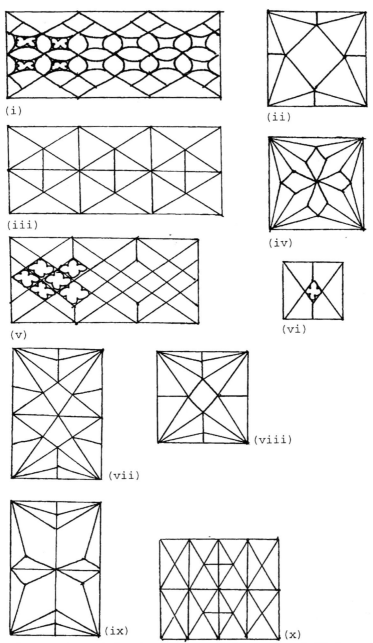

FIG. 11. Comparative vault drawings. (i) Ottery St Mary, chancel, (ii) Ottery St Mary, transepts, (iii) Ottery St Mary, nave, (iv) Ottery St Mary, crossing, (v) Ottery St Mary, Lady chapel, (vi) Ottery St Mary, Lady chapel screen, central bay, (vii) Exeter Cathedral, pulpitum east bay, (viii) Exeter Cathedral, St Edmund's Chapel (ix) Exeter Cathedral, pulpitum west bay, (x) Malmesbury Abbey, nave

Linda Monckton

the undercroft vault of St Stephen's Chapel, where Witney is known to have worked between 1292 and 1294.[51] These lozenges featured prominently in the later high vault of St Augustine's Bristol. A more Angevin-looking type of net vault appeared in the choir aisles of St Augustine's and the nave high vault at Malmesbury in the 1320s (Fig. 11 x), both of which are considered by Crossley to have provided the basis for a more sophisticated and more radical vault over the choir of Wells Cathedral *c.* 1329.[52] Sophisticated net vaults, using cusped lozenges on a large scale, were subsequently used at Ottery St Mary, also often considered to be by William Joy, the designer of the Wells choir,[53] and dating to 1338–42 (see Fig. 11 i–vi), and St Mary Redcliffe, mostly dating to the late 14th and early 15th centuries.[54] Other variations on a net-vaulting theme were deployed over the Lady chapel at Wells (see Fig. 19), generally attributed to Witney (and completed by 1326), and the south choir aisle at Wells Cathedral, after 1330 (Fig. 12 vii). By this date, a tradition of variety in vaulting in the south-west was well established. By contrast, the contemporary cloister of St Paul's was covered by a tierceron vault, a type of vault which remained popular in London and the south-east throughout the 14th century.

None of the above examples of net and lierne vaults includes a cloister walk, which is, perhaps, surprising, given the fluidity with which designs passed from the large to the small scale (and vice versa) in the early 14th century. That a pulpitum might provide the earliest surviving example of an English net vault is symptomatic of this, and a study of two cloisters, those at Exeter and Sherborne, does indeed demonstrate that cloisters were areas of architectural experiment and expression during the first half of the 14th century. The only problem is that as both no longer survive they require some form of abstract reconstruction.

Exeter

LITTLE now remains *in situ* at Exeter and, as so little has been noted in published sources, a brief history of its construction and destruction is necessary.[55] It is currently supposed that the east walk of the cloister was constructed between 1310 and 1325 to an unknown design. The basis for this is a series of ambiguous references within the cathedral fabric accounts which suggest that work to the roof of part of the cloister was going on between 1310 and 1319, and that subsequently this was vaulted, with seven heads for the vault being ordered in 1323.[56] The north walk was constructed with the nave, between about 1325 and the 1330s, and it must be for this walk that settlement for twenty-nine purbeck marble columns for the cloister was made in 1331/32, as well as references to roofing in 1330–31, presumably indicating that it was near completion.[57] Clearer documentary references exist for the west walk, plans for which were drawn up in 1377, and the construction of this and the south walk continued into the 15th century.[58] The cloister was still in use and in good condition in the early 17th century, but, having passed into secular hands after the abolition of the Dean and Chapter in 1649, all the walks were demolished, probably by the Surveyor to Cromwell's Office of Works.[59] By the late 17th century the site had been redeveloped to incorporate a Serge Market to the south and south-west, and houses to the west (Fig. 13). The area to the north is distinguished by the presence of very large and deep buttresses, necessitated by the construction of the nave vault. The gaps between the pier buttresses lent themselves to the construction of cheap two-storey houses for poor men, which became known as 'the miserable hovels'. The site was cleared by the Dean and Chapter in the 19th century, and a proposal to reconstruct the cloister was

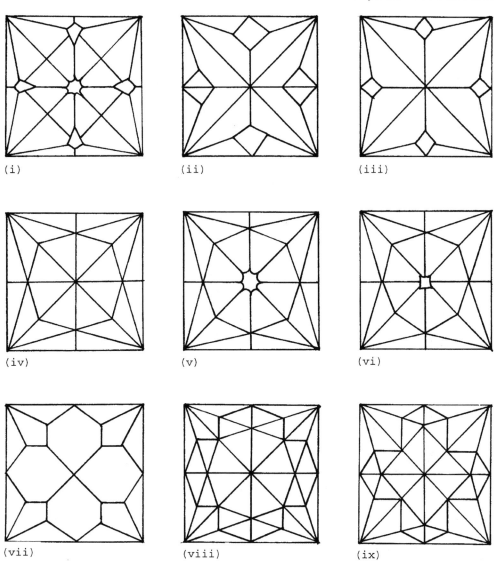

FIG. 12. Comparative vault drawings. (i) Lacock Abbey, cloister (phase one) south walk west bays, (ii) Wells Cathedral, retrochoir, central bay, (iii) Sherborne Abbey cloister reconstruction, (iv) Worcester Cathedral, cloister, (v) Lacock Abbey, cloister (phase two) south walk, (vi) Wells Cathedral, cloister, (vii) Wells Cathedral, choir aisle, (viii) Exeter Cathedral, cloister, Pearson's reconstruction (ix) Sherborne Abbey, south nave aisle

Linda Monckton

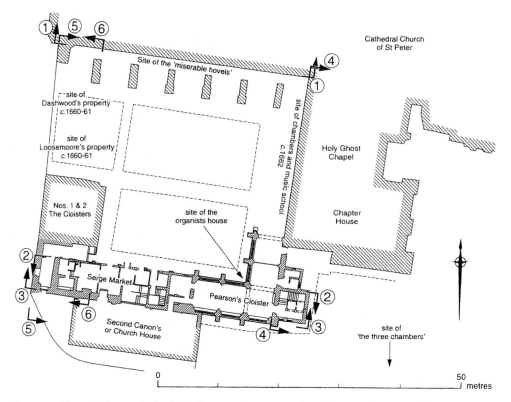

FIG. 13. Plan of Exeter Cathedral, cloister, composite plan showing location of buildings and the sections

© *Exeter Archaeology*

floated. In the event this was never done, although Pearson did construct a part of the cloister in the south-east corner, based on the discovery of architectural fragments during the 19th-century demolition works. More recent conservation work to the north side of the cathedral, combined with a second proposal to reconstruct the cloister (also unrealised at present) has led to a series of archaeological investigations of the site, carried out by Exeter Archaeology. These have provided much of the information on which the following assessment is based.

Little is known about the appearance of the earliest part of the 14th-century cloister — the east walk.[60] Of the north walk, however, constructed by Thomas of Witney, more can be said. Thomas of Witney arrived at Exeter Cathedral in 1313 to provide advice on the design and construction of the Bishops' Throne.[61] He had become master mason by 1316 and retained his position until about 1342, when it seems likely that he died.[62] For some of the time he was in charge at Exeter, he also acted as master mason for Wells Cathedral. On his arrival at Exeter the reconstruction of the Romanesque church was well underway, the choir having been substantially complete by 1310 when the choir stalls were moved into the building. Between 1317 and *c.* 1326

FIG. 14.   Exeter Cathedral: cloister, north
walk from south
Linda Monckton

FIG. 15.   Exeter Cathedral: cloister, north
walk, view east through buttresses
Linda Monckton

attention was directed towards the transepts and the fitting-out of the choir, although
it was also during this time that the east walk of the cloister seems to have been completed. Work to the nave seems to have followed on directly under Witney's supervision, and that the west end was reached by the late 1320s is indicated in the accounts.
Gifts of timber from Bishop Grandisson in 1332 and 1338 are usually taken to mean
that roofing the nave was in progress.[63]

Witney's design for the nave of the cathedral is, on the whole, relatively conservative in that it follows the basic principles of the elevation and vault design
established in the choir and presbytery several decades earlier.[64] With the construction
of the north cloister walk, however, Witney was met by an unusual set of circumstances. The high nave vault required large buttresses which projected deep into the
space which would conventionally be occupied by a cloister walk (see Figs 13 and 14).
Rather than pushing the north walk away from the side of the nave, as at Salisbury,
for example, Witney designed a cloister walk around the buttresses, creating a series
of small square bays bounded by their rhythms, rather than a continuous open walk.
Archways were cut into the buttresses so as to facilitate circulation. In each bay, as is
evident from the scars on the north nave wall and the sides of the buttresses, two
arches were constructed on each wall (Figs 14 and 15). Scant remains of wall ribs and

FIG. 16.   Exeter Cathedral: cloister, proposed reconstruction of north walk
© *Exeter Archaeology, reconstruction drawn by Richard Parker*

springers indicate that this was stone vaulted and that ribs sprang from the base of each arch, and possibly also the apex.

The north walk of the cloister has previously been assumed to follow the nave in its use of established designs. In general it has been assumed that each bay was covered by a tierceron vault supported on a central column, emulating on a small-scale, chapter-house arrangements such as those at Salisbury, Westminster and Lichfield. This idea was adopted by Exeter Archaeology in their initial report and seems to be based on an idea developed early in the 20th century by Reverend Chanter.[65] The article by Chanter provides no evidence for his proposal.[66] Exeter Archaeology's subsequent site excavation tested this hypothesis and found no evidence of a central column. Instead, evidence was found for an external buttress midway between the nave buttresses in the centre of each cloister bay, facing the garth.[67] This both means that the tracery facing the garth was divided by buttresses into two windows, and the vaulting bays were subdivided on both north and south faces (Fig. 16).

That Witney should come up with so inventive a solution to the north cloister walk is not wholly surprising. As the pulpitum shows when not constrained by earlier designs, he was capable of remarkable ingenuity. In addition to this, Richard Morris has demonstrated that, although the nave continued to use templates from the choir for the major features, those aspects of the work that were new provided an opportunity for Witney to devise a more personal contribution.[68]

The cloister walk comprised five square bays, each of which must have had four small square vaults as its basic design. The springers would have been supported on a series of marble columns (as ordered in 1332).[69] In plan, therefore, each cloister bay is most likely to have consisted of four small cross vaults. Brakspear came to the same conclusion, as is shown by his drawing of 1913 in the *Archaeological Journal* (Fig. 17), though he offers no explanation for his choice, and it is unclear whether or not he foresees the Revd Chanter's central column in each bay.[70]

The rectangular space created by the passageway through the buttresses was also vaulted in stone, as can be seen in the remaining springer in the second bay from the west (Fig. 18). As Richard Parker notes, there appears to be evidence for subsidiary ribs, possibly indicating a tierceron vault in these bays.[71] The fragmentary springer in the second bay from the east indicates a main diagonal rib, but it is not clear that any subsidiary ribs existed at this point. Assuming, therefore, that the main vault is a series of four cross vaults, how should we reconstruct its solid geometry?[72] Simple cross ribs, when used in combination across different types of severy, can be fantastically varied. As used by Peter Parler in Prague, for example, they 'became the vehicle for [his] most imaginative experiments in patterned vaulting'.[73]

As we can dispense with the notion of a central column, it is most likely that the Exeter north walk vaults were domical. Although examples of early domed-up vaults over square bays do exist in England, in particular the 13th-century vault over the consistory court at the south-west angle of Lincoln cathedral nave, more appropriate parallels are perhaps to be found in France and in Prague where domical severies are associated with the development of the net vault. The best-known are the 13th-century vaults in western France, where, like Exeter, paired arches and windows within a square space were often covered by a net vault taking a domed form. Perhaps of more relevance here, especially in view of Crossley's more recent conclusion that Parler was directly influenced by the works of Witney and Joy, are the net vaults in Prague Cathedral.[74] Here various examples of similarly patterned vaults over square bays demonstrate the possibility, for example, of a flattish crinkly vault (the west bay of Sacristy in Prague Cathedral, 1356–62), or a domed-up vault (Wenceslas Chapel, consecrated 1367).[75] In fact, the earliest net vaults in Prague and England, as cited by Crossley, are used in the context of centralised chapels with domical vaults.[76]

That Witney was already using domed vaults in miniature is clear from the sedilia in the choir at Exeter, on which he was working in 1316–17.[77] It is tempting to suggest that in the north cloister walk he designed vaults for centralised spaces that exploited the three-dimensional potential of the pulpitum net vaults in domed form, on the basis of his experience on the sedilia. That he has an interest in domed centralised spaces is most obviously shown in his design for the Lady chapel at Wells Cathedral, a building constructed between 1323/4 and 1326 (Fig. 19).[78]

This last raises the question of the date at which the Exeter north cloister walk was designed. One of the characteristics of all the work at Exeter during this period is the fact that stone and timber were being stockpiled in advance of construction. A place for the storing of stone is identified from the accounts as early as 1317, and works for the nave were surely set by this date on the basis of the continuing use of most of the templates used in the eastern arm.[79] What is not clear is whether the design for the cloister was set at this date too, which would coincide with Witney's appointment, or whether it was designed once construction work on the nave began in earnest in the mid-1320s. It is known that work proceeded on the cloister in tandem with the nave, and by 1331 (when the small columns for the cloister were ordered), both cloister and nave were well advanced.[80]

Erskine states that the cloister was clearly part of Witney's plan on arrival at Exeter,[81] and it is certainly tempting to suggest that its design was set by *c.* 1320 and building stone ordered. This would make its design either earlier or contemporaneous with that of the Lady chapel at Wells. Crossley counts the Lady chapel at Wells as

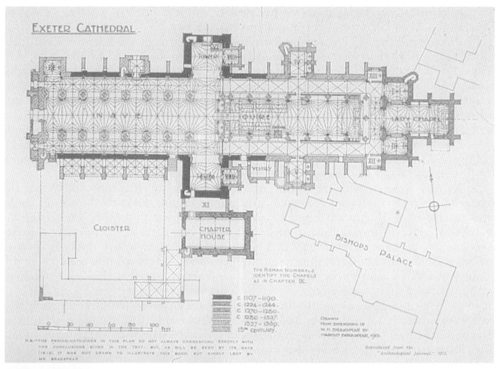

FIG. 17.   Exeter Cathedral: plan by Harold
Brakspear, 1913

FIG. 18.   Exeter Cathedral: cloister, north walk,
detail of springer in 'buttress passage'
Linda Monckton

FIG. 19. Wells
Cathedral: Lady Chapel
vault

John McNeill

'amongst [Witney's] earliest experiments in net construction'.[82] The cloister at Exeter,
however, is just as likely to be an early expression of Witney's interest in domed,
structural net vaults, which was then adapted to the larger and structurally more
complex Lady chapel at Wells.[83]

Sherborne

WHERE the interest at Exeter is in three-dimensional forms, the mid-14th-century
cloister at Sherborne instead favours the development of the lierne vault tradition and
provides evidence that vaults with lozenges were used in a variety of architectural
contexts. The cloister at the Benedictine monastery at Sherborne is attributed by
Leland to the abbacy of John Frith (1348–73) and was demolished in the 16th
century.[84] It was constructed of local Ham Hill stone, with the exception of the vault,
which was built using Beer stone. The survival of parts of the cloister *in situ*, along
with some architectural fragments excavated from the site of the chapter-house in the
1970s, show that the cloister can be closely related to work in the west porches of
Exeter Cathedral of the mid-1340s. The Exeter porches, as mentioned in the fabric
accounts, followed on from the completion of the main body of the nave and the
cloister. The designs for the south-west and central porches are attributed to William
Joy, Witney's successor at both Exeter and Wells.[85] An assessment of the remains at
Sherborne has shown that its stylistic antecedents range from London to the West
Country.[86] The main vault rib can be compared with a number of cloisters in the
south-east, all of which probably emanate from that of 1332 at Old St Paul's, whilst
the handling of the corner bays shows an awareness of the Dean's cloister at St
George's Windsor. The vault pattern, however, is firmly rooted in a West Country
tradition of progressive vault designs (Fig. 12 iii). Its basis is a tierceron vault, but
with the tiercerons interrupted by lozenges made out of liernes. It is likely that these
lozenges were cusped, as in the high vault at Wells and the vaults at Ottery St Mary,
both attributable to William Joy. More precisely, Sherborne relates to the first of Joy's

FIG. 20. Lacock Abbey: south cloister walk phase one

John McNeill

cusped designs, that over the retrochoir at Wells Cathedral of *c.* 1326 (Fig. 12 ii), and the Sherborne cloister is a rare example of its application to an 'aisle' environment. Other aisle vaults of a similar date which used liernes, include the Wells Cathedral choir (Fig. 12 vii), and St Mary Redcliffe, the latter in particular using cusped lozenges. One further cloister example can be found in the west bays of the south walk at Lacock Abbey, perhaps to be dated to the middle of the 14th century, and broadly contemporary with Sherborne. The two bays at Lacock are rather crudely executed, but are interesting for their use of a series of lozenges placed at the intersection of the major ribs (Figs 12 i and 20). These two bays seem to have formed a discreet campaign in their own right, and the rest of cloister was reconstructed to a different design in the early years of the 15th century, however their application of lozenges to complex lierne vaults in cloister walks was to bear fruit in a number of early-15th-century vaults discussed below.

The Whitefriars, Coventry

A further tradition of lierne vaulting that emanated from the Exeter pulpitum was the creation of a design omitting the main diagonal. A series of set-piece vaults follow on from this, for example Witney's own St Edmund's Chapel at the west end of Exeter Cathedral (*c.* 1328–30) (Fig. 11 viii), the pulpitum at Tintern Abbey (*c.* 1330),[87] the transepts of Ottery St Mary (*c.* 1340) (Fig. 11 ii), and Berkeley Castle great hall porch (?1344–35).[88] The design was also used in the context of at least one cloister — at the monastery of the Whitefriars, Coventry (after 1342) (Figs 21 and 22).[89] Although the master mason for this work is unknown, both William Ramsey[90] and John Box have been suggested.[91] Box is likely to have either designed or worked on the tomb of Archbishop Stratford (d. 1348) in Canterbury,[92] and may have come from Box, near Bath.[93] This design, and possibly its designer, thus straddles the south-east and the south-west, although its ultimate source is probably West Country.[94] Its use in a cloister relates directly to the West Country principles of applying highly fashionable lierne vault designs to 'aisle-like' environments at this date.

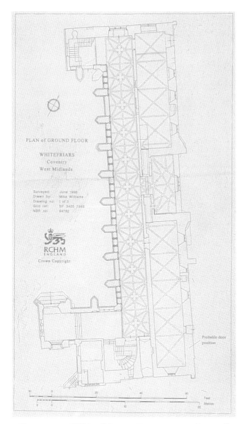

FIG. 21.   Whitefriars, Coventry: plan of
east cloister range and walk
Crown Copyright, NMR

FIG. 22.   Whitefriars, Coventry: cloister, east
walk vault
Linda Monckton

That cloisters were experimenting with the application of elaborate vault designs
in the middle of the 14th century has tended to be overlooked, largely because the
patterns of survival are themselves somewhat misleading, but what evidence there is
strongly suggests that cloister walks were afforded treatments as varied as those of
furnishings and aisles within the West Country, and contributed towards the experimentation and application of new designs. The above examples of lierne-vaulted cloisters can all be dated between *c.* 1320 and *c.* 1350, and should thus be seen as part
of a tradition preceding that, crystallised in the third quarter of the 14th century, at
Gloucester.

Exeter and Glastonbury

THE last quarter of the 14th century was witness to a further series of large-scale
cloister reconstructions, some of which, as discussed above, looked directly to
Gloucester for inspiration. Major work at Exeter Cathedral and Glastonbury Abbey,

 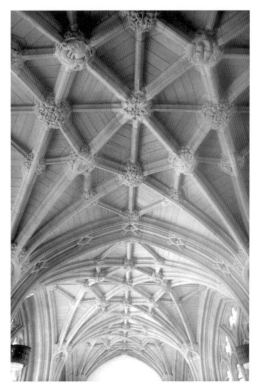

FIG. 23. Exeter Cathedral: south-east cloister
as reconstructed by Pearson

© *Exeter Archaeology*

FIG. 24. Exeter Cathedral: south-east
cloister, vault as reconstructed by Pearson

© *Exeter Archaeology*

however, provide evidence of a continuing alternative to the fan-vault design of Gloucester.

The west walk at Exeter Cathedral and the east walk at Glastonbury were constructed contemporaneously. At Exeter it is recorded that in 1377 the mason Robert Lesyngham was paid for 'supervising the work of the new cloister',[95] and that the cloister design can be dated to this year is confirmed by reference to a piece of parchment bought for the mason in order that he might set out the plan of the cloisters in the same year.[96] Work on the south and west walks seem to have been largely carried out by the late 1380s, with references to the 'crest of the cloister' in 1386,[97] although Lesyngham remained on the pay roll until 1394, and the walks were not completed until some time later (with evidence, by this time, of a shortage of funds). Glass was being installed, apparently piecemeal, at the end of the century,[98] followed by gutter work, repairs and roofing in 1418/19.[99] Some evidence for the appearance of Lesyngham's work was obtained in 1887 during the demolition of the late-17th-century vergers' houses.[100]

Lesyngham's south and east walks are now best understood from Pearson's reconstruction of the south-east corner of the Exeter cloister, as begun in 1887 (Figs 23 and 24).[101] Pearson based his vault on the discovery of at least ten fragments indicating a complex lierne vault.[102] The responses and springers also appear to be accurate copies of the fragmentary medieval remains.[103] Pearson's reconstruction of the interior wall of the cloister is plain to the east and fenestrated to the south. Parker explains that the decision to add windows to the south wall of the south walk is the most obvious departure from the medieval design.[104] The form of the vault, however, is commonly accepted as a reconstruction of the 14th-century design. It comprises fan springers leading into a lierne vault. Unlike Witney's work, which often experimented with lozenges and absent diagonals, this vault has a full complement of ridge, diagonal and transverse ribs, supplemented by liernes, to produce a central octagon intersecting with four hexagons, with foliate bosses at the rib intersections (Fig. 12 viii). The liernes forming the hexagon have a smaller, subsidiary profile to the rest of the vault and the bosses at these intersections are correspondingly smaller, making it clear that the octagon is the primary form and the hexagons secondary (Fig. 24). Hexagons can most readily be associated with the choir aisles of Wells Cathedral, designed some fifty years earlier, but the use of liernes to form polygons orbiting the central boss seems to emerge in the 1370s. That the late-14th-century sees a distinctive move away from lozenges as the primary decorative feature of vaults in the West Country is perhaps most clearly demonstrated at Sherborne Abbey. Here, the south nave aisle was remodelled, probably between 1385 and 1415, after the completion of the cloister (1349–73).[105] Rather than emulating the cloister vault's lozenges, the south nave aisle vault instead takes it lead from the cloister at Exeter, though with a square rather than an octagon at its centre — the aim being to achieve a traceried effect over a square bay (Fig. 12 ix). Unlike the net vaults in the choir at Wells and those at Ottery, which seek to minimise bay divisions, the Sherborne lierne vaults maintain a sense of compartmentalisation, perhaps to emphasise a progression of bays as a processional route.

By way of contrast to Exeter at this period, the appearance of the cloister at Glastonbury is essentially unknown, and what is known shines only dimly through some very ambiguous archaeology. Leland, however, clearly attributes the cloisters to Abbot John Chinnock, 1374 to 1420.[106] Our understanding of the cloister area is almost completely dependent on a series of publications and excavations undertaken by Bond early in the 20th century.

In his 1909 handbook to Glastonbury, Bond states of the cloisters that 'there remain but faint traces, yet these are sufficient to indicate that their nature was something similar to those of Gloucester, in regard to the vaulting'.[107] However, after each season of excavations Bond published reports in the proceedings of the Somerset Archaeological and Natural History Society. Those for 1909–10 state that the excavation of the east walk of the cloister revealed a wealth of architectural fragments, and Bond subsequently revised his assessment of the appearance of this walk stating that it was 'in character not unlike those of Wells, yet vaulted with greater richness and profusion of panel-work'.[108] It is frustrating that Bond does not illustrate the cloister fragments on which he bases this assessment.[109]

Despite the subsequent damage to his reputation aroused by his interest in psychic reconstruction, Bond was well versed in the character of the finds at Glastonbury, and provided considerable evidence for the presence of a fan vault in the 16th-century Edgar Chapel at the east end of the church. It seems likely, therefore, that had clear evidence for a fan vault in the cloister existed, Bond would not have revised his opinion. The presence of a complex lierne vault should therefore be accepted. What Bond's reports suggest is a panelled internal wall, as at Gloucester and its followers,

FIG. 25.   Glastonbury Abbey: ?fragment of
choir panelling

Linda Monckton

but with a lierne rather than a fan vault. That Glastonbury could already be counted
among Gloucester's followers is implicit in the appearance of the eastern arm of the
church, and it is worth digressing slightly to discuss this.

In 1909 Bond suggested that the early-14th-century works at the east end of
Gloucester exercised a considerable influence on the remodelling of the choir of
Glastonbury, attributed to Abbot Walter Monington (1342–74) and therefore just
preceding the construction of the new cloister.[110] The most obvious point of similarity
is the method of updating the eastern arm, which consisted of applying a screen of
Perpendicular detailing to the earlier fabric, a method common to the south transept
and presbytery/choir at Gloucester. Wilson has gone further and suggested that a fan
vault over the choir at Glastonbury should be considered a possibility.[111] The presence
or otherwise of fan vaulting at Glastonbury is a knotty matter, complicated by Leedy's
references to architectural fragments which may or may not come from the choir.
Tradition recalls that they relate to the early-16th-century eastern chapel of the abbey,
known as the Edgar Chapel, which in turn depends on Bond's interpretation of a large
boss found during the chapel's excavation (still on site but much eroded and worn)
and his own excavation reports. The fragments themselves were at one time kept in
the Abbot's kitchen, which is where Leedy saw them. They are still visible on site —
now kept against the north boundary wall of the site.[112] These are the pieces associated directly with the Edgar chapel by Bond. One further piece, however, is illustrated
by Leedy, as seen in the abbot's kitchen, and dated by him to the 16th century.[113] The
piece in question shows two lights within an almost semicircular arch, which appear
to be teardrop in shape (the bottom is lost) (Fig. 25), adjacent to which is a row of
carved fleurons in a hollow chamfer. This fragment should be dated to the late 14th
century rather than the 16th for two reasons. First, it can be compared to the fan vault
in the north-west porch of Exeter Cathedral (the location and design of the fleurons
are similar). Second, the mouchette-shaped lights closely relate in style to the panelling
of the Glastonbury choir, evidence for which remains *in situ*. If Leedy were right in
seeing this as a vault springer it would strengthen the case for a fan vault over the
choir. However, what can be deduced from this piece as regards the presence of fan
vaulting in Glastonbury in the late 14th century is complicated by the fragment's total

lack of curvature. Whether it should even be considered a part of a vault is questionable. It might belong to the spandrel of an arch and the presence of the tear drop shapes in a style commensurate with the choir panelling may yet, if more evidence comes to light, help support a theory that the panelled effect extended to every surface of the re-cast choir, including the vault.[114]

The balance of probability is that Glastonbury not only looked to Gloucester for inspiration to update its eastern arm, but also adopted the fan vault on a major scale. As Wilson argues, this would go a long way to explaining the subsequent development of vaults, such as Sherborne, in the region. The apparent absence, by contrast, of a fan vault in the cloister at Glastonbury, is therefore noteworthy. Leedy's concern, that the major constraint on fan vaulting was cost, does not apply to Glastonbury, known to be by far the wealthiest monastery in the region. Indeed, the contemporary reconstruction of some of the monastic ranges around the cloister, as demonstrated by Bond, with unusual and complex undercroft vaults to the south range, is exceptional and exceptionally expensive. Whether the monks at Glastonbury deliberately eschewed a copy of the Gloucester cloister is worth considering.

At present, most of what one might say about the appearance of the Glastonbury cloister is circumstantial. Bond describes the cloister as like Wells but richer. The Wells cloister, constructed shortly after Glastonbury, *c*. 1420, has a lierne vault with an octagonal centre and fan springers (see Figs 7 and 12 vi). It is, essentially, a simplified version of the Exeter design. By way of contrast to the large foliate central boss at Exeter, the Wells design favours a square 'ring-boss' and the ribs meet the boss with a reverse curve. Curved ribs in a grander form had been key elements in the chancel vault of Ottery St Mary (Fig. 11 i). They turn up again, probably just before the construction of the Wells cloister at Lacock. After the construction of the two southernmost bays of the south walk (see above), the rest of the cloister at Lacock was reconstructed in the early 15th century (see Figs 6 and 11 v).[115] The vault pattern is the same as Wells but the central recessed 'ring-boss' is octagonal and more obviously associated with curving ribs. The later Lacock vault, in a sense, provides a refined solution to some of the problems encountered in the adjacent mid-14th-century bays.

Both the second Lacock and the Wells designs post-date the completion of the Glastonbury cloister. Bearing in mind Bond's comments, they may represent pared down versions of the Glastonbury design. Even setting aside the obvious geographical proximity of Wells to Glastonbury, there exist good reasons to associate the two designs. Not least the close similarity between the sub-bases at Glastonbury, a number of which survive *in situ*, and those at Wells, along with the constructional technique employed in attaching the two cloisters to earlier walls at both locations.[116] This might go some way to supporting a case for a close link between masons at each place. That the Wells design is simpler than Glastonbury is clear from Bond's reference to panelled walls at the latter. Bond's reference to Glastonbury as 'vaulted with greater richness and profusion of panel-work' than Wells could imply a design more akin to that at Exeter which had the added 'panels' of the hexagons.[117]

As it happens, there is one vault in the cathedral precinct at Wells that draws together all these forms and motifs — panel work, lozenges (as previously used at Lacock cloister and Wells east end) and lierne vaults. Constructed by Bishop Beckington *c*. 1451, the vault of the Penniless Porch is a more complex version of the cloister applying 'ring-bosses' to the basic vault design at Exeter, but with the intersections providing an opportunity for further cusped lozenges (Fig. 26). It is tempting to speculate that this vault could be a close copy of the Glastonbury cloister. Another reason for risking such a suggestion is one last piece of circumstantial evidence.

FIG. 26. Wells Cathedral: precinct, Penniless Porch vault

Linda Monckton

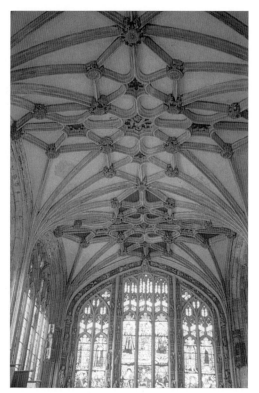

FIG. 27. St Mary's Warwick: Beauchamp Chapel vault

Linda Monckton

Between 1439 and 1462, the executors of Richard Beauchamp, Earl of Warwick constructed a magnificent chapel to the south of the chancel at St Mary's Warwick. The designer of this chapel clearly drew on a range of sources, quoting from a series of the most prestigious buildings in a broad region across the Midlands and West Country.[118] The vault of the chapel is almost identical to that of the Penniless Porch, although notably more elegant in its details and in its execution (Fig. 27). The Beauchamp Chapel vault almost certainly precedes that at the Penniless Porch, and yet both vaults show a clear awareness of the experiments in vaulting in the early and late phases of the Lacock cloister and the earlier general tradition of lozenge and lierne vaults in Wells and its stylistic hinterland. That the Beauchamp Chapel designer, in all other aspects of his design, sought out the most sophisticated models to incorporate into his design may imply that the Penniless Porch and the Beauchamp Chapel share a common source. That Glastonbury Abbey was amongst the richest architectural settings for a monastic community is well known, and it is just possible that it was the cloister at Glastonbury that provided the appropriate model. Such a cloister design at Glastonbury would demonstrate two things. First, that it was heavily indebted to a tradition of vaulting in the south-west of England as it had been practised over the previous 50 years. Secondly, that the aesthetic of the panelled surface articulation at Gloucester could be expressed not with a fan vault, but with a complex lierne.

Although it may be impossible to determine whether the Exeter or Glastonbury cloister was designed first, there remains one further area of ambiguity in relation to these designs. It is known that a mason from Gloucester designed the Exeter cloister; it is equally known that the preceding generation of work at Glastonbury was done with significant reference to Gloucester. Is it possible that the design which became the most sought after alternative to the Gloucester model was created by a Gloucester mason? Lesyngham, at Exeter, is attributed with the fan-vaulted north-west porch of the cathedral. Furthermore, the first known copy of the Exeter cloister vault design appears in the south porch of Gloucester Cathedral, constructed under Abbot Morwent (1421–37).[119] The choice of a lierne vault for the west walk at Exeter may come as much from the context of the adjacent north walk, next to which the fan vault would less easily relate. At Glastonbury the decision to panel the walls and the vault betrays a wholehearted acceptance of the principles of perpendicular architecture. An aesthetic which might as easily be achieved through lierne as fan vault designs.

The cloisters that followed Exeter and Glastonbury in the early years of the 15th century certainly favoured the simplified version. However, a number of vault designs more closely associated with the Exeter (and potentially Glastonbury) model do exist at, for example, the Fromond Chapel, Winchester College (1425–30), and Winscombe parish church tower (1430s) and the south porch of Gloucester, as above.[120] Like the Penniless Porch these are all set pieces indebted to a complex model, which appears not to have been copied so wholeheartedly in a cloister or aisle environment.

CONCLUSION

WHILST many gaps remain, the above paper is an attempt to provide an overview of cloister design from the early 14th to the early 15th century, a period which witnessed more cloister rebuilding than any other except the 12th century. It would be false to suggest that cloisters existed in a vacuum, isolated from other architectural projects, and as this paper has illustrated their design was inextricably linked with the general tradition for vaulting in the West Country in the late Middle Ages. In addition, as most obviously shown in Witney's work, cloister walks might relate to models which range from small-scale furnishings to main vessel vaults. Furthermore such an exchange of ideas between 'micro' and 'macro' remained fluid, and worked in both directions.

Standing buildings alone can provide little insight into the variety of approaches taken to 14th-century cloister design, and it is hoped that the above examples go at least some way to addressing that imbalance. More particularly, design choices made within the context of the cloister had a specific impact on both the future of fan vaulting, as has long been recognised, and, as is less well understood, on the evolution of lierne vaulting. However, to separate these two architectural approaches, as has been necessary here, creates a false dichotomy, and one that was surely not recognised in this way in the Middle Ages. Indeed, it is well established that certain technical characteristics of fan vaulting emerged from lierne vaults, most notably in the fact that the vaults of Ottery transepts and Whitefriars cloister structurally anticipate the fan.[121] Moreover, the cloisters at Exeter and Glastonbury demonstrate that lierne vaults were used to achieve comparable aesthetic goals as the fan vault. That both solutions were both acceptable and compatible is rather neatly illustrated by the construction of a chapel by Isabel Despencer for her husband Richard Beauchamp, Earl of Worcester, in the choir of Tewkesbury Abbey. Built in 1421/22, shortly after the Earl's death, the chapel is an elaborate cage chantry with an upper ceiling underscored by a high, almost flat, vault, and a lower western 'vestibule', also vaulted. The upper vault is tierceron with liernes forming an octagon at the centre, as was used earlier in cloister designs in the south-west (with the added decorative feature of quatrefoils). The lower vault is a fan vault with pendant keystones. Both designs were clearly prestigious and fashionable in the early 15th century.

Cloisters were well suited to adventurous, even experimental, vaulting, and the above examples demonstrate a continuing 14th-century tradition of invention. Many early-15th-century vaults seem explicitly derived from designs that originated in cloisters. The Lady chapel at Christchurch Priory, a variety of chantry-chapels, including the Tewkesbury-Beauchamp chapel, the Beauchamp Chapel at Warwick, even, perhaps, the Lady chapel at Wells, all derived their essential characteristics from vaults first explored in cloisters. That this is so demonstrates the significance attached to them by contemporaries.

Not all cloisters with comparable two-dimensional patterns are necessarily as closely related as some of the buildings discussed above, however. The vault of Worcester Cathedral's cloister is technically similar to that at Wells and Lacock but whilst those south of the Avon appear to be a direct simplification of the assumed Glastonbury or Exeter design, at Worcester an alternative dynamic is evident. Rather than focus on the linear qualities of the design Worcester uses liernes to focus attention on the historiated bosses that animate their junctions.

Otherwise, the West Country examples that have been the subject of this study quite noticeably avoid the historiated approach. Multiple bosses at Exeter are foliate and heraldry at the centre of the bays in the Wells east walk alludes to patronage and episcopal allegiance rather than liturgical narrative. Instead of endorsing the sense of movement — of procession — implicit in the historiated cloister, West Country cloisters focus on architectural expression as a means of characterising the spaces. Visually, it is the bay that defines one's sense of progression through the cloister, and the panelled surfaces enhance a sense of enclosure appropriate to the more static liturgical functions. The very existence of an emerging West Country tradition of complex vault designs, may be the result of masons and patrons making a conscious choice to determine the character and function of cloisters via architectural expression rather than sculptural narrative.

Aside from the influence on buildings outside the monastic enclave, the development of cloisters, therefore, has its own history. The evidence presented above suggests that by the late 14th century two alternative and prestigious models had emerged for the vaulting of cloisters. Because of the acknowledged variety of design in the 14th century, a point reinforced by this paper, the early 15th century has often been associated with a stagnation of architectural ideas. In order to challenge this traditional assumption I would like to paraphrase the late Larry Hoey. In writing about the early Gothic architecture of Anjou he stated that: 'The so-called heroic age of Decorated experimentation . . . could in fact just as easily be characterised as an age of confusion over architectural goals and dissatisfaction with achieved solutions.'[122] That two cloister models established by the end of the 14th century were then used repeatedly, could easily be taken to mean that as far as contemporary patrons were concerned, the form of the cloister had been perfected. Masons and patrons were perhaps at last satisfied that the appropriate models could not be improved upon.

ACKNOWLEDGEMENTS

I have received considerable assistance from a number of people in connection with this article and would particularly like to thank the following: John Allan and Richard Parker from Exeter Archaeology for their willingness to discuss their work, and permission to reproduce images; Jerry Sampson for our joint visits to Wells and Glastonbury; David Kendrick for assistance and provision of photographs relating to Evesham; Richard Lea for his helpful conversations concerning St Paul's Cathedral and John Schofield for access to the historic stone collection. In addition I am grateful to the staff at the Almonry Heritage Museum Evesham, Warwick Rodwell, Alexandrina Buchanan, Zoë Opacic and Pat Payne. John McNeill deserves a particular vote of thanks for his good-natured and helpful comments and keen editorial eye. Finally I would like to express my thanks to Richard K. Morris: many of the projects which form the basis for this paper were carried out jointly with him, and for those opportunities as well as for his continued support and generosity I remain in his debt.

NOTES

1. For debates over the dating of the Salisbury cloister, see T. Cocke and P. Kidson, *Salisbury Cathedral: Perspectives on the Architectural History*, RCHME (London 1993), 8–10. More recently, see T. Tatton Brown, 'Introduction', in *Salisbury Cathedral The West Front: A History and Study in Conservation*, ed. T. Ayers (Chichester 2000), 6 and note 18.

2. For which see J. H. Harvey, *The Perpendicular Style* (London 1978), 34, 43 and 50–51; C. Wilson and T. Cocke, 'Old St. Paul's Cathedral chapter house from the south', in *Age of Chivalry: Art in Plantagenet England 1200–1400*, ed. J. Alexander and P. Binski (London 1987), 369–70; and C. Wilson, 'The Origins of the Perpendicular Style and its development to circa 1360' (unpublished Ph.D. thesis, University of London, 1980), 197–226.

3. Fragments still survive, see Fig. 3.

4. See Harvey, *Perpendicular Style*, fig. 5, 54; and Wilson and Cocke, *Age of Chivalry*, 369–70.

5. The accuracy of the moulding drawings has been confirmed recently by excavations in preparation for new landscaping proposals on the south side of the cathedral. I am grateful to John Schofield for providing this information and access to the excavation.

6. Wilson and Cocke, *Age of Chivalry*, 369–70; and Wilson, 'Origins of Perp', 197–226.

7. I am extremely grateful to Richard Lea for sharing his thoughts and drawings of the chapter-house with me, and to John Schofield for providing access to the Historic Stone Collection at St Paul's.

8. Examples include the initial design for a vaulted east end to All Saint's Maidstone, constructed under the auspices of Archbishop Courtenay from 1395, and St Thomas' Chapel on Old London Bridge dated 1384–96. For which see copy of foundation charter in J. Cave-Browne, *The history of the parish church of All Saints', Maidstone* (Maidstone 1889), Appendix A (5), 233; and B. Watson, T. Birgham and T. Dyson ed., *London Bridge 2000 years of a River Crossing* (London 2001), 109–13. For discussion of these buildings in context, see L. Monckton 'The Collegiate Church of All Saints, Maidstone', in *Medieval Art, Architecture and Archaeology at Rochester*, ed. T. Ayers and T. Tatton Brown, *BAA Trans.*, XXVIII (Leeds 2006), 300–21.

9. W. Hart ed., *Historia et Cartularium Monasterii Sancti Petre Gloucestriae* (London 1863–67), I, 55, as quoted in W. Leedy, *Fan Vaulting: A Study of Form, Technology and Meaning* (London 1980), 167–68.

10. Leedy, *Fan Vaulting*, 168.

11. L. Toulmin Smith ed., *The Itinerary of John Leland, in or about the years 1535 to 1543*, II (Carbondale 1964), 61.

12. Leedy, *Fan Vaulting*, 168.

13. C. Wilson, Review of 'W. Leedy, Fan Vaulting: A Study of Form, Technology and Meaning (London 1980)', *JBAA*, 134 (1981), 138.

14. For example, see Wilson, 'Origins of Perpendicular', 259; and D. Verey and A. Brooks, *Gloucestershire 2: The Vale and the Forest of Dean*, B/E, rev. edn (Harmondsworth 2002), 427.

15. For the two main attempts to date the cloister at Worcester, see J. H. Harvey, 'Notes on the Architects of Worcester Cathedral', *Worcestershire Archaeological Society Transactions*, 33 (1956), 23–27; and R. K. Morris, 'Worcester Nave: From Decorated to Perpendicular', in *Medieval Art and Architecture at Worcester Cathedral*, *BAA Trans.*, 1 (Leeds 1978), 127 and 140–41 note 52. R. K. Morris challenges the alternative

dating and order of the construction of the walks at Worcester offered in Harvey, 'Architects of Worcester', 23–27. He suggests that work may have begun as early as 1372 preceding works on the chapter-house with a subsequent sequence of the west walk (1390s) followed by the north and south walks in the early 15th century. The volume of work to buildings adjacent to the chapter-house in the 1370s (the library and treasury), however, may make it more likely that the east walk followed on from this rather than being at the same time, and therefore after 1377, suggesting a date close to the works of the chapter-house itself. For which see J. Greatrex, 'The Layout of the Monastic Church, Cloister and Precinct of Worcester: Evidence in the Written Records', in 'Archaeology at Worcester Cathedral: Report on the Eighth Annual Symposium March 1998', ed. Chris Guy (1998), 12–18.

16. H. Brakspear, 'Lacock Abbey', *Archaeologia*, 62 (1900), 136–39; and L. Monckton, 'Late Gothic Architecture in South West England' (unpublished Ph.D. thesis, University of Warwick, 1999), vol. 1, 66.

17. My thanks to John McNeill for drawing my attention to this.

18 See for example L. Colchester, *Wells Cathedral* (London 1987), 72–76; and most recently W. Rodwell, *Wells Cathedral: Excavations and Structural Studies, 1978–93*, 1 (London 2001), 246.

19. Colchester, *Wells Cathedral*, 74; and Rodwell, *Wells*, I, 246–47.

20. For which see Wells Cathedral Fabric Accounts, Wells Cathedral Archive, transcribed by L. S. Colchester, 12–13; and Rodwell, *Wells*, I, 247.

21. Colchester, *Wells Cathedral*, 72–72; and Monckton, 'Late Gothic Architecture', 89–90.

22. Colchester, *Wells Cathedral*, 76–77.

23. J. Sherwood and N. Pevsner, *Oxfordshire*, B/E (Harmondsworth 1974), 159. For summary of development of east end of Winchester, see P. Draper and R. K. Morris, 'The Development of the East End of Winchester Cathedral from the 13th to the 16th century', in *Winchester Cathedral Nine Hundred Years 1093 to 1993*, ed. J. Crook (Chichester 1993), 189.

24. J. A. A. Goodall, 'The Aerary Porch and its Influence on Late Medieval English Vaulting', in *St George's Chapel Windsor in the Fourteenth Century*, ed. N. Saul (Woodbridge 2005), 166, 172 and 175; Wilson, 'Review of Leedy', 138.

25. Goodall, 'Aerary Porch', 179.

26. For St Stephen's Westminster, see Wilson, 'Origins of Perpendicular', 34–111.

27. Wilson, 'Origins of Perpendicular', 268–69; and Goodall, 'Aerary Porch', 178–79.

28. Wilson, 'Origins of Perpendicular', 259–77, considers the likelihood that the designer of the Gloucester cloister was familiar with works for which the south-east based mason, William Ramsey, was responsible.

29. Leedy, *Fan Vaulting*, 8.

30. D. C. Cox, *The Chronicle of Evesham Abbey: an English translation* (Evesham 1964), 50.

31. ibid., 50.

32. Cox, *Chronicle*, 19–21.

33. Cox, *Chronicle*, 58, states the rebuilding was between 1367 and 1379. Also see Leedy, *Fan Vaulting*, 8 and note 26, quoting London, British Library, Harley MS 3763, f. 176.

34. D. C. Cox, 'The Building, Destruction, and Excavation of Evesham Abbey: a Documentary History', *Transactions of the Worcestershire Archaeological Society*, 3rd Series, 12 (1990), 137.

35. Visits to Abbey Manor were made by Dr R. K. Morris and David Kendrick in February 1998 and January 2002, and with the author in April 2003. I am grateful to David Kendrick for providing photographs from these visits.

36. These could be either trefoil headed lights or partially revealed quatrefoils.

37. An example of this piece can also be found in the garden of the Almonry Heritage Museum in Evesham.

38. It must be stated clearly at this stage that all of these fragments have neither a provenance nor context, and a detailed examination of the pieces has not yet been possible. Unfortunately, since the earlier visits, some of them seem to have disappeared from the site. A similar piece, with trefoil and blind panelled decoration can be found behind the wooden shed in the garden of the Almonry Heritage Museum; this piece was attached to a solid wall rather than forming part of a free-standing screen.

39. Wilson, 'Origins of Perpendicular', 170.

40. There remains a debate about the form of the vaulting of the Hereford chapter-house. It is thought that work began *c.* 1340 but that the chapter-house was not vaulted until after 1364, at which time a contract was drawn up with the mason Thomas of Cambridge. William Stukeley visited the site in 1721, by which time the chapter-house was already demolished, and produced a reconstruction drawing which showed the chapter-house with a fan vault. This was generally accepted until questioned by Leedy (Leedy, *Fan Vaulting*, 172). Wilson preferred to adopt Stukeley's position believing that Leedy was playing down the significance of Hereford, for which see Wilson, 'Origins of Perpendicular', 274; and Wilson, 'Review of Leedy', 139. Morris, however, makes a good case for the vault being a complex lierne, more like the Tewkesbury presbytery vault than a fan vault, accepting that it may have used fan springers, for which see R. K. Morris, 'The Architectural

History of the Medieval Cathedral Church', in *Hereford Cathedral: A History*, ed. G. Aylmer and J. Tiller (London 2000), 227–29. The Morris (and Leedy) argument for a lierne rather than a fan vault is accepted here.

41. J. H. Harvey, *English Mediaeval Architects: A Biographical Dictionary down to 1550* (Gloucester 1984), 181; and Harvey, *The Perpendicular Style*, 112.

42. Leedy, *Fan Vaulting*, 207.

43 R. K. Morris, 'The Monastic Buildings', in *Tewkesbury Abbey: History, Art and Architecture*, ed. R. K. Morris and R. Shoesmith (Almeley 2003), 149–50.

44. R. K. Morris, 'The Worked Stone and Architectural Stonework', in *The Archaeology of the medieval Cathedral and Priory of St Mary, Coventry*, ed. M. Rylatt and P. Mason (Coventry 2003), 65, and for illustration see fig. 49a, 66.

45. Gloucester's direct imitators seem to be confined to a geographical area, north of Bristol. Its influence further afield was less direct. Although beyond the scope of this paper, the centre for fan vaulting designs seems to shift towards Oxford and its hinterland in the second quarter of the 15th century.

46. Leedy, *Fan Vaulting*, 11.

47. Monckton, 'Late Gothic Architecture', 70–77; and J. H. P. Gibb, 'The Fire of 1437 and the Rebuilding of Sherborne Abbey', *JBAA*, 138 (1985), 101–16.

48. J. M. Luxford, 'The Founders' Book', in *Tewkesbury Abbey: History, Art and Architecture*, ed. R. K. Morris and R. Shoesmith (Almeley 2003), 60.

49. See R. K. Morris, 'Thomas of Witney at Exeter, Winchester and Wells', in *Medieval Art and Architecture at Exeter Cathedral*, ed. F. Kelly, BAA Trans., XI (Leeds 1991), 57–84; H. Bock, 'The Exeter Rood Screen', *Architectural Review*, 130 (1961), 313–17; and P. Crossley, 'Peter Parler and England: A Problem Revisited', *Sonderdruck aus dem Wallraf-Richartz-Jahrbuch*, LXIV (2003), 62. Jean Bony considers the Bristol high vault to be the earliest net vault, which he dates to c. 1300 (J. Bony, *The English Decorated Style: Gothic Architecture Transformed 1250–1350* (Oxford 1979), 50), but the sequence of construction of the east end of St Augustine's, Bristol was reassessed in R. K. Morris, 'European prodigy or regional eccentric? The rebuilding of St Augustine's Abbey Church, Bristol', in *Almost the Richest City: Bristol in the Middle Ages*, ed. L. Keen, BAA Trans., XIX (Leeds 1997), 41–56. Morris suggested that the aisle vaults were constructed c. 1320 and the high vaults of the choir and Lady chapel in the 1330s or 1340s.

50. This was first pointed out in 1961 by Bock, 'Exeter Rood Screen', 313–17.

51. Harvey, *English Mediaeval Architects*, 339.

52. See Crossley, 'Peter Parler', 53–82, for the most recent consideration of the chronology and development of this series of vaults.

53. For William Joy, see Harvey, *English Mediaeval Architects*, 164–65.

54. For Redcliffe, see L. Monckton, 'The Myth of William Canynges and the late medieval Rebuilding of St Mary Redcliffe', in *Almost the Richest City: Bristol in the Middle Ages*, ed. L. Keen, BAA Trans., XIX (Leeds 1997), 57–67. Wilson, in 'Origins of Perpendicular', 274, implies that William Ramsey may have been involved in both the south transept at Redcliffe and at Ottery St Mary. Whilst the south transept at Redcliffe shows differences in overall style and handling to the rest of the late medieval rebuilding, the work at Ottery, and in particular the choir and Lady chapel vaults, are handled in a way so close in style, construction and date to those known to have been by Joy at Wells that here he is considered to be responsible for the Ottery designs.

55. For what follows I am extremely grateful to Richard Parker and largely dependent on his work for Exeter Archaeology.

56. A. M. Erskine, *The Accounts of the Fabric of Exeter Cathedral 1279–1353, Part I 1279–1326* (Torquay 1983), 60; R. W. Parker and J. Z. Crocker, 'Exeter Cathedral Cloisters Evaluation: Part I Reconstruction Drawings and Documentary Research', Exeter Archaeology Report No. 98.34 (1998), 7–8; and P. M. Stead and R. W. Parker, 'Exeter Cathedral Cloisters Evaluation: Part 2 Archaeological Evaluation Excavation', Exeter Archaeology Report No. 98.66 (1998), 13.

57. A. M. Erskine, *The Accounts of the Fabric of Exeter Cathedral 1279–1353, Part II 1328–1353* (Torquay 1983), 250.

58. Harvey, *English Mediaeval Architects*, 181.

59. R. W. Parker, 'Archaeo-Historical Assessment of Exeter Cathedral Cloisters', Exeter Archaeology Report 97.42 (1997), 19.

60. For summaries, see Parker, 'Archaeo-Historical Assessment'; Parker and Crocker, 'Cloisters Evaluation Part 1'; and Stead and Parker 'Cloisters Evaluation Part 2'.

61. Erskine, *Exeter Fabric Accounts*, I, 73 and 77, and II, xx; Harvey, *English Mediaeval Architects*, 339; and Morris, 'Thomas of Witney', 57–58.

62. Harvey, *English Mediaeval Architects*, 339; and Erskine, *Exeter Fabric Accounts*, II, xx–xxi.

63. Erskine, *Exeter Fabric Accounts*, II, xxx–xxxii.

64. Morris, 'Thomas of Witney', 62.

65. See Parker, 'Archaeo-Historical Assessment'.

66. J. F. Chanter, 'The Story of the Cloisters of Exeter Cathedral, 1250–1930', *Transactions of the Exeter Diocesan Architectural and Archaeological Society*, IV, 3rd Series (1929), 135–49.

67. Stead and Parker, 'Cloister Evaluation Part 2', 14–15.

68. Morris, 'Thomas of Witney', 62–71.

69. Parker has suggested that 5 were required for each bay, with 4 for bay one (i.e.: the westernmost bay of the north walk), for which see Parker and Crocker, 'Cloister Evaluation Part 1', 2; and Parker, 'Archaeo-Historical Assessment', 9.

70. H. Brakspear, 'Exeter Cathedral plan', *Archaeol. J.*, XX (1913), fig. 6, facing 518.

71. Parker, 'Archaeo-Historical Assessment', 9–10.

72. The design of the choir aisles in Wells Cathedral both share the same pattern and disposition of ribs, but the south aisle is a series of domes and the north a more conventional quadrapartite vault. It has been suggested by Dr Alexandrina Buchanan, to whom I am grateful for this observation, that this may indicate the interpretation of the same 'pattern' by different masons.

73. P. Crossley, 'Wells, the West Country, and Central European Late Gothic', in *Medieval Art and Architecture at Well and Glastonbury*, ed. N.Coldstream and P. Draper, *BAA Trans.*, IV (Leeds 1981), 92.

74. See Crossley, 'Peter Parler'.

75. Crossley, 'Wells and the West Country', 90–92.

76. Crossley, 'Peter Parler', 68.

77. Erskine, *Exeter Fabric Accounts*, II, xxx.

78. P. Draper, 'The Sequence and Dating of the Decorated Architecture at Wells', in *Medieval Art and Architecture at Wells and Glastonbury*, ed. N. Coldstream and P. Draper, *BAA Trans.*, IV (Leeds 1981), 18–29.

79. Erskine, *Exeter Fabric Accounts*, II, 250.

80. ibid., II, 250.

81. ibid., II, xxxi.

82. Crossley, 'Peter Parler', 68.

83. It is noteworthy that the south choir aisle was also constructed with domical vaults, see note 72 above, under Witney's successor William Joy after 1329. However after this domical vaults seem to pass out of use at Wells, at least in aisle and cloister spaces.

84. L. Toulmin Smith, *The Itinerary of John Leland in or about the years 1535–1543*, I (London 1964), 153 and 295.

85. Morris, 'Thomas of Witney', 65–66 and fig. 6.

86. For a fuller description of the architectural fragments and their use in a reconstruction of the cloister at Sherborne, see R. K. Morris, L. Monckton and J. West, 'The worked Stones and Medieval Architecture', in *Sherborne Abbey and School: Excavations 1972–76 and 1990*, ed. L. Keen and P. Ellis (Dorchester 2005), especially 83 to 101.

87. For which see S. Harrison, R. K. Morris and D. Robinson, 'A Fourteenth-Century Pulpitum Screen at Tintern Abbey, Monmouthshire', *Antiq. J.*, 78 (1998), 177–268.

88. For account of this vault type, its history and relationship to Tintern, see ibid., 226–28.

89. J. Cattell, 'The Standing Building with a detailed analysis of the east cloister range', in *The Church of Our Lady of Mount Carmel and some conventual buildings at the Whitefriars, Coventry*, ed. C. Woodfield (Oxford 2005), 22–47.

90. Harvey, *English Mediaeval Architects*, 244.

91. See Harrison, Morris and Robinson, *Tintern Pulpitum*, 227 and 206 and note 107, where it is suggested that the design emanates from Bristol at this date.

92. See Harvey, *English Mediaeval Architects*, 31, who attributes the tomb to Box. For an attribution to Ramsey, see C. Wilson, 'The Medieval Monuments', in *A History of Canterbury Cathedral*, ed. P. Collinson, N. Ramsay and M. Sparks (Oxford 1995), 468–69.

93. Harrison, Morris and Robinson, 227, 206 and note 107.

94. ibid., 227, 206 and note 107 for a discussion of whether this vault design was first developed in the south-east or south-west. Current evidence would appear to support a West Country origin.

95. Parker and Crocker, 'Cloisters Evaluation part 1', 11–12 quoting from D&C fabric rolls 2640; and Harvey, *English Mediaeval Architects*, 181.

96. A. Erskine, V. Hope and J. Lloyd, *Exeter Cathedral: A Short History and Description* (Exeter 1988), 45.

97. Parker, 'Archaeo-Historical Assessment', 15.

98. A. Erskine, V. Hope and J. Lloyd, *Exeter Cathedral: A Short History and Description* (Exeter 1988), 45.

99. Parker and Crocker, 'Cloisters Evaluation Part 1', 19, quoting D&C Records 2670 and 2673. For a more detailed summary of progress, see Parker, 'Archaeo-Historical Assessment', 15–18.

100. Parker, 'Archaeo-Historical Assessment', 17.

101. ibid., 35.

102. ibid., 36.

103. ibid., pl. 32 shows the vault respond that still survives in the basement of No. 1 The Cloisters and on which such assertions can be confidently based.

104. ibid., 36, referencing D&C 3593, 186.

105. Monckton, 'Late Gothic Architecture', I, 151–57.

106. Toulmin Smith, I, 289.

107. F. B. Bond, *An Architectural Handbook of Glastonbury Abbey* (Wellingborough 1909), 32.

108. F. B. Bond, 'Glastonbury Abbey: Third Report on the Discoveries made during the excavations 1909–10', *Proceedings of the Somerset Archaeological and Natural History Society*, VLI, part ii (1910), 69–70.

109. F. B. Bond, 'Glastonbury Abbey: Fourth Report on the Discoveries made during the excavations 1910–11', *Proceedings of the Somerset Archaeological and Natural History Society*, VLII, part ii (1911), 79. Plate iii does not illustrate the cloister fragments, although referenced as such in the text.

110. For attribution to Abbot Monington, see Toulmin Smith, I, 289; see Wilson, 'Origins of Perpendicular', especially 319–23, for discussion of Gloucester and Glastonbury; and Bond, *Handbook*, 31, for discussion of the influence of Wells and Gloucester on works of Monington.

111. Wilson, 'Origins of Perpendicular', 321.

112. Illustrated in F. B. Bond, 'Glastonbury Abbey: Second Report on the Discoveries made during the excavations 1908–09', *Proceedings of the Somerset Archaeological and Natural History Society*, VL, part ii (1909), facing 115.

113. Leedy, *Fan Vaulting*, 165–66 and fig. 141. This fragment is currently exhibited in the visitor centre.

114. Note for example that a flat tear-drop shaped panel would probably have existed, as, for example, at Sherborne, adjacent to a chancel arch. The fleurons imply the piece formed part of a jamb and arch.

115. Brakspear, 'Lacock Abbey', 136–39, suggests a date in the early 15th century; a date supported by the mouldings which relate closely to those at St John's, Yeovil and Sherborne Abbey (south nave aisle and related buildings, for which see Monckton, 'Late Gothic Architecture', I, 66 and 154–57, and II, fig. 5.9).

116. J. Sampson, 'Glastonbury Abbey south nave aisle: archaeological survey of the standing fabric 2004' (unpublished report for Glastonbury Abbey Trustees, 2004).

117. Bond, 'Glastonbury Abbey: Third Report', 69–70.

118. For which see L. Monckton, 'Fit for a King? The Architecture of the Beauchamp Chapel', *Architectural History*, 47 (2004), 25–52.

119. The attribution to Morwent's abbacy is generally accepted, as Morwent is known to have been responsible for the rebuilding of the west end of the nave; see for example, Verey and Brooks, *Gloucestershire 2*, B/E, 398 and 400.

120. Monckton, 'Late Gothic Architecture', I, 152–53.

121. For which see Wilson, 'Origins of Perpendicular', 265–67.

122. L. Hoey, 'An Outsider Looks at Angevin Gothic Architecture', in *Anjou: Medieval Art, Architecture and Archaeology*, ed. J. McNeill and D. Prigent, *BAA Trans.*, XXVI (Leeds 2003), 183.

Religious Politics and the Cloister Bosses of Norwich Cathedral

VERONICA SEKULES

In this paper, I argue that analysis of the imagery associated with the late medieval cloister of Norwich Cathedral priory sheds light on crucial issues of the statement of belief and purpose in the monastery, suggesting that the choice and use of imagery in this institutional environment was a direct response to challenges from other authorities. I explore some of the means by which visual imagery indicates attitudes to religious orthodoxy and worship, in terms of learning and the interpretation of scripture, of rituals and their organisation, and also through didactic ambitions to reinforce the authority of the Bible. Aspects of the choice and placing of imagery of the Norwich cloister bosses are seen as responses to particular historical and intellectual circumstances relating to broader political and religious agendas in and beyond the monastery.

LATE medieval religion is generally understood in terms of the growth of lay concerns such as patronage in towns, the rise of confraternities and professional guilds, personal devotion and the institution of new feasts.[1] For his essay in the Victoria and Albert Museum's Gothic exhibition catalogue, Eamon Duffy highlighted the burgeoning lay patronage and devotion associated with the Parish church during the 15th century:

If the high middle ages was the age of the Great Church, of cathedral and monastery, then the century and a half after the Black Death was emphatically the age of the parish church and the lay people that worshipped there ... The emergence in the course of the 14th century of the vernacular theologies associated with so-called 'mystics' like Richard Rolle of Hampole, Walter Hilton and, later, Julian of Norwich was another manifestation of the ferment produced by this democratisation and vernacularisation of religion ...[2]

This view remains a convincing and dominant one. If we concentrate on parish churches, consider who paid for them and then look at the wider pattern of patronage and religious observance, preaching, the publication of guides to lay devotion, moralising literature aimed at the layman and woman, the conclusion that the context for personal devotion really developed and broadened in the later Middle Ages is obvious and inescapable. However, the cloistered life, and what could be termed the mainstream orthodoxy of the monasteries, continued alongside these new developments. Monasteries and friaries had to reconsider their position, even if this meant trying to redefine themselves against these new vernacular and populist forces. As Andrew Brown has recently emphasised, while the institutions of the Church resorted, especially after the Black Death, to what he called the 'corporate devotion' of communal celebration such as the founding of guilds, lay devotion was often

JBAA, vol. 159 (2006), 284–306
© British Archaeological Association 2006
DOI: 10.1179/174767006X147451

self-motivated and independent.[3] On the other hand, ascetic and self-denying piety continued to be accommodated institutionally, within orthodox structures like monasteries.[4] Julian Luxford's recent study of Benedictine patronage in West Country England has highlighted the continuous role of art in the monastery as an expressive and unifying tool with a political as well as a religious role to play. He provides a sustained picture of the commissioning of works of art as being in the interests of the whole Benedictine order, in that they provided potential links between the physical development of the monastery, devotional practice, and the continual reinforcement of religious identity and belief.[5]

From the middle of the 13th century monasteries had to compete with friaries and colleges, not only for recruits, but for the care of souls; for claims to authority about the nature of piety, instruments of belief and the ways in which to pursue devotion. The shedding of unnecessary show and pomp, of hierarchy, of ceremonial, came from various quarters, from mendicant friars, beginning in the first quarter of the 13th century, and then with increased rigour after the 1380s via Wycliffe and the Lollards, who espoused an alternative asceticism which threatened the monastic establishment.[6]

NORWICH

NORMAN TANNER has described Norwich as a city of exceptional piety, indeed, possibly medieval Europe's most religious city.[7] He noted, among its 'new movements', a complex of developments during the 14th and 15th centuries, that included both the enhancement of individual and lay devotion and an increase in associated forms of social and religious organisation. These included *beguinages* and their equivalents, provision for anchorites and hermits, craft guilds and confraternities, the commissioning of and worship at private chapels, the founding of chantries and devotional practices and cults, such as pilgrimage, and the celebration of new feasts and masses for the dead.[8]

For the purposes of analysis of the new forces at work in religious life of the city, Tanner included the friaries with the established institutions, described by him as 'the old order'.[9] However, there were many circumstances in which the four main friary churches in the city offered alternatives to the parish churches and the cathedral for the local population, for choice of burial site and associated benefactions, as well as for kinds of worship.[10] Well known for their accessible and lively preaching style, they competed for attention with the Cathedral's own preaching yard. Like the cathedral, they also provided libraries and intellectual leadership, although the cathedral seems to have been the only provider of education available to lay boys rather than just for trainee monks and priests.[11]

However, an impression emerges that from the 13th to the 15th century, an undercurrent of dispute existed between the cathedral and the city, between the cathedral and the friaries and, within the cathedral itself, between the bishop and the priory. Between the bishop and the priory there were further running disagreements over governance of land and property and payment of tithes, but also over disciplinary matters concerning the admission of novices and monitoring of behaviour. On matters of protocol specifically between the prior and the bishop, there were disputes over who took precedence in church.[12] Tense relations between the priory and townspeople over rights to land and income erupted into violence directed at the cathedral in 1272 and again, but less seriously, in 1443.[13] Elsewhere I have written about the Ethelbert

FIG. 1.   Norwich Cathedral priory cloister: north and east walks
Veronica Sekules

Gate leading into the Cathedral Close from Tombland, the area under contention in these 13th-century disputes, and which had to be rebuilt as a result of damage to the fabric during the riots. I suggested that the imagery chosen for the spandrels over the main arch, of a man fighting a dragon, originally presided over by Christ displaying his wounds, was derived from a biblical reference, specifically invoked in order to reclaim the symbolic authority of the church.[14] It is precisely this idea of the strategic use of imagery which I intend to develop in analysing the cloister.

NORWICH CLOISTER AND ITS ANTECEDENTS

THE existing cloister at Norwich was begun at the end of the 13th century after the completion of the Chapter House in 1292–93 (Fig. 1 and Appendix). Both these projects are normally attributed to a need to repair parts of the precinct, following damage by townspeople in 1272. However, as was discovered during a restoration in the early 1900s when 12th-century capitals from the first cloister came to light having been re-used as building material, the new cloister was neither a straightforward replacement nor a structural repair, but a radical departure from the original design, to the extent that it might be described as a complete reconceptualisation.[15] The damage may have provided the initial impetus, but the scale of the response was far

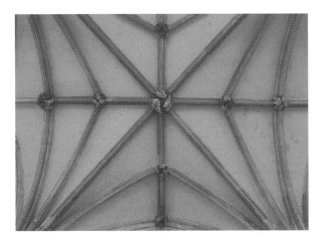

FIG. 2.   East walk showing foliate
bosses at south end
Veronica Sekules

greater than necessary. This suggests that there were other issues at work, not just practical and financial ones. The result was a sustained period of rebuilding lasting over a hundred years.

The 12th-century cloister had an open arcade supported by twin columns carrying double capitals. The capitals were carved intricately with narrative, decorative, and combat imagery. Jill Franklin has argued that they carried a number of symbolic messages, broadly concerning the struggle against evil, but that their placement was very unlikely to have been organised programmatically. She noted that there was a predominance of pagan themes and classical allusions, which led her to suggest that the imagery of the capitals was deliberately historicising, perhaps with a pedagogical or mnemonic function connected with teachings in the cathedral school.[16]

The post-1290s rebuilding, which continued through a number of different campaigns over a period of 133 years, substituted traceried arcades, and rather than being on capitals carved imagery was transposed to the ceiling in the form of roof bosses incorporated in a lierne vault (Fig. 2). Especially in the earliest phases, the general characteristics of the imagery are not so different from the 12th-century version. Green men (also with pagan and classical origins) are substituted for figures engulfed in foliage, and comical or grotesque figures form an equivalent to the combat scenes. However, in pride of place along the central ribs at the northern end of the east walk is a sequence of Passion scenes, bringing a programmatic narrative element emphatically into the scheme. This involvement with narrative becomes stronger and more explicit in the extensive Apocalypse sequence and lives of saints of the later 14th- and 15th-century phases, and there are other pedagogical techniques employed later too, such as the amplification of stories through repetition and digression. If this imagery was there to support teaching, priorities had changed markedly over the period.

The cloister rebuilding coincided with an extended phase of monastic reform concerned specifically with training and education, which was expressed in Capitular Statutes in 1277 and 1343.[17] Joan Greatrex has shown that the challenge of the friaries caused something of a crisis in the Benedictine General Chapter, leading it to recommend the abandonment of outworn observances from the past, adding new impetus to the quest for recruits who might be especially interested in learning, even though, as it turned out, their efforts were only partially successful.[18]

Even if the cloister imagery was not intended specifically for teaching, and I do not seek to tie it to a specific didactic purpose or syllabus, it is undoubtedly expressive of changing intellectual patterns and references. Indeed, the difference between the earlier and later imagery illustrates a change in emphasis within the monastery — from an open-ended allusion to moral qualities and attitudes in the 12th-century sequence, to a much clearer, more targeted collection of visual reference points directed to specific biblical narratives, hagiography and moralising story-telling, in the 14th and 15th centuries. There may be something in the changed circumstances outside the monastery, a new spirit of competition, which caused this change of emphasis.[19]

It is, I suggest, no accident that the new cloister at Norwich began in the episcopate of one of only two bishops of Norwich who was also a monk, the much venerated John Salmon, and a man who had a particular interest in strengthening the spiritual, intellectual and processional heart of the monastery.[20] Another pertinent factor was that the cloister campaign coincided with a period of expansion of the friaries in Norwich, all of whom undertook building campaigns in the first half of the 14th century.[21] This was an opportunity for the Benedictine monastery to display its wealth and distinctiveness and rebuild beyond the minimum necessitated after the riots.

There are few extant models for a vaulted cloister punctuated by figured roof bosses from as early a date as the 1290s. Martial Rose, who wrote the most recent accounts of the bosses at Norwich, claimed they were unique.[22] Certainly, in terms of the scale of the operation and the range of the imagery, they are without parallel for their date. However, Norwich is contemporary with the wooden roof bosses at the cloister at Lincoln Minster, and given the low survival rate of cloisters there may well have been precedents, both in wood and very probably in stone.[23] The wooden bosses at Lincoln are in fact comparable in their range of imagery to the first sequence of bosses at Norwich at the north end of the East walk, containing animal combats and foliage with some New Testament scenes concentrated in the section of cloister between the chapter-house entrance and the church.[24]

Dating and organisation of the sculpture

THE history of the cloister rebuilding, which lasted from 1297–1430, is summarised in a short narrative account recorded in the first register (see Appendix for a summary of the documentation).[25] Accounts for the progress of the building survive in the Communar and Pitancer Rolls.[26] Identifications of the sculpture by M. R. James have provided a foundation for later study,[27] and subsequently both Eric Fernie and Frank Woodman published suggested chronologies for the building of the cloisters based on a combination of interpretations of the accounts and stylistic analysis of the building.[28] They were principally interested in the architecture and their analyses concentrated on mouldings and tracery rather than sculpture. The most recent work on the bosses by Martial Rose followed an extensive programme of restoration, and photography by Julia Hedgcoe.[29]

Fernie and Woodman are broadly in agreement that the building of the walls on the cloister garth side, including the tracery, proceeded in a reasonably continuous sequence, following the dates of the documented benefactions from 1290 to c. 1400. Both of them based their analyses on the tracery patterns, for which the crucial interventions were thought to have been made by John and William Ramsay from c. 1335.[30] As far as the earliest parts of the campaign are concerned, they both accept that the record of John Salmon's benefaction applies to work done on the east range and the ten bays alongside the refectory. Woodman dates the sequence of Passion bosses in the east range to 1327–29 and the rest of the bosses in the east range to 1299–1314.[31] Fernie suggests a general dating for the east range, 1299–*c.* 1314.[32] Fernie then dates the south walk to 1314–30 and Woodman to 1320–29.

I think there are both stylistic and historical reasons for differing slightly from this suggested dating. My analysis starts from the premise that work on the cloister proceeded not only in different phases, but that each element of the building, that is, the arcades, their tracery infills, and the vaulting and the bosses, were not synchronised, but followed separate schedules. It follows that dating of the bosses is not necessarily tied to that of the tracery. The essential prerequisite for the vaulting and the bosses was only the arches themselves. Indeed, I suggest that the cloister arcades were rebuilt first, which would have necessitated the removal of the 12th-century arcades in the first campaigns. Evidence for this is provided by the sculpture. It is clear that, with only one or two exceptions, all the corbels forming the keystones for the arches of the arcade are part of a sequence continuous from the earliest work in the east. Many of the figurative keystones are fairly certainly by one of the artists who was involved in the vault campaigns for the east and south walks, and the foliate corbels are consistent with the soft waving style of foliage carving which was not current much beyond the 1350s (Fig. 3 a–d). This suggests that the entire cloister was laid out and its outer walls constructed by the 1350s.

The tracery infills were a separate campaign, and the vaulting and the bosses followed still later. This is where I differ most from Fernie and Woodman. I prefer to suggest that the dates associated with Salmon's bequest refer to the construction of the east and south walks, but not necessarily to all their vaulting. There is a hiatus in the funds for building from *c.* 1330 for a few years. This, I suggest, marks the completion of the east range, including its bosses. Then, clearly, substantial new work was planned and materials acquired in the mid- to late 1330s. The acquisition of an apocalypse manuscript, expenditure for which is documented in the Communar and Pitancer rolls for 1346, can be linked to this phase, and I believe marks the start of the vaulting campaign for the south range. [33] Furthermore, work on vaulting in the 1360s, which Fernie and Whittingham attributed to the west walk, cannot apply to that part of the building as work on some of the lower parts was not started until 1411 (see Appendix), and it is much more likely that the south walk vaulting continued until the end of that phase in 1364. Meanwhile, work on the west walk tracery bays was continuing throughout the 1340s. Fernie suggests that the ninth bay, constructed of wood, was an economy measure built around the time of the Black Death, when the cathedral also lost two of the master masons. Then, according to the documents, the first three bays of the north walk were constructed in the early 1350s, with the rest of that walk, including its upper parts but excluding the vaults.

While I agree with Fernie's dating of the outer walls and tracery, for the roof bosses, I would prefer to suggest a slight modification:

East walk: 1320–30;
South walk: 1346–64 (with a possible extension into the south-west corner until *c.* 1380);
West walk: 1411–25;
North walk: 1423–28.

Layout of the bosses

AN important aspect of the power and importance of the cloister for the monastery was the fact that it was enclosed and faced inward, serving as the main vehicle of

FIG. 3a.   Keystone for arch on west side of
east walk
Veronica Sekules

FIG. 3b.   South walk arch keystone
Veronica Sekules

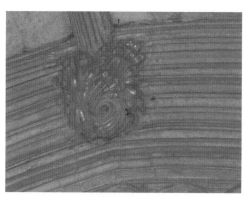

FIG. 3c.   West walk arch keystone
Veronica Sekules

FIG. 3d.   North walk arch keystone
Veronica Sekules

circulation for the monks between their living accommodation and places of worship.
It also functioned as a place of learning, both literally and symbolically.[34] The
sculpture is carefully organised so as to allow some measure of reading from any
direction, while making it clear which views were favoured for important routes and
processions.[35]

The figures of the east walk bosses are designed to be seen the right way up by a
viewer who is walking from the church to the chapter-house, but the Passion narrative
sequence works the other way, from south to north (Fig. 4). While Fernie remarks that
the bosses therefore make sense whichever direction one is walking in, it is also important to note that the culmination of the narrative is the Judgment imagery of the
Prior's door, very much a part of the experience, and that a directional reading from
south to north should take priority.[36] The rest of bosses in the east walk, south of the
chapter-house, are mainly foliate, but in the south walk, the subject of the imagery

Fig. 4.   East walk: Resurrection
boss surrounded by foliate bosses
Veronica Sekules

changes quite suddenly to the Apocalypse. Here we can observe the same phenomenon, of narrative and composition going in opposite directions, meaning now that
the heads are the right way up when walking from west to east and the narrative
sequence goes from east towards west. So, a viewer starting at the prior's door would
begin seeing images the wrong way up as they turned the corner to go west. There is
also a difference in the placing and emphasis of the narrative. The Passion narrative in
the east walk is carried by the main boss at the centre of each bay (Fig. 4). All the
subsidiary bosses are decorative. In the south walk, the Apocalypse narrative is
continuous along the central spine and furthermore, the bosses linking the ribs at the
intersections between the bays also carry the main narrative. These changes in how
the bosses are organised reinforce the idea that there was a break between the sculpture campaigns in the east and the south walks. As the viewer turns from the south
walk northwards into the west walk the images are still the wrong way up, but the
narrative sequence continues running clockwise from the south walk. It is only as one
turns the corner from the north end of the west walk to walk eastwards into the north
walk that the images and the sequence are in parallel, that is, they are both going in
the same direction, and are seen the right way up by someone walking along from
west to east.

The direction of boss images seems to have been designed, aesthetically at least, to
make sense in terms of approach from the two church doors: from the prior's door to
the infirmary entrance at the south-east corner, and then again from the nave door in
the north-west corner, the bosses are the right way up not only when travelling east,
but also when travelling south, right round to the south-east corner. If this follows
processional routes, as Gilchrist suggests, it implies that the west door was the main
processional exit from the church for going in either direction, and that the east door
was used for access to the chapter-house and infirmary.[37]

However, there are also variations in terms of the directions the bosses face within
each bay, which reflect design changes made during separate building campaigns. In
the east walk, the central bosses carrying the narrative face the same way and the side
bosses, mainly foliate, are without direction. In the south walk, and the two southern
bays of the west walk, the central bosses face the same way and the side bosses, only

some of which carry the main narrative, face outwards away from them (Fig. 9B). For the rest of the west walk and the north walk, the four side bosses face in towards the central boss, and the bosses on the bay-dividing ribs face the same way as the central boss (Fig. 14). In both these walks, the main narratives also extend across the whole vault. All these directional variations suggest a break between the east and south walks, and another between the south-west corner and the west and north walks. These anomalies and changes in details of the layout are consistent with the changes in decisions about the imagery I outline below.

IMAGERY AND ARTISTS, SUBJECTS AND CONTEXT

The Passion in the East Walk

THE bosses of the east walk form two phases, one incorporating the Passion sequence north of the chapter-house, the other, consisting mainly of foliage and green men, extending south from the chapter-house to the south-east corner. At the north end subsidiary bosses and corbels carry genre scenes and four figures of the evangelists. The Passion scenes clearly lead up to the prior's door into the church, against the arch of which figures are placed radially, centring on Christ in Majesty displaying his wounds, flanked by two angels holding symbols of the Passion, St Peter as Pope (holding the Church), St Edmund, St John the Baptist, and Moses. Apart from the obvious Christ in Judgement, it emphasises, as has often been pointed out, the old law and the new law as well as authority, temporal and spiritual, a theme to which we shall return (Fig. 5).[38]

The Passion sequence extends to five scenes in this walk: The Flagellation (Fig. 6), Christ carrying the cross, the Crucifixion, the Resurrection, and the Harrowing of Hell. It may not be a coincidence that this was the first major programme of imagery at Norwich following the expulsion of the Jews in 1290, after which emphasis on the Redemption through Christ may have served to reaffirm the core of the Christian faith. The genre scenes which border the Passion sequence include combats between men and animals, acrobatic feats, a woman snatching her washing back from a child who is evidently trying to steal it; and, as Eric Fernie noted, a man defecating right over the head of the bishop's door (Fig. 7). Comparisons have frequently been made with East Anglian manuscripts, such as the Ormesby Psalter which was probably illuminated at or near Norwich in several phases between the 1280s and c. 1320, especially with the range of marginal scenes.[39] Indeed, elements of both the lively and the softer figure styles can be closely paralleled in the work of the 'great master of the manuscript' which dates from its later phases, shortly before the manuscript was given to the cathedral by Robert Ormesby, a monk here.[40]

At least two artists, or modes of carving, seem to have been employed in carving the figures and bosses of the east walk. One artist created long thin figures, often contorted or seen at angles and swathed in drapery, and was responsible for the prior's door and the Evangelist corbels. The other, who carved the Passion bosses, made stockier and less mobile figures in fairly conventional broadfold drapery (Figs 6 and 7). It is possible that the foliage bosses and green men at the south end of the east walk were carved by a third artist, as they make a distinct group, both in terms of how they are arranged and in terms of their style. According to Woodman, they also compare in terms of their date (Fig. 2). Work in each of these styles continues in the south walk. There, another artist appears, specialising in multiple small figures.

FIG. 5.   Prior's door: detail
Veronica Sekules

FIG. 6.   East walk: Flagellation
Veronica Sekules

FIG. 7.   East walk: defecating figure
Veronica Sekules

The First Apocalypse Series

THE first sequence of Apocalypse scenes begins in the south walk with thirty-seven scenes from the Apocalypse; the rest of the bosses are decorative and foliate, or support combat scenes, or refer to other biblical episodes (a John the Baptist narrative, and a sequence devoted to the life of the Virgin Mary which extends to the cloister garth wall ribs). The Apocalypse bosses carry the story from the first twelve chapters of Revelation: the opening of the seven seals, the appearance of the four horsemen and the sounding of the six trumpets, until the 'War in Heaven' (Fig. 8). The choice of scenes in this walk is broadly consistent with those in the group of Anglo-French apocalypse manuscripts, some of which have been associated with Norwich.

The table of images in Apocalypse manuscripts published by Lucy Freeman Sandler suggests the following correspond most closely to the range of scenes at Norwich: Brussels Apocalypse MS Bib Roy II. 282, an Anglo-French book which had been in Flanders since the 15th century;[41] and London BL Royal MS 19.B.XV, which has exactly the same range of scenes, but is of a different style, belonging to the Queen Mary Psalter group.[42] Both of these manuscripts (and the small group to which they relate), date from the first quarter of the 14th century. It is not clear whether the Apocalypse manuscript purchased for the cathedral in 1346 was specially made, or was second-hand and made some decades earlier.

The Dublin Apocalypse (Dublin, Trinity College MS 64), dating from 1310–20, which has been related to Norwich work in the Ormesby psalter group, is, unfortunately for us, the least relevant to the cloister scheme in terms of the range of its pictures. However, as the only manuscript which has reorganised the compositions into a vertical format, it is perhaps the one which allows us to imagine how pictures which were being used as models had to be altered to suit different contexts.[43] For some of the bosses the compositions have had to be ingeniously adapted in order to fit the cramped and rounded spaces, especially those by the second small-figure artist, including, for example, the Adoration of the Lamb (Fig. 9A). Stylistically, these more crowded compositions recall those found in initials in manuscripts of the 1360s, especially those associated with the Bohun family commissions, where we see similar attempts to crowd multiple figure compositions into tiny spaces.[44]

It is perhaps significant that the south walk sequence at Norwich ends at the corner next to the entrance from the refectory with the message from chapter 12 of the Apocalypse, of the clarification of the divisions between good and evil suggested by the War in Heaven, and the casting out of Satan, with its message from verse 12, 'Rejoice oh heavens and ye that dwell in them. Woe for the earth and the sea: because the devil is gone down to you, having great wrath, knowing that he hath but a short time' (Fig. 10).[45] This forms a natural break and, indeed, the next two bays introduce several different kinds of subjects. These include a gateway apparently being approached by a variety of figures including a giant knight, two men in a sword fight, and a windmill to which a woman on horseback is delivering a sack of corn, all of which echo subjects and styles which occur in margins and borders in manuscripts, brasses and other art-forms such as misericords. The windmill scene echoes a similar composition in the borders of the brass to Adam de Walsoken at St Margaret's church, Kings Lynn, which dates from after 1349. A similar scene is also found in Alexander manuscripts, such as Oxford, Bodleian Library, MS 264 (Fig. 11). As Lynda Dennison has pointed out, these images were in use as part of an Anglo-Flemish

FIG. 8.   South walk: Second Trumpet

Veronica Sekules

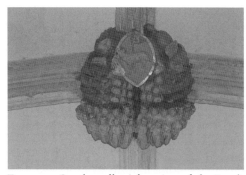

FIG. 9A.   South walk: Adoration of the Lamb

Veronica Sekules

FIG. 9B.   South walk:
Seventh Trumpet. Note
directions of heads

Veronica Sekules

FIG. 10.   South walk: War in Heaven

Veronica Sekules

FIG. 11.   South-west corner bay:
windmill

Veronica Sekules

crossing of cultures in the second half of the 14th century, which she related very convincingly to the circle of Bohun manuscripts of the 1340s to 1350s.[46] Fernie and Whittingham attribute this work to the next documented building phase which relates to the area from the towels to the guest hall, funded by the Simmonds donation of 1412, which was spent from 1415 onwards.[47] This would suggest a hiatus between work on the south and the west walks of almost half a century. But it seems on this stylistic evidence that work on the south-west corner preceded this by a few decades and followed on closely in date from the south walk campaign.

It may be significant that one of Norwich's prominent intellectuals, Adam Easton, a monk at Norwich, who then became an academic at Gloucester college Oxford, was recalled to Norwich from 1357–63, to combat the mendicants who were 'loosing their backbiting mouths at everyone'.[48] Adam Easton argued strongly in favour of the primacy of ecclesiastical authority over and above the secular authority of the crown. His writings are thought to have explained his rise to prominence with the Papacy and he became a cardinal in 1381. He was then out of favour for a while, but was reinstated in 1389. He wrote an important condemnation of heresy and may indeed have set the Papacy against John Wycliffe, initiating the whole anti-Lollard movement, including the heresy trials and witch-hunts of the first half of the 15th century. He bequeathed his considerable library of 228 books to Norwich Cathedral Priory, which were transported from Rome to Norwich in six barrels in 1407, ten years after his death.[49] Thus, Easton would have been present at the priory during the building of the south walk of the cloister, and, even though a large part of his career was spent elsewhere, he clearly was an intellectual force with influence far beyond this period and context.[50]

It is against this background that the next phases in the installation of the cloister bosses are to be understood, as being contemporary with, and a direct response to, problems raised by the Lollard heresy at the beginning of the 15th century. For the monastery, a reforming ascetic movement strongly motivated to preach and teach, such as the Lollards, posed a threat even greater than that of the mendicants a century earlier. At the time that Easton was installed in Rome, they had potentially a strong popular appeal because they communicated in the native tongue, promoted preaching and reading the Bible in the vernacular, and rejected pomp, ceremony and the irresponsible exercise of power. They also wanted to strip worship of the trappings of mystery, challenging beliefs associated with the sacrament, and claiming that the doctrine of transubstantiation did not do proper honour to it. They were also consistently and strongly anti-images, holding they constituted a distraction from proper prayer.[51] It is a moot point how organised they were and how coherent a movement existed.[52] Especially at Norwich, Tanner maintains that heresy never was a real threat, that religious life was too secure and conservative.[53] Margaret Aston, in her article 'Lollardy and Sedition, 1381–1431' suggests otherwise, not specifically at Norwich, but argues that for England generally there was a strong current of radical anti-establishment attitudes directed against religious organisations and practices, as well as against secular lords and values. These included claims that any holy and worthy person could have the same status as a priest and could celebrate mass even though they may not have been formally ordained by a bishop.[54] Such was the perceived threat that the death penalty was instituted against relapsed and impenitent heretics for the first time in England in 1401.[55]

It is in what must have been an atmosphere of heightened tension that the monastery can be seen to be bracing itself during the ensuing phase of the cloister campaign from 1415 until its completion in 1428.

The Second Apolcalypse Series: Retribution and Salvation

PROGRESS was made steadily from 1415, and for the next ten years the west walk campaigns continued. Two artists were involved at first: John Watlington as the 'gravour' for the main bosses for 33 weeks, and Brice the Dutchman (who may have been the conduit for Flemish imagery), who was employed for 46 weeks. Each boss took two weeks to carve, so between them they carved about a third of the bosses for the whole walk (See Appendix). Payments were recorded for James Woderof and his brother John in 1420–21 to carve the bosses for three bays. Fernie and Whittingham identify these as those in front of the guest hall door, which are of simpler hemispherical shape and include a boss relating to the benefaction of Robert Knollys and his wife Constance Beverley. The artists were joined in the next year by John Horn, who remained a principal carver until the end of the cloister campaign.[56]

In the second bay of the west walk, there is a major change in the approach to the imagery. The Apocalypse sequence continues, taking the narrative forward from chapter 13 onwards, but it is not a straightforward continuation. If one compares the scenes with Sandler's list of Apocalpyse subjects from 14th-century manuscripts, there are some 22 extra scenes at Norwich which do not appear in the manuscript series. The emphasis is different from the more conventional sequence of the south walk. It is not consistent with the Alexander commentary tradition from Saxony either.[57] Instead of there being an average of three scenes per chapter of the Apocalypse as in the south walk, the west walk averages seven. The highest number is for Chapter 16, which is illustrated by 14 bosses; Chapter 17 is illustrated by 11 bosses and Chapter 19 has 10. Chapter 16 is concerned with the pouring out of the seven bowls of wrath of God upon the earth, the proliferation of pain, plagues and blasphemy. This seems to reinforce the message with which we were left at the end of the south walk, of an earth which is subject to waves of evil forces. Chapter 17 is concerned with the whore of Babylon who comes in for particular condemnation. Illustration of these themes is not confined to the bosses relating just to these chapters. Altogether there are 30 images to do with the plagues, brought out at Norwich not so much by stressing the afflictions but more by an emphasis on the means of retribution. Rather than being a specific reference to plague, such as the great plague of 1349 that had interrupted progress on the cloisters, it may be more appropriate to interpret this emphasis on plague as a metaphor in Apocalyptic imagery and writings for the unleashing of irrational forces.[58]

In the whore of Babylon sequence, retribution is particularly directed at the ten kings, who appear repeatedly, clearly bringing out the association in the text with the 'kings of the earth who committed fornication with her' (Fig. 12). This could be taken either as a sign of a particular force directed against secular authority, or as a warning against dangers of corruption. Conversely, the power of salvation is frequently reinforced through the image of the authority of Christ, but it is not the avenging Christ with the sword in his mouth, who shall 'rule them with a rod of iron' of chapter 19 but Christ as merciful judge. There are ten bosses concerned with salvation drawn from chapter 19 illustrating repeated images of homage to Christ framed in the mandorla, emphasising the reconciliatory function of the Last Judgement (Fig. 13).

Aspects of these values, especially messages reinforcing appropriate authority and role models, are given further emphasis in the two legends which are woven into the Apocalypse series in the west walk: the four bosses devoted to the legend of St Basil and the Emperor Julian the Apostate, and three bosses featuring the legend of the

FIG. 12. West walk: Unclean spirits entering the ears of kings
Veronica Sekules

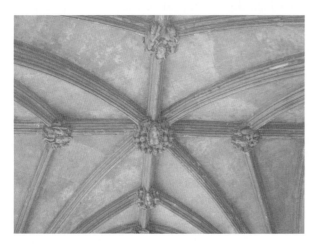

FIG. 13. West walk: Salvation scenes
Veronica Sekules

Christian of Constantinople. The legend of St Basil shows him as a champion of religious authority over secular. The story concerns an antagonistic relationship between Basil, Bishop of Caesarea, and the Emperor Julian, which arose over a gift from Basil, which the Emperor spurned. The Virgin Mary came to Basil's assistance, and upon his instigation, raised from the dead his friend and champion, Mercurius, whom Julian had killed for his faith in God. Mercurius then killed Julian in order to exact retribution for them both.

This illustrates the championing by the Virgin Mary of the authority, faith and generosity of a Bishop and Doctor of the church against the Emperor, and there were a number of reasons why it may have been chosen. There had been a long history at Norwich of conflict between ecclesiastical and secular authority. As mentioned above, this had been very much part of the reason for the riots in 1272. It is also evident from the seal of the priory that they saw themselves as a directly equivalent to secular power. As T. A. Heslop noted, their first seal of 1125–40 represented the figure of Christ presiding over the city walls, in a direct echo of the gold bulls of contemporary German kings and emperors.[59] The second seal of 1258 continues this theme, emphasising the status of Christ as king in its legend. Heslop suggests that this overt homage to a higher authority as king was in direct response to the difficulties in Henry III's reign in that year.[60] In the context of Lollard heresy there were once again issues over whose status was under threat, whose responsibility it was to counter-attack. The questions of authority and adherence to principles of faith must have been much on their minds.[61]

The second story, of the Christian of Constantinople, is also pertinent in the context of challenges to authority. It concerns a Christian who borrowed a sum from a Jewish money lender and then travelled abroad, leaving an image of the Virgin Mary as surety. The repayment of the sum becoming due, he sent it in a casket by sea. The Jew found the casket but refused to accept that the repayment was legitimate. In doubting it he also, by implication, doubted the miraculous power of the Virgin, and her image therefore condemned him. As well as being patently anti-Jewish, for which there was a strong tradition at Norwich, the story is explicitly about the power of images and therefore comes as a direct challenge to those forces of Lollardy which were rising against them.

The North Walk, Saints and Sacrament

IN 1415–16, bosses were being carved by John Watlington and Brice the Dutchman. The rest of the west walk bosses were carved by John Horn who had joined the team in 1421. From 1423 there is documented work to the roofs of the north walk where he continued working until it was completed in 1428. In 1427–28, William Reppys was paid for carving six keystone bosses at 6s. 8d. per boss (see Appendix). Assuming it was still taking two weeks to carve a boss, this sum is comparable to the 4s. per week for 15 weeks, which was being paid to John Horn. It is possible that William Reppys was not based on site if he was being paid per item rather than for his time.

The Apocalypse series being complete, the north walk comprises new material consisting of episodes from stories of saints' lives. These include the Virgin Mary, St Lawrence, St Eustace, St Edward the Confessor, St George, St Thomas Beckett, St Clement, St Peter, St Paul, St James the Great, St James the Less, St John the Evangelist, St John the Baptist, St Benedict, David and Goliath, King David and the lion, St Nicholas, St Giles, St Edmund, St Lucy, St Catherine, St Denis, St Stephen, St Martin, and St Eustace (Fig. 14). It is not a specifically Norwich litany: there are no local saints apart from St Edmund. Significantly however, the sequence contains: virgins, martyrs, apostles, confessors, archbishops, bishops, popes, monks, and kings, both biblical and historical.

However, as well as the images of saints and confessors, near the east end of north walk another change in imagery takes hold with the introduction of a small series of bosses returning to post-Resurrection events especially associated with the emphasis of Christ's Real Presence. They lead to the prior's door continuing the east walk sequence, but as the earlier work the direction in which they are seen when walking from west to east is the reverse of the narrative order, so it begins with the Ascension, then the post-Resurrection appearances of Christ: the Supper at Emmaus, Noli me Tangere, the Sealing of the Tomb, the Maries at the Sepulchre (Fig. 15). These bosses are surrounded by others which are distinctly Eucharistic in symbolism, emphasising

FIG. 14.   North walk: Supper at Emmaus
Veronica Sekules

FIG. 15.   North walk: Thomas Becket
Veronica Sekules

FIG. 16.   North walk: Mary Magdalen
Veronica Sekules

the Real Presence, such as the Pelican in her Piety, the Princess and the Unicorn, Doubting Thomas and 'The Jew of Bourges', which records a miracle of the Virgin involving administration of the sacrament to a Jew who was protected by it during a trial of endurance (Fig. 16). The reinforcement of the orthodox doctrine of the sacrament is clear, and it cannot be an accident that these bosses are contemporary with the activity of the Lollard persecutions and immediately precede the Norwich heresy trials of 1428–31.[62]

One final question remains. Who would have seen the cloister and what would have been the point of taking such care with the choice of imagery? The most important audience had to be the monks. There is evidence of there being a particularly learned community here. Joan Greatrex's researches have shown that Norwich was a centre of learning on a par with Canterbury and Worcester, at least in the records of monks who attended university, attaining an average of one in seven, as opposed to the one in twenty which was the minimum required by papal legislation.[63] So, as stated before, the cloister as the seat of learning and the symbolic heart of the monastery would have been an obvious locus for a display of doctrine. Barbara Dodwell refers to customs of reading in the cloister where the medieval book cupboards survive in the east and south walks, though mostly now sealed shut. The cloister also played a part in the liturgy as a place of procession, as already discussed above.[64]

Harper-Bill and Rawcliffe suggest that visitors from outside would not have been uncommon, that the citizens of Norwich must have had frequent recourse to the cathedral for commercial as well as religious reasons, and that 'the great and the good would doubtless have been taken round the new cloister to admire the striking sequence of Apocalypse bosses'.[65] Indeed the guest hall opened onto the cloister, in front of which was carved the boss paid for and recording the heraldry of Sir Robert Knollys and his wife Cecily. However, during Bishop Alnwick's Lollard heresy trials at Norwich in 1428–31, another reason for visiting the cloister emerged. One of the forms of public penance for defendants was to be flogged during ritual circuits around the cloister. Thomas Wade, tailor of Norwich, was instructed in 1428 to attend barefooted, bare-headed and wearing only shirt and breeches, for floggings on processional circuits of the cloister on three consecutive Sundays. It is not clear whether the punishment was thought to be appropriate to his sin, but perhaps the force of the images would have struck him as he was whipped past them.

Margery Baxter of Martham, who was tried for heresy in 1429, believed that the devils who fell to earth with Lucifer entered the images in churches and continued to dwell in them, causing people to commit idolatry if they honoured them.[66] Kathleen Kamerick discussed this episode as indicative of Margery's understanding of the real power of images.[67] Underlying her disapproval was possibly fear of the consequences of submission to them. One wonders if she knew the relevant boss in Norwich cloister, and was speaking from experience, as her interpretation is unusually vivid (see Fig. 10). But the significant point to which Kamerick draws attention is of the perceptions of evil lurking within even the most sacred imagery, and that to the Lollards idolatry was perceived to have the dangerous potential to unleash the demonic. If this fear was widespread, and Kamerick makes out a strong case that it was, then it is would be quite understandable if the bosses of the cloister at Norwich were expressly, and increasingly, designed to present a corrective view, as well as an incontrovertibly holy context for devotion and scholarship in the monastery.

Taken as a whole, the cloister boss imagery can be seen as equivalent to a spread out façade scheme of the kind that became standard on great churches from the mid-13th century, as for example at Amiens, Reims, Wells, Lichfield, and Exeter. All of them have versions from, or permutations of, the Passion and Resurrection, Christ in Judgement, Christ displaying his wounds, visions of heaven and hell, and combined these with similar kinds of litanies which incorporate different estates and ranks of authorities, secular and religious. It is conceivable that the broad sequence of imagery around the cloister, its underlying range and content, was planned more or less from the start, or at least from the moment the design changed in *c.* 1330, to introduce the Passion and Apocalyptic sequences.

APPENDIX

TABLE SUMMARISING DOCUMENTARY EVIDENCE FOR CLOISTER BUILDING AT NORWICH

Documentary references	Summary interpretation & comments
In 1297, work on cloister begun at the entrance to the chapter-house, by Lord Ralph Walpole, Bishop of Norwich (1288–99). Walpole and Uppehall 'made' three bays of the cloister in addition to the chapter-house. Walpole's benefaction was recorded on an inscription stone on west side of the cloister in front of the chapter-house entrance; a stone on the east side of the cloister, north of the chapter-house entrance records Richard Uppehall as founder of the new work.	These benefactions mark the beginning of the work to the wall fabric. There are two doorways in this part, one into the chapter-house, and one external entrance from the east.
Remaining five bays towards the church, the 'prior's' north-east door into the church and the bays towards the infirmary entrance, from that entrance to the bays where the towels are hung, was made at the expense of Lord John Ely, Bishop of Norwich, other friends and the offices of the Pitancer at dispensation of the monastery. 1324–25: expenses for 'ogives' and lead.[68]	This was the work paid for by Bishop John Salmon (1299–1325). Donations were made by his executors in 1326–27, 1329–30, and at his tomb. This work refers to the whole of the east walk and the first ten bays of the south walk. The position of the 'towels' is not certain, but Fernie and Whittingham suggests that they were located in the south-west corner bay next to the refectory entrance.[69] They suggested that the vaulting of the east and south walks were completed during this period, but I think references to vaulting, which are scarce, refer only to the east walk.
1330–35: interruption to progress. 1335–36: donation from Bishop Ayermin (1325–36) marks start of new phase supervised by John and then William Ramsay (till 1349). There is also an unidentified image of a man and woman on the centre boss of the south walk, presumably depicting benefactors. 1343–49: Simon Lillie is master mason. I think, rather than work on roofing the west walk, as suggested by Fernie and Whittingham (see below re Simmonds benefaction of 1411–12 and later documentary references to construction of its lower parts of west walk), this new phase from 1345–64 is likely to mark the phase of roofing the south walk, especially marked by the purchase of the apocalypse manuscript to inform the imagery. 1345: works begin in earnest with purchases of stone from Caen, Purbeck and Corfe, Quarr, Barnack and Dublin. 1346: purchase of apocalypse manuscript.[70] From 1348–50, then till 1364 work on roofs.	

APPENDIX (CONTINUED)

Documentary references	Summary interpretation & comments
1349: Fernie associates the construction of a bay of wooden tracery in bay 9 of the west walk with a reduction in funds around the time of the Black Death.[71]	Judging from the sequence of the sculpture of the keystones of the centre bays on the garth side, work of construction of these bays continued more or less uninterruptedly throughout the 14th century. However, the expenditure in the C&P rolls suggests that work may have moved from the south range to the north, maybe simultaneously with the west range.
1352–59: work in progress in the north walk, perhaps continuing from northernmost bays of west walk. Master William de Norton and John Attegrene the younger are associated with that work.[72]	This must refer only to the construction of the first three bays from the west, as the style of the tracery of the remaining seven is definitely later.
Walter Berney of London left money in a legacy of 1382 and is buried in the cloister.	There were very few lay burials in the cathedral and he may be related to another noted by Tanner, John Berney, who was a wealthy local merchant and probably steward to the priory, whose will of 1374 asked that he be buried in St Anne's chapel where one of his wives lay already.[73]
1382–94: Berney's benefaction being spent. Robert Wadherst (who had worked at Westminster Abbey) was master mason.[74]	Fernie and Whittingham attribute this expenditure to the completion of the tracery of the cloister garth bays for the north walk. It is possible that work on the upper storeys included a start on vaulting; however, this is unlikely given other north walk evidence for 1420s below.
In 1412, £100 given by Geoffrey Symond or Simmonds, rector of St Mary in the Marsh, for part from 'where the towels hang, with the door of the refectory, and the lavatories, and the door to the Guest hall entrance, the lavatories and entrance to guest house hall'.[75]	The legacy of Geoffrey Simmonds has been associated with the expense of building the south-west corner and also with vaulting the north-west half of the north walk.[76] The money was spent between 1414–22, and could refer to the doorways and lavatories in the outer wall and the fabric up to the guest house, as well as expenditure on vaulting.[77]
From guest house hall entrance to the north-west entrance to the church, including the vaulting, by executors of John Wakering, former bishop (1415–25). James and John Woderof were master masons and John Horn carved the bosses.	Then for nearly ten years — west walk campaigns. The rest of the west walk was accounted for by the bequest of Bishop Wakering, with the exception of at least one boss opposite the Guest Hall, which was paid for by Robert Knowles and his wife Constance and has their heraldry on it. In 1415–16, the bosses (C&P rolls attribute this to the south-west corner, 41) were carved by John Watlington — who is paid a lot; Brice the Dutchman does the rest — two weeks per boss.

APPENDIX (CONTINUED)

Documentary references	Summary interpretation & comments
1423–24: payments for roofing in north walk. North part against the church and the vaulting against the church at the expense of Master Henry Well for 210 marks, £20 given on behalf of the Pitancer's office by John Hancock, mentioned in First Register summary. Henry Wells, archdeacon of Lincoln's donations were 1423–24 and 1427. John Hancock's donation, of 1425–26, also went towards the north walk.[78]	These payments went towards the completion of the vaulting of the north walk. 1427–28: John Horn continued as 'gravour' for 15 weeks at 4s. per week and William Reppys was paid for six keystones at 6s. 8d. each. These have been associated with the easternmost post-Resurrection scenes. Nicholas Blackamour was the labourer.[79]
1430: completion of building of cloister in bishopric of William Alnwick and in the third year of office for Prior William Wursted.	

NOTES

1. See, for example, M. Aston, *The Fifteenth Century: the Prospect of Europe* (London 1968), 117–75; R. N. Swanson, *Religion and Devotion in Europe c.1215–c.1515* (Cambridge 1995), 235–56, and E. Duffy, *The Stripping of the Altars, Traditional Religion in England c.1400–c.1580* (New Haven and London 1992).

2. E. Duffy, 'Late medieval Religion', in *Gothic, Art for England 1400–1547*, ed. R. Marks and P. Williamson (London 2003), 56–67.

3. A. Brown, *Church and Society in England 1000–1500* (Basingstoke 2003), 146–56.

4. Brown, *Church and Society*, 161–2.

5. J. Luxford, *The Art and Architecture of English Benedictine Monasteries 1300–1540, A Patronage History* (Woodbridge 2005).

6. M. Aston, 'Lollardy and Sedition', in *Lollards and Reformers: Images and Literacy in Late Medieval Religion*, (London 1984), 17–19.

7. N. P. Tanner, *The Church in Late Medieval Norwich 1370–1532* (Toronto 1984), 155; N. Tanner, 'Religious Practice', in *Medieval Norwich*, ed. C. Rawcliffe and R. Wilson (Hambledon and London 2004), 137.

8. ibid., 57–112.

9. ibid., 1–55.

10. ibid., 93, 97, 119, 120–21.

11. ibid., 271–72.

12. ibid., 160ff.

13. ibid., 145ff.; N. Tanner, 'Cathedral and City', in *Norwich Cathedral, Church, City and Diocese, 1096–1996*, ed. I. Atherton, E. Fernie, C. Harper Bill and H. Smith (Hambledon 1996), 259–62; C. Rawcliffe and C. Harper Bill, 'The Religious Houses', in *Medieval Norwich*, ed. C. Rawcliffe and R. Wilson (Hambledon and London 2004), 85.

14. V. Sekules, 'The Gothic Sculpture', in Atherton et al., *Norwich Cathedral*, 199–202.

15. See J. A. Franklin in *Medieval Sculpture at Norwich Cathedral*, ed. Alan Borg *et al.* (Norwich 1980), 5–27.

16. J. A. Franklin, 'The Romanesque Sculpture', in Atherton *et al.*, *Norwich Cathedral* (1996), 116–35.

17. J. G. Clark, 'Monastic Education in Late Medieval England', in *The Church and Learning in Late Medieval Society. Studies in Honour of Barry Dobson*, ed. C. Barron and J. Stratford, Harlaxton Medieval Studies, Vol. XI, (Donington 2002), 25–26.

18. J. Greatrex, 'Monk students from Norwich Cathedral Priory', *The English Historical Review*, CVI (1991), 555–56.

19. C. Reeves, 'Creative Scholarship in the Cathedrals 1300–1500', in Barron and Stratford ed., *The Church and Learning*, 160–69. I would suggest that the imagery of the cloister is evidence for exactly the

kind of 'creative scholarship' which Compton Reeves seeks in his article. He neglects to consider any visual evidence, but the reliance on a variety of scholarly sources for these images is clear, as well as being in themselves an impressive exercise in exposition of learning.

20. Rawcliffe and Harper Bill, 'Religious Houses', 81.

21. ibid, 105–06.

22. M. Rose and J. Hedgecoe, *Stories in Stone, The Medieval Roof carvings of Norwich Cathedral* (London 1997), 30–39.

23. At Worcester Cathedral Priory, the cloister was rebuilt from the 1370s incorporating a traceried glazed enclosure around the garth and a vaulted ceiling decorated with figured bosses. This is of a quite different style and tradition from Norwich, suggesting that there were very probably a number of different models which may not have been directly connected. See also the article by Linda Monckton in this volume.

24. C. Brighton, *Lincoln Cathedral Cloister Bosses* (Lincoln 1985), 10–15.

25. E. Fernie, *An Architectural History of Norwich Cathedral*, (Oxford 1993), 166–67.

26. E. Fernie and A. B. Whittingham, *The Early Communar and Pitancer Rolls of Norwich Cathedral Priory with an Account of the Building of the Cloister* (Norfolk Record Society 1972), 31–43.

27. M. R. James, *The Sculptured Bosses in the Cloisters of Norwich Cathedral* (Norwich 1911); D. H. S. Cranage, *Norwich Cathedral Cloister* (Norwich 1938), incorporating articles by E. W. Tristram.

28. Fernie, *An Architectural History*, 166–79; F. Woodman, 'The Gothic Campaigns', in Atherton et al., *Norwich Cathedral*, 158–96.

29. *Norwich Cathedral Roof Bosses* (CD-Rom, Norwich Cathedral 2000); Rose and Hedgecoe, *Stories in Stone*; M. Rose, *The Norwich Apocalypse* (Norwich 1999).

30. Woodman, 'The Gothic Campaigns', 168–70.

31. ibid, 165–74.

32. Fernie, *An Architectural History*, 164–77.

33. Fernie and Whittingham, *Communar and Pitancer Rolls*, 38.

34. B. Dodwell, 'The Monastic Community', in Atherton et al., *Norwich Cathedral*, 236 and fig. 14. A context for an interpretation of imagery of cloisters, which would have been taken very seriously in the Middle Ages, was the tradition of symbolic reading. See the introduction by Michael Evans to Brighton, *Lincoln Bosses*, 1–3.

35. R. Gilchrist, *Norwich Cathedral Close, The Evolution of the English Cathedral Landscape* (Woodbridge 2005), 68–92.

36. Fernie, *An Architectural History*, 177.

37. Gilchrist, *Norwich Cathedral Close*, 88, states that processions worked their way in clockwise fashion from the prior's door round to the west door following the sequence of imagery from the Passion to the final image of the Apocalypse, the siege of Jerusalem, the church itself symbolising the holy city.

38. Fernie, *An Architectural History*, 173–75.

39. Rose and Hedgecoe, *Stories in Stone*, 30.

40. L. F. Sandler, *Gothic Manuscripts 1285–1385* (London 1986), vol. I, 49–51; vol. II, frontispiece and illus. 96–98.

41. ibid., vol. I, illus. 134–36; vol. II, 64, no. 55.

42. ibid., vol. I, illus. 161–64; vol. II, 69, no. 61.

43. ibid., vol. I, illus. 107–08; vol. II, 52–53, no. 46.

44. ibid., vol. I, illus. 355, 362, 366.

45. Margery Baxter of Martham, who was tried in 1429 in the Norwich heresy trials, believed that the devils who fell to earth with Lucifer entered the images in churches and continued to dwell in them, causing people to commit idolatry if they honoured them. See N. P. Tanner ed., *Heresy Trials in the Diocese of Norwich*, Camden Society, 4th series, 20 (London 1977), 13, 49. See below, note 66.

46. L. Dennison, 'The Artistic Context of Fourteenth-Century Flemish Brasses', *Transactions of the Monumental Brass Society*, XIV (1986/91), 1–38.

47. Fernie and Whittingham, *Communar and Pitancer Rolls*, 41, roll 1068 for the years 1411–12; roll 1070 for the years 1415–16.

48. B. Dodwell, The Monastic Community', 247–48; W. A. Pantin ed., *Documents Illustrating the Activities of the General and Provincial Chapters of the English Black Monks*, Camden Society, 3rd series, 3 (London 1937), 28–29.

49. H. C. Beeching and M. R.James, 'The Library of the Cathedral Church of Norwich', *Norfolk Archaeology*, 19 (1915–17), 71, 79.

50. Greatrex, 'Monk Students', 556, points out that Easton's career lost him to Norwich. Nevertheless, I would maintain that his intellectual influence had sufficient impact to suggest contact was maintained with his ideas.

51. See the essays on 'Devotional literacy' and 'Lollards and Images' in Aston, *Lollards and Reformers*, 101–33, and 135–92.

52. Aston, *Lollards and Reformers*, 9.

53. Tanner, *The Church in Late Medieval Norwich*, 55, 150–51, 164–65.

54. Aston, *Lollards and Reformers*, 16–17.

55. ibid., 38–42.

56. Fernie and Whittingham, *Communar and Pitancer Rolls*, 42, roll 1073–74.

57. There are, for example, few correspondences with the apocalypse panels by Meister Bertram now in the Victoria and Albert Museum.

58. L. A. Smoller, 'Of Earthquakes, Hail, Frogs and Geography, Plague and the Investigation of the Apocalypse', in *Last Things. Death and the Apocalypse in the Middle Ages*, ed. Caroline Walker Bynum and Paul Freedman (University Park and London 2000), 156–87.

59. T. A. Heslop, 'The Medieval Conventual Seals', in Atherton et al., *Norwich Cathedral*, 443–50.

60. Heslop, 'Conventual Seals', 449–50.

61. Aston, *Lollards and Reformers*, 1–47.

62. M. Groom, 'England, Piety, Heresy and Anti-Clericalism', in *A Companion to Britain in the Later Middle Ages*, ed. S. H. Rigby (Oxford 2003), 389, points out the problematic nature of the term and concept of Lollardy, but his remark that dissent was usually defined by those whose task it was to prosecute it is of some interest here.

63. Greatrex, 'Monk Students, 558, 559.

64. Dodwell, 'The Monastic Community', 232–33.

65. Harper-Bill and Rawcliffe, 'The Religious Houses', 77.

66. N. P. Tanner, *Heresy Trials*, 13, 49.

67. K. Kamerick, 'The Cause of all Evil: Idolatry in Late Medieval England', in *Popular Piety and Art in the Late Middle Ages. Image Worship and Idolatry in England 1350–1500* (New York and Basingstoke 2002), 13–42.

68. Fernie and Whittingham, *Communar and Pitancer Rolls*, 35; roll 1041, 100, roll 1042, 105.

69. ibid., 33.

70. ibid., 38.

71. Fernie, *An Architectural History*, 170.

72. Fernie and Whittingham, *Communar and Pitancer Rolls*, 38.

73. Tanner, 'Cathedral and City', 278–79.

74. Fernie and Whittingham, *Communar and Pitancer Rolls*, 39–40.

75. Fernie, *An Architectural History*, 166.

76. Fernie and Whittingham, *Communar and Pitancer Rolls*, 41.

77. Fernie, *An Architectural History*, 170, note 40.

78. ibid., 171, note 41.

79. Fernie and Whittingham, *Communar and Pitancer Rolls*, 43.

REVIEWS OF BOOKS

Forensic Archaeology: advances in theory and practice. Edited by JOHN HUNTER and MARGARET COX. Abingdon, Routledge 2005. 256 pp., 50 figs, 25 b/w photographs. ISBN 9780415273114, £65.00 (hb); ISBN 9780415273121, £24.99 (pb).

During an era where television and literary fiction are dominated by forensic studies it is hardly surprising that there is an ever-growing number of people interested in this area of expertise. In turn this has lead to a sudden influx in the number of related texts becoming available, subsequently making it hard to determine those with the most beneficial and varied content. First and foremost it should be noted that not only is this volume edited by two of Britain's leading forensic archaeologists, both of whom have published extensively on the subject, but contributors comprise an array of prominent academics, researchers and field experts, all of whom are well known to everybody currently engaged in forensic archaeology. Secondly, this could be regarded as a continuation or 'updated version' of a previous Routledge publication, *Studies in Crime: An Introduction to Forensic Archaeology*, also co-edited by John Hunter, which became a core text to forensic archaeology and anthropology students across Britain following its publication in 1996.

This volume is split into eight distinct chapters, each exploring one of the many facets of forensic archaeology. The introduction gives a good overview of the subject as a vocation and discusses both the need for forensic archaeology in Britain and the difficulties associated with combining general archaeological techniques with criminal investigations. The two following chapters cover the many techniques employed during the search for and the location of human remains and rather nicely provides a broad introduction to the use of geophysical surveying in a criminal context. Chapters are also dedicated to the recovery of evidence, the often-problematic issue of excavating mass graves in a forensic context and a very basic introduction to the identification of human remains. Furthermore, a unique feature of the book is the inclusion of a chapter dedicated to providing a basic overview of the legal system, including court structures, ethics, expert reports and the giving of evidence, although a significant drawback is that it is geared specifically to the English and Welsh legal system. The two most notable absences from this volume that are featured prominently in 'Studies in Crime' are the chapters relating to the decay of human remains and to the dating the burial from time of death.

Overall, the layout of the text is clear and easy to follow, more so than its precursor, *Studies in Crime*. Good use is made of figures, tables and photographs throughout the book to make specific aspects of the text clear and accessible to the reader. However, unquestionably the volume's most outstanding feature is the number of case studies used to highlight different techniques and associated difficulties. This is particularly true of the chapters relating to the search and location of remains and the recovery of forensic evidence.

In summary, this very reasonably priced volume provides a good, easy to follow introduction to the field of forensic archaeology in Britain, broadly covering all aspects of the job from search and recovery to the presentation of evidence in a legal setting. It may be warmly recommended as a good overall text for students thinking of branching into forensics and for people with a general interest in this type of work.

LYNNE COWAL

The Past from Above. Edited by CHARLOTTE TRÜMPLER. London, Frances Lincoln, 2005. 415 pp., 268 pls (256 in colour). ISBN 0 7112 2478 1. £50.00. (Originally published as *Flug in die Vergangenheit*, Munich: Schirmer/Mosel, 2003.)

This is probably one of the most important general books on aerial archaeology to have been published in the last decade. Its purpose has been to publish to a very high standard a large selection of oblique colour air photographs taken by Georg Gerster, one of the world's finest and best-known aerial photographers. Its starting point was an exhibition of aerial photographs

JBAA, vol. 159 (2006), 307–22
© British Archaeological Association 2006
DOI: 10.1179/174767006X147479

of archaeological sites throughout the world at the Ruhrlandmuseum, Essen. This had been initially inspired by the former director of the museum, Walter Sölter, whose book on the subject, *Das römische Germanien aus der Luft*, played such an important role in awakening and furthering interest and research into the use of aerial photography in archaeology in Germany when it was published in 1981. The book bears witness to the magnificent achievement of Gerster, who in forty years as a photographer has flown over most parts of the world to assemble an unrivalled collection of unique images of archaeological sites and landscapes in fifty-one countries. At the same time it displays some of the most important architecture, planned settlement and ritual landscapes from prehistory and particularly from the ancient civilisations of the Old and New World. Many photographs will be an important source of archaeological data, particularly those taken in countries and areas that can now be flown over only with difficulty, if at all, such as Iraq, Iran, Syria, Israel and Palestine. Although not stated in the book, this endeavour has followed in the steps of Poidebard and Sir Aurel Stein, whose work and that of their successors has been given a scholarly survey in *Rome's Desert Frontier from the Air* by Kennedy and Riley (Batsford, 1990).

The book is introduced by two interesting chapters. The first, by the editor, attempts to provide a history of aerial archaeology and the work of its pioneers. This has, of course, been done before by several acknowledged scholars and experts in the field. But this is a rather fresh view by an archaeologist coming to the subject anew, from the mainstream of classical and museum based studies in Germany. Whilst it has long been generally acknowledged that the greatest advances in the field have been pioneered and developed by British based workers, Trümpler makes a valiant case for German pioneers, such as the archaeologist Theodor Wiegand (1864–1936) who asked pilots to photograph archaeological sites during reconnaissance flights in the Middle East during the First World War. There is an interesting overview of the work of the most important British pioneers, particularly O. G. S. Crawford (who Trümpler points out had claimed to have invented the subject) and Alexander Keiller, and later Major G. W. G. Allen and John Bradford, but this has a number of minor inaccuracies. Also, her account of the most important developments in the understanding of archaeological landscapes through the study of the vast amounts of data provided by crop-marks, soil-marks and earthworks in Britain and other parts of Europe, is only sketchily reviewed. The major developments since the Second World War are not discussed and the enormous contributions of 'private fliers' and organisations such as Cambridge University, the Royal Commissions on Historical Monuments for England, Wales and Scotland, and more recently English Heritage and sister organisations on the Continent, are not mentioned. However, the chapter is illustrated by some fine monochrome and extremely early photographs such as Lieutenant P. H. Sharpe's oblique record of Stonehenge in 1906, often claimed to be one of the first photographs relating to aerial archaeology. Trümpler quite rightly doubts this, referring back to Nadir's balloon views of Paris in 1858 and suggesting that there must have been others taken in the second half of the 19th century. Gerster bases the second introductory chapter on his own private log as an aerial photographer. It is written in his own journalistic style but provides many fascinating insights into his technique, for those of us who continue to practice in the field.

The main body of the book is taken up with the magnificent photographs themselves, most filling a whole page. They are all then reproduced at a smaller scale at the end of the eleven main sections, each accompanied by a written commentary of about 320 words with one or two references, by a series of 29 contributors. These include for British and Irish sites, Robert Bewley, who has recently headed the Aerial Survey Branches of RCHM(E) and English Heritage, and Barry Raftery, Professor of Celtic Archaeology at University College, Dublin. It is rather interesting that this method of presenting the evidence was first pioneered by Crawford and Keiller in 1928, in what is probably the greatest work ever published on the subject, *Wessex from the Air*, and this tradition was continued by the Cambridge University series of surveys edited by J. K. St Joseph and others, such as *Roman Britain from the Air* (1983) and *Medieval England, An Aerial Survey* (2nd edn, 1979). But the text of this book in no way approaches the depths of scholarly interpretation and discussion to be found in these seminal works. Instead, it concentrates on reproducing the photographs to the highest standards of modern printing. Most of the photographs are of landscapes of standing structures; buildings of every kind, villages, towns, tombs, temples, churches, etc., often in a ruinous condition, but the aerial view providing startling evidence of pattern and planning. Few and far between are the traditional crop-marks and earthworks which make up the daily bread and butter of most professional aerial archaeologists.

The individual sections are arranged thematically. For example, one of the first illustrates 'villages and towns — settlement types'. These include urban landscapes such as the cities of Hatra in Iraq, Hamadan in Iran and Xinjiang and Gaochang in China. But also included are Rome, Ostia, Jerash, Apamea, Volubis, Pompeii and Carnuntum. The section on 'palaces and royal residences' includes Herodium, Masada, Tivoli, Montmaurin, Knossos, and Persepolis, but also several lesser known but equally spectacular sites. An interesting grouping is a series of urban and rural shrines which include 'festival sites and places of assembly' such as the theatres, amphitheatres and stadia at Salamis, Leptis Magna, Dodona, Merida, Agos, Miletus, Nicopolis, Aphrodisias, Pergamon, Trier, Orange, and the Gallo-Roman sanctuary at Sanxay, France.

Under the category of 'fortresses and bulwarks' there are some very fine images of Iron Age and Dark Age fortresses in Europe, particularly British and Irish sites such as Ismantorp, Dún Eochla, Dún Aengus, The Hill of Tara, Barmkin, Hambledon Hill, and Maiden Castle. Roman and medieval fortified sites include Castel Sant'Angelo, Jublains, Irgenhausen, Trelleborg, The Krak des Chevaliers and Carcassonne. The sections on 'graves and cemeteries' and 'sacred sites' contains some surprising new insights into less well known monuments in Egypt and the Middle East, the Classical World and prehistoric Europe, particularly in their layout, pattern and planning within their wider landscape setting. They also contain remarkable photographs of major sites in the Far East and the New World. Particularly surprising are the images of the Temple of Apollo at Didyma, St John's Basilica at Ephesus, St Simeon's Monastery in Syria and the fortified church at Viscri in Romania.

This book is not a great work of scholarship in the old-fashioned sense, neither is it a coffee-table book. It is rather something much better: a volume of unique and amazing images of mankind's built heritage. Many will provide new data and insights into well-known locations, some designated as 'World Heritage Sites' by UNESCO, but also many other lesser known but no less important sites throughout the world. It will also provide a most accessible teaching aid for those of us who try to bring our subject to the widest possible audience.

GRAHAME SOFFE

Roman Mosaics of Britain. Volume II. South-West Britain. By STEPHEN R. COSH and DAVID S. NEAL. London, Illuminata Publications for the Society of Antiquaries, 2005. xiii + 406 pp., 389 illus., many in colour. ISBN 0-9547916 1 4. £160.00.

The second volume of this amazing enterprise has now appeared, covering south-west England, including the counties of Wiltshire, Dorset and Somerset. In the 4th century, and the majority of mosaics here are late, this comprised a good part of the wealthy province of *Britannia Prima*, wealthy even in terms of the rest of the Western Empire; this book (together with volume IV on Gloucestershire, Oxfordshire and South Wales) are going to provide that proof, if any were needed for a world readership. This volume includes some wonderful and important mosaics. Amongst them are the Orpheus mosaic from Newton St Loe (No. 209.2), now sadly fragmented, which this Association can be proud of having brought again to scholarly attention in its Bristol Transactions volume. Another Orpheus pavement, totally anomalous, was also in a sad state after having been 'lost' and forgotten on a Wiltshire Estate after its discovery in 1729. The Littlecote mosaic (248.1) is best known from the tapestry by the owner's wife, until a couple of decades ago one of the treasures of Littlecote House but now sadly in a private collection. It is wonderful to have this, Vertue's engraving and Luigi Thompson's meticulous painting of what survives as well as photographic details, but the complete mosaic as restored should have been shown. Cosh and Neal ascribe both mosaics to a Southern Dobunnic group of mosaicists. Also of the highest antiquarian interest is the wonderful series of floors from Frampton, Dorset (168.1–5). Here we can appreciate the first discovered mosaic in James Engleheart's painting of 1794 alongside Samuel Lysons's more professional engraving, or could if Engleheart was not shown at too small a scale. The major chamber in this intriguing complex is replete with myth scenes, an inscription and a

Chi-Rho. Explanations have ranged from its being a display of the 'villa' owner's scholarly erudition, learned mythological and literary allusion being a keynote of life amongst the polite society of the region, to pagan or Christian chapel or perhaps a Christian-Gnostic cult room. However the mosaics need to be seen alongside the sensationally important Hinton St Mary mosaic (172.1) sharing very similar portrayals of Bellerophon slaying the Chimaera and the Chi-Rho, though here the latter is the backing for a head of Christ. This wonderful mosaic can be enjoyed in David Neal's engraving but the printers have badly let him down in the inexcusably muddy photographs. At the time of writing we have all been even worse let down by the British Museum who have sliced up the mosaic and put it in store, all but the Christ-bust. Unfortunately this, one of the earliest representations of Our Lord as World-Ruler (*Cosmocrator*), can only be fully understood in the context of the hounds chasing the deer and the tree of life. It is all most probably an exegesis on Psalm 22 and surely deserves more respect.

Other wonderful mosaics include the fragmentary hexagon from Keynsham (mosaic 204.9) whose Europa and the bull, temporarily liberated from a packing case under Keynsham town hall, is proving one of the sensations of the Constantine exhibition in York. Here, fortunately, the colour pictures are properly produced. If the love of Ovid prompted the mythological display here, Low Ham (207.1) uniquely takes its subject matter from an illuminated manuscript of Virgil. Alas the photos are again not up to standard and we lack the usual Neal or Cosh paintings, but at least this mosaic is available in Taunton museum. Once again one marvels at the work of mosaicists based in Dorchester and its region.

The compilers have done their best to be as up-to-date as possible and have included the recently discovered floors at Lopen (206.1/206.2) and Bradford-on-Avon (234.1) both splendid largely geometric compositions, though dolphins and cantheri may have appealed to Christians and at the latter destruction of a section of the contiguous floor in the 5th century was a consequence of the insertion of a font (a 'post-Roman structure' as the authors call it).

The great virtue of the volume is to lay the evidence before the reader. Apart from its clear value as a source for scholarly research, an enduring monument to the passion of a very few people for Romano-British mosaics it prompts the question of why people enthuse over often vulgar and violent mosaics from North Africa and elsewhere when we have such treasures in England. Then, on reflection, the answer comes back that we have shockingly neglected these lovely works of art, destroyed, hacked up, put into store or at best inadequately displayed the very evidence that should give the lie for ever to the ignorant notion that the art of Roman Britain was, even at its best, second rate. It is the modern Britons who are a philistine nation; not their Romano-British forebears.

MARTIN HENIG

Imago Dei. Sculpted Images of the Crucifix in the Art of Early Modern Malta. By SANDRO DE BONO. Malta, Superintendence of Cultural Heritage, 2005. 61 pp., 39 col. pls. ISBN 99932 58 01 6. No price stated.

This colourfully-illustrated monograph presents an engaging selection of Maltese painted and sculpted crucifixion scenes produced between 1530 and 1798. The time bracket is neatly demarcated by the arrival and departure of the Knight's of St John, whose presence exposed Malta to wider European influence and whose patronage propelled the island into an era of unprecedented artistic production.

The first chapter reveals that the introduction of the sculpted crucifix to Malta cannot currently be dated to earlier than the 16th century. This may prove a surprise to those acquainted with the proliferation of the sculpted image of the crucifixion throughout mainland Europe from the 9th century onwards. However, this fact serves to emphasise the importance of the early modern period in the stimulation of the artistic output of the Maltese archipelago and the merit of its study, a canon to which this publication makes a valuable contribution.

Drawing on an array of works notable for their polychromy, used to full effect in the enthusiastic application of gore, the author effectively explores three key themes and their influence on the sculpted crucifixion: Necessities of Rituals and Cult, The Quest for Reality and Transactions between Core and Periphery. This thematic approach, arranged in three chapters that combine individual case studies with events from Maltese history, enables the author to draw succinct conclusions from a complex story. The case studies include examples of local work and also influential imports. One such import, the distinctive Lando Crucifix, the prototype for a number of later crucifixion scenes, was at one time reputed to have been painted by the Devil himself, though we are informed that the painting brought from Piacenza to Malta by the Knight of Malta, Fra. Felice Conte de Lando, today enjoys the less diabolical attribution of 'unknown authorship'. The Transactions chapter focuses most rigorously on influence from abroad, but this is the theme to which the monograph returns with frequency throughout its chapters. It is from Rome, Sicily and Spain that the major artistic currents of the continent were transmitted to Malta and triggered development in local work. The publication is a good introduction to these local works, a compelling oeuvre that has not previously been widely discussed. *Imago Dei* is the fruit of thorough research, brought together as a well-organised and scholarly consideration of a familiar object-type, which forms a complex aspect of Maltese heritage.

SIMON CARTER

Observation and Image-Making in Gothic Art. By JEAN A. GIVENS. Cambridge, Cambridge University Press, 2005. xiv + 231 pp., 8 col. pls, 63 figs. ISBN 0 521 83031 1. £45.00.

This is a remarkably original and important book whose interest extends far beyond the period with which it purports to deal. The questions posed about how artists saw and transmitted 'reality' in the high Middle Ages are equally relevant for Antiquity, the source (via Pliny's *Natural History*) of many anecdotes about virtuoso artists, as well, no doubt, of other cultures whose art has been recognised as naturalistic. Classically, 'pattern books' are invoked as though everything descended through endless versions from some ideal prototype, though as is rightly stated here, copies degenerate from the original. Givens draws on a wide range of evidence, including the varied and naturalistic leaves carved in the Chapter House at Southwell (most of us, like the author, must have first encountered the subject through Nikolaus Pevsner's classic King Penguin book), Matthew Paris's *Chronica majora*, the notebook of Villard de Honnecourt and Frederick II's *De arte venandi cum avibus* to demonstrate that this is not so, and the wide range of ways in which reality was accessed then and now. If Villard's lion (fig. 16) supposedly taken *al vif* is rather diagrammatic compared with what we might expect of a lion from the time of Durer onwards, it does include certain features not found in the usual bestiary lions, and its somewhat human-like face is perhaps a product of the artist's imagination and proves nothing about 'medieval' attitudes in general. Matthew Paris's representations of the elephant are to modern eyes more impressively naturalistic and were in fact taken from the beast given by Louis IX of France to Henry III; he is shown in one case with a human figure indicating scale (fig. 11) and in another with a separate representation of its trunk showing how the animal used it (pl.v). Matthew's drawings of the jewels of St Albans (pl.iii) would pass muster in a modern book about medieval jewellery, but his achievement is extraordinary in the case of the Great cameo, where it was shown (in *JBAA*, 139 (1986), 147–53) that the scalloped surround dated not long before Matthew's time; however he also managed to convey a very accurate record in most particulars of a Tiberian cameo showing *Divus Augustus*. Equally fascinating is the way Frederick II accurately represented or had represented, the flight of migrating waterfowl.

Realism might have a very practical use, as around the borders of the Pilkington Charter (pl. vii) where the beasts of the chase which Roger of Pilkington had the right to hunt were given a visual form. Images could represent more abstract notions, whether indicative of the precedence of ecclesiastics in a chapter house, or as premonition of secular hierarchy. The Southwell chapter house carvings are suggestive of the paradise garden, which is normally signified in ecclesiastical contexts by a cloister. The book is indeed dominated by plants, the ways in which they were reproduced, and although sometimes there is evidence of copying, both in sculpture and illumination, and of workshop tradition, so that the same design is used more than once in a building (figs 47 and 48), again and again one is struck by meticulous observation, sometimes from nature and sometimes in cut and dried specimens. Incidentally, exactly the same processes can sometimes be seen in relief carvings of the Augustan age, an altar showing crossed plane-tree branches for example which have always put this reviewer in mind of the 'leaves of Southwell'. This need not surprise us; for too long we have tended not to seriously engage with making connections between Renaissance art and what went before, so that we are (unjustifiably) surprised by artistic productions which reflect the *real* world!

That world today is equally at home with abstraction, with its diagrams of the London Underground and technical drawings of all kinds; this is in line with the famous Canterbury waterworks plan inserted into the Eadwine Psalter (pl. iv) or the simpler plan of that at Waltham Abbey. These and the maps and charts also draw on a version of reality, which may indeed have ancient precedents (the Peutinger Table and *Notitia Dignitatum*, known from a number of medieval copies, merit a brief mention here) but Matthew Paris's map (fig. 58) for example adds an enormous amount of detail to earlier cartographic representations of Britain dependant on his own, current knowledge. As Givens shows again and again, what is shown and how it is represented, depends on the nature of the particular audience for a book illustration or a sculptural scheme.

The illustrations both in black and white and colour are excellent, and very well chosen, and how seldom can one end a review by praising the excellence of the author's literary style. She has indeed achieved her object of providing us with 'an expanded sense of visual culture in the Latin West'. It is very much to be hoped that the book, which all students of art history should read, will soon be reissued in paperback.

MARTIN HENIG

A History of Ely Cathedral. Edited by PETER MEADOWS and NIGEL RAMSAY. Woodbridge, Boydell Press, 2003. xxx + 434 pp. ISBN 0 85115 945 1. £29.95 (hb).

Cathedral histories have been appearing steadily for several years, and this one devoted to Ely Cathedral is among the best. Fourteen contributors, several responsible for more than one chapter, write about every aspect of the building's history: as abbey, cathedral priory and secular cathedral; its documentation, history, architecture and decoration; the liturgy, library and archives, restoration and the clergy. As far as possible matters are brought down to 2000 and beyond. The book contains a lucid narrative of the development of this great institution showing both how it was at a particular period and how its past informs the present. The few weaker contributions are more than balanced by the strength of the scholarship as a whole, and the volume is well written and readable.

Only two chapters out of 18 are primarily concerned with the architecture and decoration of the great church, but this is fully justified since they are covered extensively in other literature, to which full reference is made. The other chapters provide information that is less accessible elsewhere. There is a strong focus on Ely Cathedral as a legal entity, and this expands and deepens the art history. The documentary record is discussed in various ways: by Simon Keynes's assessment of the early history down to the establishment of the see in 1109; by Nigel Ramsay in three chapters on the library and archives; and by others who take the story of the restorations and the post-Reformation Deans and Chapters to the present day. All provide a valuable source for anyone who wants to do some more research into aspects of the building, with full references in the footnotes and an evaluation in the main text of the material itself, be it a chronicle, a cartulary or secondary works by antiquaries and historians. Ely Cathedral is thus grounded as a living building, inseparable from its Fenland surroundings and — for part of its history — from Cambridge. Our understanding benefits from this wider picture.

The chronological divisions are set at important moments in the evolution, with continuity maintained in the coverage of all aspects. The large number of coloured and half-tone plates are well chosen: we see the building recorded at various dates with many less familiar views and details; other artefacts and documents are also illustrated, together with a splendid array of clergy, from medieval tombs to later engravings, oil portraits and photographs. Some plate references have gone awry (and Canon Raven, promised as pl. 51(c), has emerged as Bishop Gordon Walsh). There are other signs of editorial haste in inconsistent citations in the footnotes; but it is nevertheless a pleasure to have references on the page rather than at the end of the book. The cathedral authorities and the publisher are to be congratulated on keeping the price of the volume within everyone's means. Owing evidently to some generous grants, it is a bargain.

NICOLA COLDSTREAM

Gold and Gilt, Pots and Pins. Possessions and People in Medieval Britain. By DAVID A. HINTON. Oxford, Oxford University Press, 2005. xi + 439 pp.,108 figs, 26 col. pls. ISBN 0 19 926453 8. £30.00.

In most studies of the Middle Ages 'material culture' is largely represented by architecture and by the major arts of sculpture and painting. Occasionally a jewelled shrine will make an appearance to remind us of what has been lost from the furnishings of abbeys and cathedrals, and coins, of course, tell us about the economy. With the exception of a series of sumptuous exhibition catalogues, Hinton's book breaks new ground. Moreover, it is conceived on an ambitious scale, running from the end of Roman Britain to the eve of the Reformation, and embracing Wales, Ireland and Scotland as well as England. For those of us who have written on small finds from excavations over the years, and felt that this has brought us close to the men and women who used and often loved some small item of jewellery or a distinctive knife or a pot, only to see our work relegated to a mere appendix at the end, Hinton provides a massive vindication, by demonstrating conclusively that such objects are throughout history key indicators to social change. Moreover they can often be used with written sources (where they exist) to flesh out a social history and explain social change.

One is astonished by the grasp of evidence here. The main text moves effortlessly from one type of material to another, and every statement can be followed up through copious endnotes, which demonstrate how little the author has missed. Hinton's discursive notes, nowadays discouraged, are so often informative, picaresque and entertaining that we seem to be listening in on a learned after-dinner conversation. Thus, for example, the Wilton Diptych (pp. 224–25) leads to note 39 on pp. 352–53 on Richard's hart badge, though the comment by Langland on the disgusting taste of the peacock seems to be a *non sequitur* until one realises it belongs below with note 46!

The author seems very much at home in most periods. Although the title of chapter 1, 'Adapting to Life without the legions', seems to envisage the old chestnut of legions withdrawing, the general feel of the chapter is one of cultural change and interaction between groups, not yet fully explained but certainly not the result of blanket conquest. Readers might be warned that many people (including the reviewer) believe the Shepton Mallet Christian pendant (p. 268 note 37) to be a forgery, but by and large this is an admirable summary of this difficult period. Hinton's work really shines with the coming of Christianity and the development of insular cultures, Pictish, Irish and especially English, here returning to the theme of his 1974 catalogue of Anglo-Saxon Ornamental Metalwork in the Ashmolean. Kings and Ecclesiastics often seem to be trying to assert a Christian *Romanitas* but this is a feature of all medieval art, except possibly the pagan Vikings, who at least left a legacy of craftsmanship especially in silver.

There are some interesting and unexpected trends. For instance, students of Architecture and Sculpture see the Norman conquest as initiating a sort of cultural Renaissance, but when one turns to jewellery and precious personal items the event appears to mark something of a hiatus between the golden age of Anglo-Saxon art (as represented by the Pentney brooches, allotted two pages of colour plates, and the Alfred Jewel and other *aestels*) and the luxury of the high Middle Ages. The burden of Norman taxation must, indeed, have been heavy.

From the second half of the 12th century, however, there is a wealth of material illustrating the power of feudal relationships, wealth and piety. Some of the jewellery of this period is outstanding and it is a pity that more was not shown in the excellently reproduced colour plates. We could have done with one or two gold and silver seals, and such masterpieces of the medieval jeweller's art as the gem encrusted silver-gilt New College jewel in full colour. However, it is a little churlish to complain about a book that points the way towards a sociological and anthropological study of other periods (such as Greece and Rome), similarly based on objects from daily life. It is doubtful, however, that it will ever be better done than here in this truly classic work.

MARTIN HENIG

Decorated Medieval Floor Tiles of Somerset. By BARBARA J. LOWE. Taunton, Somerset Archaeological and Natural History Society and Somerset County Museum Service, 2003. vi + 160 pp.,
  17 figs. ISBN 086 183 366X. £14.95 (pb).

It is a pleasure to welcome this long-awaited volume: the result of many years work, started in 1961 when the author examined the medieval floor-tiles from excavations at Keynsham Abbey. The work resulted in a booklet on the Keynsham tiles, published in 1978 (*JBAA*, 132 (1979), 119–20).

Some six hundred tile designs from 68 sites (Bristol and Bath are not included) are published here, arranged thematically by design motif. This approach has distinct advantages for the field-worker trying to find a design parallel, but it removes a wide variety of designs from the particular groups to which they belong. This makes it difficult to reconstruct any individual group. Each numbered design is described and provenanced, a group and dating suggested and parallels given. Following the published designs each site is listed with cross references to the designs.

The introduction contains a general review of floor-tile production, though some of the groups referred to have no relevance to Somerset: especially 'plain tile mosaic', 'sgraffito', 'line-impressed' and 'Penn': these could have been excluded. It is a pity that several articles in this Association's publications have not been taken into account. The plain tile mosaic at Canterbury Cathedral ('pre-1220') has been reassessed by Christopher Norton and Mark Horton, who con-clude that the tile mosaic pavement cannot be associated with the altar step in use in 1220, but must belong to a later arrangement, which dates the tiles to *c.* 1285–90 (ibid., 134 (1981), 58–80). This affects Lowe's dating of the mosaic group present in Somerset.

More relevant is Lowe's discussion of the so-called Wessex school. To give a fuller appreciation of how the Somerset material fits into this, Norton's work should have been mentioned. It is disconcerting that Norton's excellent publications are not cited more frequently. He has shown that the earliest tiles from Winchester Castle and Marwell Manor can be dated to the early 1240s, predating the inlaid mosaic roundel from the King's Chapel, Clarendon Palace, ordered in 1244 and the pavement in the Queen's Chamber at Clarendon Palace, ordered between 1250 and 1252 (*BAA Trans.*, VI (1981), 78–93; *BAA Trans.*, XVII (1996), 90–105). For the art historical contexts of Wessex and French tiles Norton's important paper, which discusses the relationship of the decorated mosaic roundel at Notre-Dame at Cunault, Anjou, with the Clarendon Palace roundel and the Wessex school should have been mentioned (*BAA Trans.*, XXVI (2003), 210–34). It is unfortunate that Cunault is printed as Canault on page 9.

While Warwick Rodwell's volumes on Wells Cathedral, which must be well known to the majority of our members, are noted, Jane Harcourt's paper on the Cleeve Abbey, Somerset, tiles published in this *Journal* might have been given a fuller airing (153 (2000), 30–70). Alan Vince's appendix on the petrology of the Cleeve tiles concludes that two groups (4 and 5) can be identified as products of a well-known factory whose tiles 'were widely distributed around the Bristol Channel'. Lowe, adding to her then completed text, states that they are 'products of a tile kiln in the Gloucestershire area' (p. 12), revising her entries for Cleeve, where, wrongly, a Wessex origin is suggested.

The tiles of Group 4 in the frater pavement at Cleeve are large well-made inlaid heraldic tiles 198 to 208 mm square, showing the arms of England, de Clare and Edmund, earl of Cornwall. It has been accepted generally that the occurrence of the arms of de Clare and Edmund commemo-rate the marriage of Edmund and Margaret de Clare in 1272. Harcourt noted that 'no other heral-dic tiles of this size were produced by the tilery at the time'. However, this reviewer's excavations at Blackfriars, Gloucester, found not only the same three large arms as at Cleeve, but also another large tile in the same fabric showing the arms of Berkeley. Part of the same design from Wells has been published by Rodwell but was not then recognised.

The frater pavement at Cleeve Abbey seems an unlikely place to commemorate the marriage of 1272, and the arms of Berkeley in this group open up the question of another interpretation. The Berkeley connection suggests a Gloucestershire origin in the late thirteenth century for placing the four arms together. This would seem to be confirmed by a collection of smaller tiles of the same group from St Bartholomew's Hospital, Gloucester. The inclusions in the fabric are insufficiently distinct to pinpoint the location of the kiln. The presence of tiles of the same group in south Wales, mapped (Group 9) by J. M. Lewis in his 1999 study *The Medieval Tiles of Wales*, which is an example for all to follow, suggests production somewhere in the Severn Valley, or near the Bristol Channel.

Lowe lists many tiles, usually referred to as '?Worcester type', 'Droitwich', or 'South Worcestershire'. These, too, have a wide distribution in the Severn basin and south Wales (Lewis, Group 20). Although some of these were made at Droitwich, tile wasters from a tile-kiln found in Silver Street, Worcester, now support a Worcester origin. The most important comparable sites are Worcester Cathedral, where there are five *in situ* pavements, datable to 1377–80 (*BAA Trans.*, 1 (1978), 144–60), and Gloucester Cathedral, where tiles surround the tomb of Edward II and are present in the sanctuary: they probably date to the furnishing of the remodelled choir, dated by Christopher Wilson to about 1360. Significantly, later designs have been found at St Oswald's Priory, Gloucester, dated by Vince to within a decade of two of *c.* 1400. These are well represented at a number of sites in Gloucestershire.

Certainly, two of the tile groups found in Somerset serve to illustrate the importance of the Bristol Channel in the transport of medieval tiles: and this is reinforced by the distribution of tiles of other groups not found in Somerset. Lowe's important work places Somerset medieval tiles in an important archaeological context with tiles in the South-West, south Wales, Gloucestershire and Worcestershire.

We owe Barbara Lowe an enormous debt of gratitude for bringing her extensive research programme to a successful publication. That the volume is so well designed and produced is due to Peter Ellis. There are a few minor inconsistencies in the citing of works in the bibliography but these do not detract from a work of substance.

LAURENCE KEEN

Greater Medieval Houses of England and Wales. Vol III, Southern England. By ANTHONY EMERY. Cambridge, CUP, 2006. 725 pp., numerous illus. ISBN 052158132X. £175.00.

Acton Court: The evolution of an early Tudor courtier's house. By KIRSTY RODWELL and ROBERT BELL. London, English Heritage, 2004. 444 pp., many b/w illus., col. figs, fold-outs. ISBN 1873592639. £80.00 (pb).

The completion of Emery's *magnum opus* puts all scholars of medieval architecture in his debt. Bringing (we are told) the total number of houses considered to over 750, in almost 1,900 pages and about as many illustrations, he has left his third and largest volume for southern England. The study is divided into three sub-regions: Thames Valley, London and the South-East, and the South-West, each with its own historical introduction. Again there are careful lists of licences to crenellate, and a scattering of essays on a variety of themes (e.g. lodgings, secular art, and the value of Leland and the Buck brothers). A discussion of the impact of the Hundred Year's War is a nice opportunity for a timely reminder that castles such as Bodiam and Amberley, often these days regarded as play-castles, were in fact built at a time of a very real and imminent threat of coastal attack.

This part, as with the whole work, is of great practical value for its clear analysis of better and less well-known buildings, often with outline plans explaining development rather more readily (e.g. Knole) than vastly detailed ground plans which would have taken a lifetime to assemble. The accounts of individual houses are anything than merely architectural, and show a constant awareness of the nuances of family history and local geography. As before, the term 'greater' houses is allowed to include quite a variety of greater and lesser buildings, such as colleges and granges, and not just those of the aristocracy and upper gentry. Unfortunately some (e.g. Cowdray) are just too late to get under the bar as 'medieval', but then it would have been an even longer task to complete so successfully.

If Emery represents the best kind of a collective general study, then *Acton Court* by contrast represents the very best of a particular study. It reports on an extraordinary project to investigate and record the remnant of a great house through the archaeology of its fabric and buried remains before releasing it again for private use. The house would be remarkable in any case, but has the added interest for the clear association of a major building phase in the surviving part with a royal visit by Henry VIII in 1535. Much of the history of the house comes from the excavation of lost portions, admirably done and clearly and attractively presented, but the fabric analysis has been equally archaeological and informative, and its reporting is a model of how this can best be done, both for the narrative treatment and the presentation of architectural details (and again the pleasing illustrations).

The overall phasing is explained briefly in the introduction, and then the history is given (though a predictable editorial fascism has made the admirable history section almost unreadable by disallowing the use of footnotes). The main sequence of building development is then presented as a single archaeological account, whether from below or above ground, with separate sections on internal decoration and the architectural context for the Tudor house. Star items include the highly sophisticated wall paintings in latest 'antik' style, a Kratzer sundial, and the best in international tableware apparently bought for the king's visit amongst many other finds of domestic rubbish. The decision by English Heritage to expend so much effort on Acton Court, and for once to dig properly rather than 'preserve in situ', has been amply rewarded. For a model publication that deserves to be used as an exemplar the price of *Acton* is excessive, whereas with Emery for what you get the excessive price seems almost reasonable.

JULIAN MUNBY

The Idea of the Castle in Medieval England and Wales. By ABIGAIL WHEATLEY. Woodbridge and Rochester, NY, York Medieval Press in association with Boydell and Brewer, 2004. 174 pp., 17 col. pls, 5 b/w illus. ISBN 1 903153 14 X. £40.00.

Occasionally the workings of the Zeitgeist seem to be undeniable: how else to explain the publication in 2003 of C. Whitehead, *Castles of the Mind* (Cardiff) and, a year later, the volume under review? Although both books consider castles in allegory and metaphor, Wheatley's is of more immediate interest to historians of art and architecture, since her purpose is to consider what the term 'castle' meant to people in medieval England (and Wales, despite the title) and how the building designs absorbed and reflected literary traditions.

By taking account of chronicles, charters, stories, seals and illustrations of castles in other media, Wheatley challenges traditional approaches to castle studies. She builds on recent work on meaning and symbolism to suggest that the interpretation of the castle as a fortified aristocratic residence introduced by the Normans is too limited. She argues that for contemporaries the Latin *Castellum* resonated far more than the French *Castel*. The word covered a wider variety of fortified enclosure; and it appeared in both Latin literature and Latin translations of the Bible, thus achieving Antique as well as spiritual validity. Wheatley's exposition, although clear, is too complicated to be given fully here. She ranges from Biblical connotations to legends of Troy, Rome and Jerusalem, exploring the symbolism of Christ's entry to Bethany, the Virgin as castle, and foundation myths that saw the towers of ancient, legendary cities as representing civic harmony.

She argues persuasively that the imperial connotations detected in such castles as Colchester and Caernarfon reflect an interest in Britain's Roman past. The polychrome masonry banding at Caernarfon was based not on the Theodosian walls of Constantinople, as suggested by the late Arnold Taylor, but on standing Roman masonry visible in several places in England including London and, one might add, Wroxeter.

Unlike several recent productions this book does not read like the PhD thesis on which it is based. Wheatley guides her readers through the maze with signposts and summaries. Her authorial intrusions (e.g. 'I seek to show') are mildly tiresome, but seem to reflect current trends in scholarly writing. The reference on p. 138 to the tomb of Edward II should, given the context, be amended to that of Edward I.

Wheatley has provided much material for us to think about in trying to understand castles in their time and place. She has made a significant contribution to the opening up of castle studies. Here castles achieve parity with churches in being legitimate subjects of symbolic and allegorical enquiry, and the book is a welcome addition to the growing literature that addresses these questions. Pevsner's famous distinction between Lincoln Cathedral as architecture and a bicycle shed as building should perhaps be modified: architecture is a building of whatever kind that carries meaning. BAA members can feel proud that the award of an Ochs Scholarship helped Wheatley to finish her work.

NICOLA COLDSTREAM

Stonehenge. By JULIAN RICHARDS. English Heritage, 2005. 48 pp. ISBN 1 85074 933 7. £4.99 (pb); *Birdoswald Roman Fort.* By TONY WILMOTT. English Heritage, 2005. 40 pp. ISBN 1 85074 956 6. £3.50 (pb); *Goodrich Castle.* By JEREMY ASHBEE. English Heritage, 2005. 48 pp. ISBN 1 85074 942 6. £3.50 (pb); *Lindisfarne Priory.* By JOANNA STORY. English Heritage, 2005. 40 pp. ISBN 1 85074 943 4. £3.99 (pb); *Belsay Hall, Castle and Gardens.* By ROGER WHITE. English Heritage, 2005. 48 pp. ISBN 1 85074 924 8. £3.99 (pb); *Apsley House: The Wellington Collection.* By JULIUS BRYANT. English Heritage, 2005. 48 pp. ISBN 1 85074 932 9. £3.99 (pb); *Old Sarum.* By JOHN MCNEILL. English Heritage, 2006. 40 pp. ISBN 1 85074 981 7. £3.50 (pb); *Kenilworth Castle.* By RICHARD K. MORRIS. English Heritage, 2006. 52 pp. ISBN 1 85074 980 9. £3.99 (pb); *Caerwent Roman Town.* By RICHARD J. BREWER. CADW, 3rd edn, 2006. 56 pp. ISBN 1 85760 216 1. £3.50 (pb); *Chepstow Castle.* By RICK TURNER. CADW, rev. edn 2006. 56 pp. ISBN 1 85760 229 3. £3.50 (pb); *Blaenavon Ironworks and World Heritage Landscape.* By PETER WAKELIN. CADW 2006. 64 pp. ISBN 1 85760 123 8. £3.50 (pb).

A review of the new CADW guidebooks in the pages of this journal (*JBAA*, 155 (2002), 329–31) noted how superior the Welsh series of guidebooks was to those then on offer from English Heritage. Clearly some people with influence in English Heritage shared such thoughts, and the result is a new series of more scholarly guidebooks. There is no copyright on good ideas and it has to be said at once that the influence of CADW screams out from every page and from the material on and in the card covers. The first part of this review will make a few comparisons as to style and format, and the second will deal with content.

The covers of the CADW guidebooks with their Times New Roman titles, and sweeping views of the monument achieve a classic simplicity, aided by the attractive daffodil yellow spine, the back cover having a map of nearby monuments in Wales. English Heritage adopts a thin and, to my eyes, rather ugly sans serif typography, and somewhat garish spine and back cover with pictures of highlights of the site to tempt the casual browser. Inside the Welsh series at the front are a well written publisher's blurb and, at the back, an invaluable list of key dates; English Heritage has a series of thumb-nail 'highlights', and at the back a bibliography, which in the Welsh series is printed at the back of the text, and sites to visit in the area. In the case of the *Goodrich* guide one may be surprised to learn that Kenilworth is quite near. Most people would think White Castle, Grosmont, Skenfrith and Chepstow were rather closer as well as more apposite to Goodrich, but then they are across the border in Wales. At least that misleading information will now lead one to one of the best and perhaps the most attractive of the English Heritage guides, Richard K. Morris's *Kenilworth*, assuredly a must for any visitor to the site! Both series have reconstructions of the monuments in order to find one's way about, but English Heritage has greater concern with telling the visitor that there are car parks, loos and refreshment facilities. Both have plans of the monuments though the typography style of those in the Welsh series remains far better.

The Welsh guidebooks measure 254 by 210 mm, a handy size in the frequent howling gales one finds in Wales, but also convenient in the study. English Heritage has two sizes, all 289 mm in height but whereas the longer volumes are 210 mm across, *Birdoswald*, *Goodrich* and *Old Sarum* are 'slimline' at 160 mm. Neither feels quite right, the larger volumes are too cumbersome and the others feel mean. Visitors to the Wye valley will find this especially jarring if they visit all the castles mentioned above.

As for content, there is less to choose between the two series, and sometimes comparisons are difficult to make. There is no prehistoric monument in Wales with quite the significance of *Stonehenge*, and of course there are many specialist (and not-so-specialist) books and papers on it and its landscape. While English Heritage as an organisation still struggles to find a solution to the problem of presenting a World Heritage site as it should be shown, preferably without roads, car-parks, loos or souvenir shops, Julian Richards has done a good job in text, photographs and reconstruction drawings at doing just that. With *Birdoswald*, comparison can be made with, for example, CADW's volume on *Caerleon*. Alas, the temptation to dumb down, so evident is some earlier English Heritage guidebooks rears its head again in, for example, the inadequate and misleading description of the intaglios on p. 3 while the reconstructed Roman sculpture of Vulcan and Jupiter 'as it might once have looked' on p. 5 seems to have strayed from a children's comic. Dumbed down too is the history of Hadrian's Wall on p. 23 while in discussing the 5th century we find the superfluous statement 'it is part of the archaeologist's job to form theories that can be tested by future work'. Tony Wilmott has written superbly on Birdoswald elsewhere and presumably the brief about English Heritage going up-market did not reach the far north. Fortunately Jeremy Ashbee in his *Goodrich* has managed to write a castle book as informative and wide ranging as those that have come out on the west bank of the Wye, and is only let down by deficiencies of format (mentioned above). Details like the map showing the movements of Countess Joan and her household in 1296/97 accompanied by a vignette from the Luttrell Psalter, comparative details from Welsh castles and an intelligent guided tour give one some hope for the future. So too do John McNeill's *Old Sarum* and Joanna Story's *Lindisfarne*; the former takes us from Iron Age hillfort to imaginative reconstruction of Norman castle and cathedral and the continued existence of the site as a Rotten Borough; the latter takes us beyond the medieval Priory to consider the importance of the site in terms of Celtic and Northumbrian Christianity. Both guides show us that English Heritage has no lack of really good, imaginative writers. Belsay has the well-preserved ruins of a peel tower well described in Roger White's guidebook to *Belsay*, though most of this volume is taken up with the early 19th-century house. Another house only recently taken over by English Heritage is *Apsley House*, unlike Belsay, still a showcase of the opulence showered on the hero of the war against Napoleon. Julius Bryant has certainly provided a much-needed guidebook which puts all that gold and gilt in context.

There are, nevertheless, important questions to be asked. Research is constant and the Welsh guidebooks are forever being updated. The reviewer has before him the new edition of Rick Turner's 2002 CADW guide to *Chepstow Castle* recently reviewed in this Journal and now carefully revised and with a considerable amount of new material reflecting the very latest research and criticism. Richard Brewer's guide to *Caerwent* has similarly been greatly augmented for a third edition and now appears in the splendid new format. These are classic sites in every way for the Medieval Castle and Roman Town and ideal introductions to these subjects even for a reader living far away from Wales. Will *Belsay* and *Apsley*, for example, be similarly updated in a year or so? Will they too become classics? Let us return to Blake's 'Satanic mills' at Stonehenge, a World Heritage site, and at first glance utterly different from the mills at *Blaenavon*, that other World Heritage site, though the visitor may well find herself similarly awed by this colossal wreck of an Industrial Landscape. But the guidebook CADW has produced is simply longer, more scholarly and trail blazing in every way. The plans, photographs and text bring back (perhaps to haunt our sanitised age) the human costs of the Industrial Revolution. At three quarters of the price and a third as long again as *Stonehenge*, it surely deserves an award.

Without the continuing vitality and increasing standards of the Welsh series this review would have doubtless been much shorter and more complacent. After all, the English Heritage guides appear, at last, to be moving in the right direction, and undoubtedly visiting the monuments discussed in most of them will be more pleasurable in future. But too many questions still remain. Some concern individual guides: Will the deficiencies still apparent in the *Birdoswald* guide be made good? Others are concerned with format: The slimline versions are mean looking and in the case of *Goodrich*, especially, is shown up painfully by the design qualities of the guides to nearby CADW properties. Is it too late to go over to the Welsh format entirely?

MARTIN HENIG

The Victoria History of the Counties of England. A History of the County of Chester Vol. V Part 1, The City of Chester: General History and Topography; Vol. V Part 2, The City of Chester: Culture, Buildings, Institutions. Edited by C. P. LEWIS and A. T. THACKER. Woodbridge, Boydell & Brewer for the Institute of Historical Research, 2003/2005. xvii + 288 pp./xxiv + 398 pp., numerous illus. ISBN 1 904356 00 1/1 904356 03 6. £90.00 each.

Medieval Trim, History and Archaeology. By RICHARD POTTERTON. Dublin, Four Courts Press, 2005. 464 pp., numerous illus. ISBN 1 85182 926 1. £50.00.

New Winchelsea Sussex. A Medieval Port Town. By DAVID and BARBARA MARTIN. King's Lynn, Heritage Marketing for UCL Field Archaeology Unit, 2004. 222 pp., numerous illus. ISBN 0 9544456 51. £24.50 (pb).

As the *Victoria County History* gets on with its job of completing the history of the English counties the occurrence of major cities is naturally rather rare, and it is the more to be welcomed that Chester is the subject of not one but two volumes (divided into (1) general history and topography, and (2) culture, buildings and institutions). There can be few places where an historical narrative can be written of the Roman period, but Chester benefits from a long tradition of archaeological investigation, as well as more recent work on the fabric of the medieval town. The narrative of the early medieval town, and its growth as a regional centre, garrison, and port is masterly. It brings out the proximity to the border with Wales, and the importance of the port for the trade with Ireland, and the export of Cheshire salt, and at the same time provides a firm but readable guide through the thickets of constitutional history of the burgesses and their emerging privileges won from the King and Earl. In all these areas people working on other towns will have recourse to *Chester* for comparative material and the benefits of a modern approach to old questions. The 'topography' section intervenes between historic and modern Chester to explain the growth of the town and provide a narrative of the built city. The second volume, like the first, is fully illustrated (now integrated into the text) and treats of the cathedral, castle and defences in full, and with a special section on The Rows as well as transport, markets and mills. It would have been useful to have had a proper mapping of town fields and commons, but that is a minor quibble for a job that has been so well done.

Medieval Trim is a superb monograph on a single medieval town, and one of Ireland's finest, with its remarkable castle, defences, churches and hospital. The confident treatment of historical, topographical and archaeological sources makes for a well balanced account, and the town is placed in the context of the Lacy lordship of Meath, and the landscape of this heartland of the pale that survived (just about) the late medieval shrinkage of the Anglo-Norman settlement. The administration and urban topography are well described, and there is a full investigation of the fascinating castle, and effectively a detailed archaeological inventory of all the existing remains of buildings in the town (with further details in a series of historical and archaeological appendices). Although the Irish *Historic Towns Atlas* is moving at some speed, with an excellent output, there is a clear need for more exhaustive monographs of this kind.

New Winchelsea is a major re-investigation of the well-known story of the classic hill-top Sussex *bastide*, left high and dry by a silting harbour, to which much new insight is brought as the result of detailed survey and investigation. This is partly represented in a companion volume in which the excavations were published (D. Martin and D. Rudling, *Excavations in Winchelsea, Sussex 1974–2000* (2004)), but the work we have here is more of an historical and architectural account. The origins of the town are discussed, and there is a re-examination of the internal topography of the tenement layout (the opportunity should have been taken to republish the famous rental from which the town plan has been derived). The Martins have conducted a searching investigation of the remaining cellars (almost the sole remnant of the vanished town) and provided a thoughtful discussion of their function, reaching towards what seems apparent from elsewhere that the more elaborate ones were probably wine taverns. The churches and defences are also described and discussed, and there is a good general narrative of the growth and disappearance of the town. Winchelsea has long deserved a proper account such as this, and its price should ensure the wide circulation it deserves.

JULIAN MUNBY

SHORT NOTICES

Archaeological fantasies. How pseudoarchaeology misrepresents the past and misleads the public. Edited by GARRETT G. FAGAN. Abingdon, Routledge, 2006. 417 pp., illus. ISBN 0 415 305993 4. £25.00 (pb).

An important collection of a dozen papers on world-wide aspects of the misrepresentation of the past through delusions arising from the wild outskirts of nationalism and religion to plain commercial dishonesty of those who make books and television programmes, for all of whom the truth matters little. The value of the book lies in its careful dissection of particular instances and the demonstration of the relationship between the fantasies of charlatans with post-modernism and new-age tosh, and the sad readiness of 'the public' to be led astray by paranoid nonsense about pseudoscience as much as pseudoarchaeology.

The Beautiful Burial in Roman Egypt. Art, Identity, and Funerary Religion. By CHRISTINA RIGGS. Oxford, Oxford Studies in Ancient Culture and Representation, 2005. xxiii + 334 pp., 126 figs, 12 col. pls. ISBN 0 19 927665 X. £80.00.

Although there have been several studies of mummy portraits from the Fayum, this study is pitched far wider and surveys painted shrouds, coffins and funerary art in general where naturalistic Graeco-Roman features are incorporated into traditional [Pharaonic] Egyptian funerary ritual and iconography. Riggs not only considers funerary art that is fully Hellenised, but many other works where the native traditions remain paramount. With a thoroughly approachable text, and a large body of little known but often beguiling paintings and mummy cases this is an important and unusual contribution to the art-historical understanding of the Roman Empire. In the Archaising traditions of Western Thebes as well as elsewhere, the early medievalist will want to ask questions about the birth of Coptic art. This book is produced to high standards and can be commended in every way except for the exorbitant price, which will militate against it achieving the wide circulation it deserves.

Celtic Gods. Comets in Irish Mythology. By PATRICK MCCAFFERTY and MIKE BAILLIE. Stroud, Tempus Publishing, 2005. 224 pp., 68 figs. ISBN 0 7524 3444 6. £15.99 (pb).

Dramatic celestial events occurring in Irish mythology that were described as supernatural (and therefore often disregarded by scholars) can also be interpreted as deriving from actual observations of real phenomena, such as comets. A re-examination of many such stories also calls upon scientific evidence (such as dendrochronology and ice cores) to look again at the chronological context, and inevitably turns to the cataclysmic natural events in the middle of the 6th century which are increasingly being seen as playing a major part in Dark Age history.

The Sutton Hoo Sceptre and the Roots of Celtic Kingship Theory. By MICHAEL J. ENRIGHT. Dublin, Four Courts Press, 2006. 387 pp. ISBN 1 85182 636 x. £50.00.

This full-length study of one object from the Sutton Hoo burial places the sceptre in the context of pre-Christian British theories of kingship, drawing on a wide range of celtic iconography and literary sources.

Early Anglo-Saxon buckets. A Corpus of Copper Alloy- and Iron-bound, Stave-built vessels. By JEAN M. COOK. Oxford University School of Archaeology: Monograph No. 60 (distributed by Oxbow Books), 2004. 128 pp., numerous illus. ISBN 0 947816 64 X. £18.00.

A careful consideration of over 200 examples of wooden buckets with metal fittings, this valuable study has sadly appeared as a posthumous volume, partly due to the generous assistance given by

Jean Cook to helping others complete their studies. Her archive has been ordered and published by colleagues, as a fitting memorial to her scholarship, and an important study in its own right.

Anglo-Saxons. Studies presented to Cyril Roy Hart. Edited by SIMON KEYNES and ALFRED P. SMYTH. Dublin, Four Courts Press, 2006. 317 pp. ISBN 1 85182 932 6. £55.00.

A fine collection of seventeen essays on Anglo-Saxon literature, medicine, law, charters, landscape, chronicles and the Danelaw by leading Saxonists, to celebrate the life and writings of Cyril Hart (with bibliography). Noteworthy are Metcalf's paper on money circulation in the Danelaw, and Owen-Crocker on sources of the Bayeaux tapestry, while Fox and Oosthuizen have interesting contributions on landscape reconstruction in Dartmoor and Cambridgeshire.

Sandlands. The Suffolk Coast and Heaths. By TOM WILLIAMSON. Macclesfield, Windgather Press, 2005. 164 pp., 72 illus. ISBN 1 905119 02 X. £18.99 (pb).

Hedgerow History: Ecology, History & Landscape Character. By GERRY BARNES and TOM WILLIAMSON. Macclesfield, Windgather Press, 2006. 152 pp., 59 illus. ISBN 1 905119 04 6. £18.99 (pb).

These attractive and accessible studies are two examples in the Windgather Press series on the 'Landscapes of Britain'. *Sandlands* is a landscape history of the Suffolk coastal belt, chronicling the changes (largely disappearance) of wetlands, heaths and woodland in recent centuries, not to mention the older and well-known cases of the loss of towns at Dunwich and Aldeburgh. *Hedgerow History* is an attempt to use botanical and historical sources (in part based on a detailed Norfolk study) to take hedgerow studies beyond species counting, and ends with some important advice on the nature of 'landscape character'.

'Outrageous Waves'. Global Warming and Coastal Change in Britain through Two Thousand Years. By BASIL CRACKNELL. Chichester, Phillimore, 2005. 320 pp., 185 illus. ISBN 1 86077 344 0. £19.99.

Anyone who has worked on the history of a coastal site in England will be aware of occasional references to medieval storms and tide surges. Only now with Cracknell's careful assembling of diverse evidence from a multitude of places and sources has it been possible to show wider patterns of activity that do seem to add up to a medieval phase of 'global warming'. Whatever lessons this may have for the future, the general picture will be of value in providing a broad context for the rise and fall of coastal settlement.

Royston Grange. 6000 Years of Peakland Landscape. By RICHARD HODGES. Stroud, Tempus Publishing, 2006. 160 pp., 100 figs, 26 col. pls. ISBN 0 7524 3653 8. £17.99 (pb).

A classic study of upland settlement somewhere in the Peak District (the site is omitted from the location map!), this shows how a topographical and archaeological study of stone boundary walls can take elements of the existing landscape back to the Roman and prehistoric era. This revised edition in a more popular series should encourage other studies of this nature elsewhere in these islands.

The Malvern Hills. An Ancient Landscape. By MARK BOWDEN et al. London, English Heritage, 2005. 69 pp., numerous illus. ISBN 1 873592 82 5. £8.99 (pb).

As might be expected, this contains the exquisite results of measured field surveys and delightful aerial photos as the apogee of landscape archaeology, while somehow managing to miss out on much discussion of the medieval landscape history (i.e. the relationship of the Malverns to surrounding settlements, landuse, and boundaries).

Barentin's Manor. Excavations of the moated manor at Harding's Field, Chalgrove, Oxfordshire 1976–9. By PHILIP PAGE, KATE ATHERTON and ALAN HARDY. Oxford, Oxford Archaeology (Thames Valley Landscapes Monograph No. 24), 2005. 198 pp., numerous illus. ISBN 0 947816 623. £19.95.

The remarkable excavation of a well-documented moated site became a text-book example even before it was published, but it has been worth the wait for the final exposition of the never-ending changes to the crowded group of buildings, the finds and ecological history set against the changing fortunes of the gentry family of Barentin.

The Catesby Family and their Brasses at Ashby St Ledgers, Northamptonshire. Edited by JEROME BERTRAM. London, Monumental Brass Society, 2006. 122 pp., 48 illus. ISBN 0 9543271 3 6. £20.00 (pb).

An exemplary study of this family group of brasses based on surviving remains and antiquarian sources (which has indeed led to the identification and recovery of missing elements), family history and heraldry (the last being a final contribution of the late John Goodall, the indefatigable antiquary, of whom an excellent portrait is included).

A History of the Stained Glass of St George's Chapel, Windsor Castle. Edited by SARAH BROWN. Windsor, St George's Chapel Monograph No. 18 (distributed by Oxbow Books), 2005. 263 pp., numerous illus. ISBN 0 9539676 3 8. £30.00 (pb).

A comprehensive account of the glass by various authors, covering medieval, Netherlandish and 18th-century glass; glass by Willement, Clayton & Bell, and Piper; and a substantial section on heraldic glass.

The Choir-Stalls at Amiens Cathedral. By CHARLES TRACY and HUGH HARRISON. Reading, Spire Books, 2004. 208 pp., 125 illus. ISBN 0 9543615 6 3. £49.95.

A masterly study of the early-16th-century stalls at Amiens, favoured by Ruskin. The spirited carving of the misericords and end panels, along with the exuberant canopies necessarily requires consideration of stylistic influences to explain the wonderful combination of Flamboyant Gothic and Italian renaissance detail, and this is given together with an instructive account of a full structural analysis of the joinery of the stalls.

A History of English Glassmaking AD 43–1800. By HUGH WILLMOTT. Stroud, Tempus Publishing, 2005. 157 pp., 90 figs, 28 col. pls. ISBN 0 7524 3131 5. £10.99 (pb).

A welcome summary of the archaeology of glass production from the Romans down to the Georgian era, all the more welcome for bringing together the scattered results of archaeological investigation and linking them to the economic history of the industry.

ALSO RECEIVED

Digital Archaeology. Bridging Method and Theory. Edited by T. L. EVANS and P. DALY. Abingdon, Routledge, 2006. 255 pp., illus. ISBN 0 415 30150 4. £17.99 (pb).

From the Air. Understanding Aerial Archaeology. By KENNETH BROPHY and DAVID COWLEY. Stroud, Tempus Publishing, 2005. 190 pp., 82 illus. ISBN 0 7524 3130 7. £19.99 (pb).

Prehistoric Figurines: Corporeality in the Neolithic. By DOUGLASS BAILEY. Abingdon, Routledge, 2005. 256 pp., numerous illus. ISBN 0 415 331528. £25.99 (pb).

Fossils. A very short introduction. BY KEITH THOMSON. Oxford OUP, 2005. 160 pp., illus. ISBN 0 19 280504 5. £6.99 (pb).

The Last Imaginary Place. A Human History of the Arctic World. By ROBERT MCGHEE. Oxford OUP, 2006. 296 pp., numerous illus. ISBN 0 19 280730 9. £20.00.

Local Responses to Colonization in the Iron Age Mediterranean. BY TAMAR HODOS. Abingdon, Routledge, 2006. 264 pp., illus. ISBN 0 415 37836 2. £65.00.

ANNUAL REPORT OF THE COUNCIL FOR THE YEAR ENDED 31 DECEMBER 2005

1 CONSTITUTION AND AIMS. The British Archaeological Association is a registered company limited by guarantee (no. 2747476) and a registered charity (no. 1014821). It is concerned to promote and further the study of archaeology and the preservation of antiquities, to carry out and encourage research into art, architecture and antiquities, and to publish material in furtherance of its activities. The Association organises an annual lecture programme and conference, and publishes an annual *Journal* in addition to the *Transactions* of its conferences.

2 GOVERNING BODY. The Officers and Members of the Council are the Board of Directors of the Limited Company and the Trustees of the Charity. The Officers and Members of Council during 2005 were as follows.

President:	Nicola Coldstream, M.A., Ph.D., F.S.A.
Vice-Presidents:	
Past Presidents:	Sir David Wilson, M.A., Litt.D., Fil.Dr., Dr Phil., F.B.A., F.S.A., F.R.Hist.S. (1963–68)
	Professor Peter Kidson, M.A., Ph.D., F.S.A. (1980–82)
	Richard D. H. Gem, O.B.E., M.A., Ph.D., F.S.A. (1983–89)
	Laurence J. Keen, O.B.E., M.Phil., F.S.A., F.R.Hist.S., M.I.F.A. (1989–2004)
Elected:	John Cherry, M.A., F.S.A., F.R.Hist.S.
	John Coales, F.S.A.
	Brian K. Davison, O.B.E., B.A., F.S.A., M.I.F.A.
	Peter Draper, M.A., F.S.A.
	Professor Eric Fernie, C.B.E., B.A., F.B.A., F.S.A., F.R.S.E.
	William Filmer-Sankey, MA, D.Phil., F.S.A.
	Michael F. Flint, F.S.A.
	B. Graham Maney
	Kenneth S. Painter, M.A., F.S.A.
	Glenys Phillips, M.D.
	Professor George Zarnecki, C.B.E., Ph.D., D.Litt., F.B.A., F.S.A., F.R.Hist.S.
Honorary Director:	Jennifer S. Alexander, B.A., Ph.D., F.S.A.
Honorary Secretary:	John McNeill, M.A., F.S.A.
Honorary Assistant Secretary:	Antonio da Cruz, B.Eng.
Honorary Treasurer:	Stuart Bedwell (*to 3 May*)
	John Dunlop, B.A., F.C.M.A. (*from 5 October*)
Honorary Membership Secretary:	John Jenkins
Honorary Editor:	Martin Henig, M.A., D.Phil., D.Litt., F.S.A.
Honorary Assistant Editor:	Lauren T. Gilmour, M.A., Ph.D., F.S.A., A.M.A.
Honorary Reviews Editor:	Julian Munby, B.A., F.S.A.

The Council met on 2 February, 4 May, 5 October and 7 December. The AGM was held on 5 October.

3   MEMBERSHIP. The membership at 31 December 2005 was as follows

	2005	2004
Ordinary members:	257	274
Retired members:	155	163
Student members:	24	29
Life members:	71	72
Institutional members:	176	176
	683	714

278 of the individual members are also guarantors of the incorporated Company. The effect of the rise in subscription rates, which came into force in 2005, may have contributed to the slight fall in membership. None the less, the Council remains committed to trying to increase the numbers involved in the Association's activities.

4   ACTIVITIES DURING 2005. The following lectures were held in the rooms of the Society of Antiquaries from January to May and from October to December.

5 January 2005:   'Lord Leicester's remodelling of Kenilworth Castle for Elizabeth I' by Dr Richard K. Morris.
2 February 2005:   No lecture was possible owing to a power cut at Burlington House.

2 March 2005:	'The Hôtel Saint-Pol, Paris; Main Residence of the Valois Kings' by Mary Whiteley.
6 April 2005:	'Who, Where, What and Why? Trondheim Cathedral and its Decoration in the 12th Century' by James F. King.
4 May 2005:	'Architecture and Patronage at Croxden Abbey' by Dr Jackie Hall.
5 October 2005:	'The Façade of the Great Church from the 4th to the 12th Centuries: Some Observations' by Barrie Singleton.
2 November 2005:	'This Little Westminster: The Chantry-Chapel of Sir Henry Vernon at Tong, Shropshire', by Heather Gilderdale Scott.
7 December 2004:	'The Priory in the Flowerbeds, Felley Priory, Nottinghamshire' by Dr Jennifer Alexander.

The Association particularly wishes to record its admiration for the stoicism shown by February's disappointed lecturer, Mr Barrie Singleton, and its thanks to Dr Jennifer Alexander for stepping in at very short notice in December.

A Twelfth-Night Party was held after the 5 January lecture and the President hosted a reception after the 4 May lecture.

The 2005 conference was held at Bircham Newton, Norfolk, between 23 and 27 July. Organised around the theme of 'Medieval Art, Architecture and Archaeology in King's Lynn and the Fens', it was attended by 105 members and guests. A total of 22 papers were read in the Birches Conference Centre at Bircham Newton, with additional site presentations as and where appropriate. On the Sunday the Conference ventured to King's Lynn, where it divided into three groups so as facilitate access to Clifton House, Thoresby College, St Margaret, St Nicholas, and the Red Mount Chapel. On Monday visits were made to the parish churches of Walsoken, West Walton, Walpole St Peter, and Boston, as well as the castle and collegiate church at Tattershall; and on Tuesday to St Lawrence and the castle at Castle Rising along with Castle Acre Priory. The Association was honoured with receptions at the Stone Hall in King's Lynn, where the mayor of Lynn, Councillor Trevor Manley, along with Dr Brian Ayers, County Archaeologist, welcomed the Association, and at Castle Acre Priory, where Richard Halsey addressed the Association on behalf of English Heritage. The President was in attendance throughout the conference, hosting a reception on the first evening. The Association would like to record its gratitude to all those who helped open doors and assisted in the smooth running of the Conference, particularly David Higgins, Paul Richards and Kate Weaver in King's Lynn, Ian Harper at West Walton, Lord Howard at Castle Rising, and Janet Hubbard at Castle Acre Priory. Grateful thanks are also due to the Conference team, namely John McNeill, Conference Convenor, Anna Eavis, Conference Organiser, and Robert Gwynne, Conference Secretary. Finally, there are two individuals without whom the conference would have been much the poorer, Emma Day of the Birches Conference Centre, and David Pitcher of King's Lynn and West Norfolk District Council. The Association extends heartfelt thanks to both.

Preparations for the Prague Conference, to be held in July 2006, are well in hand.

The Brick Section (Chairman Terence P. Smith, M.A., M.Litt., Secretary Michael Hammett, A.R.I.B.A.) promotes all aspects of brick and brickwork and is affiliated to the British Brick Society. The Annual General Meeting was held on 18 June in Fakenham and was followed by afternoon visits to East Barsham House and the Rectory at Great Snoring.

The Association is represented on the Council for British Archaeology by David Stocker, on the York Archaeological Trust by Professor Peter Lock, on the Committee for the British Archaeological Awards by Brian Davison, and on the Standing Conference of National Period Societies by Dr Ron Baxter. Laurence Keen represents the Association on The Standing Conference on Portable Antiquities.

The members of the Association continue to enjoy the privilege of reading in the library of the Society of Antiquaries. The reciprocal arrangement whereby the Association and the Royal Archaeological Institute allow attendance at each other's lectures also continues. The Association is delighted to note the year witnessed the 80th birthday of its past-president Professor Peter Kidson, and the 90th birthday of its vice-president Professor George Zarnecki.

5   PUBLICATIONS. The *Journal of the British Archaeological Association* for 2005 (Volume 158) included papers on the Vatican Rotunda, the Vernon Chantry-Chapel at Tong, and 16th-century wall paintings at Great Ponton. It was distributed to members in January 2006.

6   THE OCHS SCHOLARSHIP. The Ochs Scholarship, set up with a generous bequest from Miss Maud Lilian Ochs, is intended to enable students and other scholars to complete theses and research projects. The Council was delighted to award the first scholarships in May 1995. From the six applications received for the 2005 scholarship three awards were made:

Claudia Marx: *Theory and Practice in the Restoration of English Cathedrals in late-Victorian England: Peterborough Cathedral in Comparison* (£1,000)
Mavis Nwokobia: *Picturing Pompeii: Victorian Classical Painting and the Legacy of Vesuvius* (£1,000)
Agnieszka Roznowska Sadraei: *'Pater Patriae': St Stanislaus and the Art of the Polish Kings 1200–1490* (£1,000)

All but two of the nineteen 1995–2004 scholars have now completed their theses or research projects. Advertisements for the 2006 scholarships were circulated in late 2005.

7   FUTURE CONFERENCES. The Council has agreed on a provisional programme for future conferences. Although the precise dates of the later conferences have yet to be decided, the cities and regions covered will be Prague on the 7–12 July 2006, Coventry and Warwick in July 2007, and South-West Ireland in July 2008.

THE BRITISH ARCHAEOLOGICAL ASSOCIATION

STATEMENT OF FINANCIAL ACTIVITIES FOR THE YEAR ENDED 31 DECEMBER 2005
(Including income and expenditure account)

	Notes	Current Year	Previous Year
INCOME AND EXPENDITURE			
Incoming Resources			
Grants and Donations		£1,500	£4,339
Annual Subscriptions		14,926	19,605
Conference Income		29,690	29,413
Royalties Receivable from the Sale		898	1300
of Transactions			
Investment Income and Interest		9,919	10,303
Tax Refund		1,727	1,210
Sundry Income		99	40
Total Incoming Resources		£58,759	£66,210
RESOURCES EXPENDED			
Charitable Expenditure	1	56,134	63,195
Total Resources Expended		£56,134	£63,195
NET INCOMING RESOURCES FOR THE YEAR		£2,625	£3,015
OTHER RECOGNISED GAINS AND LOSSES			
Unrealised Gains/(Losses) on Investment Assets		31,858	15,521
NET MOVEMENT OF FUNDS		34,483	18,536
Fund Balances Brought Forward at 1 January 2005		274,107	255,571
Fund Balances Carried Forward at 31 December 2005		£308,590	£274,107

BALANCE SHEET AS AT 31 DECEMBER 2005

	Note	31/12/05	31/12/04
FIXED ASSETS			
Investments	2	£281,910	£250,052
CURRENT ASSETS			
Stock on Hand	240		240
Debtors	2,299		363
Cash at Bank	20,455		21,418
Cash on Deposit	20,303		19,422
	43,297		41,443
Creditors			
Amounts falling due within one year	16,617		17,388
NET CURRENT ASSETS		26,680	24,055
NET ASSETS		£308,590	£274,107
FUNDS (UNRESTRICTED)			
General Fund		£125,038	£111,423
Life Membership Fund		10,577	9,690
Reginald Taylor and Lord Fletcher Fund		10,182	9,106
Ochs 150 Fund		162,793	143,888
		£308,590	£274,107

For the year in question the company was entitled to the exemption conferred by Section 249A(1) of the Companies Act 1985. No notice has been deposited under Section 249B(2) of the Act in relation to the financial year. The Council acknowledge their responsibilities for:

a. Ensuring that the Company keeps accounting records which comply with Section 221 of the Companies Act 1985; and
b. Preparing Accounts which give a true and fair view of the state of affairs of the Company as at the end of the financial year, in accordance with the requirements of Section 226 of the Companies Act 1985, and which otherwise comply with the requirements of the Act relating to Accounts, so far as applicable to the Company.

The Accounts have been prepared in accordance with the special provisions of Part VII of the Companies Act 1985 relating to small companies and with the Financial Reporting Standard for Smaller Entities (effective January 2005).

The accounts were approved by the Council on 3 May 2006 and signed on its behalf by Dr Nicola Coldstream, President.

NOTES TO THE ACCOUNTS FOR THE YEAR ENDED 31 DECEMBER 2005

		2005	2004
1.	**CHARITABLE EXPENDITURE**		
	Conference Transactions Preparation	£3,654	£8,940
	Donation to Society of Antiquaries	0	700
	Journal Expenses	12,682	15,801
	Lecturer's Expenses	425	0
	Hire of Rooms (Soc. Of Antiquaries)	3,168	2,899
	R. Taylor and Lord Fletcher Prize	312	0
	Ochs Scholarship	3,025	3,740
	Conference Expenses	26,047	26,383
	Conference Scholarships	600	1,200
	Administrative Costs	2,092	1,616
	Subscriptions Payable	162	0
	Travel and Subsistence	874	562
	Accountancy Fees	1,360	1,058
	Bank Charges	1,560	296
	Public Liability Insurance	173	0
		£56,134	£63,195

2.	**UNLISTED INVESTMENTS** (Unit Trusts)		
	Market Value at 1 January 2005	250,052	£234,531
	Unrealised Gains/(Losses)	31,858	15,521
	Market value at 31 December 2005	£281,910	£250,052
	Cost at December 2005	£180,706	£180,706

		2005		2004	
INVESTMENTS		*No*	£	*No*	£
CAF Balanced Growth Fund		51,891.14	79,316	51,891.14	66,888
CAF Income Fund		32,283.33	21,065	32,283.33	20,435
COIF Investment Fund		5,961.67	62,091	5,961.67	53,674
COIF Fixed Interest Fund		15,493.59	20,758	15,493.59	20,568
Mercury Charishare		17,885.202	74,939	17,885.202	65,227
Mercury Charinco		12,326.426	23,741	12,326.426	23,260
			£281,910		£250,052

REGINALD TAYLOR AND LORD FLETCHER ESSAY PRIZE

The Reginald Taylor Essay Prize, first awarded in 1934, was originally awarded on an annual basis, more recently biennially, for the best unpublished essay submitted on any subject of arthistorical, archaeological or antiquarian interest within the period from the Roman era to AD 1830, whenever such an essay was adjudged of suBcient merit.

With the aid of a bequest from the late Lord Fletcher, the prize was re-established in 1996 as the *Reginald Taylor and Lord Fletcher Essay Prize* with an award of £300 and a bronze medal. Details of the competition, which is not restricted to members of the Association, can be obtained from the Honorary Editor (please enclose a stamped addressed envelope). The winning essay may be read at a meeting of the Association and will be considered for publication in the Journal at the discretion of the Editorial Committee.

The list which follows gives all winners of the Reginald Taylor Essay Prize.

1934 John Salmon	'St Christopher in Medieval Art' (*JBAA*, N.S. XLI (1936), 76–115)
1935 Miss E. Carleton Williams	'The Dance of Death in Painting and Sculpture in the Middle Ages' (*JBAA*, 3rd ser., I (1937), 229–57)
1936 Miss Margaret L. Gadd	'English Monumental Brasses, with special reference to processes of manufacture and distribution' (*JBAA*, 3rd ser., II (1937), 17–46)
1937 Miss Rosamond J. Mitchell	'A Pilgrimage to Jerusalem in 1458' (*JBAA*, 3rd ser., III (1938), 65–81)
1938–39 Miss Kathleen Edwards	'The Houses of Salisbury Close in the Fourteenth Century' (*JBAA*, 3rd ser., IV (1939), 55–115)
1940 Miss M. M. Morgan	'The Abbey of Bec-Hellouin and its English Priories' (*JBAA*, 3rd ser., V (1940), 33–62)
1941 K. D. Manor Dauncey	'The Intrusive Element in Anglo-Saxon Zoomorphic Art' (*JBAA*, 3rd ser., VI (1941), 103–26)
1942 Arthur Furneaux Hall	'A Three-tracked Roman road near Colchester' (*JBAA*, 3rd ser., VII (1942), 53–70)
1944 Revd W. Lillie	'English Roodscreen Painting' (*JBAA*, 3rd ser., IX (1944), 33–47)
W. Bonser	'Epidemics in the Anglo-Saxon Period' (*JBAA*, 3rd ser., IX (1944), 48–71)
1945 F. W. Cole	'Church Sundials in Medieval Times' (*JBAA*, 3rd ser., X (1945–47), 77–80)
1947 R. P. Howgrave-Graham	'Westminster Abbey: the sequence and Dating of the Transept and Nave' (*JBAA*, 3rd ser., XI (1948), 60–78)
1948 J. P. C. Kent	'Monumental Brasses: A new classification of Military Effigies, 1360–1485' (*JBAA*, 3rd ser., XII (1949), 70–97)
1949 Arnold Taylor	'Master James of St George' (*English Historical Review*, LXV (1950), 433–57, reprinted with additions and corrections in Arnold Taylor, *Studies in Castles and Castle-Building* (London and Ronceverte, West Virginia, 1985), 63–97)
1950 Donald Nicol	'Dodona's Grove'
1951 R. E. Oakeshott	'Some Medieval Sword Pommels: an essay in analysis' (*JBAA*, 3rd ser., XIV (1951), 47–62)

1953 Miss Rotha Mary Clay	'Further studies of Medieval Recluses' (*JBAA*, 3rd ser., XVI (1953), 74–86)
1955 Eustace Remnant	'The problem of the cloister of Jumièges (*JBAA*, 3rd ser., XX–XXI (1957–58), 107–38)
D. Vinter	'The prisoners of Stapleton Jail, near Bristol: 1780–1814'
1956 M. W. Norris	'German schools of Monumental Brasses' (*JBAA*, 3rd ser., XIX (1956), 34–52)
1957 Ian McD. Jessiman	'The Piscina in the English Medieval Church' (*JBAA*, 3rd ser., XX–XXI (1957–58), 53–71)
1958 Ronald F. Jessup	'Barrows and Walled Cemeteries in Roman Britain' (*JBAA*, 3rd ser., XXII (1959), 1–32)
1959 W. Wareham	'The Reconstruction of a Romanesque Doorway' (*JBAA*, 3rd ser., XXIII (1960), 24–39)
D. F. Renn	'The Anglo-Norman Keep' (*JBAA*, 3rd ser., XXIII (1960), 1–23)
1962 G. D. S. Henderson	'The Sources of the Genesis Cycle at Saint-Savin-sur-Gartrempe' (*JBAA*, 3rd ser., XXVI (1963), 11–26)
1963 Mrs A. N. Harris	'The Gloucester Candlestick' (*JBAA*, 3rd ser., XXVII (1964), 32–52)
1964 Miss K. J. Galbraith	'The Sources of the Biblical Subjects at Malmesbury' (*JBAA*, 3rd ser., XXVIII (1965), 39–56)
1965 Martin Biddle	'Nicholas Bellin of Modena: an Italian artificer at the courts of Francis I and Henry VIII' (*JBAA*, 3rd ser., XXIX (1966), 106–21)
1966 Robin S. Cormack	'Byzantine Cappadocia: the archaic group of wall-paintings' (*JBAA*, 3rd ser., XXX (1967), 19–36)
1967 Alan Borg	'The development of Chevron Ornament' (*JBAA*, 3rd ser., XXX (1967), 122–40)
1968 Laurence Keen	'A series of seventeenth- and eighteenth-century lead-glazed relief tiles from North Devon' (*JBAA*, 3rd ser., XXXII (1969), 144–70)
1970 Peter Fergusson	'Roche Abbey: the source and date of the eastern remains' (*JBAA*, 3rd ser., XXXIV (1971), 30–42)
1972 David McLees	'Henry Yevele: disposer of the King's Works of masonry' (*JBAA*, 3rd ser., XXXVI (1973), 52–72)
1973 Lawrence Butler	'Leicester's church, Denbigh: an experiment at Puritan worship' (*JBAA*, 3rd ser., XXXVII (1974), 40–62)
1974 David Parsons	'The Pre-Romanesque church of St-Riquier: the documentary evidence' (*JBAA*, CXXX (1976), 21–51)
1976 Robin Emmerson	'Monumental Brasses: London Design c. 1420–85' (*JBAA*, CXXXI (1978), 50–78)
1977 Loveday Gee	'"Ciborium" tombs in England 1290–1330' (*JBAA*, CXXXII (1979), 29–41)
1978 Anne C. Anderson	'Continental roughcast beakers of the first and second centuries A.D.' (*Roman Pottery Research in Britain and North-West Europe*, eds A. C. and A. S. Anderson: BAR International Series 123 (Oxford 1981), 321–47)

1980 Christopher Norton and Mark Horton	'A Parisian workshop at Canterbury. A thirteenth-century tile pavement in the Corona Chapel, and the origins of Tyler Hill' (*JBAA*, CXXXIV (1981), 58–60)
1981 Stephen Heywood	'The ruined church at North Elmham' (*JBAA*, CXXXV (1982), 1–10)
1982 Catherine Milburn	'Pershore Abbey: the thirteenth-century Choir' (*JBAA*, CXXXVII (1984), 130–44)
1983 Eric Cambridge	'The Early Church in County Durham: A Reassessment' (*JBAA*, CXXXVII (1984), 65–85)
1984 Sara E. Jones	'The twelfth-century reliefs from Fécamp: new evidence for their dating and original purpose' (*JBAA*, CXXXVIII (1985), 79–88)
1985 Alan Richardson	'Some evidence of early Roman military activity on the southwest Pennine Flank' (JBAA, CXL (1987), 18–35)
1987 Phillip Lindley	'"Una grande opera al mio Re." Renaissance Gilt-Bronze effigies in England — Continuity or Change' (*JBAA*, CXLIII (1990), 112–30)
1988 Sally Woodcock	'The Building History of St Mary de Haura, New Shoreham' (*JBAA*, CXLV (1992), 89–103)
1991 Giles Worsley	'Inigo Jones: Lonely Genius or Practical Exemplar?' (*JBAA*, CXLVI (1993), 102–12)
1995 Daniel Beaumont	'The Social and Cultural Milieux of the Irish Protestant élite in the early eighteenth century. The travels of Pole Cosby, a gentleman from the Queen's County, *c.* 1700–*c.* 1740' (*JBAA*, CXLIX (1996), 37–54)

Winners of the Reginald Taylor and Lord Fletcher Essay Prize.

1996 Adrian B. Marsden	'Between Principate and Dominate: Imperial Styles under the Severan Dynasty and the Divine iconography of the Imperial Family on coins, medallions and engraved gemstones, A.D. 193–235' (*JBAA*, CL (1997), 1–16)
1998 Sally Dixon-Smith	'The Image and Reality of Alms-Giving in the Great Halls of Henry III' (*JBAA*, CLII (1999), 79–96)
2000 Carol Davidson Cragoe	'Reading and Rereading Gervase of Canterbury' (*JBAA*, CLIV (2001), 40–53)
Kate Heard	'Death and Representation in the 15th century: The Wilcote Chantry Chapel at North Leigh' (*JBAA*, CLIV (2001), 134–49)
2004 Heather Gilderdale Scott	'"this little Westminster": The Chantry-Chapel of Sir Henry Vernon at Tong, Shropshire' (*JBAA*, CLVIII (2005), 46–81)

THE OCHS SCHOLARSHIPS

Maud Lilian Ochs died on 24 June, 1991. In her will, she left the residue of her estate to the British Archaeological Association. The bequest, enhanced by other donations, amounted to £104,106, and was paid to the Association during 1994.

At its meeting on 4 May 1994, the Council resolved to use the fund to provide scholarships for two categories of researcher:
1) Students in the final year of a postgraduate degree
2) Independent scholars

The annual sum set aside for scholarships is £5,000. This maintains the capital base of the fund. It was also decided that scholarships should be awarded each May, and are tenable for a maximum of one year. This means that all applicants are required to submit a timetable, showing that their projects are capable of completion within one year. The administration of the scholarship is a duty of the Hon. Secretary.

OCHS SCHOLARS: 1995–2005

1995	Tim Ayers	The Painted Glass of Wells Cathedral
1995	Gill Chitty	John Ruskin and the Historic Environment
1995	Helen List	English Aristocratic Tombs; Ecclesiastical and Secular
1995	David Williams	Corpus of Late Anglo-Saxon Stirrup-Strap Mounts
1996	Kathleen Lane	Architectural Sculpture in Romanesque England
1996	Julia Watson	Patrons and Sculptors in Late 14th-Century France
1997	Linda Ebbatson	History of Archaeology: Context and Discourse 1845–1942
1997	David Haycock	The intellectual Writings and Context of William Stukeley
1998	Tara Hablin	Religious Representation in West Country Plasterwork
1998	Peter Hammond	The Clay Pipe Manufacturing Industry of London
1999	William Bowden	The Archaeology of Late Antique Epirus
2000	Duncan Givans	English Romanesque Tympana c. 1050–c. 1200
2000	Abigail Wheatley	The Idea of the Castle in Late Medieval England
2001	Zoë Opacic	The Emmaus Monastery at Prague and the Patronage of Charles IV
2001	Kate Welham	Compositional Homogeneity of Medieval Glass
2002	Jackie Hall	Croxden Abbey: Buildings and Community
2003	Judith Cannell	The Archaeology of Woodland Exploitation in the Greater Exmoor Area from the Early Medieval Period to the Nineteenth Century
2003	Elizabeth Worth	Historic Building Reconstruction since c. 1877: The Creation of Popular Images in the Age of Transition
2004	Thorste Hanke	The Development of Post-Medieval Roof Architecture in North-East Britain
2005	Claudia Marx	Theory and Practice in the Restoration of English Cathedrals in Late-Victorian England
2005	Mavis Nwokobia	Picturing Pompeii: Victorian Classical Painting and the Legacy of Vesuvius
2005	Agnieszka Sadraei	'Pater Patriae'. St Stanislaus and the Art of the Polish Kings (1200–1490)